I0729522

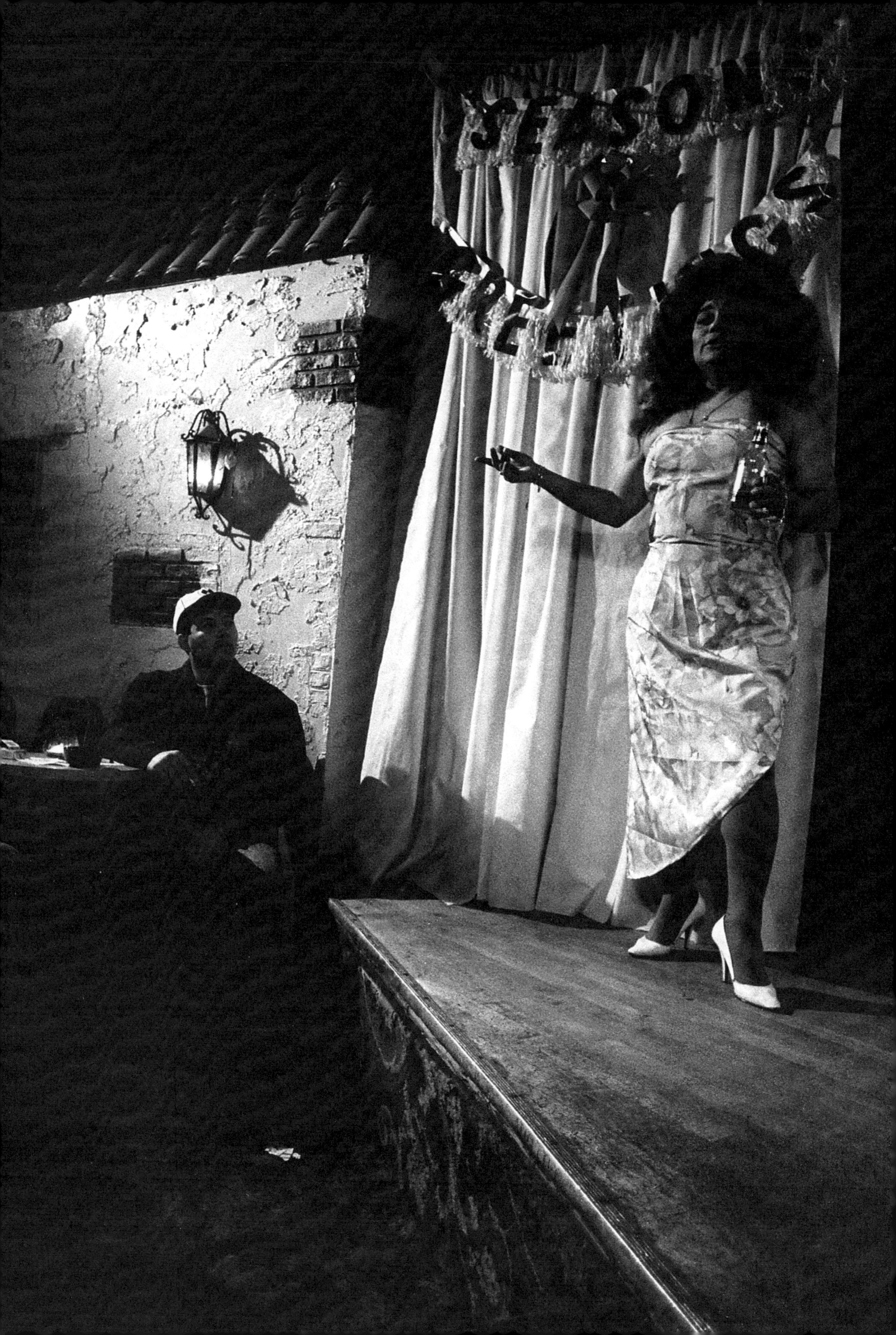

SEASON'S
GREETINGS

Edited by **Hedi El Kholti** and **Lauren Mackler**

Reynaldo Rivera

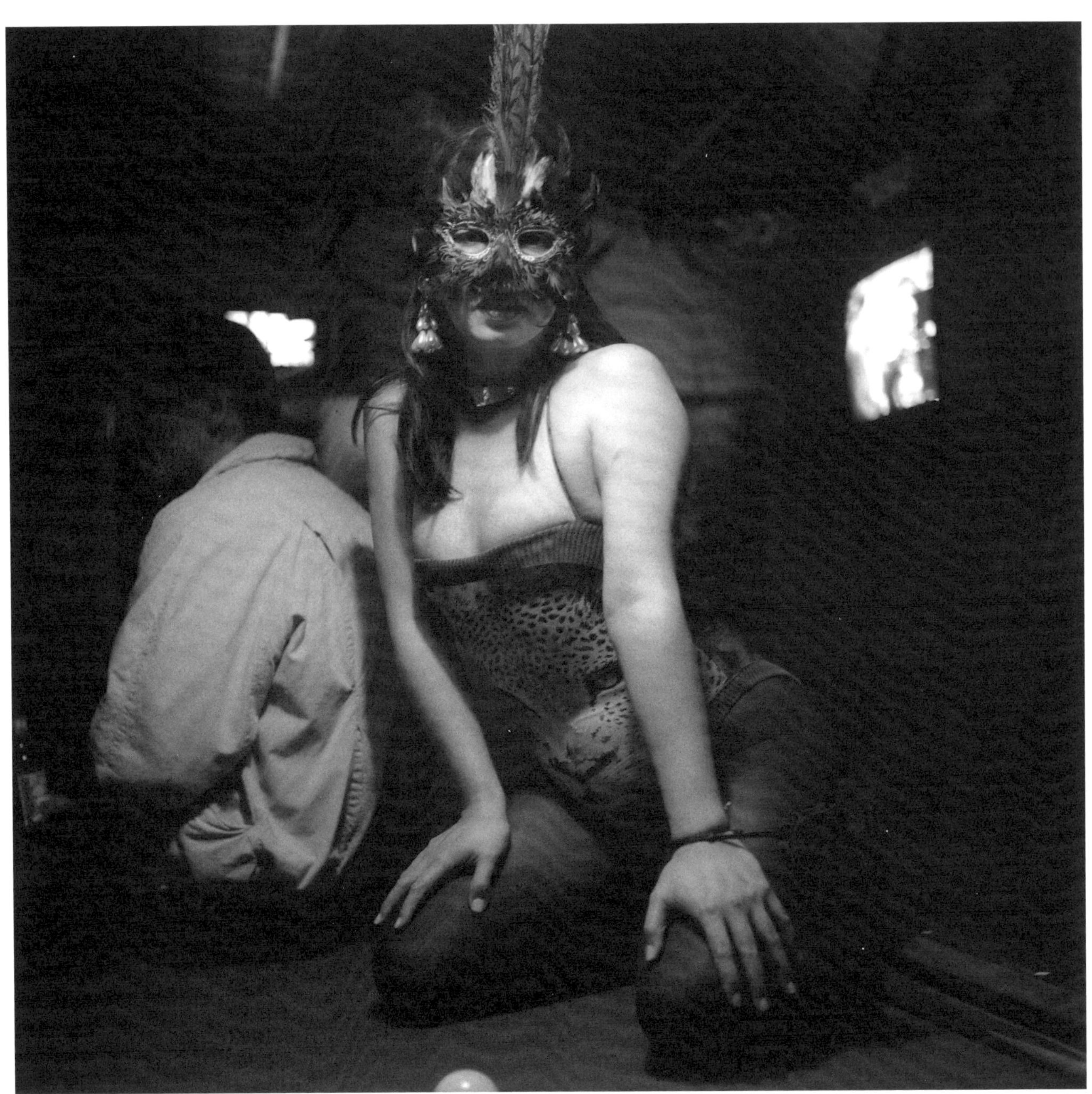

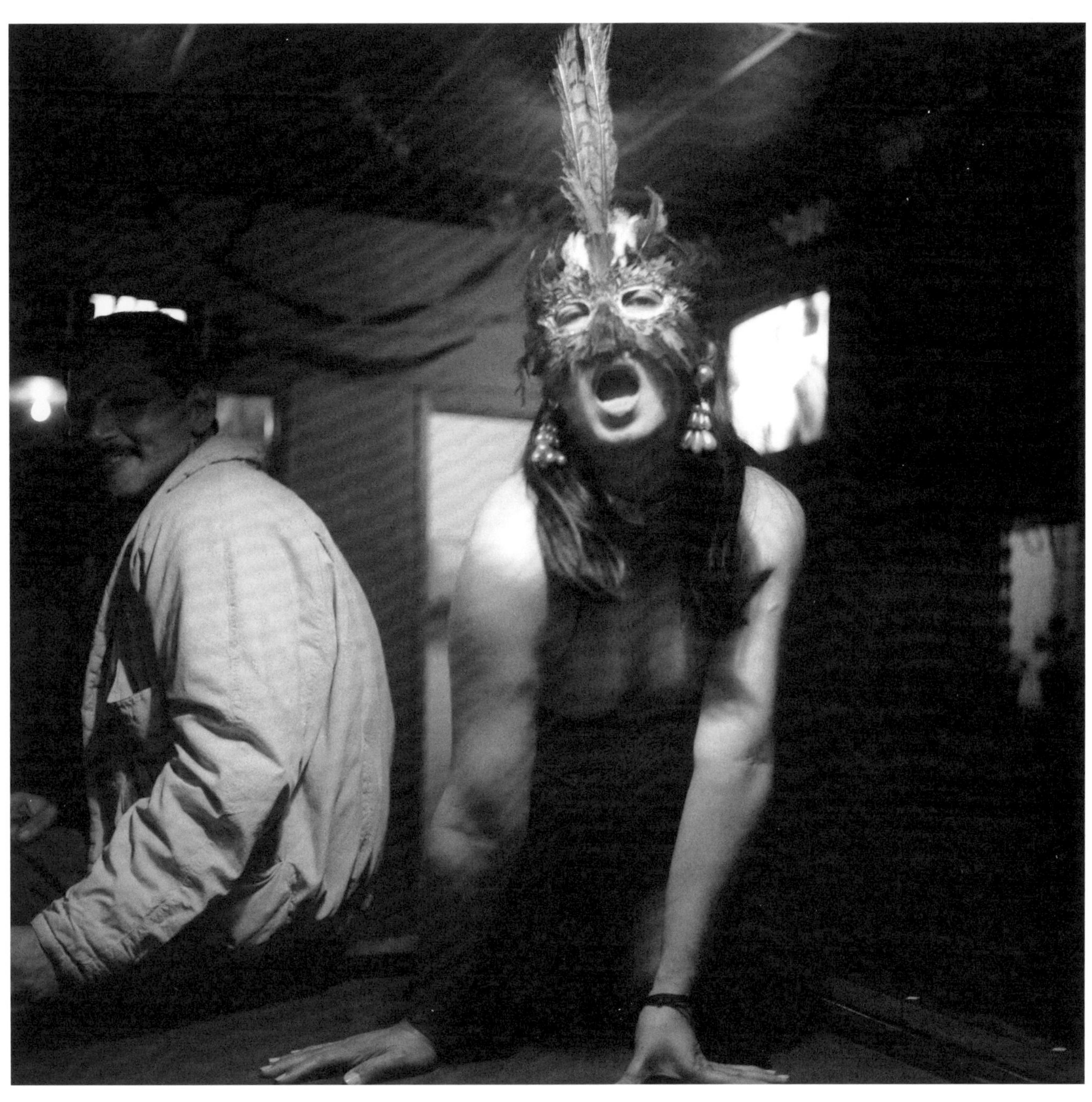

Performer, Little Joy Jr. (1997)

semiotext(e)

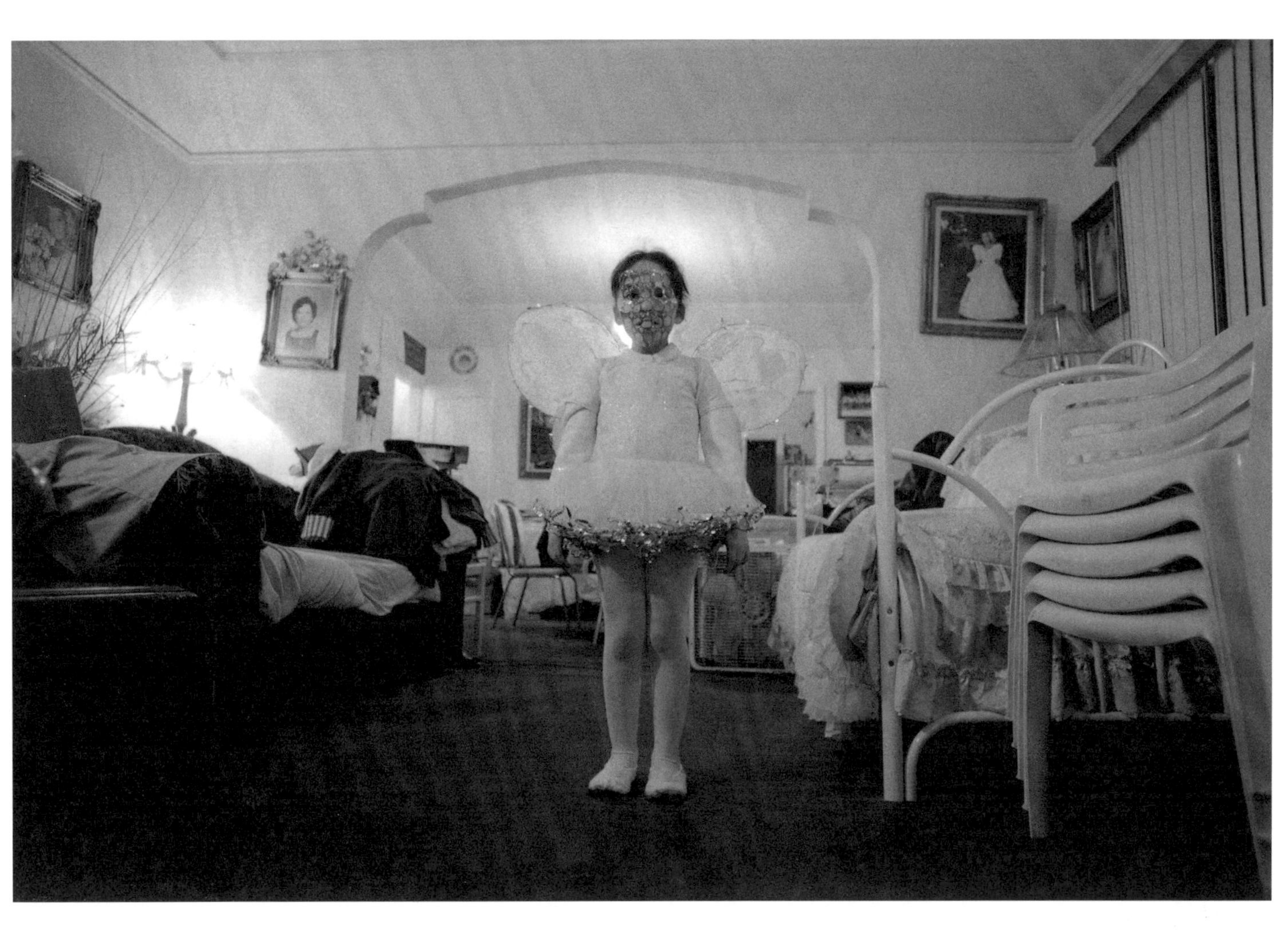

Neighbor's Child, Halloween (1997)

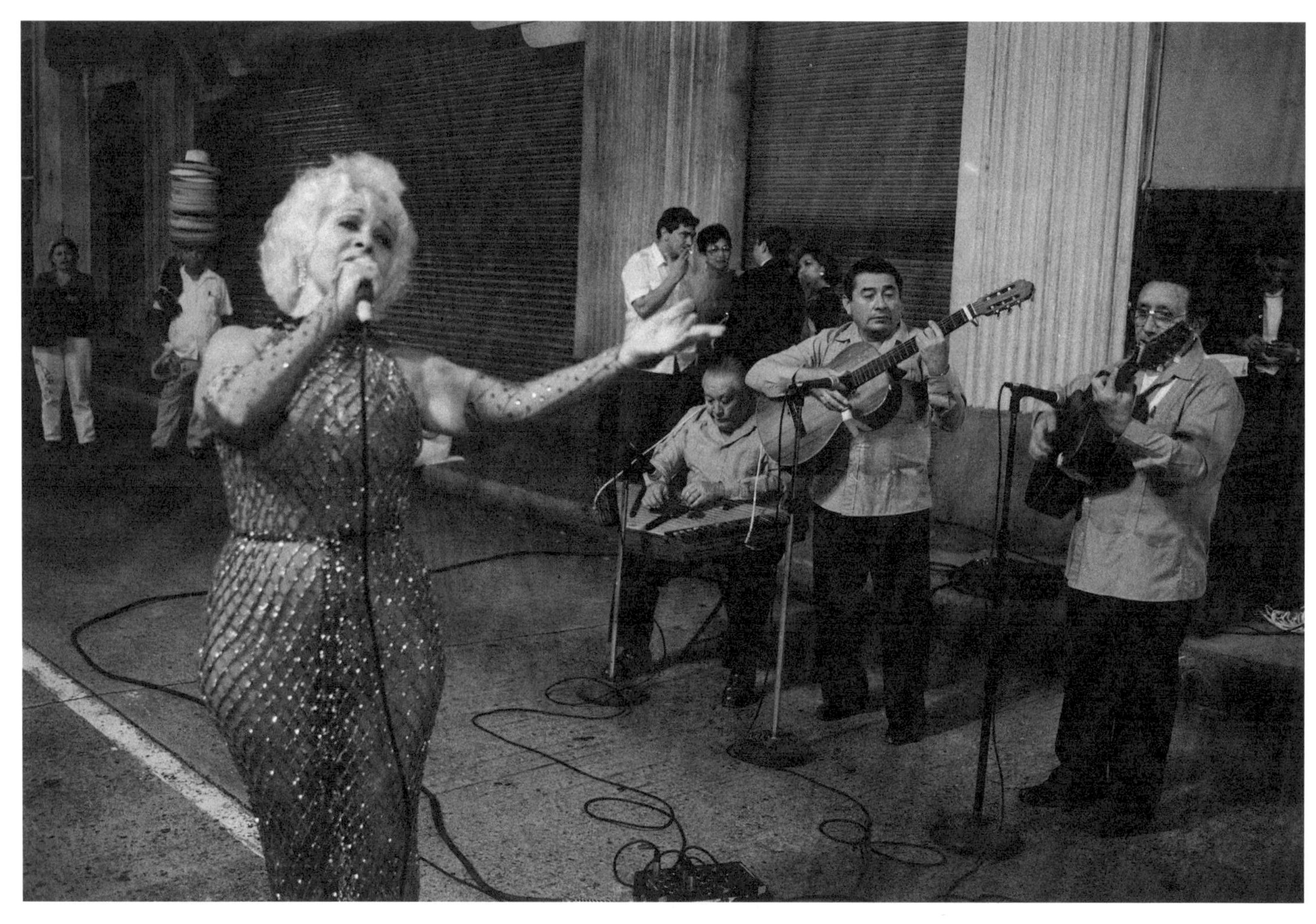

Festival del Bolero, Merida (1993)

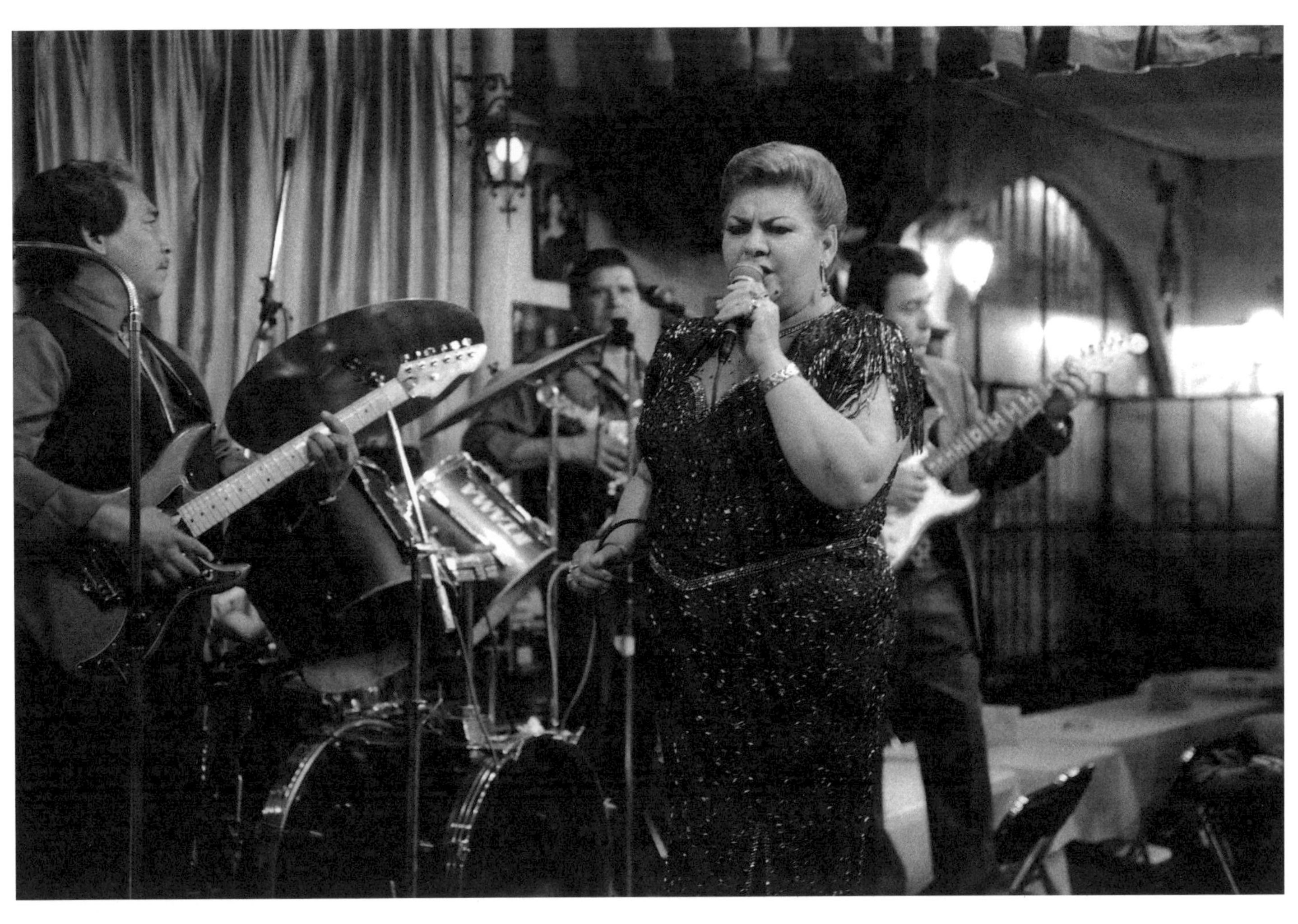

Paquita la del Barrio, Mexico City (1995)

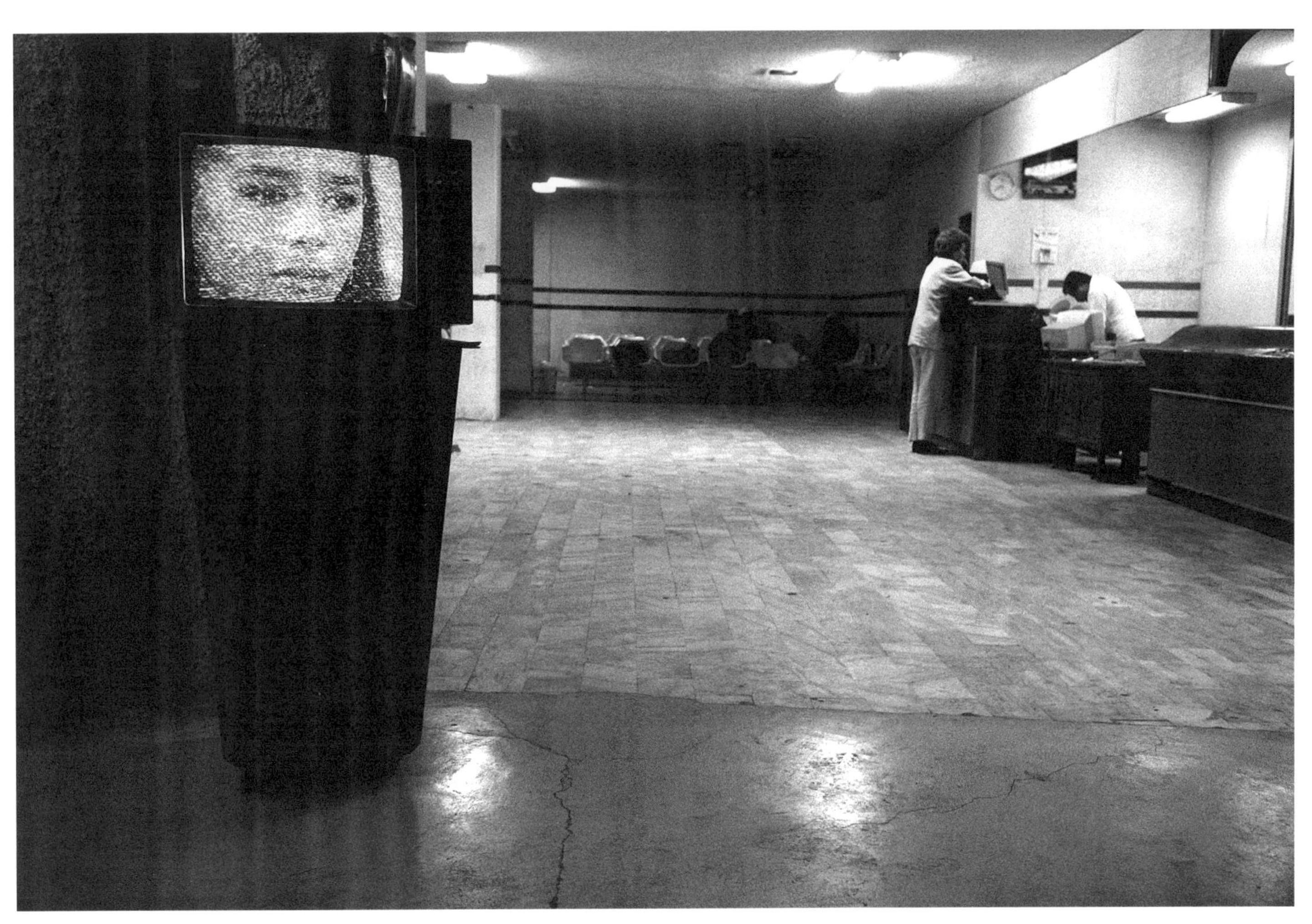

Bus Stop, Mexico (1991)

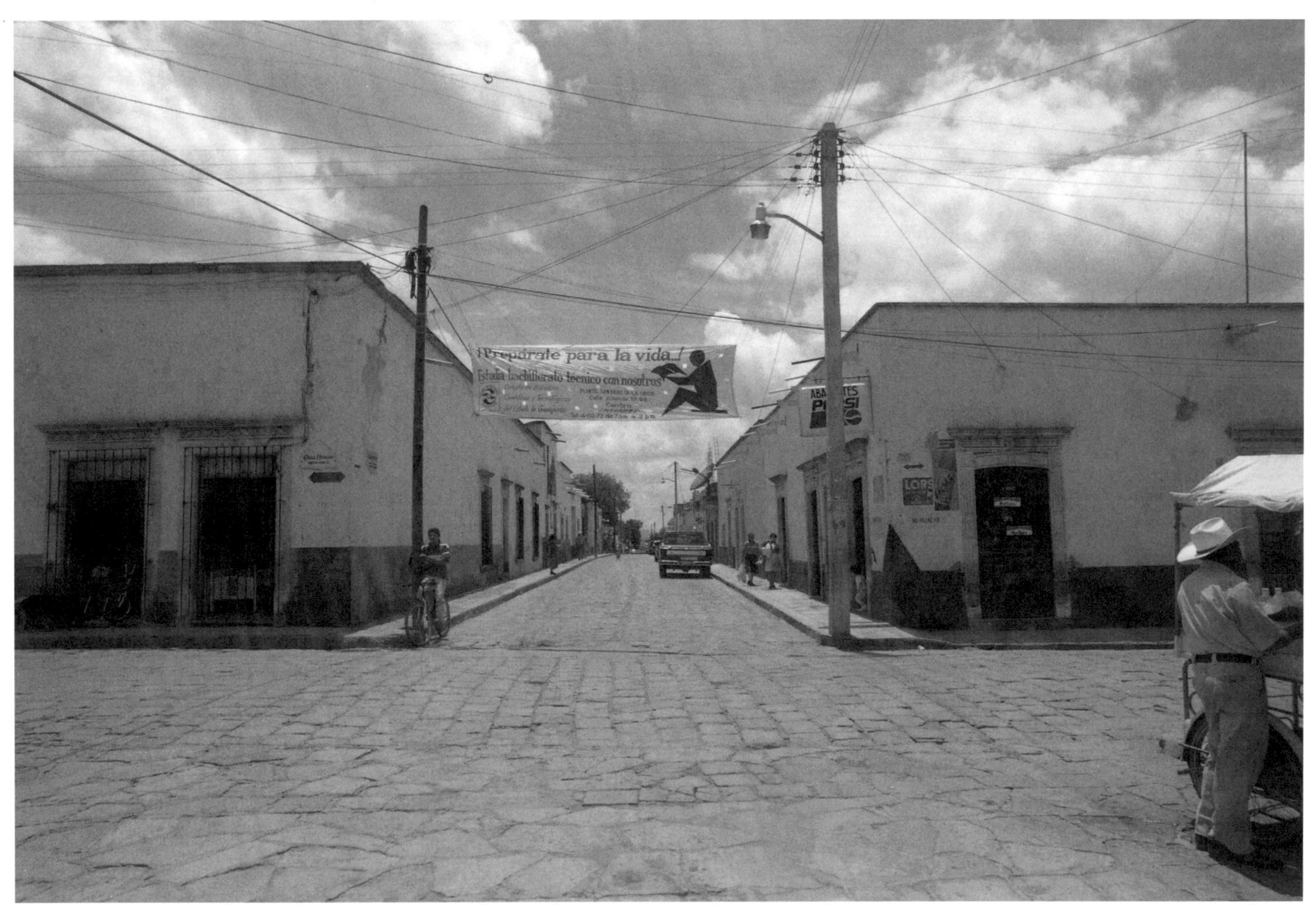

Some Provisional Notes Toward A Disappeared City by Chris Kraus

1.

Stockton — LA — Mexicali

In the opening shots of John Huston's 1972 film *Fat City*, the camera tracks slowly along the main street of Stockton, California, past clusters of street drinkers, hustlers, and out-of-work fruit pickers: handfuls of prematurely old men whose lives are spent in rotation between flophouse hotel rooms, liquor stores, city missions, culverts, and parks. The black men hang together, talking animatedly in small groups, sitting dazed on park benches. Dressed like a down and out pimp in a dapper sports jacket and mismatched pants, a skinny Mexican man stands sentry outside a hotel. A white guy with a Jesus Christ beard and long hair, maybe 30 years old looking 50, sits alone on a curb looking crazed.

Reynaldo Rivera and I drove up there last winter to visit the scenes of his earliest work. Not much in Stockton has changed in the half-century, except now the main street is virtually empty and the street life has moved about half a mile east.

There, small bands of derelict people on synthetic drugs are camped along sidewalks and medians, living underneath tarps or in tents. Others sell drugs out of apartments in the old, formerly working class two-family houses. Rivera first came to Stockton in 1976, when he was 11 or 12. The sad down and out world that appears in *Fat City* lives on as a frightening bazaar for the homeless mentally ill, who are also stoned out of their minds. It was a Sunday morning in bedlam. When Reynaldo warned me against driving to Stockton alone, I didn't believe him, but driving around the neighborhood slowly, I saw he was right.

Downtown, the Hotel Cosmos has been turned into low-rent apartments. The St. Leo Hotel, where Reynaldo stayed with his dad when they came up from Mexicali to do seasonal work, was boarded and shuttered. Rows of corniced brick pre-war buildings, vacant except for a few 99 Cent stores, were awaiting developers who'd yet to arrive. Stockton is just seventy-five miles east of booming Oakland, but it became the largest American city ever to file bankruptcy in 2012. Four years later, the inspiring, progressive 26-year old Michel Tubbs became the city's first black mayor. Tubbs, a protégé of Oprah Winfrey and Barack Obama, is a Stanford alum and a child of south Stockton. Still, that Sunday morning, a thin gray mist

San Diego de la Unión, Mexico (1987)

15

that felt viscous moved through the air, pulling us into an emotional microclimate of utter despair that we weren't aware of until we left town. Even in 2018, Stockton felt like a toxic terrarium. Both of Rivera's parents were mexican-born, but they met in Stockton, where his mom fled when she was 16 and pregnant. A family friend introduced her to his dad, who was more than 20 years older. They married soon after so that her first child would not be born out of wedlock. He promised to help with her immigration papers, and she followed him back to Mexicali, where he lived most of the year. "That's the weird thing," Rivera recalled. "Somehow we all end up in Stockton."

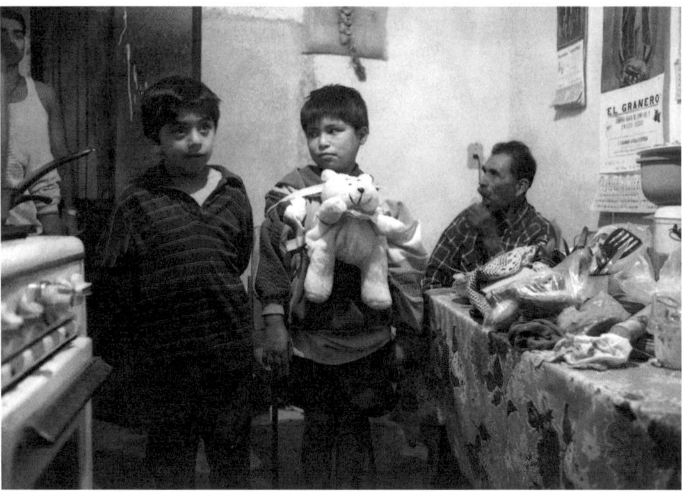

Rivera thinks he started picking cherries in Stockton in 1976, when he was 12 or 13. His early life took place in constant migration between his estranged parents in Mexicali, Santa Ana, Stockton, Pasadena and LA, so it's hard to be sure. When he was 5, he and his older sister Herminia were kidnapped from their mom's Pasadena house by their father. By this point, his parents were splitting up. Rivera's father was seeking revenge, but once he achieved it, he had no idea what to do with two little kids. He dropped them off with his sister and mother in San Diego de la Unión, the small town in Guanajuato where he was born. Rivera and his sister did not know these relations. They'd never been to Guanajuato before. Everything about San Diego de la Unión was strange and frightening. The house had no running water, no phone or TV, and Rivera recalls his grandmother's erratic, abusive behavior. He remembers his hands being burnt on the stove; he remembers being dragged through the town by his feet and no one doing anything about it. He remembers being confused by how quickly things could change, and how the moment could vanish without any trace, leaving nothing behind except for his emptiness. He and Herminia went to Mexican primary school. They stayed for four years, until they were finally tracked down and sent back to their mother.

"The earliest memories I had of feeling something was suffering," Rivera tells me. "That feeling you have when someone leaves you."

Returning to San Diego de la Unión for the first time in 1987, Rivera photographed gangs of small kids, not unlike his sister and him, climbing the wrought iron bars on a scarred stucco building. The stone streets around the town square are empty of traffic. Stillness and boredom breathe through the afternoon. The photographs capture the dreamlike dislocation of childhood migration, the shock of discovering the existence of parallel worlds, and how unfixed and arbitrary what you'd understood until then as reality actually is. He would photograph Herminia many times over the years: as a young girl in downtown LA and years later, in Mexico City and at his Echo Park house on Laveta Terr. with the artist Daniel Martinez and other friends. In all of these photos, she appears as a dreamy-romantic muse. But at the same time, she's graced with a toughness, an intact sense of herself and her place in the world that she maintains as a young girl, alone and looking straight at the camera, and in her 20s and 30s, when she becomes one of a circle of friends.

Rivera and Herminia were returned to their mother in 1975. By then, she and her two older daughters had moved south to Glendale. Coming back to California, he and Herminia were now set apart from their two older siblings by birth and by culture. Kathy and Connie, the two older girls, were Chicanas, born in the US, whereas Rivera and Herminia were born in Mexicali and had already partly grown up in San Diego de la Unión. On a good day in Santa Ana they were called Mexicans. The rest of the time they were known as TJs, chuntaros, or wetbacks.

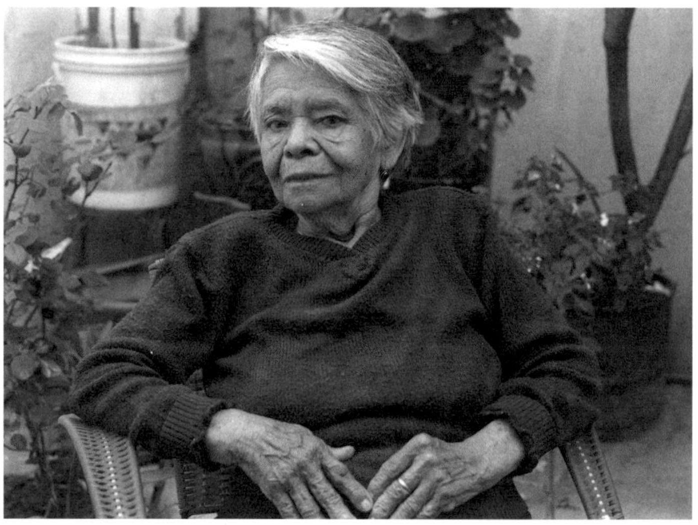

Enrolled in the fourth grade when he was 10 or 11, Rivera was already confused. And then, his life could change again any time his father appeared. His dad liked to grab his only son for impromptu custodial visits that could last weeks, even months as he moved between LA, Mexicali, and Stockton. His father's two principal occupations were seasonal work in a Campbell's Soup cannery in San Joaquin Valley, and fencing stolen merchandise on both sides of the border. Sometimes he brought Rivera along when he had business in downtown LA. They stayed at the Alexandria, or the Cecil, or one of a half-dozen other transient hotels that catered to workingmen, winos, and drifters. His dad ran a de facto office on Second and Main out of a pool hall.

Was it 1976 or 1936?

At 12, Rivera had yet to read John Rechy's *City of Night* or John Fante, but the sense of LA as an archeological site that pervades all of his work was perhaps born here.

Juan Manuel, Mexico (1999)
Herminia Rivera, San Diego de la Unión (1987)

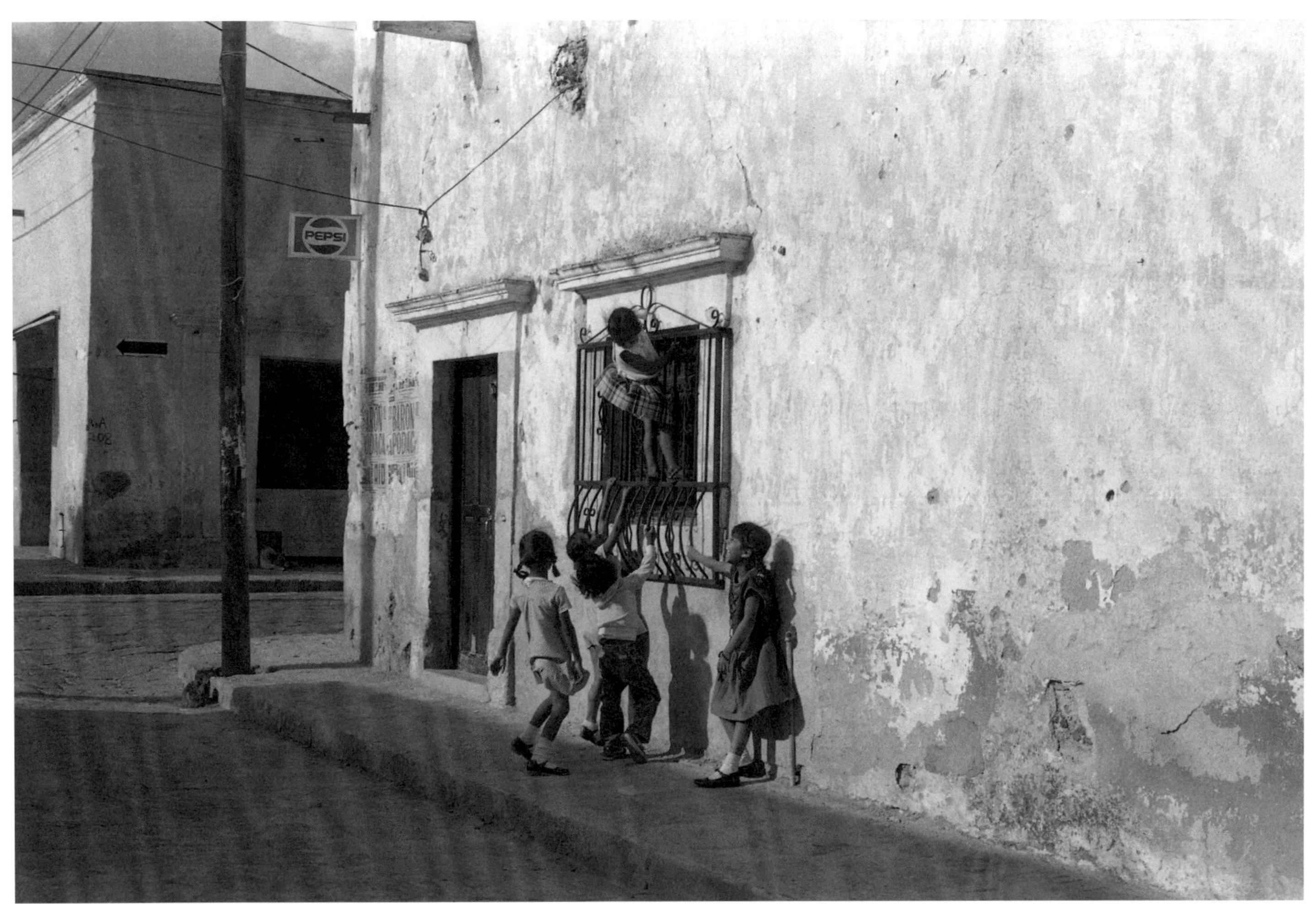

Through Rivera's work, the city becomes a place where all of the histories moving underneath the skin of the present can become visible. His photos of friends at Echo Park and East LA house parties in the early '90s; pictures of old buildings in downtown LA and photos of breakdancers grabbed from the street feel suspended in time, suffused with a presence that seems to include things that aren't physically there.

"You'd sit on these chairs in the pool hall," Rivera recalls, "and people would come by. If you were a regular, they'd come to you with all of their stolen stuff. It was boring, sitting around, waiting for someone to come in. Although sometimes, it could be fun, when we'd go to their houses and look at the stuff. There was a really old fat lady he did business with. She was in touch with the local thieves, she gathered their stuff, and we'd go to her place to look. I remember lots of gold watches. Downtown LA was full of those places, all of them gone."

During cherry season, his dad took him to work along-side him in Stockton. These trips—in late April, May, and early June—didn't necessarily correspond to the school year. Rivera's life followed his father's whims and migrations. Although, he recalls, there was nothing unusual at the time about a 13-year old boy picking fruit in the fields. He can hardly remember the work, but he remembers the boredom, and the stale, shared hotel rooms at the St. Leo, the St. Julien, and other, much sketchier, places. He remembers transient men, drinking, card playing, and business transacted in Spanish. His father moved stolen goods back and forth between Stockton and downtown LA. Rivera found it all pretty boring. Instead, he went to thrift stores and second-hand bookstores and collected 50-year old film magazines. An elderly Fillipina who worked in a used bookstore downtown let him take antique movie and photography books for free. He discovered Lisette Model...her gelatin prints from the 1940s, the fat woman bather at Coney Island, the blurred high-heeled leg on the sidewalk in front of an old-fashioned car, and the work of Brassaï, Kertész, and E.J. Bellocq. The images were proof that another life form existed. He read all the time, to a point where he felt like he'd teleported himself out of Stockton by reading about movie stars, films, and photographers day and night.

For company, he took up with the homeless. He became friends with a man and a woman, a brother and sister, who hung around outside one of these stores. The man, paralyzed from the waist down, was confined to a wheel chair, but he had elaborate Vietnam tattoos. His sister had once been a beauty queen, but she looked ravaged and frightening after her face was disfigured by one of her tricks. Rivera, comparatively clean cut, became their mascot. He was a nice, white Mexican boy helping an older man in a wheelchair. Together, they could go anywhere. So they robbed stores. His ambition then was to be homeless as well.

"One day," he recalls, "I got busted. I was fucked up out of my mind, we had drank and I'd smoked a lot of pot. I was sitting in the shoe department of this little department store Mariani's in the middle of the hood, just getting my bearings.

Kids, San Diego de la Unión (1989)

I was so loaded, and didn't want to go home to my dad. 'Cause it was already late. Apparently somebody told my dad about the drama that happened earlier in a liquor store, which happened to be the one where he bought his beer and his sandwich. And my dad found me there, and beat the shit out of me. So, yeah, that was Stockton. It was an awful, depressing place. But I remember those homeless people very fondly."

Back at home with his mom in Pasadena, Rivera liked to ditch school, stay home and watch movies. His favorite show *Hollywood Presents* came on at noon, and it featured month-long festivals of the complete oeuvres of Hollywood stars like Greta Garbo, Jean Harlow, and Marlene Dietrich. Silent films from the '20s, the Hollywood Golden Age, and eventually Mexican Golden Age cinema. The movies burned into his brain, and he felt hypnotized by them.

After watching these films, he started looking at the elderly SRO residents during his sojourns to Stockton through different eyes. These worn out old pensioners in their 80s and 90s had lived through that time. They'd seen silent films. Through them he could access a world of impossible strangeness and glamour. He asked them about movies and stars: What about this actress? What was this place? And they loved talking to him, no one in mid-1970s Stockton, CA, could not care less about how they remembered their youth. A movie theater downtown put on a matinee festival of Golden Age Mexican cinema, and he discovered the work of Lucha Reyes. He decided her song *La Tequilera* was written about him. *Como buena mexicana sufriré el dolor tranquila*...Like a good Mexican, I will suffer pain quietly...He collected boxes of magazines from the '20s and '30s. He knew that era better than the one he was living in.

At school and at home in Santa Ana, he was always in trouble. He got arrested for selling drugs in sixth grade and sent back to his father in Mexicali. When he returned to LA to start seventh grade, his mom was living in Pasadena. He got briefly involved with the South Side Pasa gang, but by the time he was 14 he was finished with school and he moved back to Mexicali.

His father had purchased a liquor store in the border-adjacent, working class Puerto Nuevo neighborhood from a friend who was going to prison. Rivera worked in the store, not sure what his next move would be until he watched his dad shoot a prominent gangster during a minor dispute over the purchase of a beer. The gangster stumbled out onto the street, where he died. His dad fled immediately, taking Rivera's green card along with him. Rivera, 14, was left with the corpse. When the victim's friends came around seeking revenge they didn't realize he was the son, and asked him where is that fucker? Rivera had no idea. He cheered them on while they emptied the register and tore up the store.

After that, he had to leave fast, but without his green card, he had no way to cross over. He spent his last $10 on a motel and some vodka, then he was broke. He'd never imagined having no money. For two weeks he slept in the streets. At one point he asked a street vendor for a hot dog that, after not eating for a while, looked like the best thing on earth. Finally, he ran into a friend who helped him get back to Calexico, where he found his dad at the bus terminal, about to get onto a bus to LA. After the shooting, they couldn't go back to Mexicali. Together, they went to LA.

His father returned to Stockton in early July, as he did every year, for his seasonal job at the Campbell's Soup cannery. The cannery was a unionized job, and he had seniority. After the liquor store drama, Rivera's father got him a Teamster's card and a job at the cannery. He was almost 15 and could pass for 18. Rivera had sworn to never pick cherries again. The cannery job was equally boring, but the money was better. He could pay his own way without getting involved in his dad's schemes. That summer, when he saw a Yashica in a pile of stolen stuff at the hotel, he realized he wanted a camera. "And then the genie came out of the bottle. I thought if I could capture these moments, keep them on file, I could find some kind of order. It was everything to me. I started capturing, documenting, for lack of a better word, the things that I saw. It was a kind of alchemy. It became my thing."

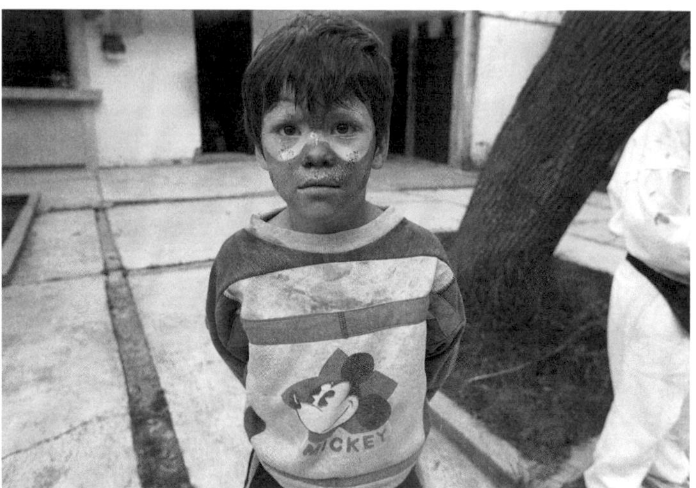

2.

Como Buena Mexicana sufriré el dolor tranquila

He started taking photos of people around the hotel—not his dad or his friends, but of the women who cleaned. He asked an elderly woman named Minnie to pose like a star in an old silent movie. The results made him want to do more. In these early photos, the dull, rundown and depressing St. Leo Hotel and the grandmotherly lady who called him lil chicken were transformed into something bigger and better than life. Photography was clearly the next best thing to making a movie. He dropped his rolls at a downtown Photomat; most of the prints came back blank. When he asked the girl working there what he'd done wrong she told him about f-stops and focusing. He was thrilled when he finally began getting images back. He worked the cannery job for four months each summer. The rest of the time, he lived in LA. He left the cholo and gang world behind him and didn't look back. In Stockton, he played old records by Edith Piaf, Billie Holiday, Bessie Smith, and Louis Jordan on an old victrola he'd found in a secondhand store. And he followed new bands. In LA, he went to clubs, bleached out his hair and wore vintage clothes. He reconnected with his cousin Trizia, who was "the most beautiful and cool girl I'd ever seen." Through Trizia, he met the photographer Michael Rush, a veteran of the 1960s

Child, Mexico City (1993)

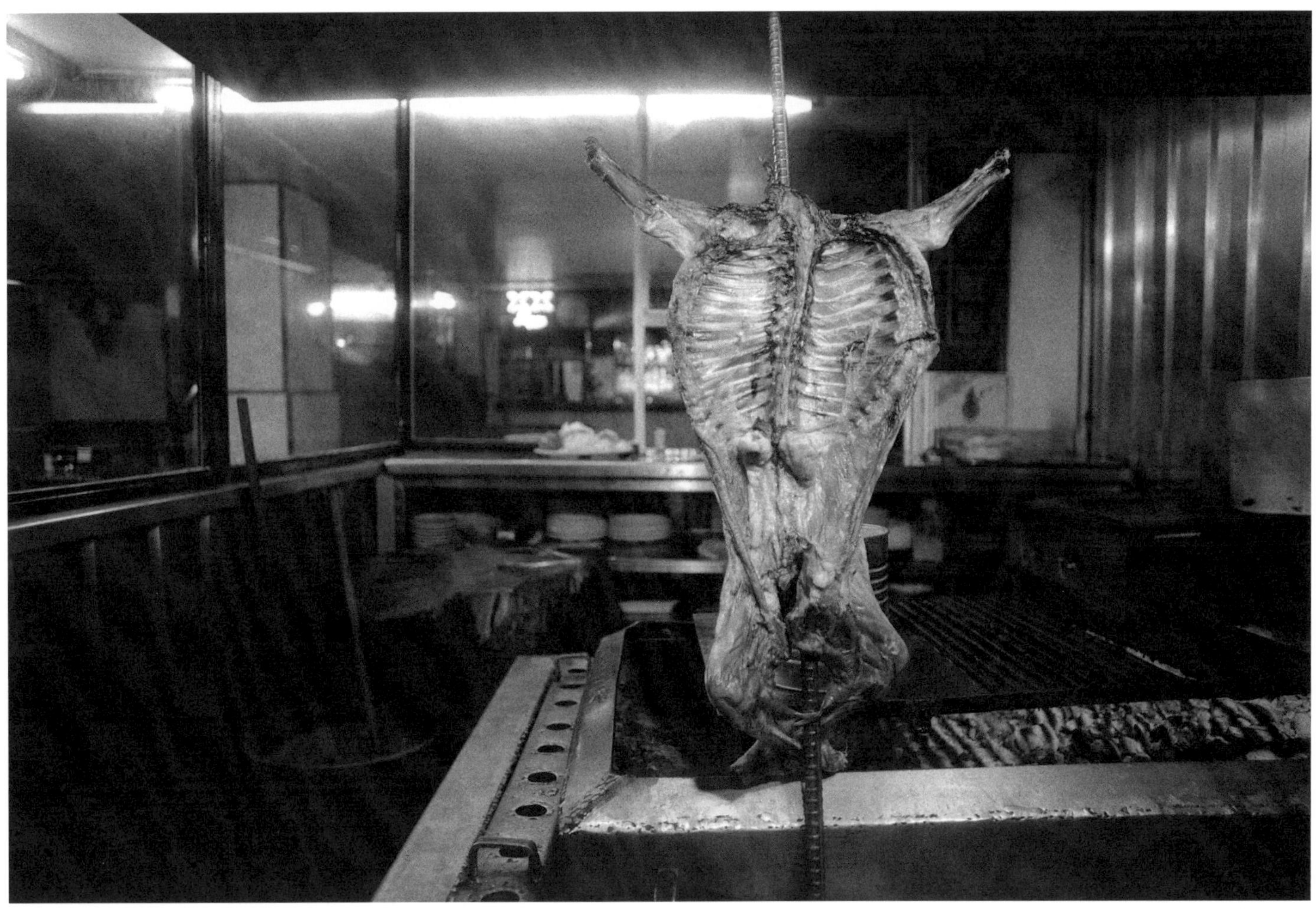

London underground scene. Michael taught him more about photography, and they both introduced him to cocaine.

There was a lot of cocaine, and eventually things would blow up. But in the early '80s, Trizia and Michael were his gateway to another world. Through them he met Myriam Sorigue and Alex Jordanov, a French couple living in Hollywood. Alex Jordanov worked for Celluloid Records and started Radio Club, the first rap club in LA. Myriam liked Rivera's work. Myriam set him up with his first photography job, taking photos for Ice-T's girlfriend. He bought a new Pentax K1000 camera, and took the 1983 black and white glamour photos of fresh, pixie-ish 19-year-old Herminia in the hallway of an old rooming house, in an alley behind industrial buildings downtown. "In LA, I started documenting everything around me. It was my way of being able to hold onto things. Moments that ordinarily would have disappeared, I would take home to relive over and over. It was some kind of insanity. Because photography was always so expensive, I really had to be careful about how I used my film, because I had no money when I wasn't working in the cannery. I shot a roll here, a roll there."

Rivera lost almost all of his earliest work in 1985. By then, Michael and Trizia's lives had taken a much darker turn, with their drug habits out of control. They were sharing a house. Once, in a rage, Trizia locked him out and when he came back to retrieve his things, most of his negatives were no longer there. He still has the photographs he took in Mexico City in 1983, of the room in Tepito where his step-grandfather was killed. At that time, Tepito was still an underclass neighborhood known for its open-air markets of counterfeit and stolen goods. Rivera and his father had traveled there, weeks after the murder, to help his grandmother deal with property matters. She and her late husband had owned the semi-communal slum building where the murder occurred. "In Mexico, buildings like this are called vecindades—I don't know where this word comes from. They have courtyards in the middle, called patios, and the deeper inside the vecindad, the poorer you were. There was a song, very popular in Mexico in the '40s, called *Quinto Patio* (Fifth Patio). My grandfather was killed by a man with a machete, the boyfriend of someone who lived there. This lady was getting beaten. He went to help her, and the guy just chopped him up. So I went in the room, with my dad, to check the place out. And I took photos of all the blood splattered everywhere. There was a big, framed saint on top of a table, splattered with blood. It was such a creepy image. My step-grandfather was such a nice man, the only one that showed us any kindness. We really felt his departure. That was the first time I went to Mexico City as an adult." The photos Rivera took in that room are anomalous to the rest of his work. They are a literal document of a horrific and filthy crime scene gone stale. Images of landscape and streets produced in subsequent trips are emotionally rich triggers of portent and imminence. In a photograph taken while traveling in Central America, a passenger boat moves through an empty, dark lake under a cloud-leaden sky, and the bland windowless hall in **Bus Stop**, *Mexico (1991)* feels thick with echoes and ghosts.

Untitled, Mexico City (1993)

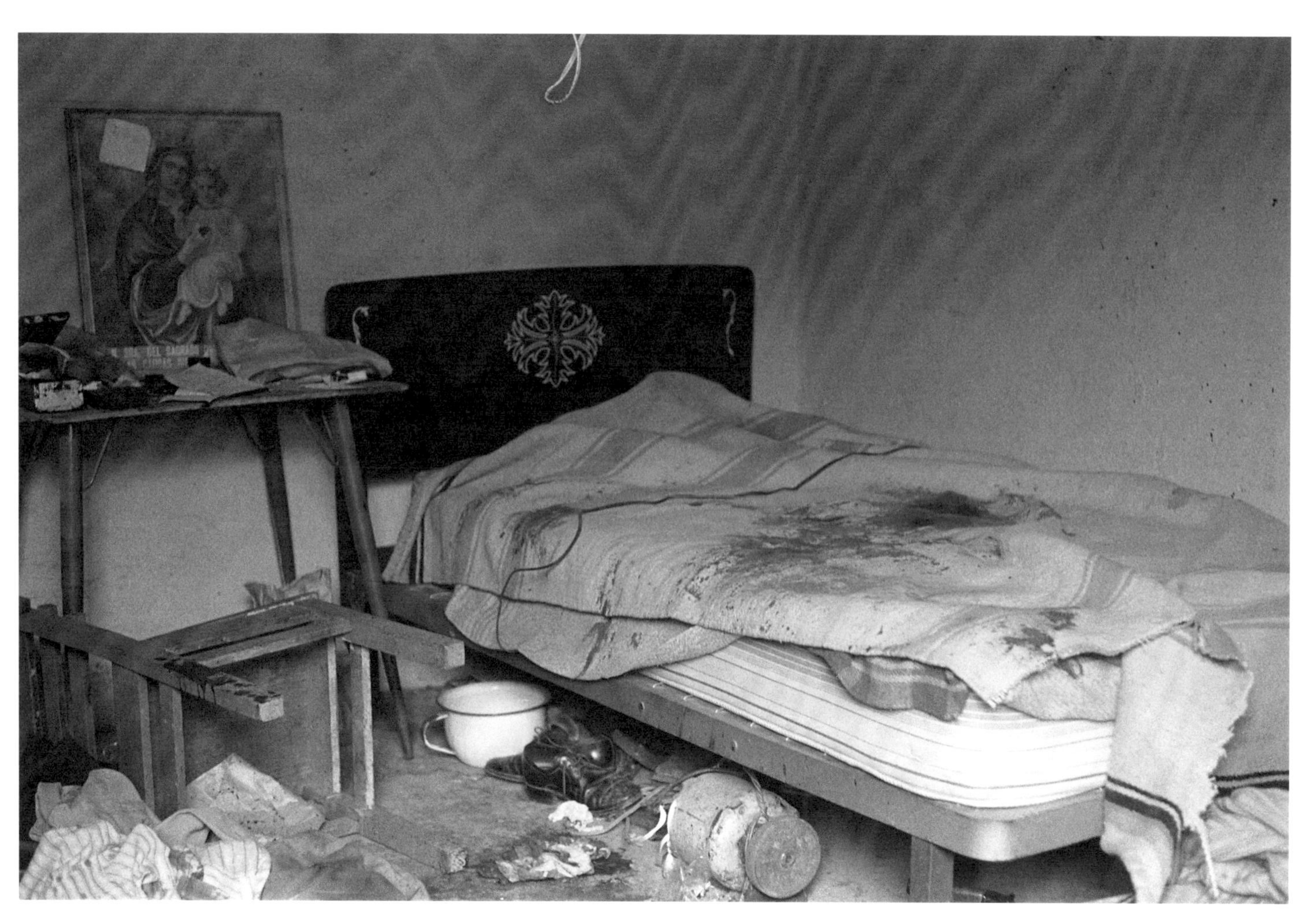

Crime Scene (step-grandfather), Mexico City (1983)

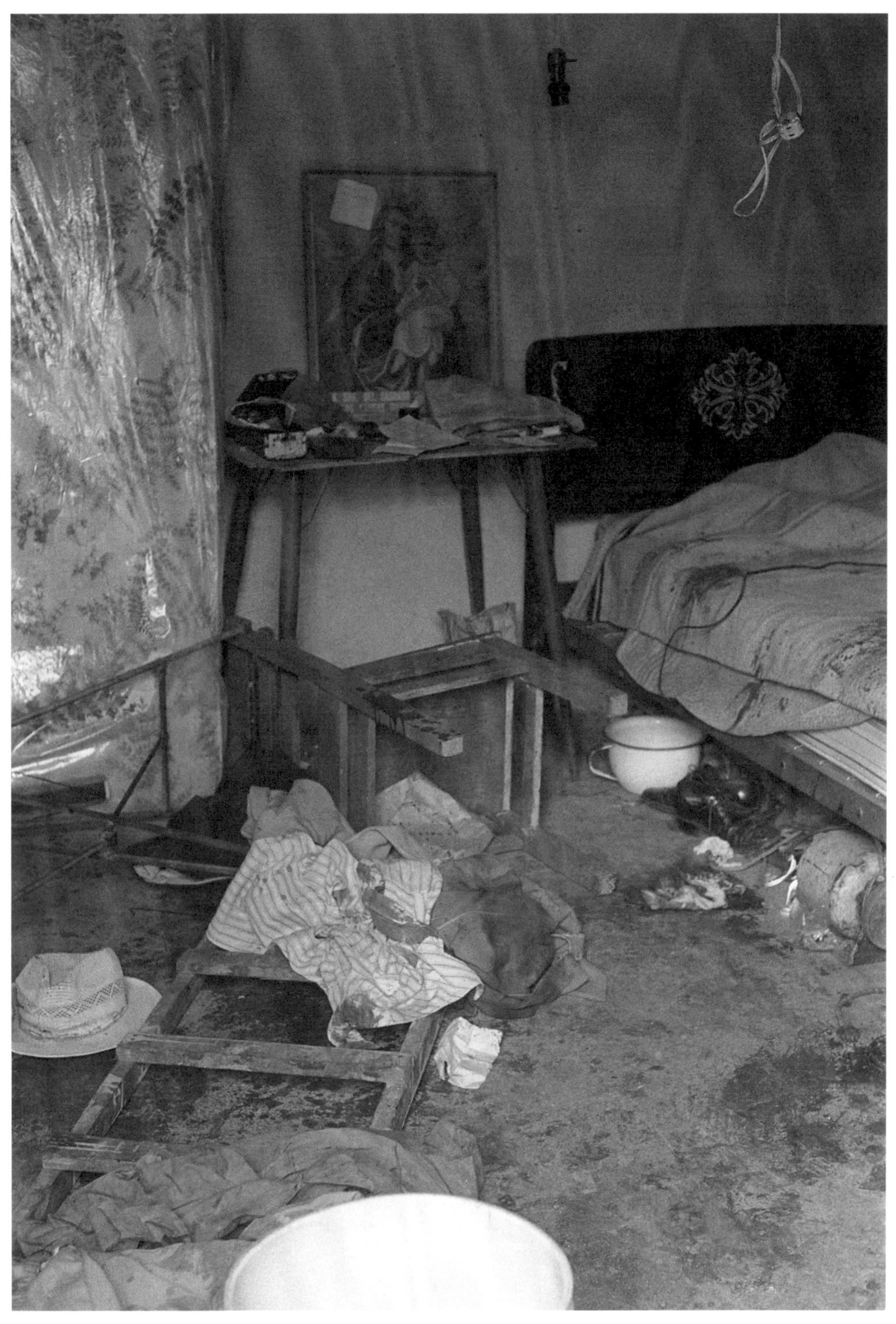

Across his body of work, Rivera depicts people enmeshed in their own private worlds who completely transcend their surroundings through the force of imagination and their inner lives. This remains true, whether the subject is photographed in a garden (**Roberto Gil de Montes**, *Echo Park (1995)* p.198), a public toilet (**Julie**, *Hollywood (1985)* p.214) or a house party in pre-gentrified Echo Park (**Elyse Regehr and Javier Orosco**, *Downtown LA (1989)* p.111).

I think this is a primary difference between Rivera's work and Nan Goldin's, to whom his portraits of drag queens, trans women, and other friends might be compared. Goldin's subjects in *The Ballad of Sexual Dependency* are downwardly mobile: middle class kids who took a wrong turn, captured in louche dens of bohemian squalor during emotionally intimate scenes. Her color-drenched portraits of drag queens taken five years later in *The Other Side* are deliberately realistic. Jimmy Paulette's face looks like a death mask in *Misty and Jimmy Paulette in a taxi, NYC* (1991). His makeup is overdone, his fishnet midi is ripped, and the two of them look like pissed off punk girls confronting the sun after a long debauched night.

Rivera's photographs of drag performers taken in Latino gay bars in LA between 1989 and 1997 reflect a different kind of collaboration. He sees his subjects less as they "are" than how they most wish to be seen, lending himself to their dreams and illusions of glamour. And why shouldn't these dreams be realized? Wearing a blonde wig and a long taffeta wedding-cake dress, Yoshi floats off the dirty linoleum of the Mugy's stage (**Yoshi (owner)**, *Mugy's (1995)* p.159). Wrapped in a towel and a turban, Tina stands on an old wooden chair with a dollar tip tucked under a bra strap, but she's in heaven. Her eyes closed, the pale shadow rests on her lids and her head tilts gently back as she moves to the music. She's so forcefully channeling fragile delight that you have to look twice before seeing her masculine triceps and shoulders (**Tina**, *Mugy's (1995)* p.174).

By the time he was 19, Rivera stopped going to Stockton for seasonal work. A musician friend introduced him to friends at the *LA Weekly*. He got a job as a janitor, where he stayed for about a year. Being involved with the paper gave him access to concerts and fashion shows. He took pictures at these events for his own pleasure, and later on sold his prints to the *Weekly*. Between 1985 and 1990, he photographed dozens of artists and bands, including Chaka Khan, Nick Cave, Sade, Vaginal Davis, Bob Dylan, Siouxsie Sioux, Echo and the Bunnymen, Depeche Mode, Tom Petty, Ray Charles and many others. None of these shoots were assignments. "I got to choose the people I wanted, and I would photograph them however I wanted to. Because for me, they were the same as my other photographs. I was doing the work for myself. Except for the concert photos, I usually took the photos at their homes, or in other scenarios that were interesting. There'd be times when I got to spend the whole evening hanging out. The pictures of Siouxsie, we took at her birthday party. I remember people saying they didn't look like photos they saw from regular shoots. They looked like art photos, as opposed to commercial photography. Maybe it's because I wasn't thinking, oh, I'm doing this for my career, to put on my resume, so I can sell it—I'm doing this for myself. Photography, for me, was that space between reality and make believe. It kept me protected."

His friend Gloria Ohland, then an editor at the *LA Weekly*, brought him along to fashion shows by designers like Christian Lacroix, which he photographed onstage and off. Although most of the negatives for these photos have been lost, I imagine them as precursors to the pictures Rivera would take several years later, an enormous body of work, of performers in Los Angeles drag clubs.

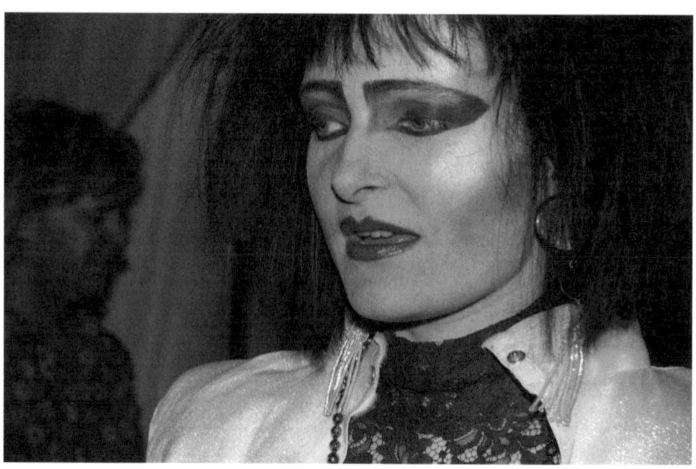

The concert photos he took during those years are remarkable for the relations that they reveal between performers, and the act of performance itself. They provide psychological insight into the dynamics at work among band members. His photographs of Eurythmics performing in 1985 at the Whiskey feature Annie Lennox scowling, seducing, and exhorting the audience, supported by an energy field running between her and guitarist Dave Stewart that feels almost visible. His photographs of Depeche Mode's 1988 concert emphasize the carefully measured moves of lead singer Dave Gahan's performance. Photographing Chaka Khan's show at the Wilshire Bell a year later, Rivera turns from the stage and considers the audience at this small venue, completely connected to the performance, almost as one.

Rivera's approach to producing these concert photographs wasn't exactly a matter of framing, exposure or angle. "At the end of the day, it's how you picture the world. And this is where one photographer is different from another. At the concerts, it would be about finding that moment—the way I want them to look. Sometimes, out of 200 frames, you get two really good ones. Sometimes I didn't get anything. But if you look at my band photos, I think you'll see I made the effort to give them more depth. To make it a multi-dimensional image, as opposed to a flat concert photo. I've never been into this. I needed them to say something, if that makes any sense. I always look for the image to speak for itself. Whoever looks at the photo, it's going to say something. My photos are very documentary, laying testament to things that happened. But at the same time, it's about creating a narrative, a movie. And I see the people as characters. You can say this about all of my work. Sometimes I ask myself why I spent so much money, which at that time was so scarce, on photography. I was constantly creating the movie I wanted to be in, as opposed to the one I was born into."

The photographs sold to the *LA Weekly* comprise just a small part of Rivera's body of work. Throughout the '80s and

Siouxsie Sioux, birthday party, Hollywood (1986)

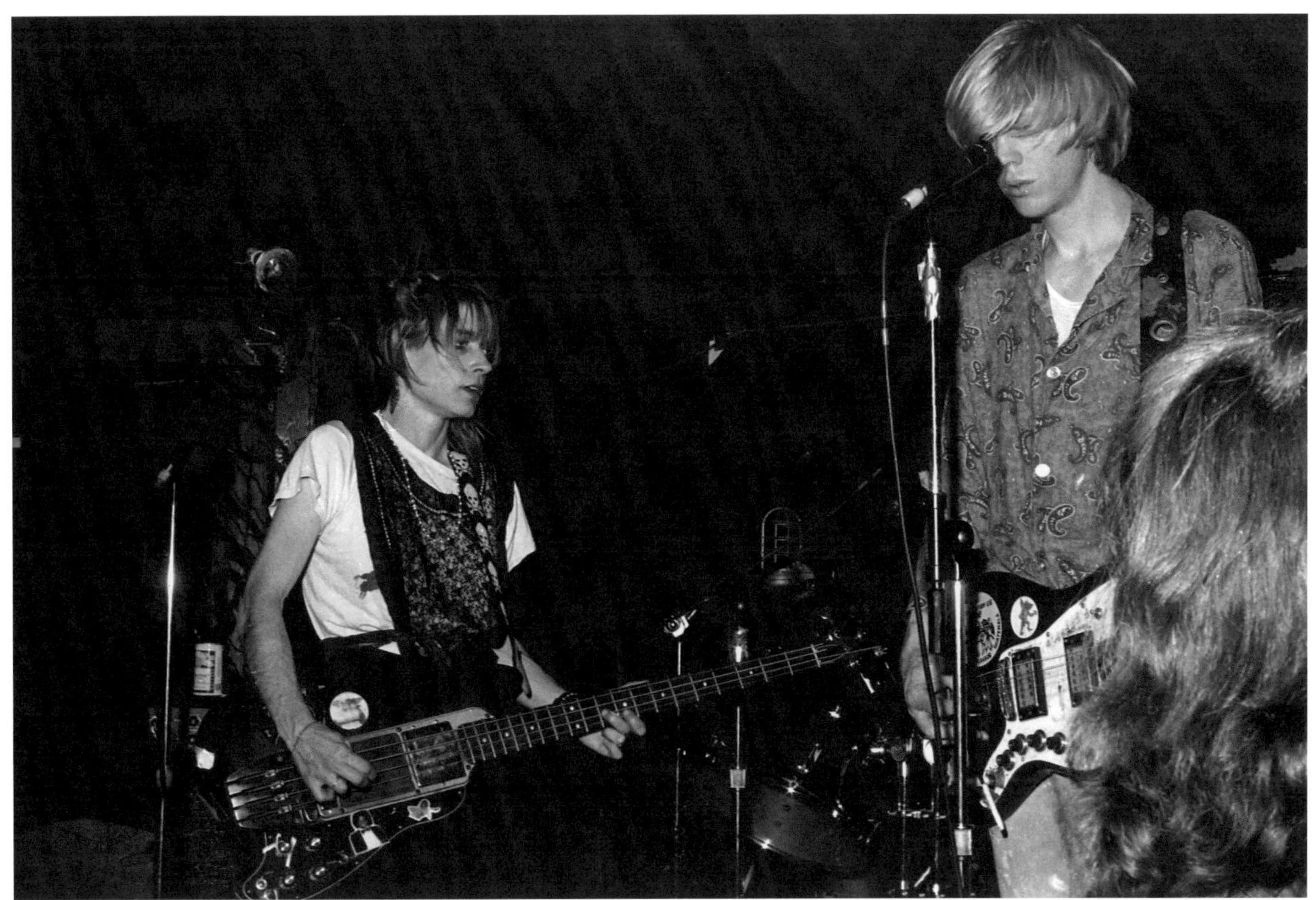

'90s, he continued taking pictures of parties and people around him. He traveled to Mexico, Berlin, and Central America, sometimes staying for months. Photography was that space between reality and make believe...The photos he took during these travels often loop back to his literal childhood, as well as his childhood fabulations and dreams. The slick surfaces and glowing street-lights during and after a summer monsoon in Mexico City recall the Paris streets seen by Brassaï, Germaine Krull, and Ilse Bing. The gestures, hairstyle and dress of a bolero performer seen in the street evoke the glamour of Mexican film stars of the golden era, but triply filtered through the passage of a half-century, poverty and old age. A tenement courtyard evokes the Tepito vecindade where his grandfather was murdered; a boy on a metal chair gazing into the camera could have been him two decades before. His photographs of indigenous children selling things in the street could have been ripped from an old *National Geographic* magazine or *The Family of Man*; they belong to another world. Later, he travels south to Chiapas and Guatemala. He stops at the edge of a village where a traveling show has set up an old Ferris wheel. The place feels as lost and remote as San Diego de la Unión seemed when he was a child.

"The photos were part of something I was documenting. And so all my work looks—if you put it back to back, it doesn't matter what the subject is, it's like one big movie. Whether I was taking photos at fashion shoots, concerts, at home or the clubs in LA. They are all of the same kind of atmosphere. Usually dark."

In 1988, Rivera's sister Herminia returned from Seville, where she'd been studying flamenco. Together with their sister Connie, they rented a house near MacArthur Park. The city's Department of Cultural Affairs was funding a Photography Center nearby, offering free workshops and printing facilities to neighborhood youth. Rivera's friend, the photographer Laura Aguilar, was in charge for a while. He got a job running the dark room. He extended his printing skills, and produced a lot of new work. The following year, they moved to a bigger apartment on Laguna Avenue, a big slice of a crumbling apartment building across the street from Echo Park Lake.

Rivera's then-boyfriend moved in. The house became a kind of center, open to anyone who arrived and needed to stay for a while. "Having my sisters guaranteed never a dull moment. I was thinking about how fortunate we were, to have each other when we were young. When we left home we had no money or education. But they all had many friends and were involved in the arts—Connie with acting, Herminia with dancing flamenco. Herminia was working at a punk rock venue called The Vex in East LA, so she knew a lot of people in the Chicano music scene. We knew a lot of people, and we would pool our friends at all the parties we had." They were broke most of the time, and Rivera sold off the collection of records and books he'd gathered in Stockton, but there was always a pot of lentils or beans on the stove. All kinds of people came by, and their Echo Park house became one of LA's most cosmopolitan salons. They had movie nights, discussions, dinners, Halloween galas and holiday parties, and regular

Sonic Youth at Anti-Club, Hollywood (1985)

23

parties at least once a month. Cindy Gomez performed in their living room.

Rivera documented it all. He had a Rolleiflex 2.8 camera he'd bought for $75 from a woman in Echo Park. Between 1989–1998, he produced a remarkable body of work taken at the houses he shared in Echo Park. The photographs range from portraits to group photographs to performance documentation and snapshots, but all produced at that moment, that I've never seen documented before, where for a brief moment LA was a glamorous outpost where all kinds of people of different races and countries, queer and straight, privileged and street, mixed.

The Riveras stayed at the place on Laguna for five years, and eventually moved over to Laveta Terrace, where he remained with his partner Bianco until 2002 when the building was sold.

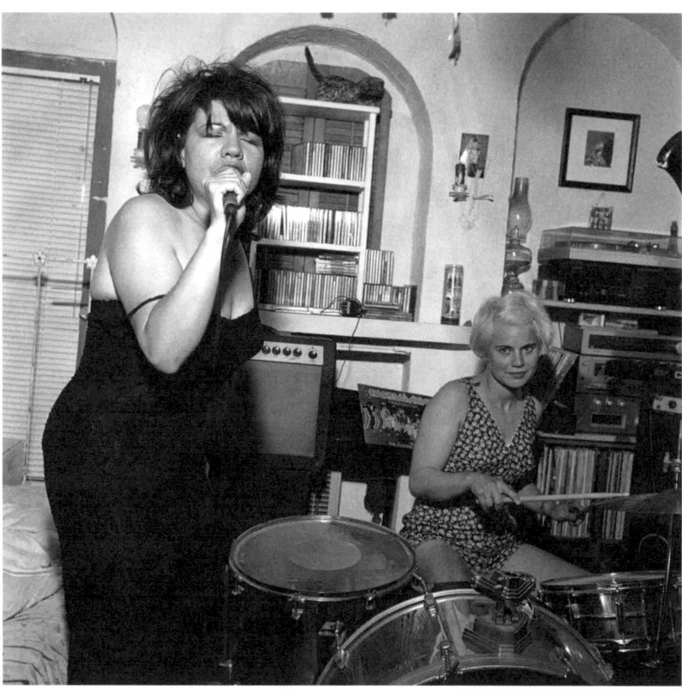

3.
Se agradece todo, hasta lo fingido

During his first visits to the Hollywood club in the mid-1980s, Luis Bauz writes in his story *La Plaza*, "the crowd was 90% Latino, and its main attraction was the female impersonators—an amazing show. What is better than to drink a whiskey sour, contemplating feathers, dance sequences, very cheap jewelry and lip syncing? All the famous Latin American, Spanish and even American divas were performing behind a crystallized illusion: Raffaella Carrà, Amanda Miguel, Olga Guillot, Lucha Villa..."

Rivera went to La Plaza a few times with friends in the late '80s. Located on the same block of La Brea as Pink's hot dog stand, the club was hardcore Mexican and Latin American, and no English was spoken there. "The neighborhood then, it was just dead. There was nothing besides Pink's on that street. It's amazing how many of these neighborhoods

that now look so chic were once, not that long ago, Latino neighborhoods. Like Silver Lake, Griffith Park, even Pasadena—they completely wiped us clean." It wasn't unusual for gay Mexican writers and artists like Rivera and Bauz to stop by for 2-for-1 Margaritas and check the place out. The club remains open, now catering mostly to tourists and students, but at that time it was a big open room with long side-by-side tables, like a church or cheap banquet hall. The raised stage had a homemade-looking sparkly backdrop, but every set ended with a turn through the hall, where performers would collect tips.

La Plaza was one of several other LA Latino drag bars like the Silverlake Lounge, Little Joy, Club Mugy's and Le Bar at a time when Latino gay and drag bars were the same thing. Miss Alex was one of La Plaza's stars. Most performers remained in one place, but she rotated between clubs. Rivera became interested in her and photographed one of Miss Alex's shows at La Plaza in 1989. She has large breasts, round buttocks and thick, shiny hair cut in a bob, and she's wearing a lace bodysuit barely laced up at the front. Miss Alex—born as a boy in a small Veracruz village—hadn't fully transitioned, but at the time, few people had. And what would be the point of performing for someone who'd completely transitioned to female? One of the rules of the clubs that performers had to still have a penis. As Rivera recalls: "It wasn't a matter of transvestite or transgender. In those days, everyone was a transvestite. There was no variant. In those days, no one differentiated between transgender and trans, because there was no trans. It seemed like the majority of the performers were transgender, because most of them lived as women, or as much as they could."

Miss Alex came by the Laguna apartment and Rivera interviewed her about her early life. She told him she'd been 12 or 13 when a tour bus of transvestites came to perform in her village. Late at night, after the show, they all went to the park to turn tricks. When they were discovered, armed, angry residents ran them out of town, threatening to kill. Hating his life in the town and having nothing to lose, Alex left with them, and arrived in Mexico City, where she became Alejandra. But it was 4 a.m. when they talked, and then she left, so the story stopped there.

One night, Rivera took his Mexico City friend, the photographer Armando Cristeto along to the Silverlake Lounge to see Miss Alex perform. "I was like, oh, I want you to go see this person I know, I think it's fun, blah blah blah. And when we got there, he was stunned. He said, oh my God, that's Miss Alex! You don't know this, but in Mexico, she's huge—she writes a column for La Jornada, 'Letters From Hollywood,' and everyone over there thinks she's living this Hollywood lifestyle. If only they knew! Well, in a way she's telling the truth. Her letters were from Hollywood. East."

"Armando told me the story about the muscle builder. By the time he knew her, she'd become the toast of the town. She was in her late teens, very well known. And she was gorgeous. She met a photographer, was also very well known over there. He was photographing a muscle show of body-builders. And one of the guys that he photographed, what's it called? Adonis? It's a very famous photo of his. But this guy, Adonis, is apparently who she fell in love with. And they had

Cindy Gomez, Echo Park (1992)

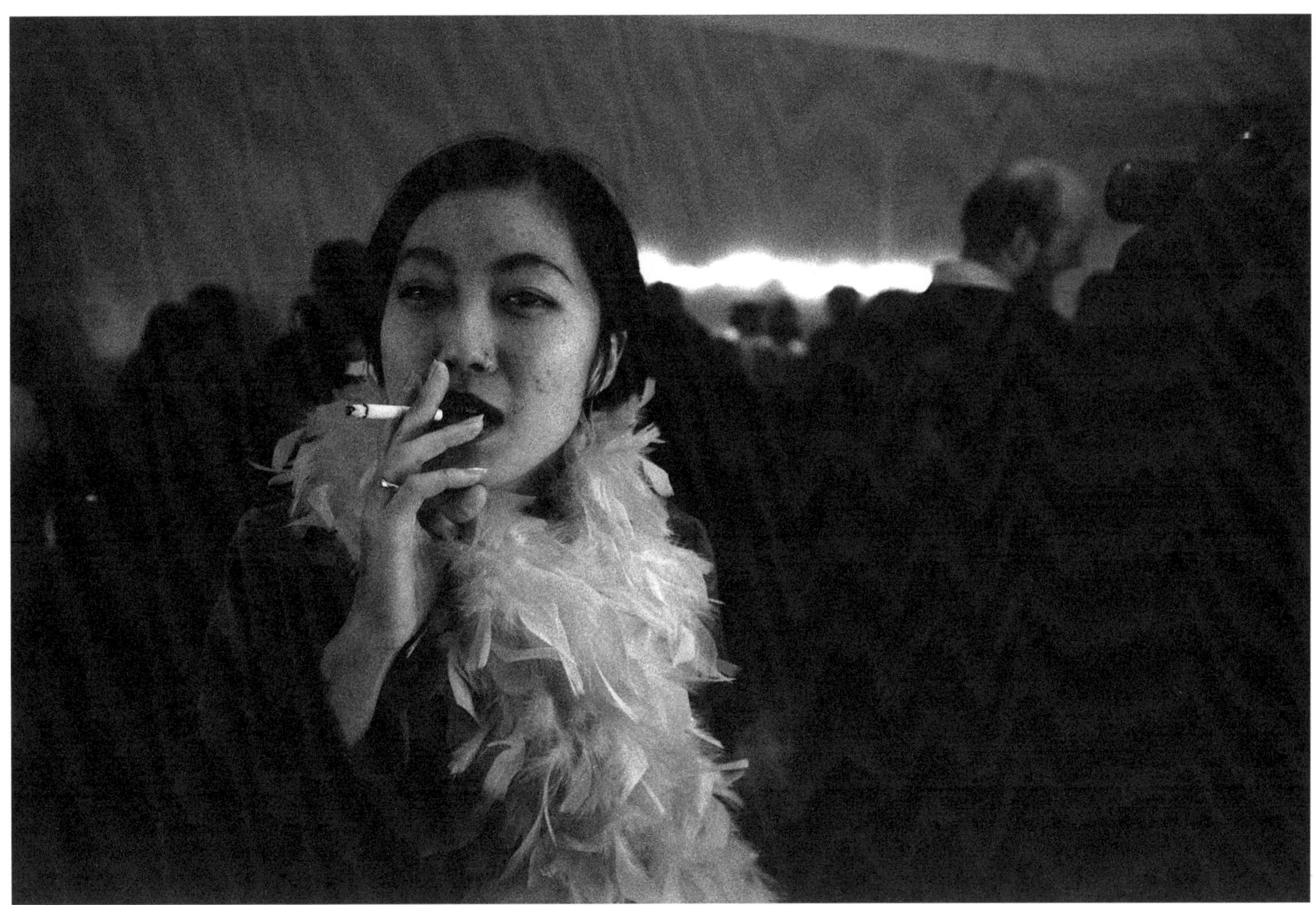

this romance. She was head over heels. And they were both at the top of their game—the *crème de la crème* in certain social circles in Mexico City. Then he moved to the US to compete, and she followed him. And that was the last anyone heard of her, except for these 'Letters From Hollywood'. But at a certain point, this Adonis obviously dumped her. She was friends with Carlos Medina, and I think he got her the La Plaza gig. And she ended up staying here, and resorted to—what most of them do (p. 129).

"You would never have known about her past. That she was a writer, or knew all these super famous people in Mexico City. All the stuff that was between the pages…I mean, the lives some of these girls had had, you would never guess. She was gorgeous in the mid-'80s, but by the time I photographed her in 1990, she was a mess. But still a star. Even after she started getting fat and swollen, she navigated the world like a person of importance. All I knew at first was at face value— that she was a little messy and crazy and interesting. But interesting in, like, a jacket is interesting—in a very superficial way. But as I got to know her, and all of this stuff, I found it just very deep. It was not like the cliché.

"Most of the trans population resorted to prostitution. That was the real 'tragedy.' Everyone always viewed this section of society as tragic. Even within the so-called gay community, they were always viewed with disdain. And in a way, they had tragic lives. But it all stemmed from their social, financial, situation, from not being able to get work. Who would hire a transvestite in those days? They couldn't

get a job pumping gas, you know what I mean? And so what are you supposed to do? It was their inability to get financial stability that was the tragedy. It made for a very unstable life. And when you live this kind of life, you have a lot of crazy shit happen to you.

"I realized, by the end of the '90s, that almost everyone in these photos was dead. Angela and Laura are the ones who did well. They lived like women, and they didn't have tragic endings. But the others? Melissa del Llano went to Mexico to get injections that would get rid of the wrinkles in her face and give her cheekbones. She ended up looking like a pin-cushion, totally deformed. She had an allergic reaction to the silicon they injected her with, and she suffered with this until she died. Paloma died, Olga died. And it wasn't any long, drawn out sickness. One day they're here, the next, you hear they died. When I went back, they were like, oh, she had a heart attack. Miss Alex ended up dying at County USC. She had a stroke. She smoked a lot of crack."

Rivera, and his Silver Lake friends Luis Bauz and Carlos Medina, started going often to the clubs. It became their derive. The clubs were Mexican and gay, and a lot more entertaining than artist bars or the bourgeois homosexual scene in West Hollywood. Their credibility at La Plaza was cemented when Rivera brought his mom along one night to see the show. Rogelio, the main waiter in charge of seating, had always harbored a particular dislike for Rivera and his friends. When his mom and Rogelio saw each other, they em-braced and wept. They were old friends from the gay scene in

Untitled, Echo Park (1992)

the 1970s. He'd been afraid of coming out, but she helped him
and even wrote a song for him and talked him out of getting married.

Rivera gained the trust of the performers by taking
photos of their shows and making prints for anyone who
wanted them. He made everyone look the kind of "good" they
most craved, even when they normally didn't. Photographed
between sets at La Plaza, Olga is a stocky, older man who looks
like Félix Guattari (p.59). In his images of her performances,
Rivera sees through the literal physical evidence of Olga's
gender to the spirit that animates her. Her arms may be hairy,
but wearing a blonde wig tousled into a bubble-cut she
projects the spirit of a little girl. Her key-lit eyes are soft and
limpid. Or, more accurately: Rivera isn't documenting what is
literally before him. He's documenting Olga's inner life, her
dreams and fantasies. His photographs transform dissonance
into glamour.

The performers saw him as a friend, and within two
years, he gained access to the dressing room, which was where
he knew he had to be. "For me, the most interesting part
always happened between closed doors in the dressing room.
That's where all the interesting shit was going on. The stage
was like the outcome. It was almost like a come down, at least
for me. Almost all my images from then on where taken in
the dressing room—that's where you heard all the gossip and
the fights.

The backstage photos taken at La Plaza in 1992–1993
are of an old-fashioned theatrical or dance production put on
by a troupe of traveling performers who know each other well.
The scenes recall the backstage life in Paris music halls Colette
describes in *The Vagabond*. Olga sits alone, writing at the
dressing table in a bra and panty hose (p.56); Melissa del Llano
adjusts her ostrich boa while Olga, dressed as a man, strides
darkly by, and Gabi combs her wig, looking in the mirror (p.50).
Wearing a vest and a long-sleeved white shirt, the waiter
Rogelio perches on the make-up table. Angela, wearing a tight
crushed velvet dress and heels, sprays her hair, while Olga,
un-costumed, still wearing his round rimless glasses, looks
on. Rogelio looks like a kind of impresario; Angela's a show-
girl, and Olga projects the aura of a European intellectual.
Garments larded with feathers, taffeta ruffles and sequins spill
out of an open closet. It's girlie heaven.

Except for Miss Alex, the performers didn't move
around from club to club. Rivera began connecting with performers from the other clubs and photographing them. At Club
Mugy's, an Asian, Filipino and Latino drag bar at Hollywood
and Western, Rivera made friends with Ou (also known as
Tina), a Thai performer who did a show impersonating
Michael Jackson: a man, dressed as a woman, impersonating
a man. Photographed at Rivera's home on Laveta Terrace
(p. 205) Ou is a slight, slender man. In drag, his stature seems
to double. His repertoire included a Japanese geisha in kimono,
a Chinese dragon-lady in a beaded gown and diamond
choker, and a Marilyn Monroe emerging from the shower
wrapped up in a towel. By day, Ou worked at a hair salon on
Hollywood Blvd.

Club Mugy's had a different, more artistic spin than
La Plaza. "It was a shit hole, pretty much. You can see that in
the photos. There was just a little stage. Unlike the Latino drag
bars, where everyone was trying to be really glitzy, the girls
at Mugy's were much crazier." Yoshi, the bar-owner, was best
known for his kabuki flamenco routine.

Rivera first exhibited the club photographs in 1995 at
Julie Rico. "I was careful not to use the word transvestite
anywhere. Because I didn't want that kind of sensationalism.
Because I didn't see that, there. They were beautiful photos of
performers, who were performing. There's a whole social layer
going on, behind this. The period when they were taken was
just before all these big transvestite movies came out. All of a
sudden, they became popular. They were still fucked, but they
were in the media.

"The gallerist really wanted to push the sensationalism,
a 'transvestite show.' A guy from Jane's Addiction really liked
the work. But I just got turned off with where they were going
with this. I didn't want any part of it. I've never wanted this
work to be about that. In my mind, it was never the intention.
When I photographed these people, I was just documenting a
moment that I found beautiful and interesting.

"When I had the idea of doing this book, I saw it as a
way of leaving a kind of document, saying, We were here.
We were once here, and this was once a very ethnically diverse
city, with Vietnamese, Mexicans, whatever. We were all mixed
in together. All these neighborhoods were ethnically diverse.
I mean we were all there, everyone. It was just Latino,
obviously. Most of us were poor, but then again we were living
in a different time, where you could live with a minimum wage
job. You could quit your job to go out for lunch, because you
knew you could just get another shitty job. You weren't afraid
of losing your apartment. At Laguna Avenue, I paid $375.
The place was a dump, but it was cheap. It was a cool place
to live in.

Thinking about putting together this book, I wanted
to leave a different story. There's so little written by Latinos
here in the southwest, for us, by us, or about us. There's such
a small trace of us. That's why we always feel like we just
got here. Because we can't seem to connect to this past, ever."

26

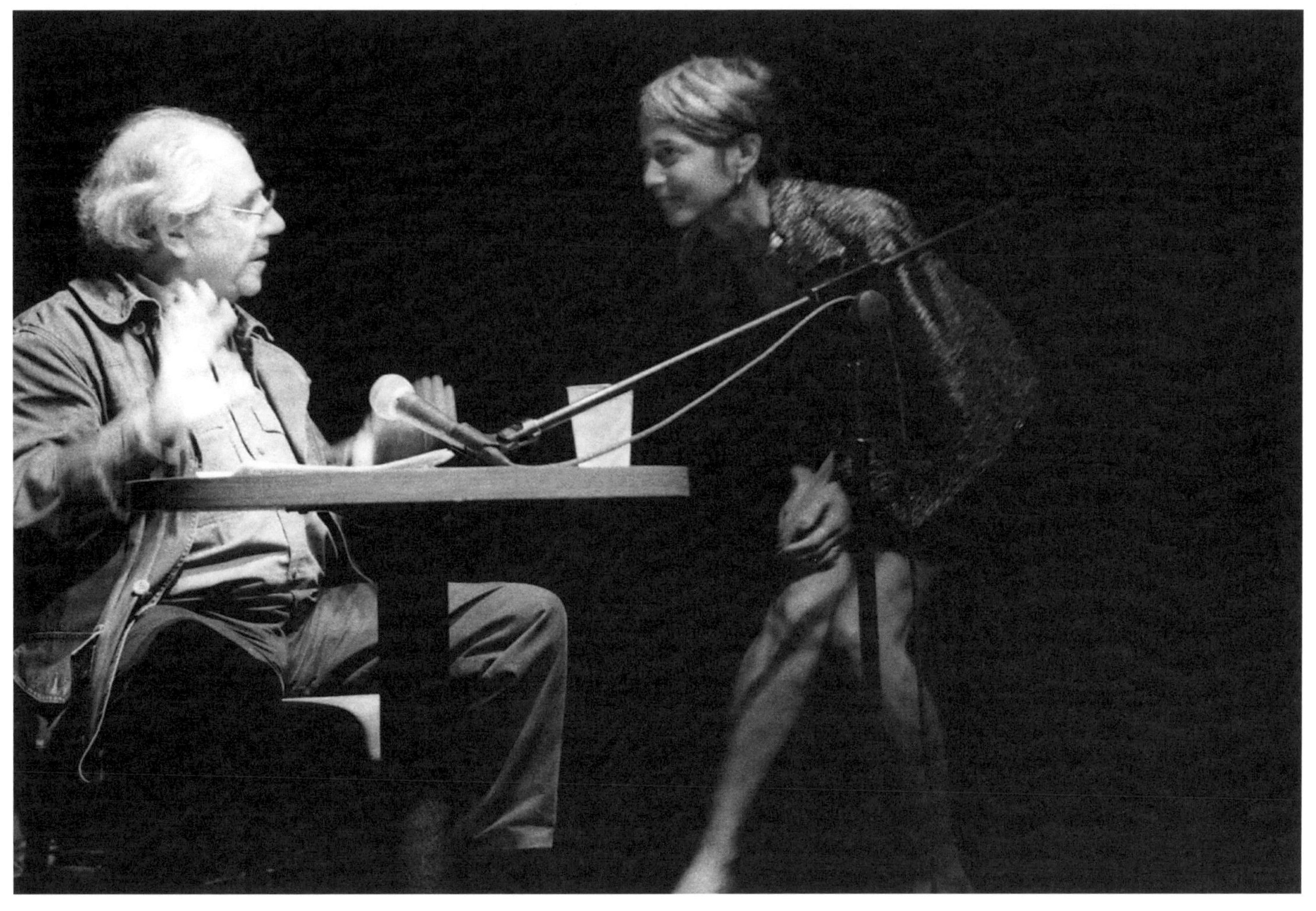

Jean Baudrillard and Chris Kraus, Chance Event (1996)

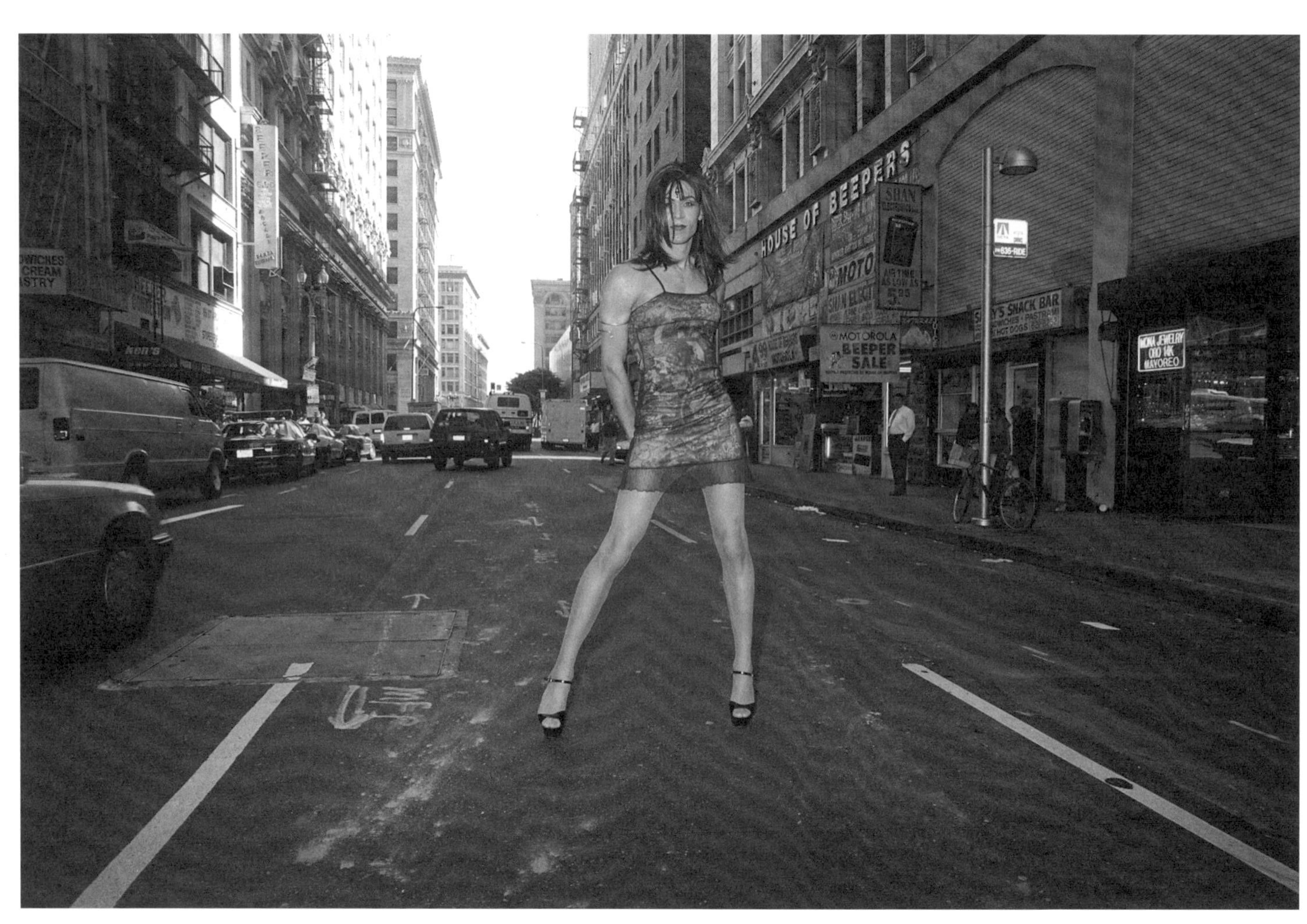

Untitled, Downtown LA (n.d.)

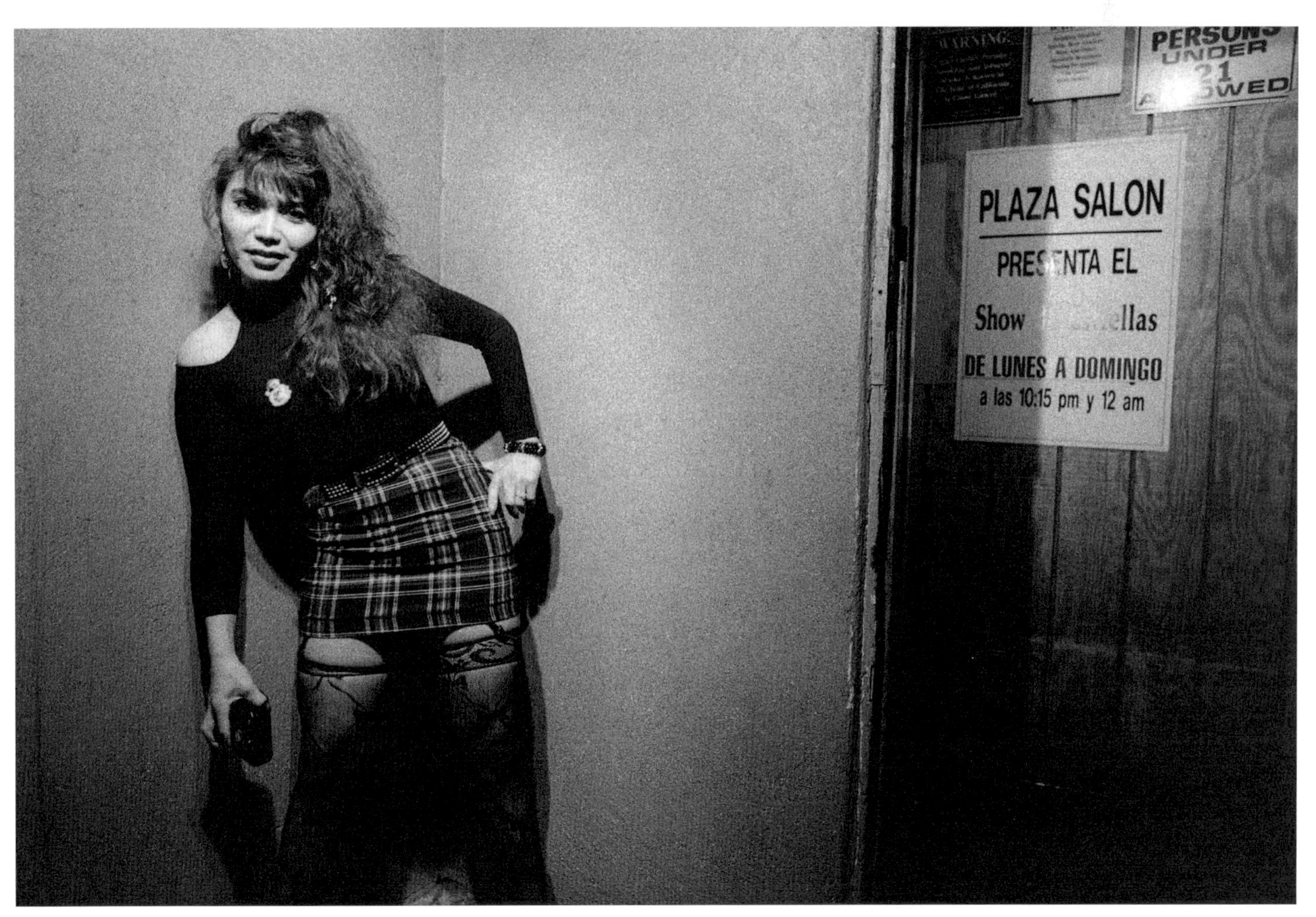

Patron, La Plaza (1994)

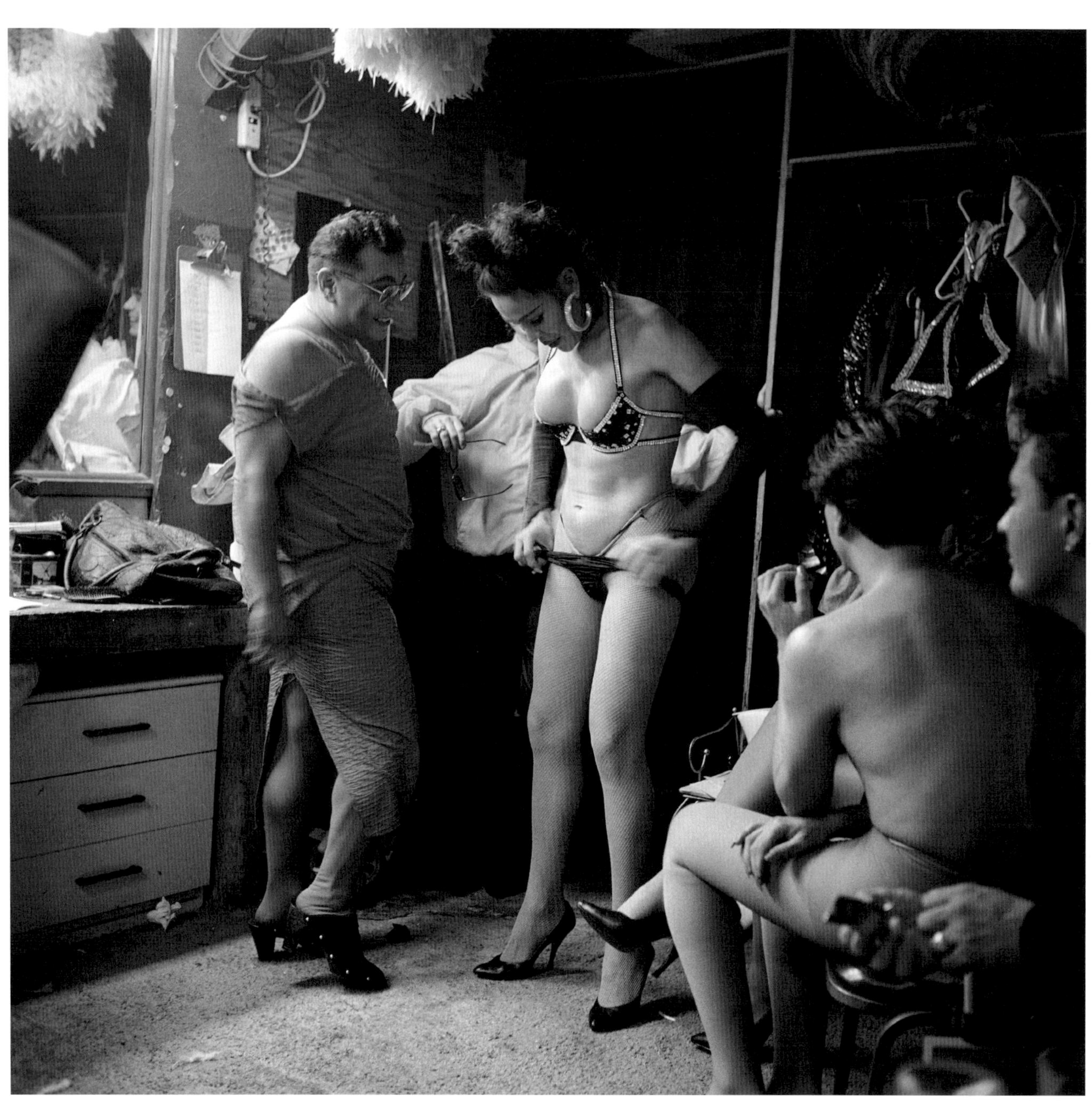

Olga, Angela, and Paloma, La Plaza (1993)

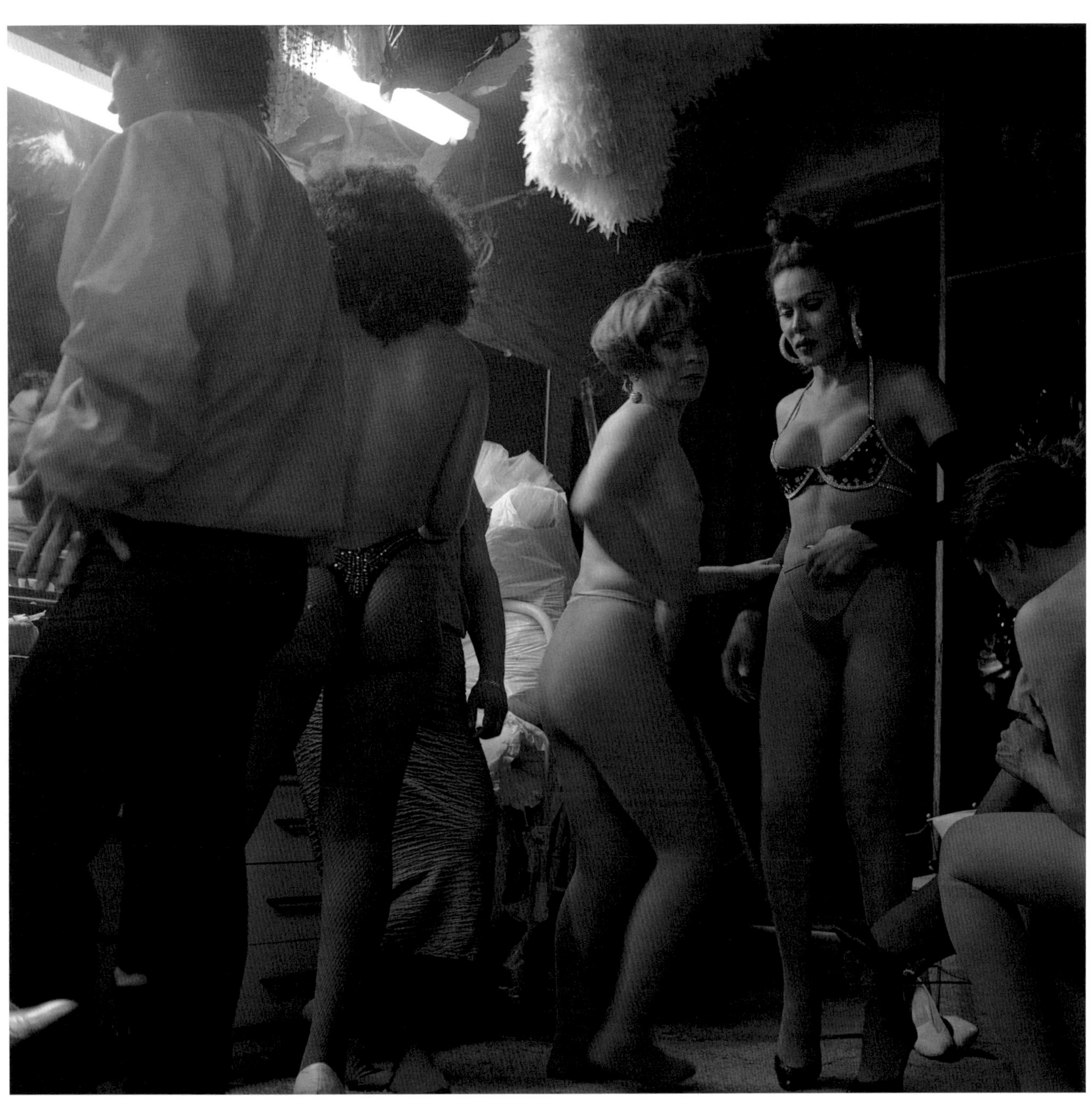

Gaby (back), Melissa, and Angela, La Plaza (1993)

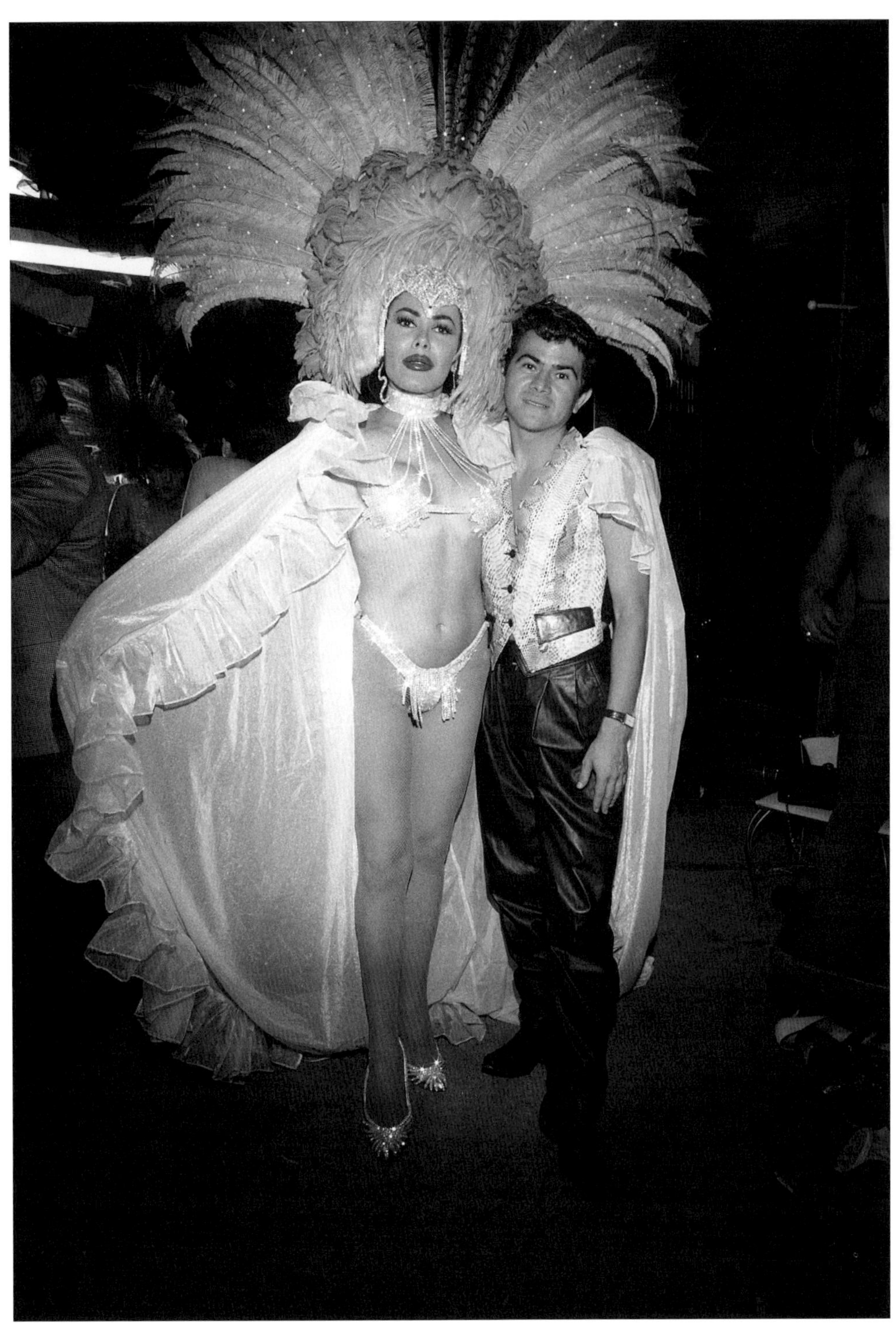

Angela, La Plaza (1993)

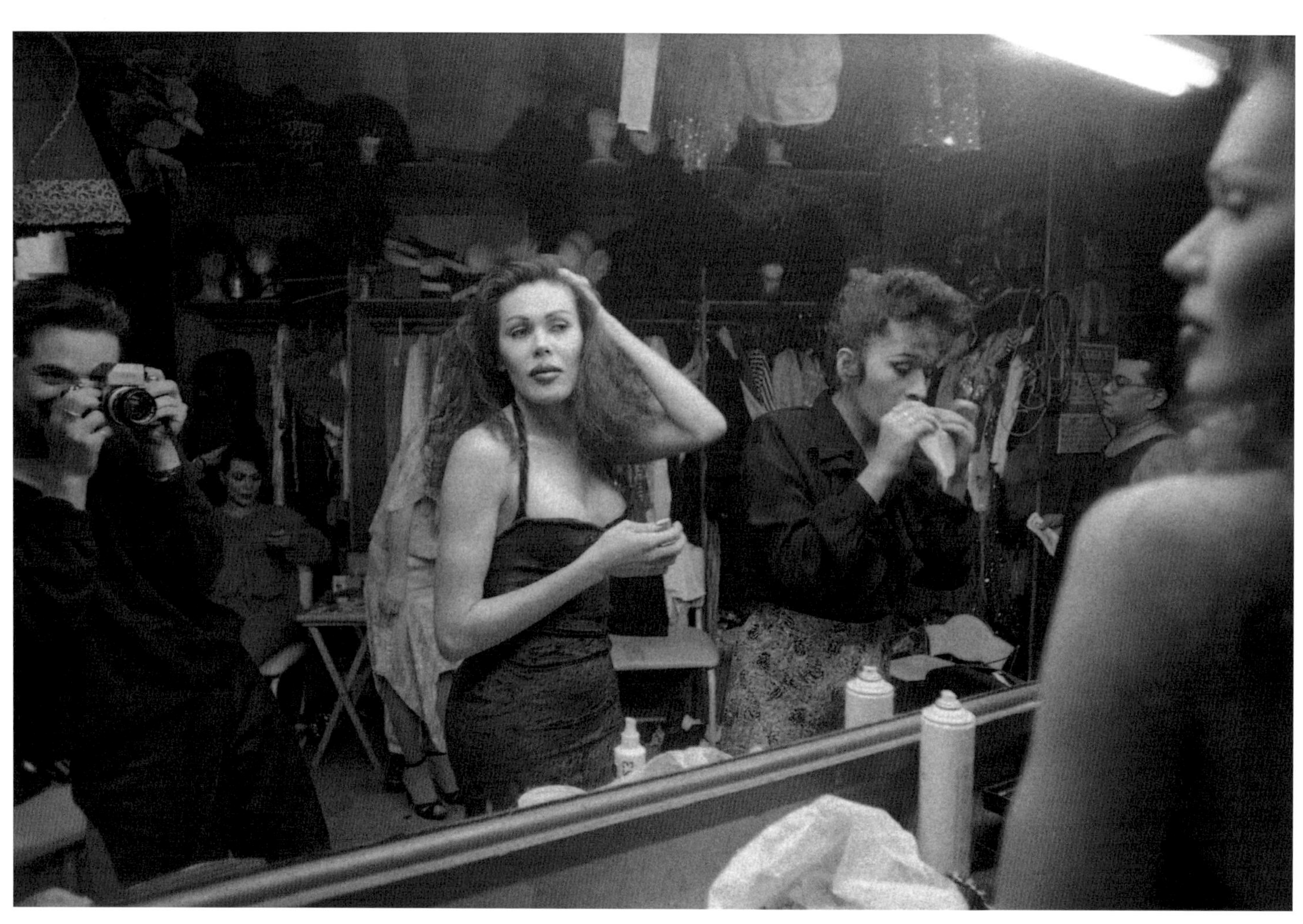

Reynaldo, Miss Alex, and Angela, La Plaza (1993)

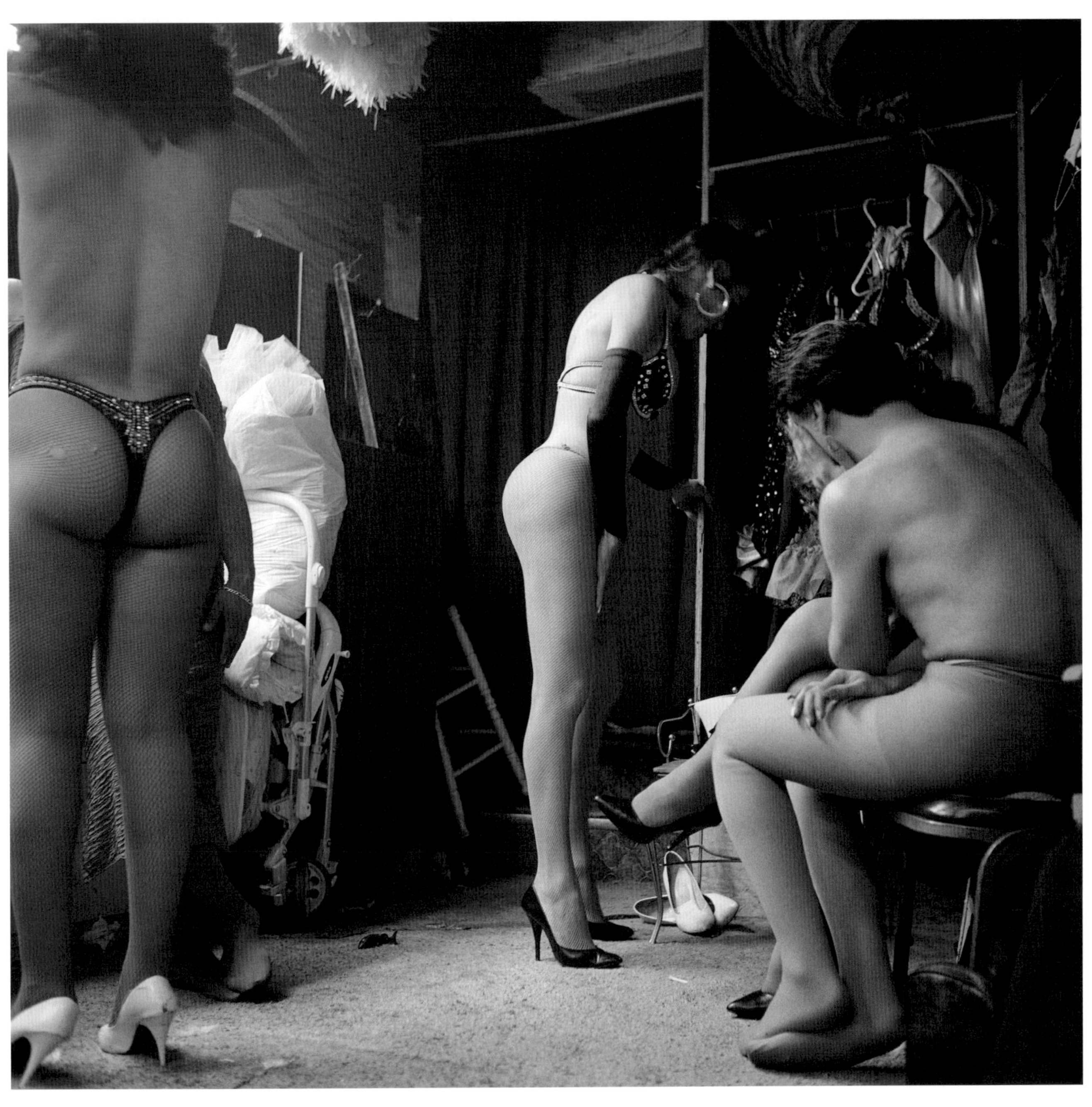

Angela, La Plaza (1993)

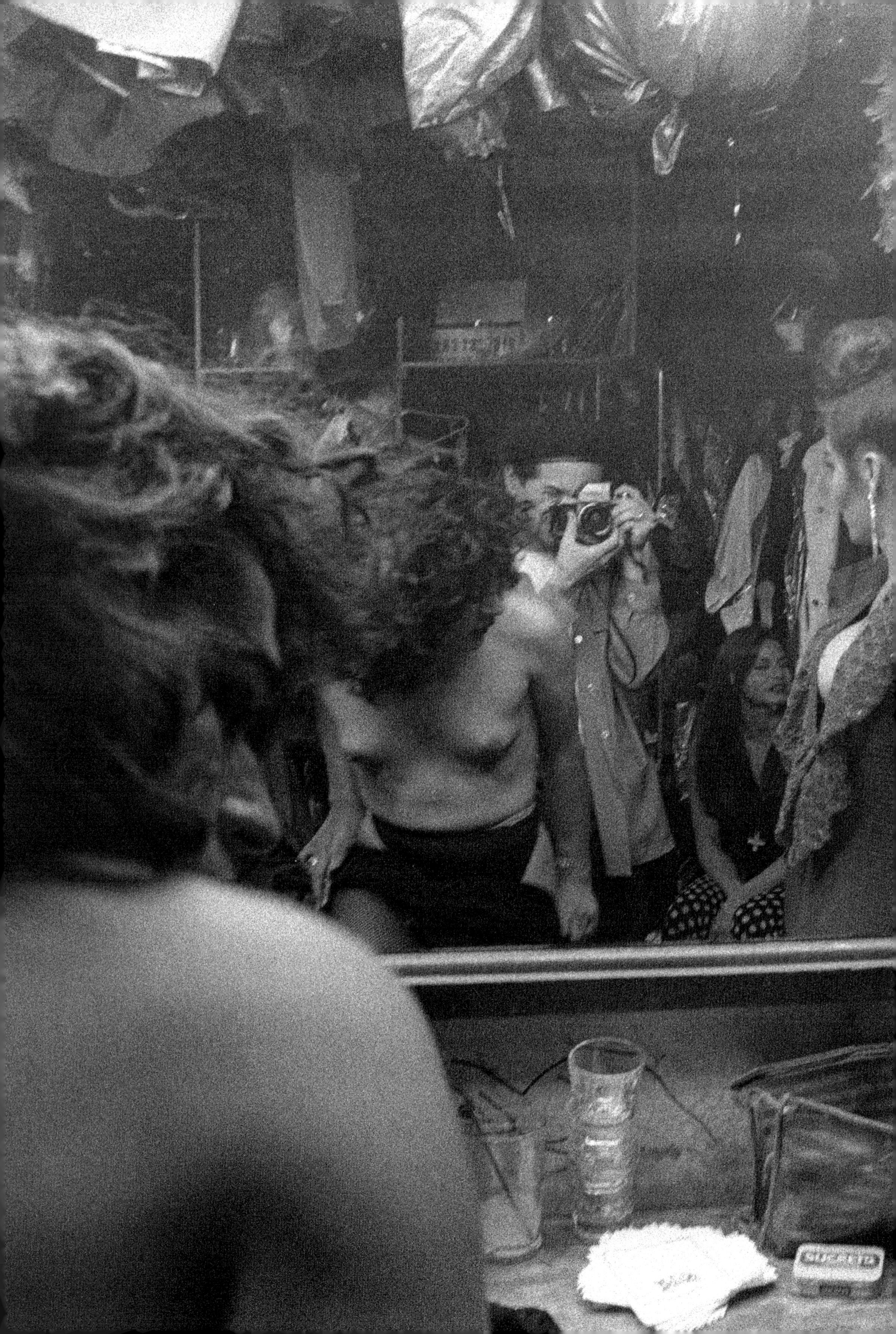

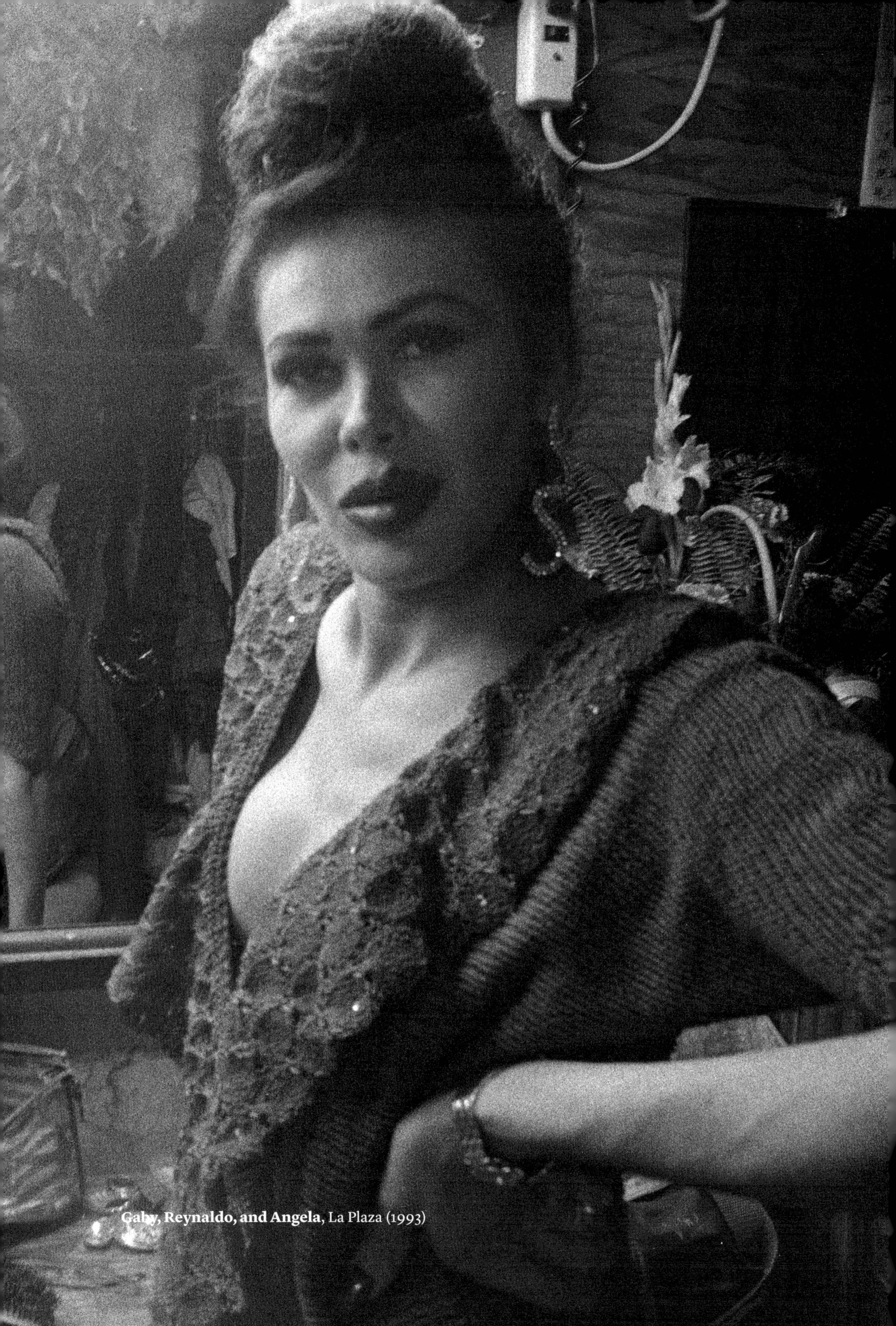

Gaby, Reynaldo, and Angela, La Plaza (1993)

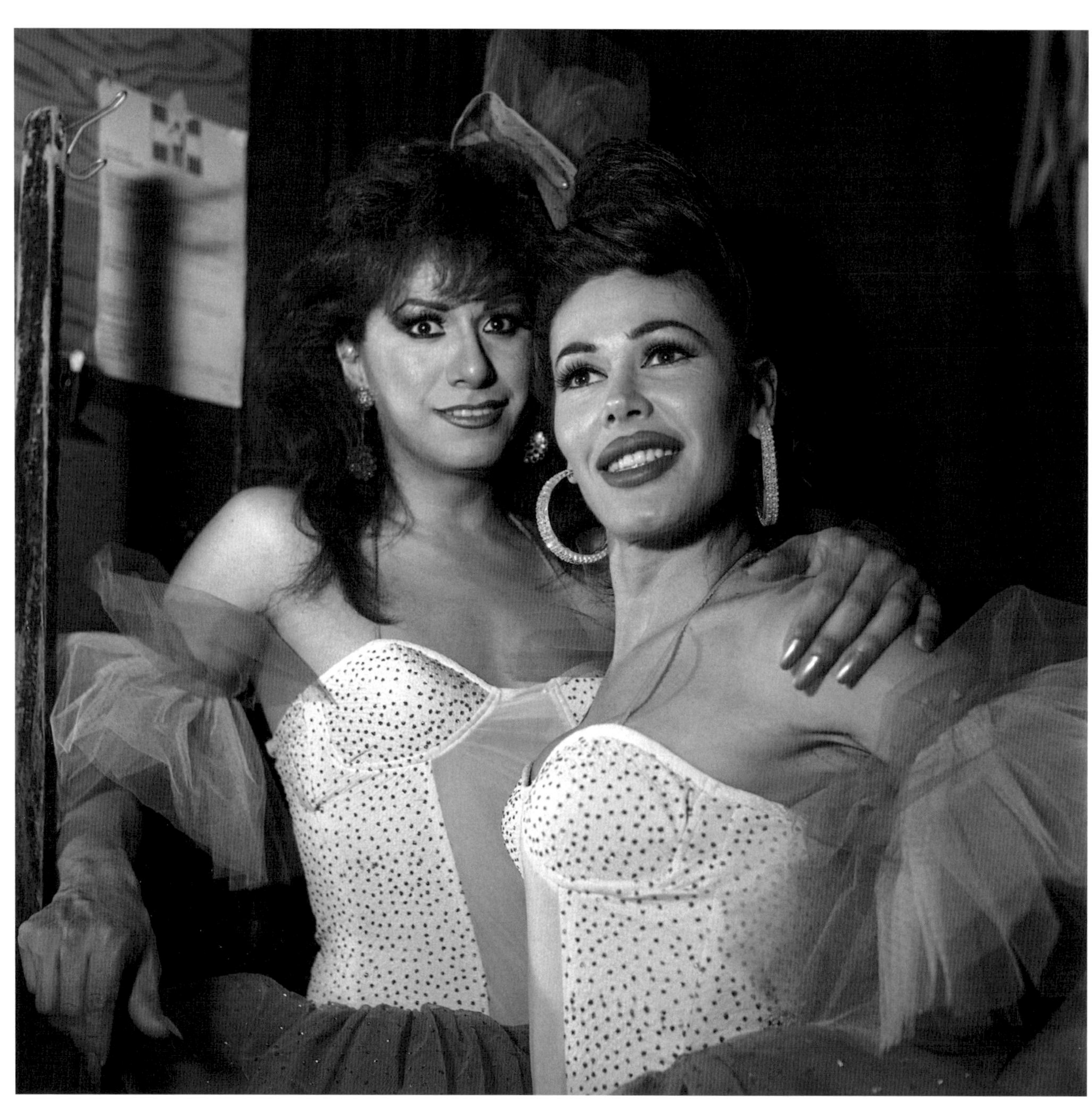

Angela and Paloma, La Plaza (1993)

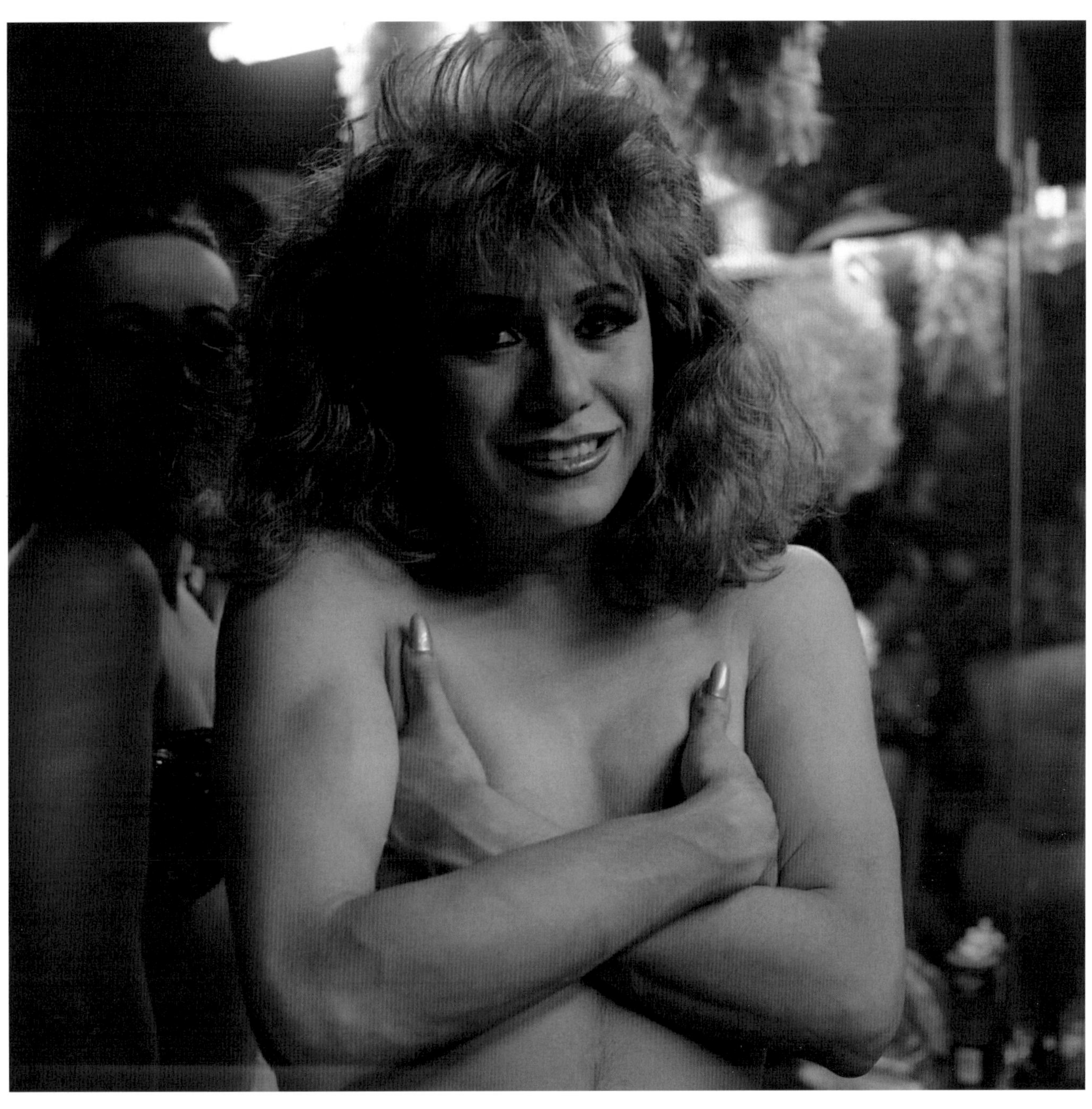

Melissa and Paloma, La Plaza (1993)

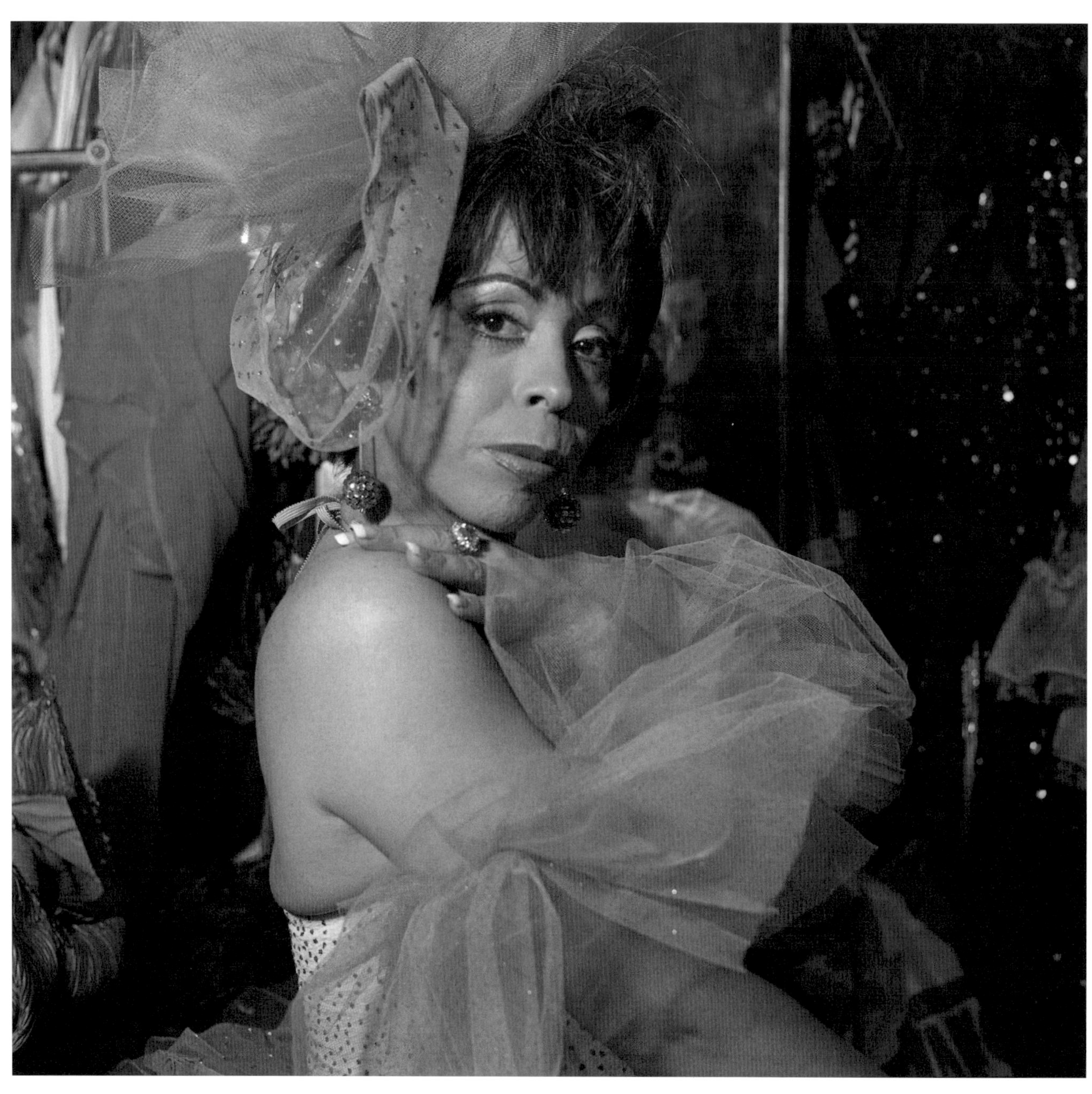

Melissa, La Plaza (1993)

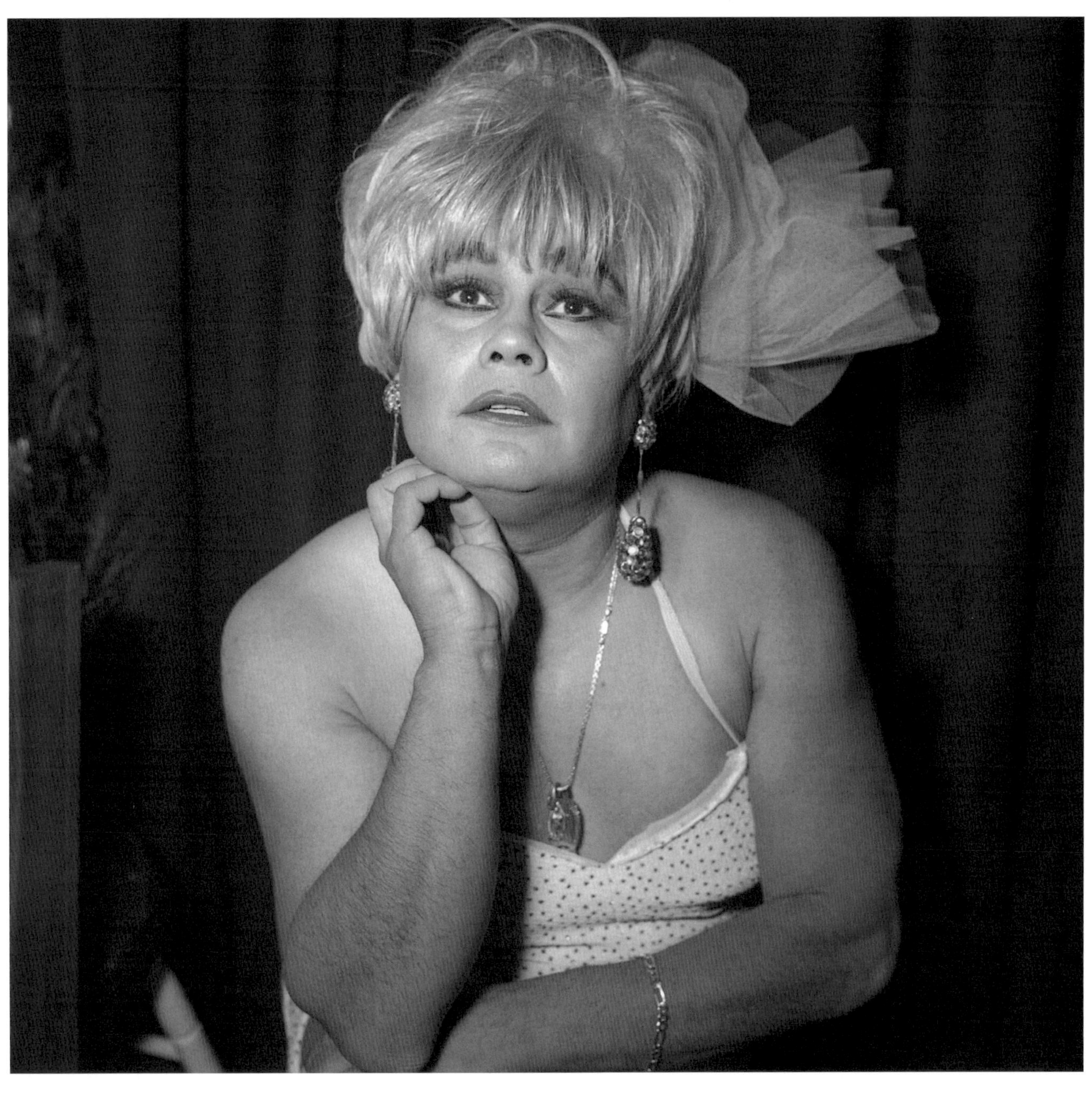

Olga, La Plaza (1993)

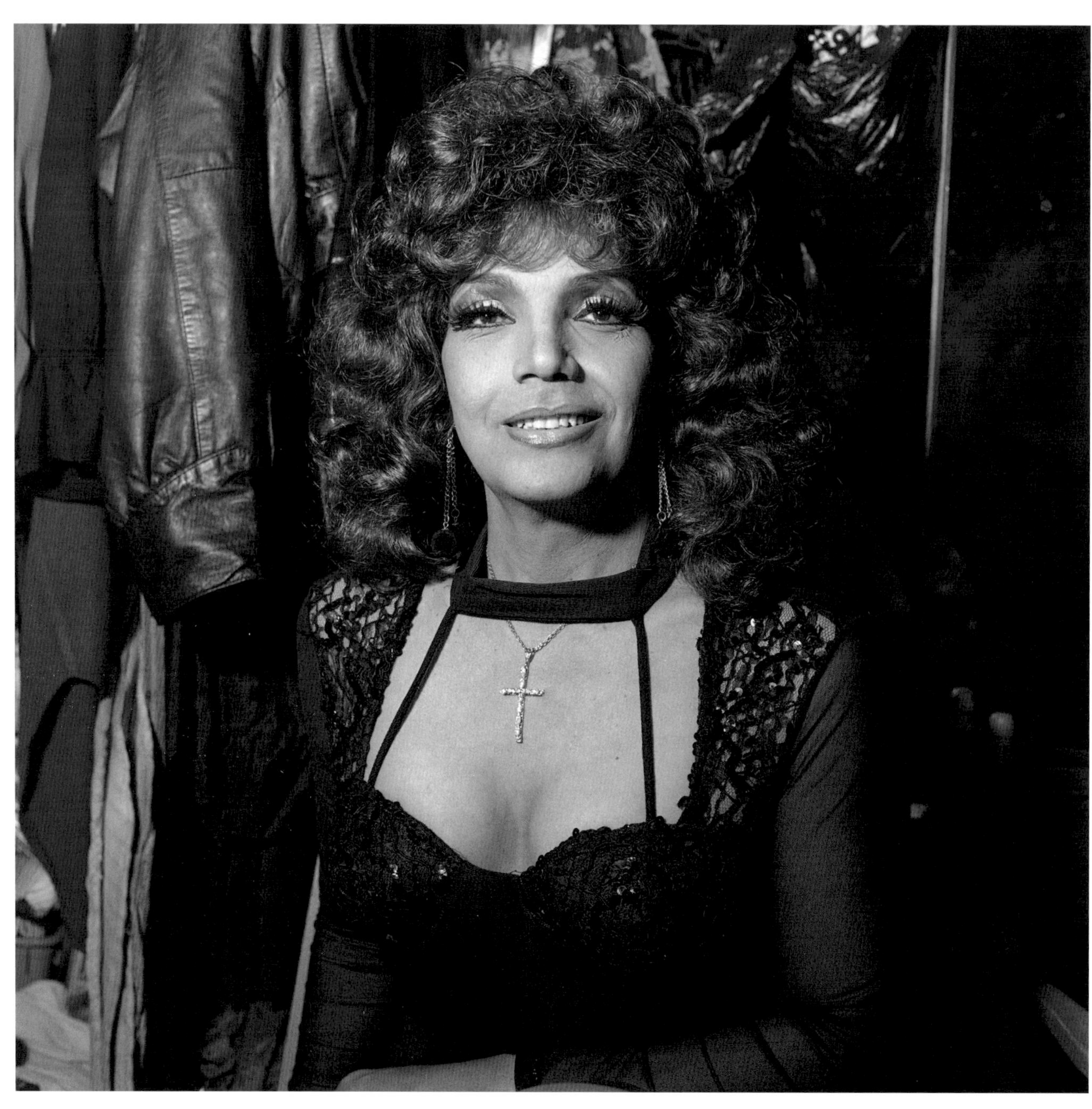

Performer, La Plaza (1993)

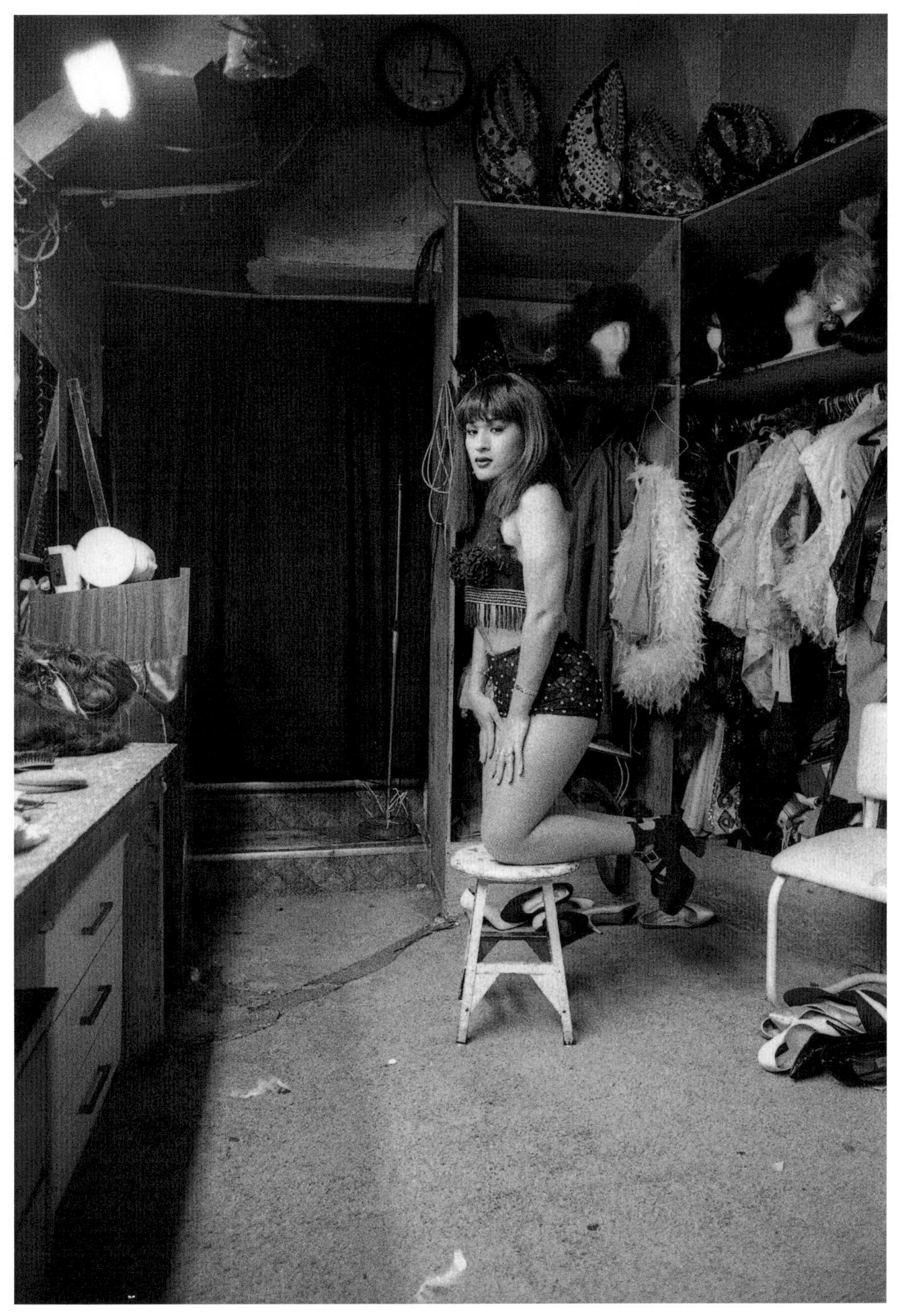

Gaby, La Plaza (1993)

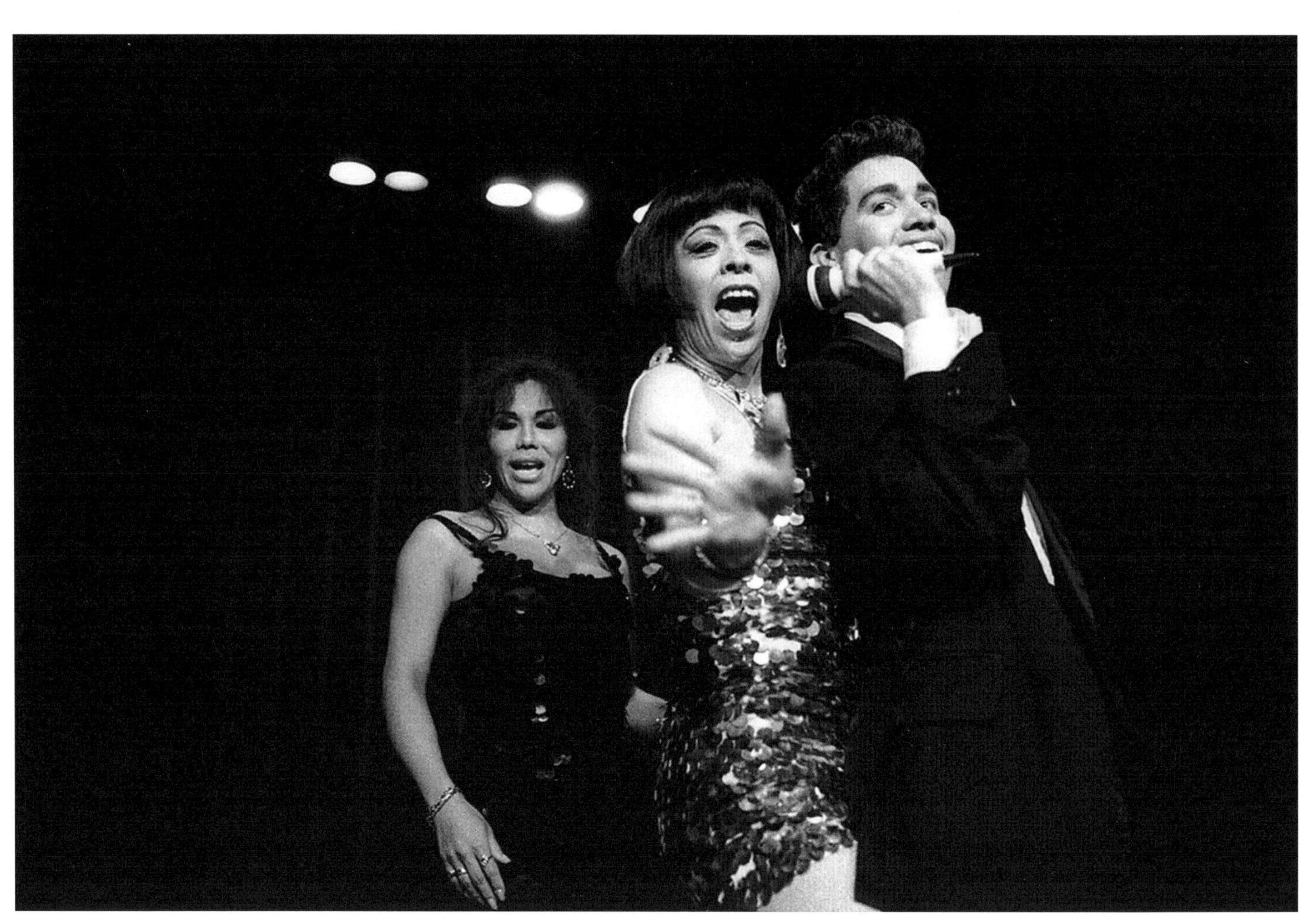

Laura and Melissa, La Plaza (1994)

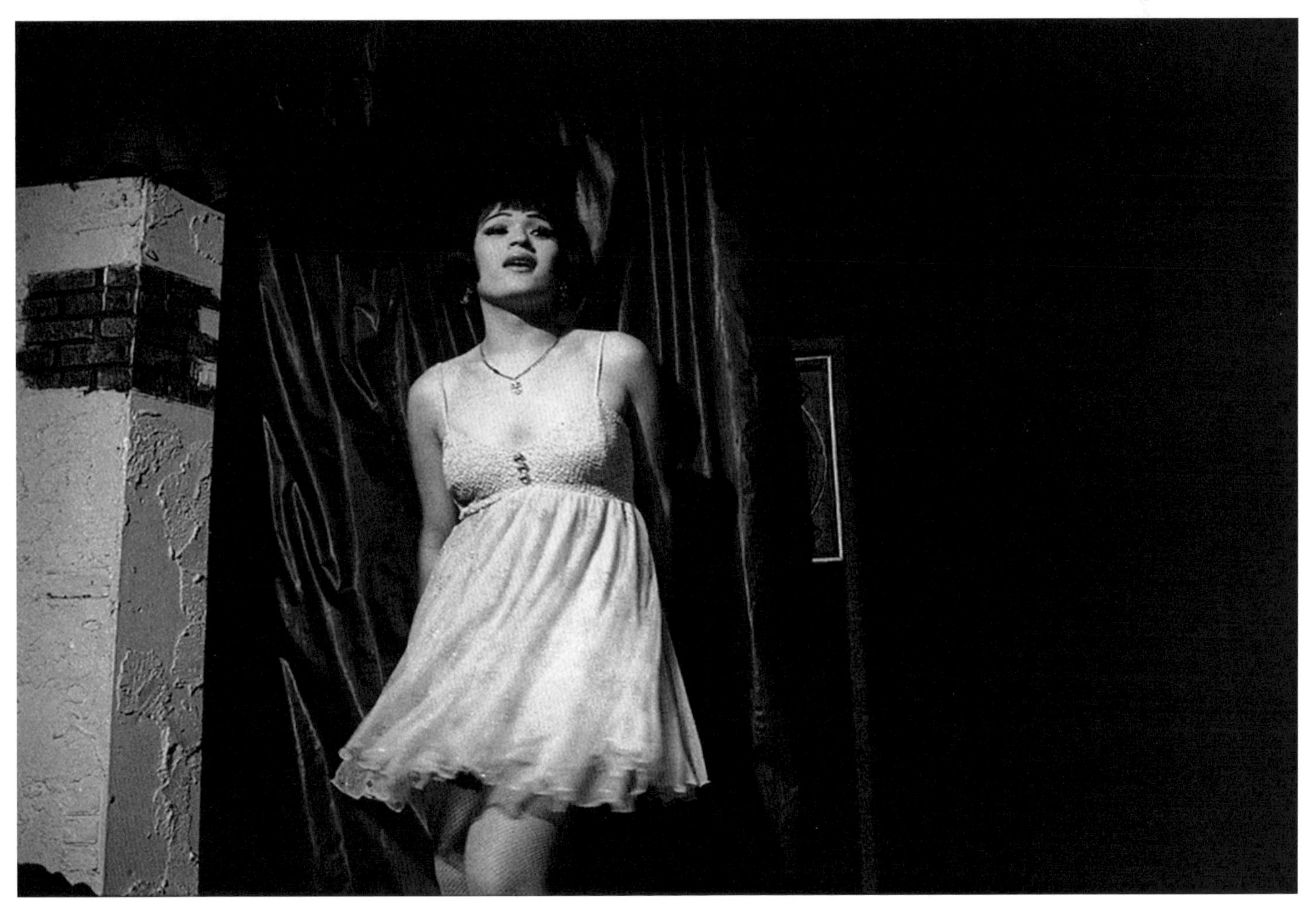

Gaby, La Plaza (1994)

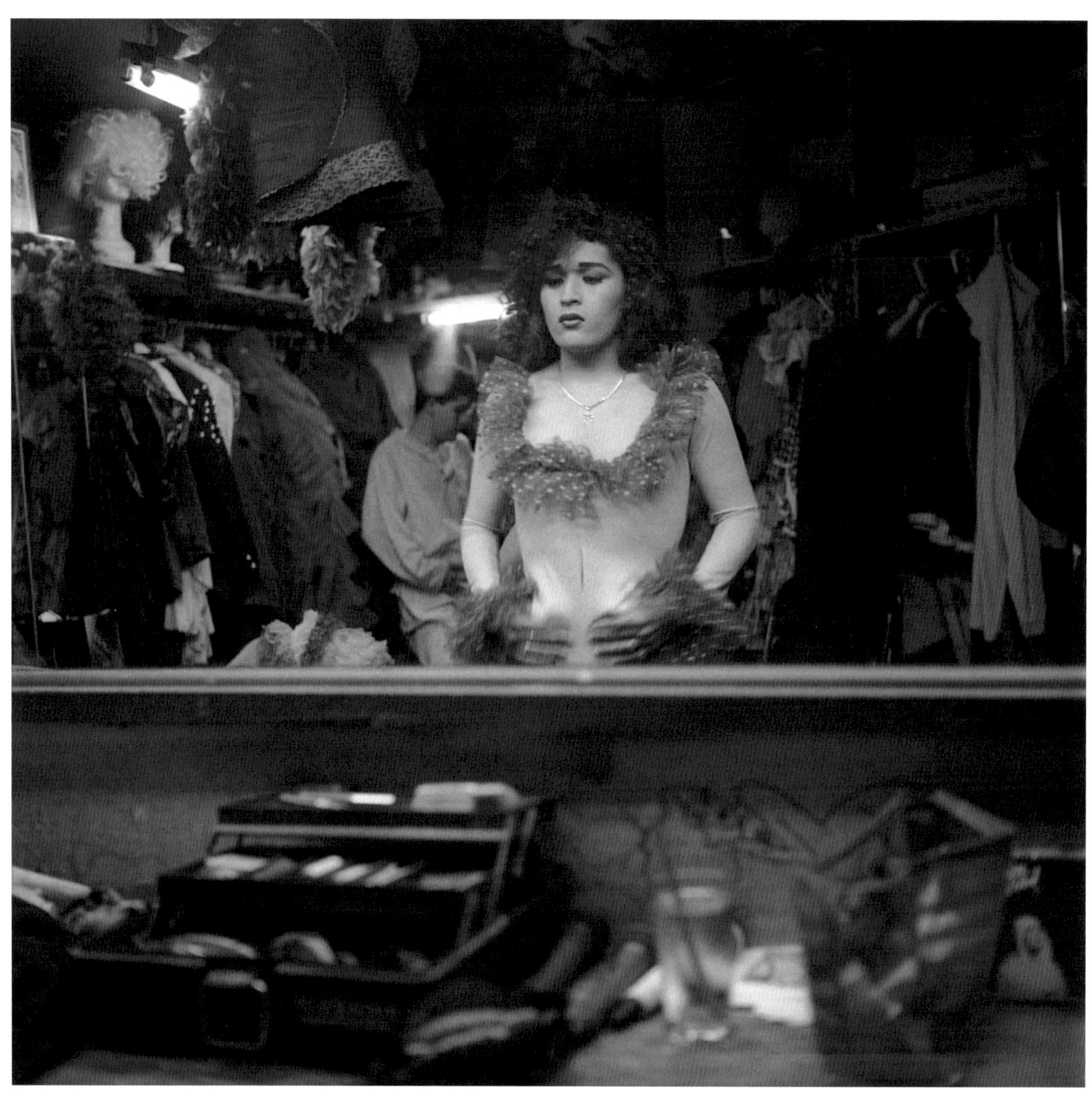

Gaby, La Plaza (1993)

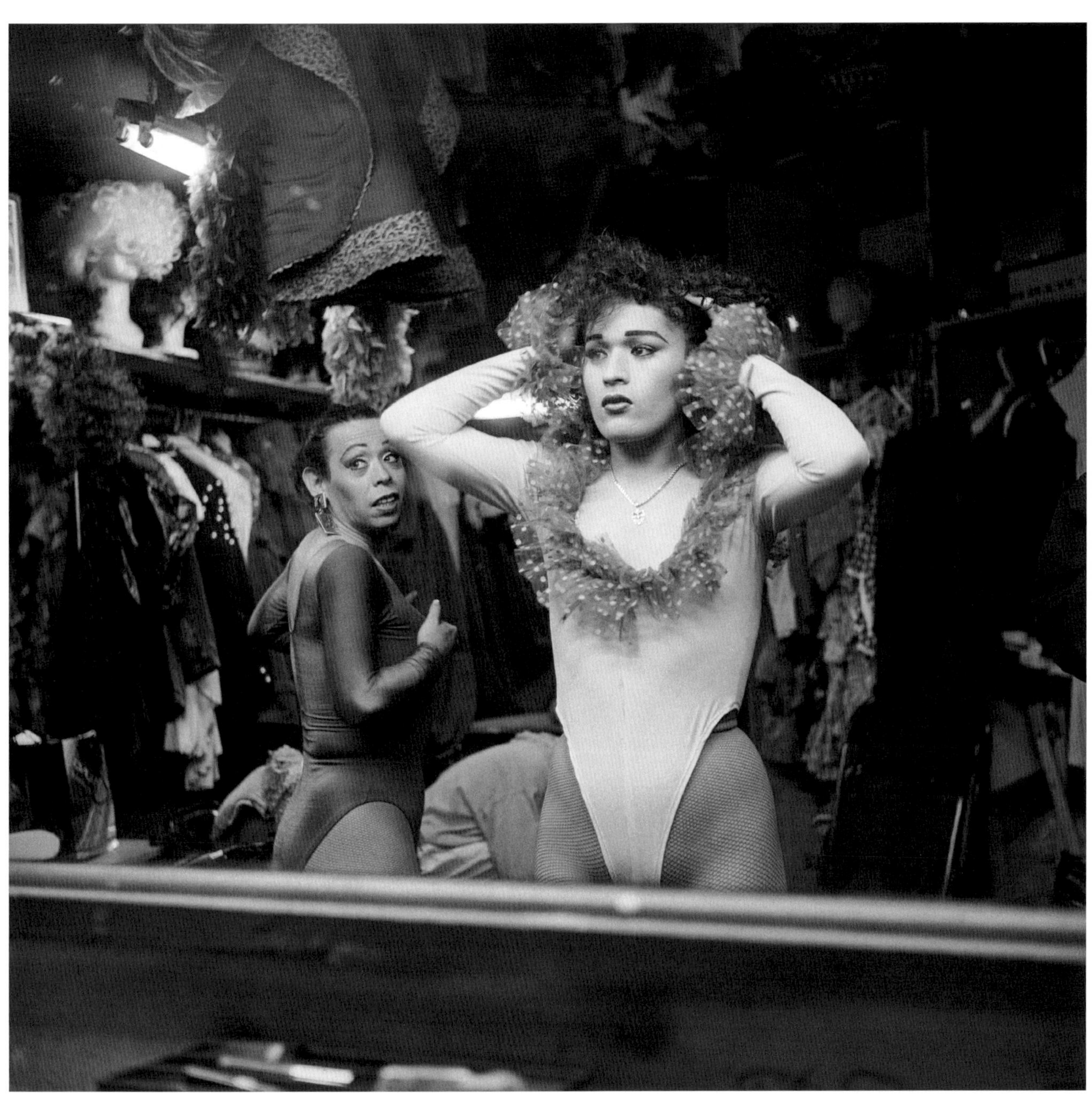

Gaby and Melissa, La Plaza (1993)

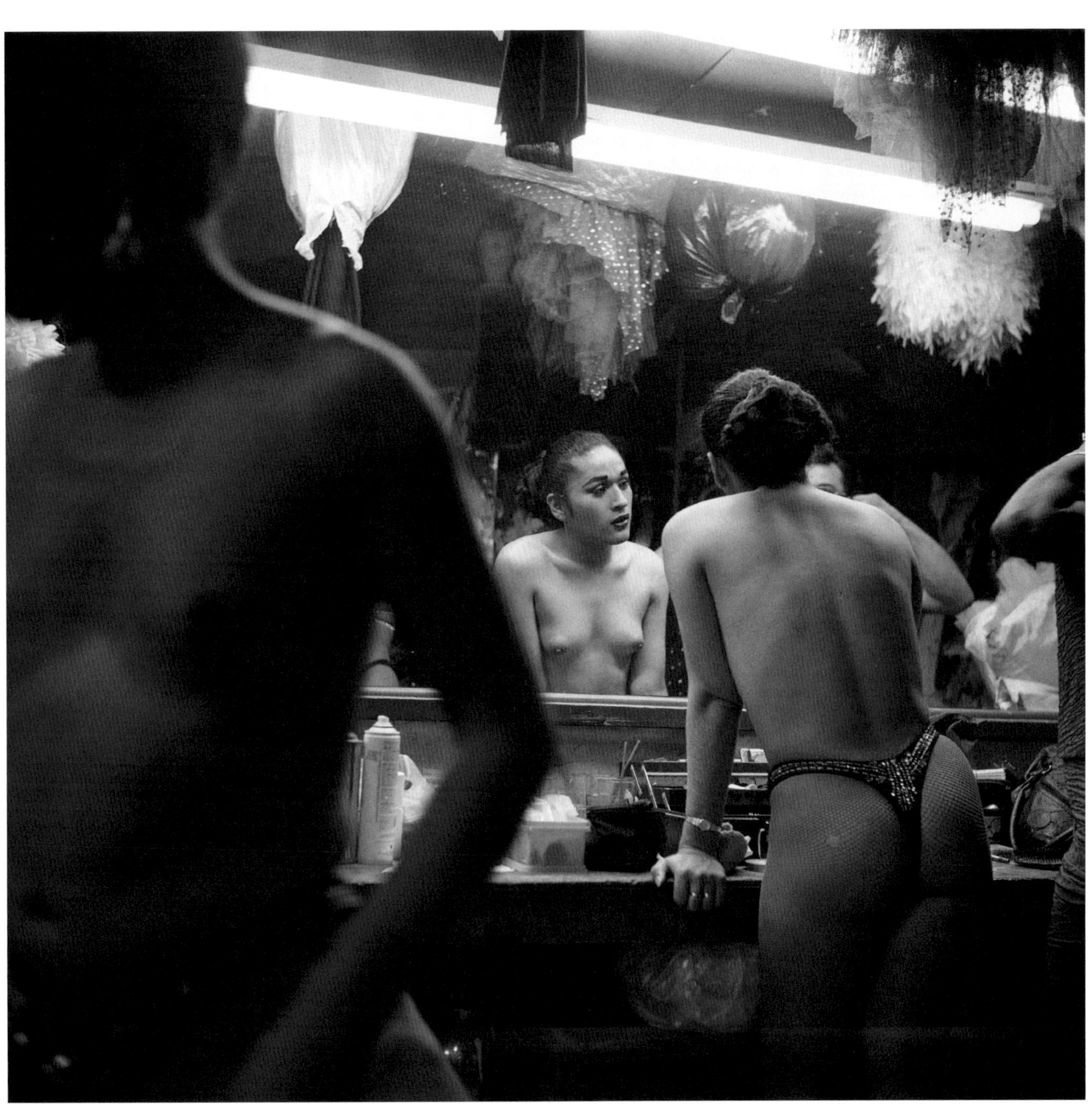

Melissa and Gaby, La Plaza (1993)

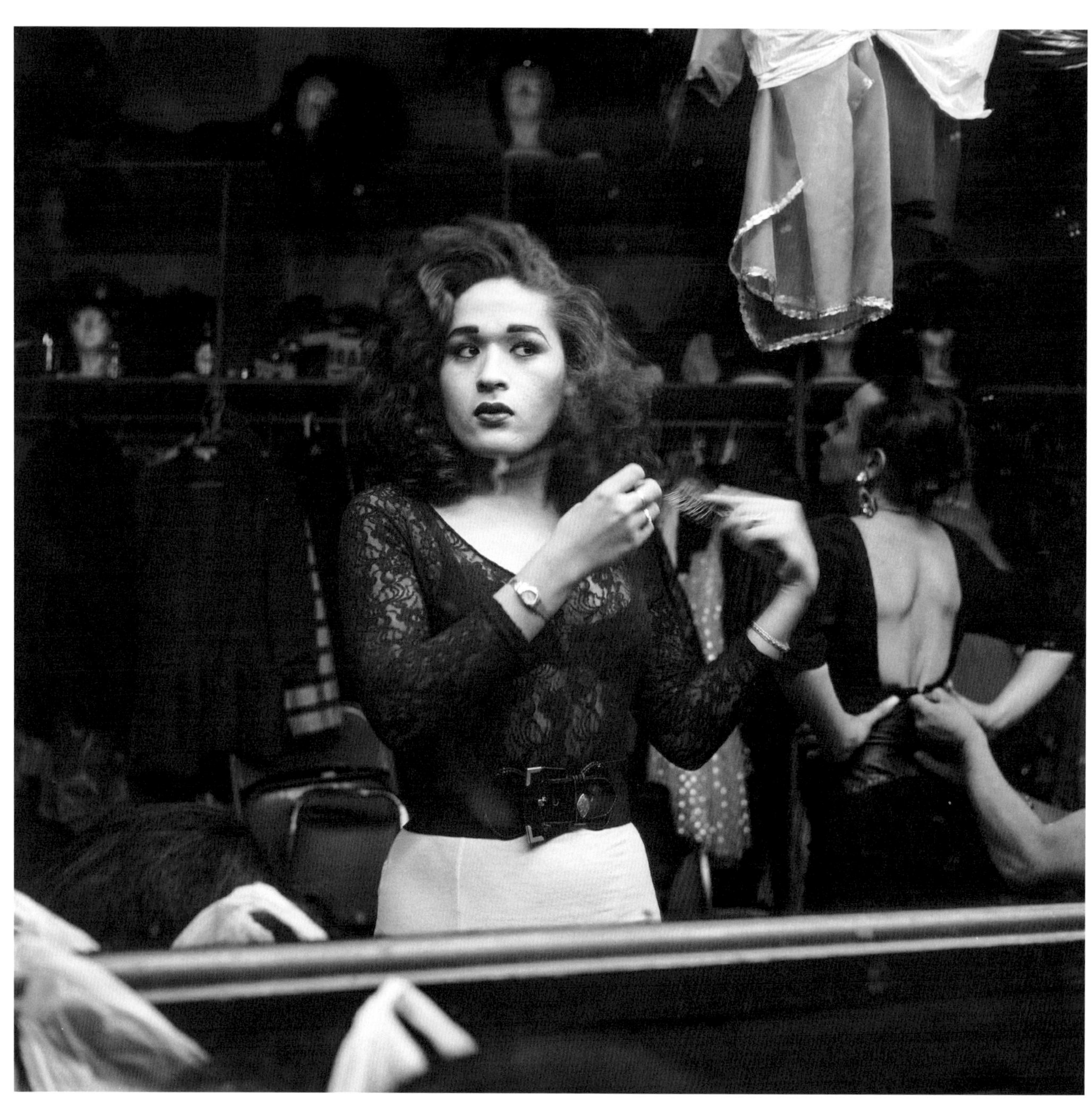

Gaby and Melissa, La Plaza (1994)

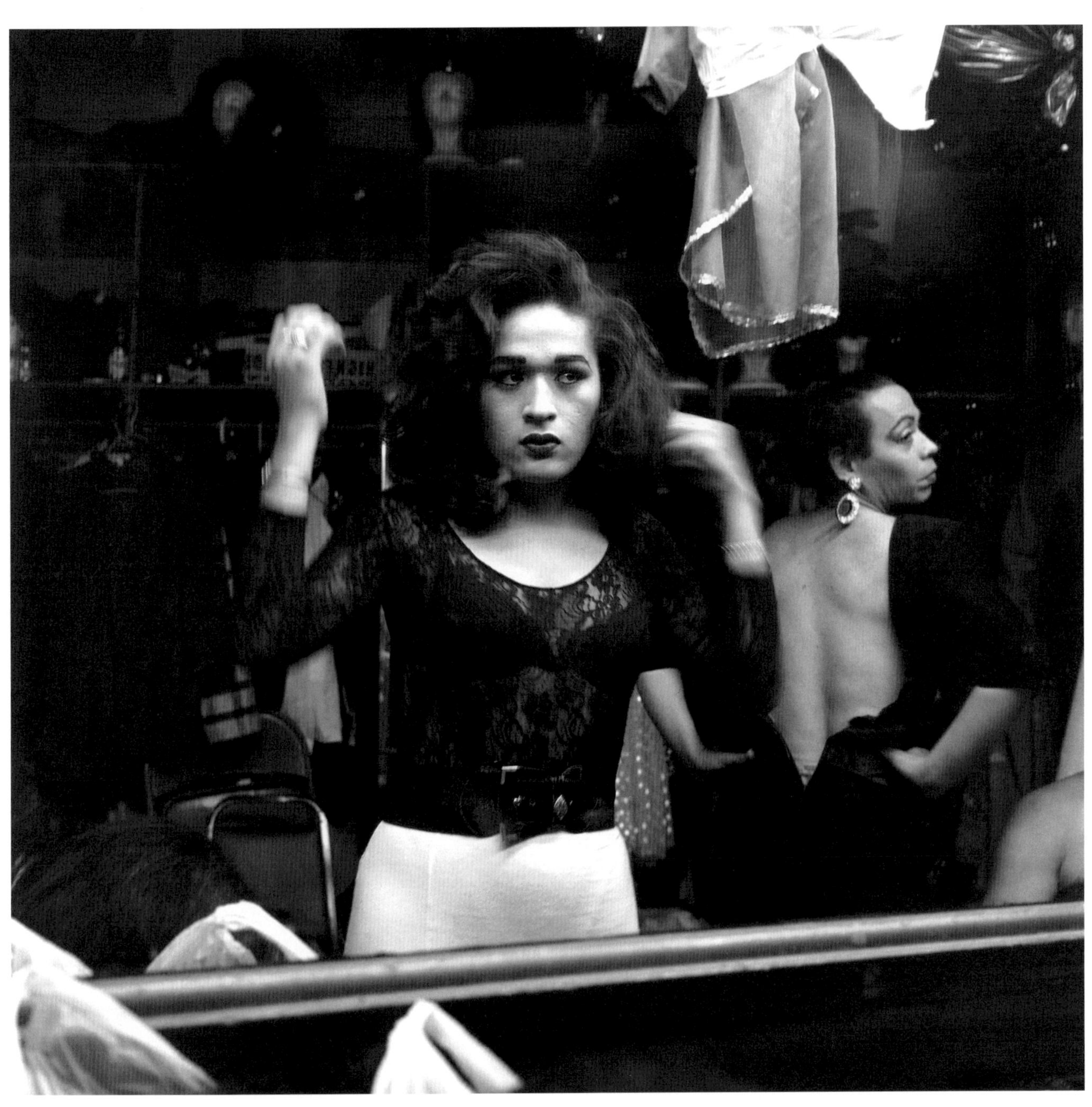

Gaby and Melissa, La Plaza (1994)

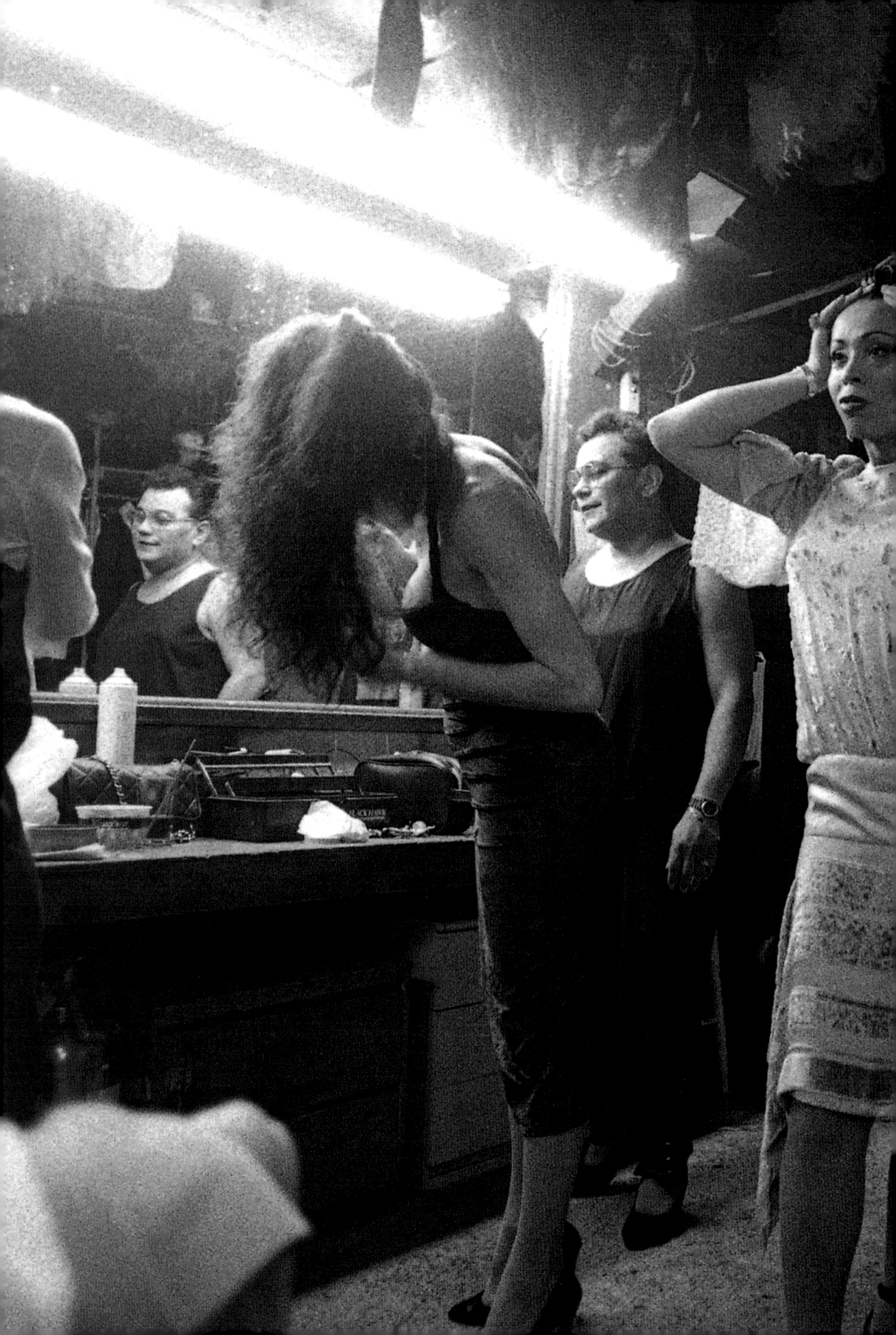

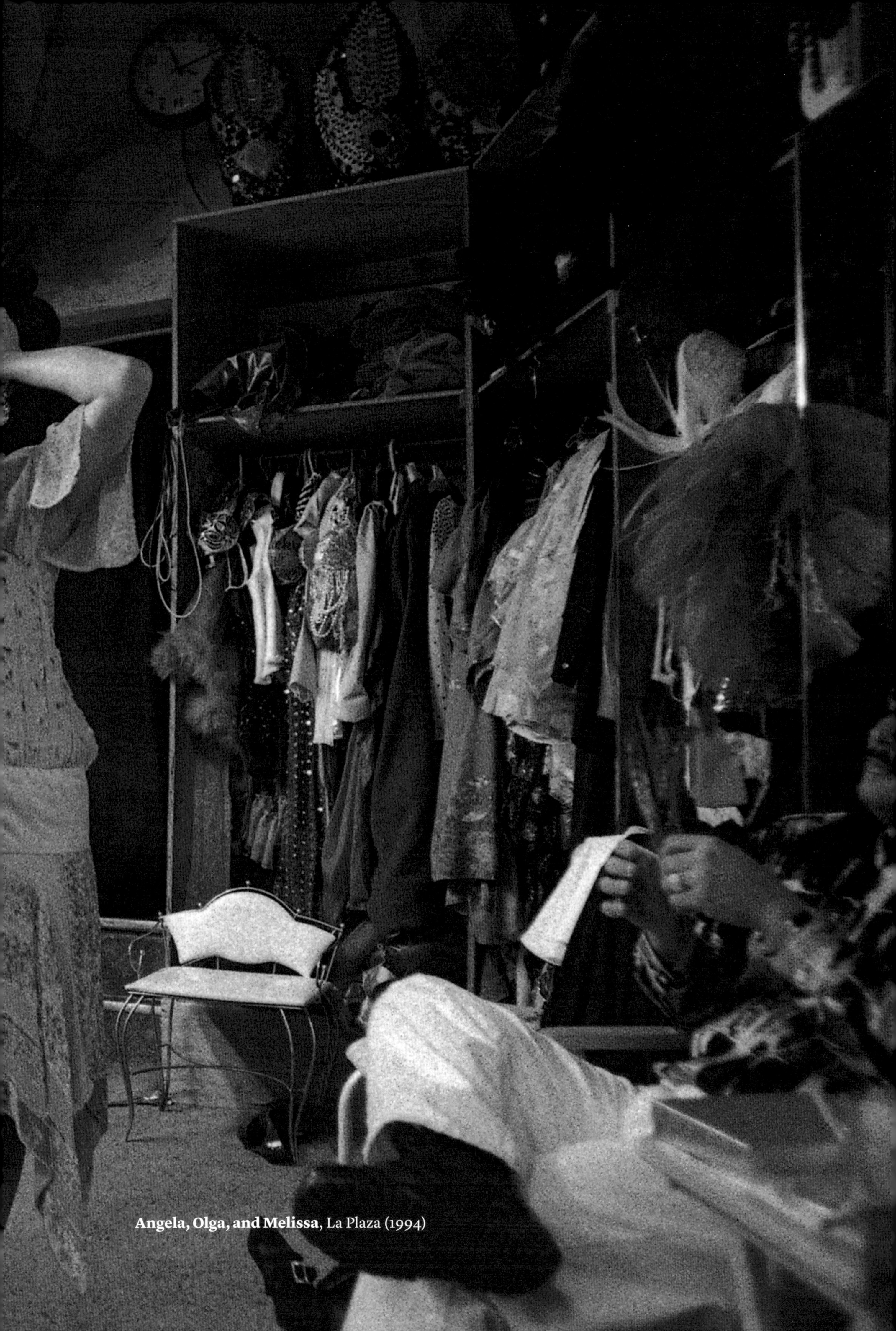

Angela, Olga, and Melissa, La Plaza (1994)

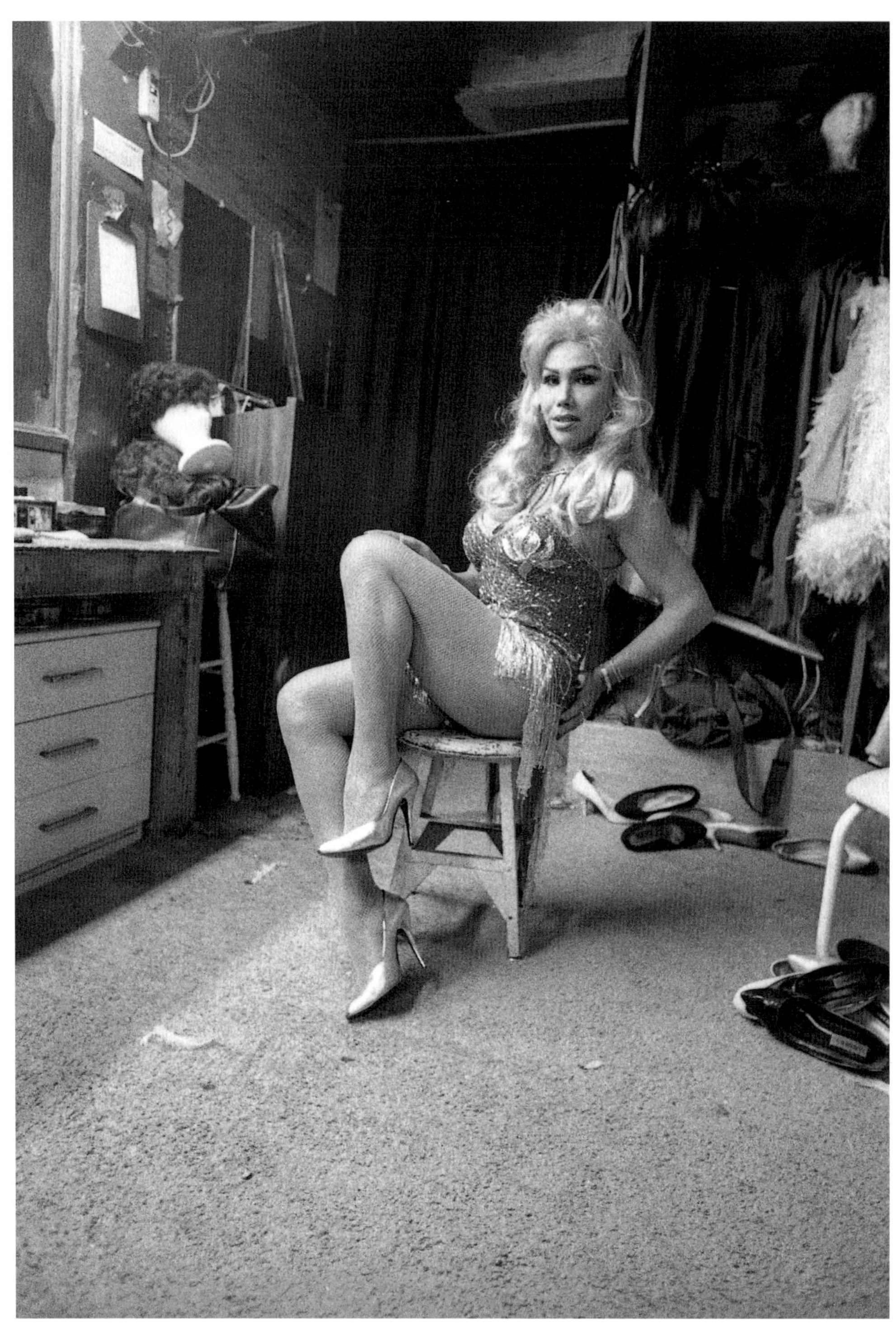

Laura, La Plaza (1994)

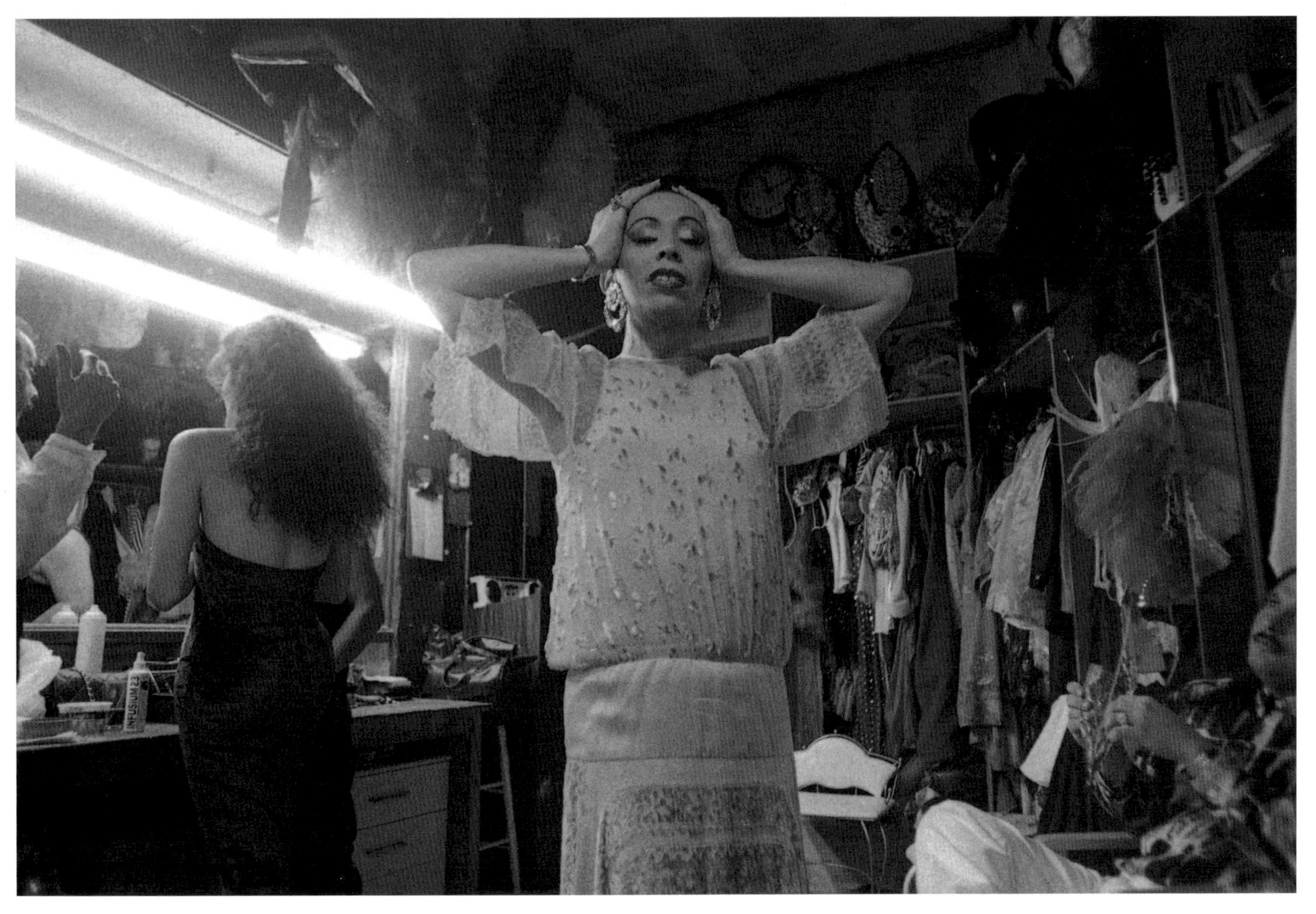

Melissa, La Plaza (1994)

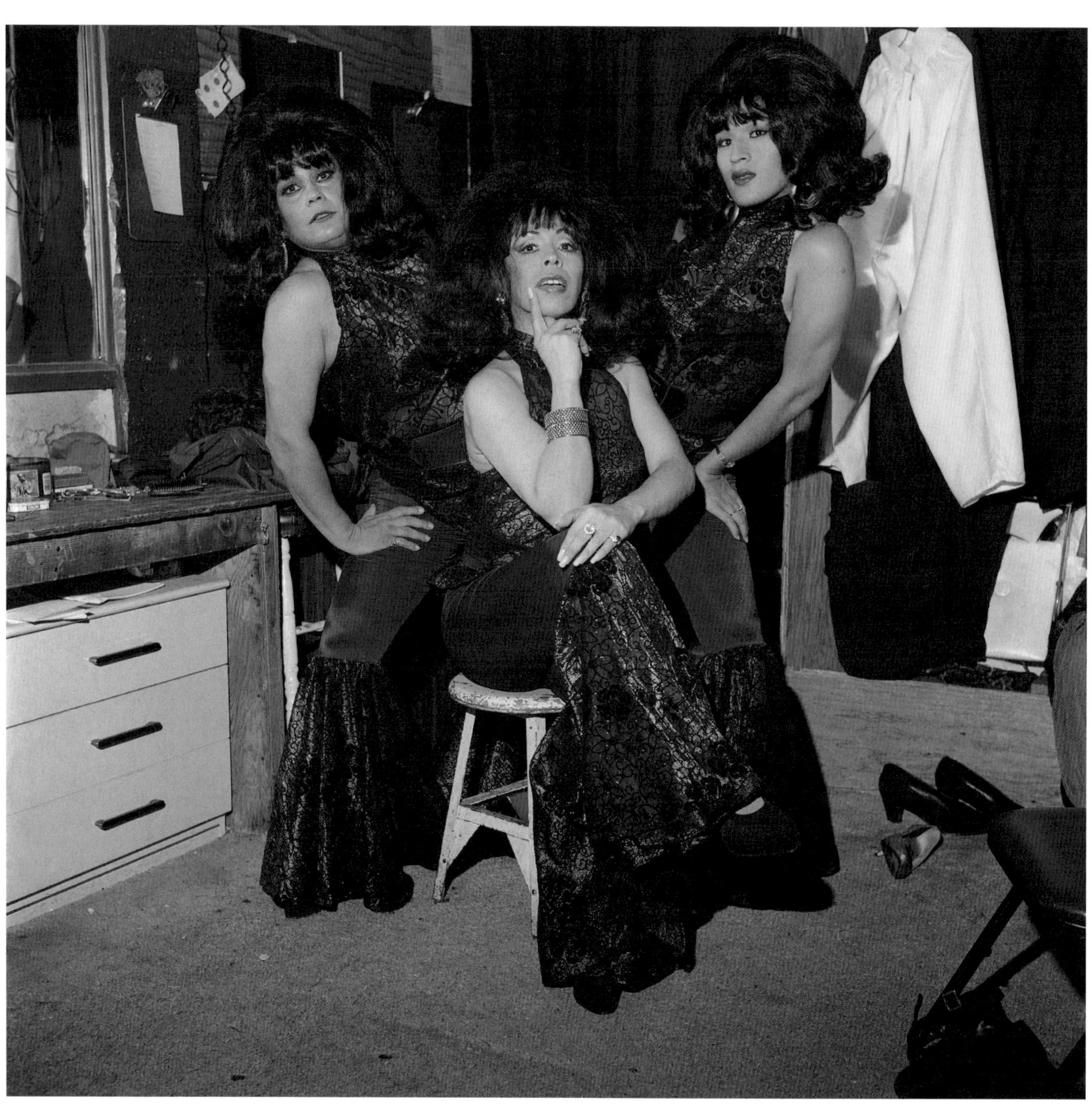

Olga, Melissa, and Gaby, La Plaza (1993)

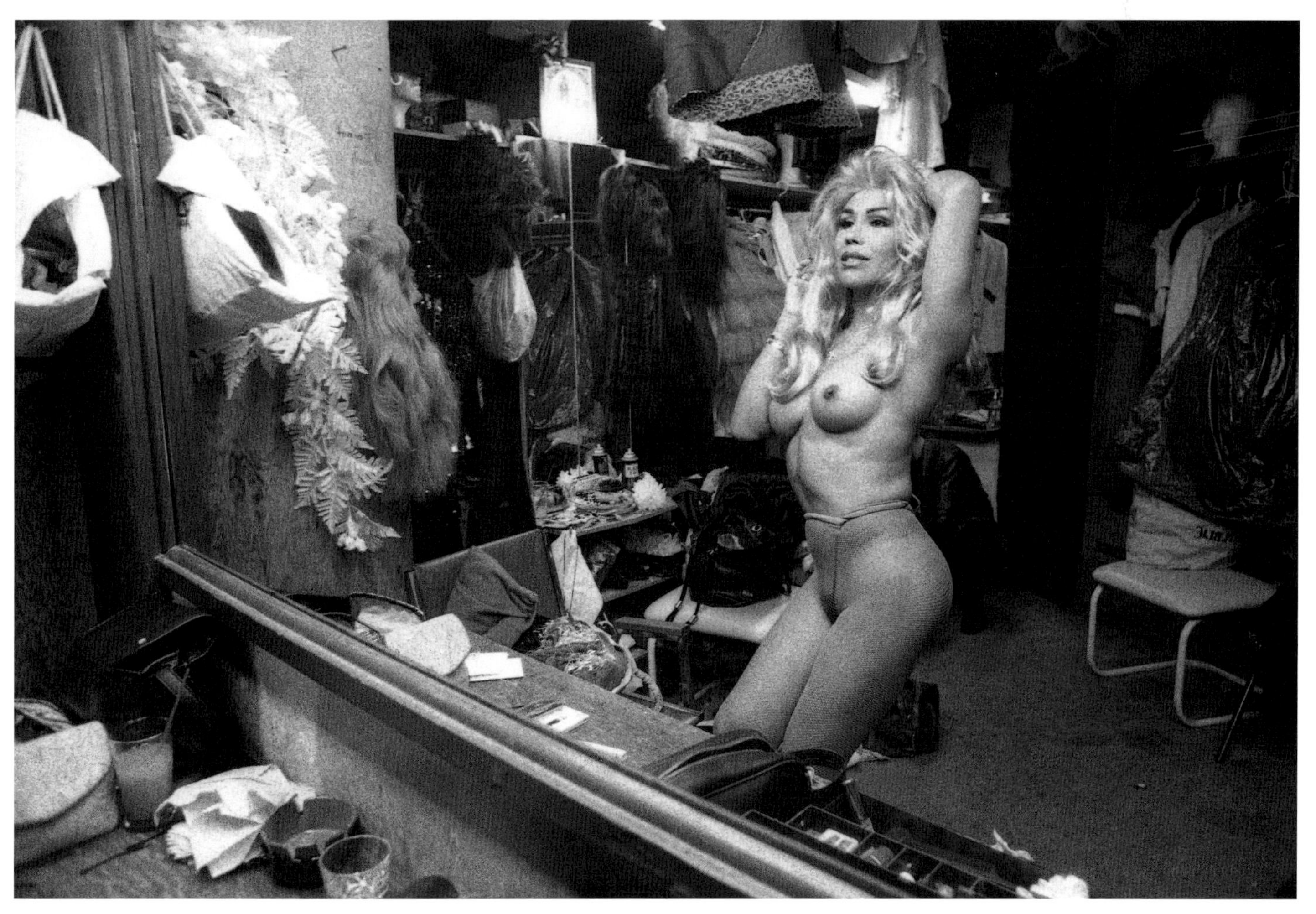

Laura, La Plaza (1994)

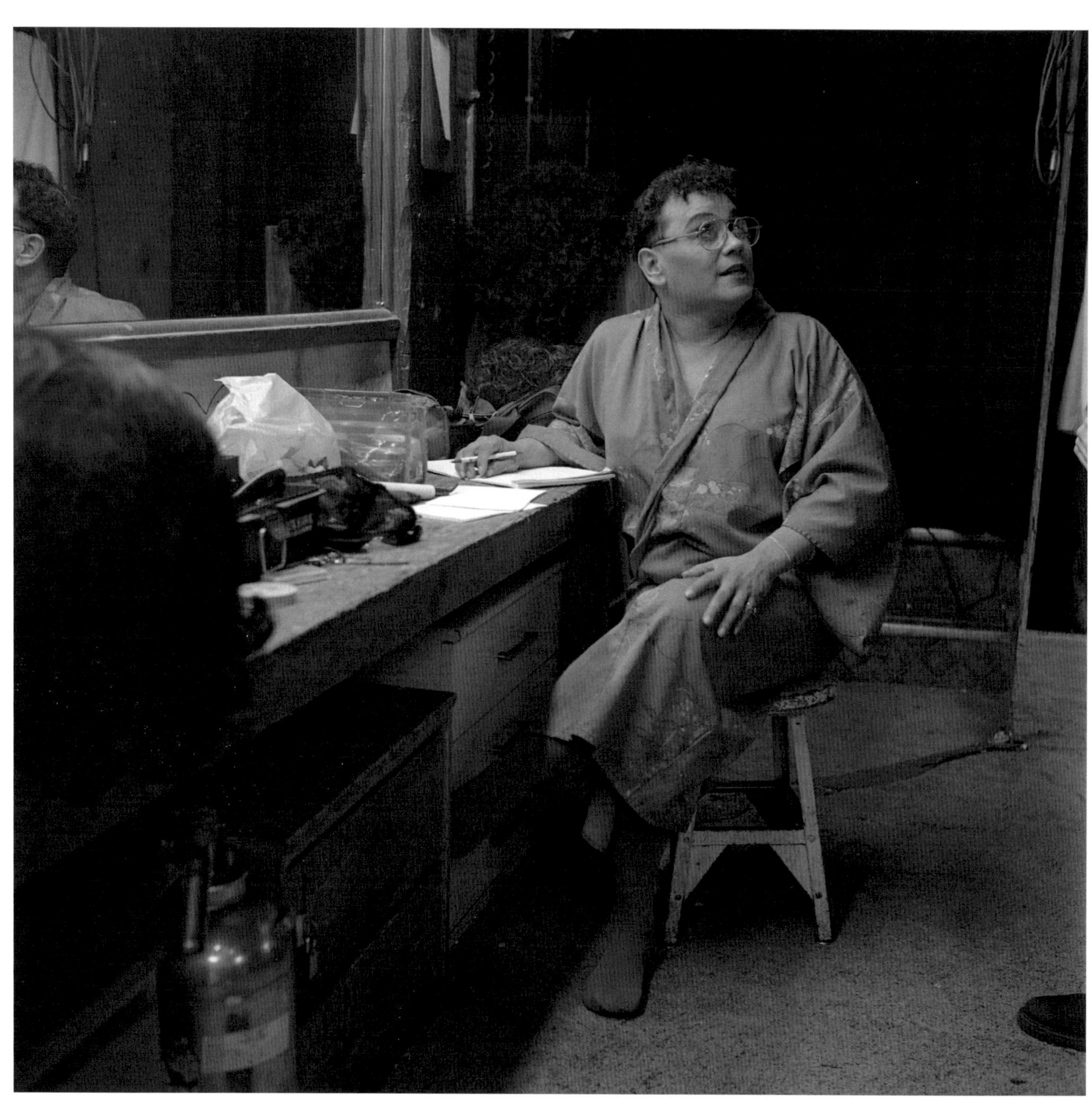

Olga, La Plaza (1993)

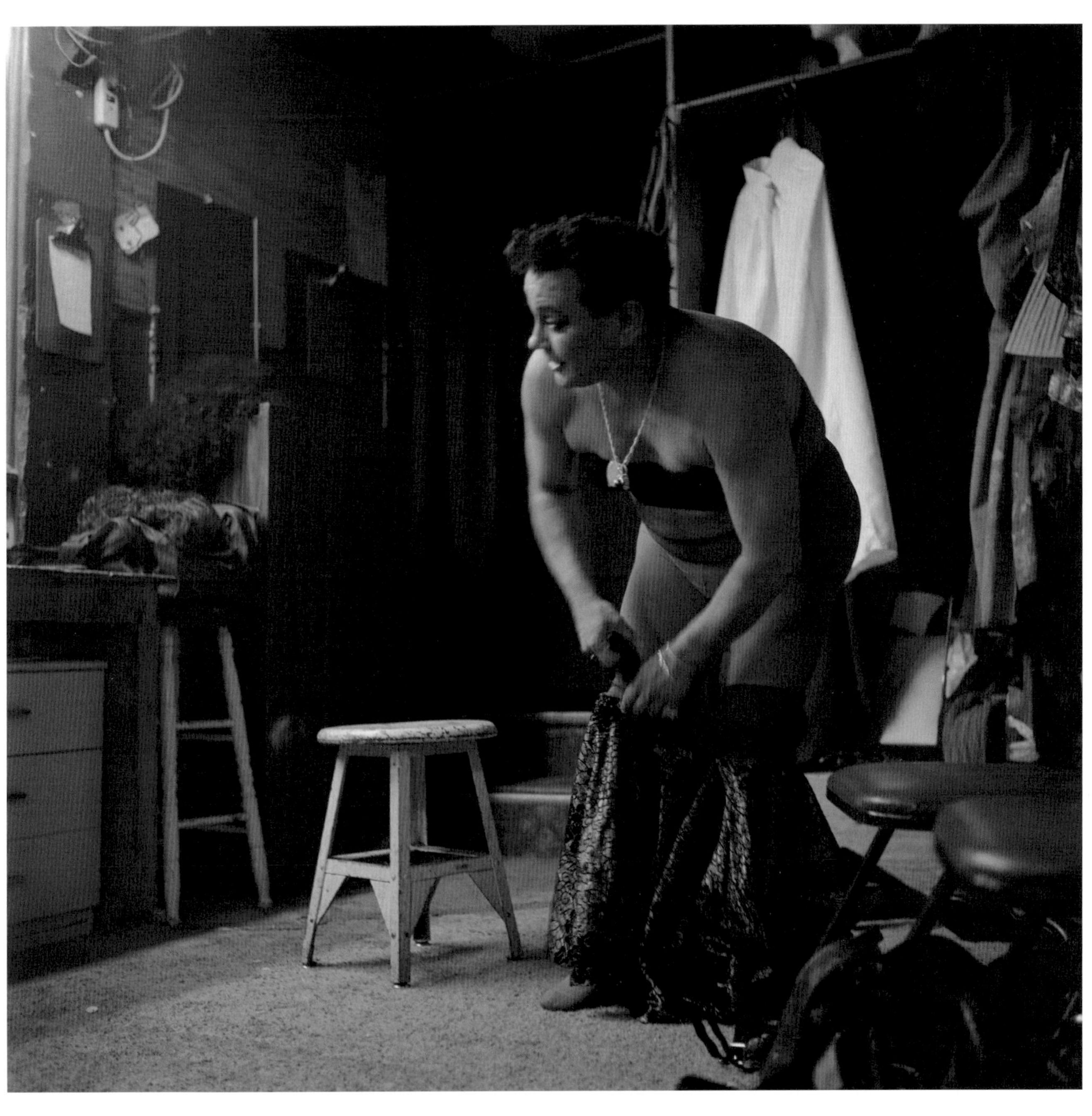

Olga, La Plaza (1993)

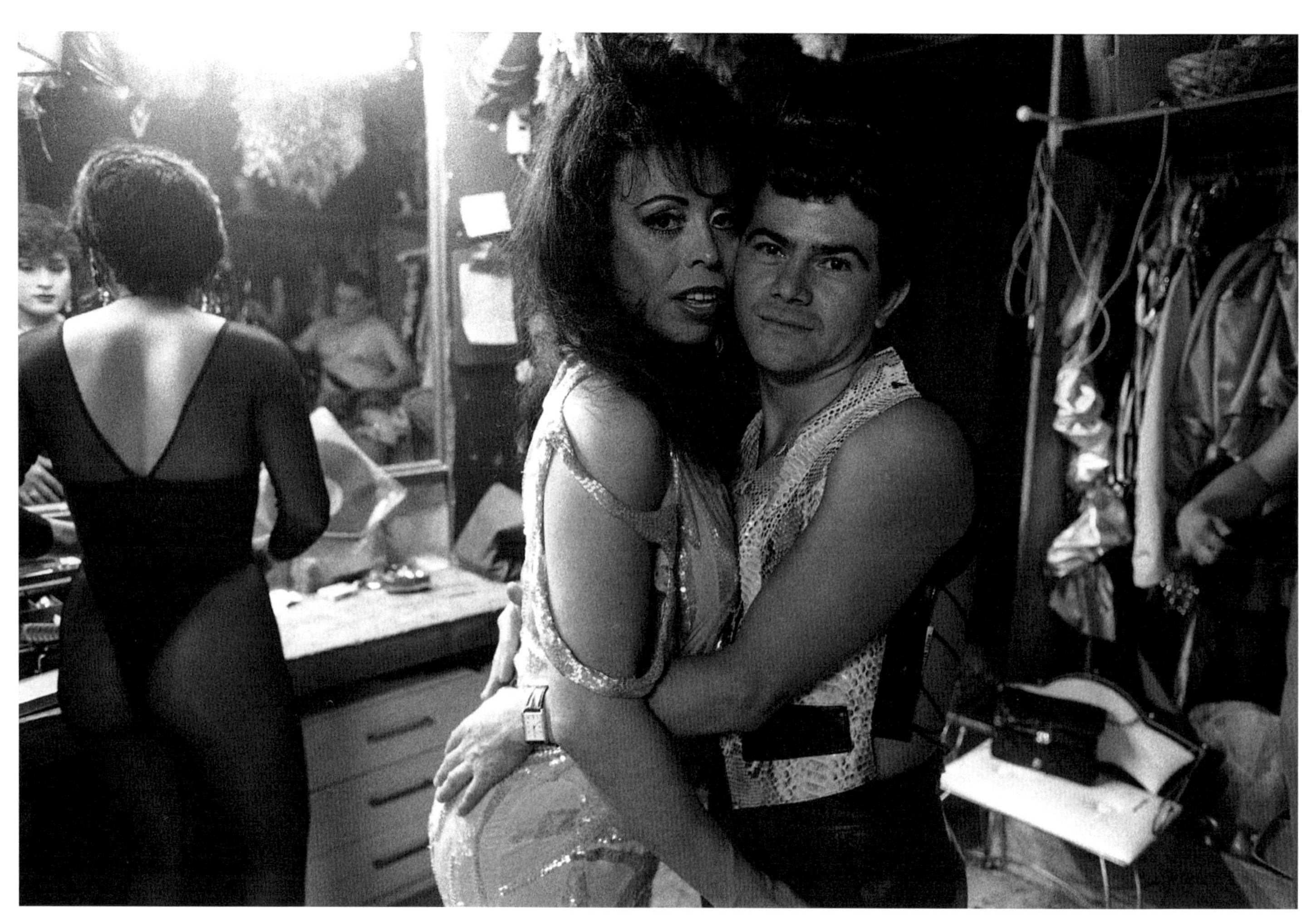

Melissa, La Plaza (1994)

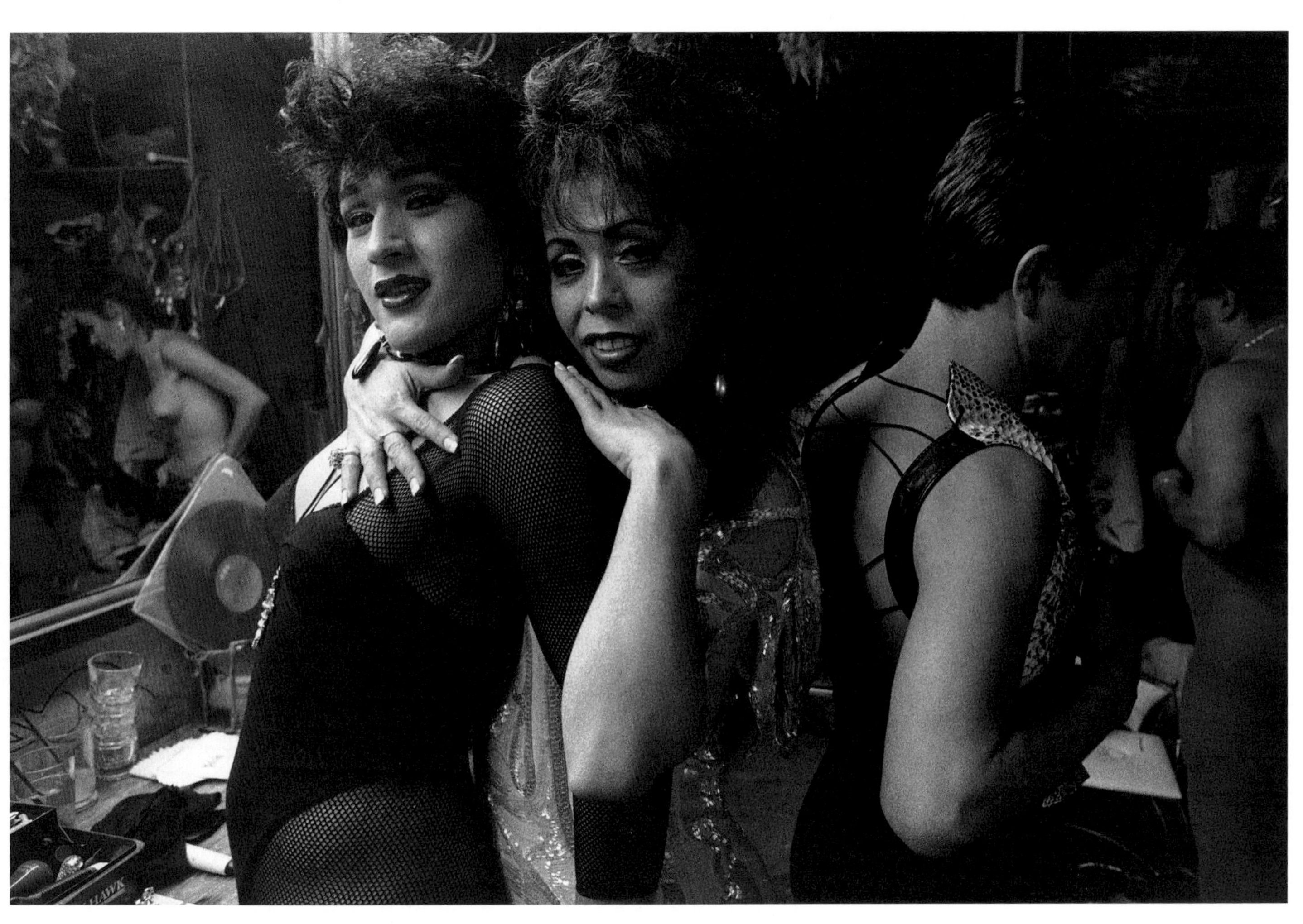

Gaby and Melissa, La Plaza (1994)

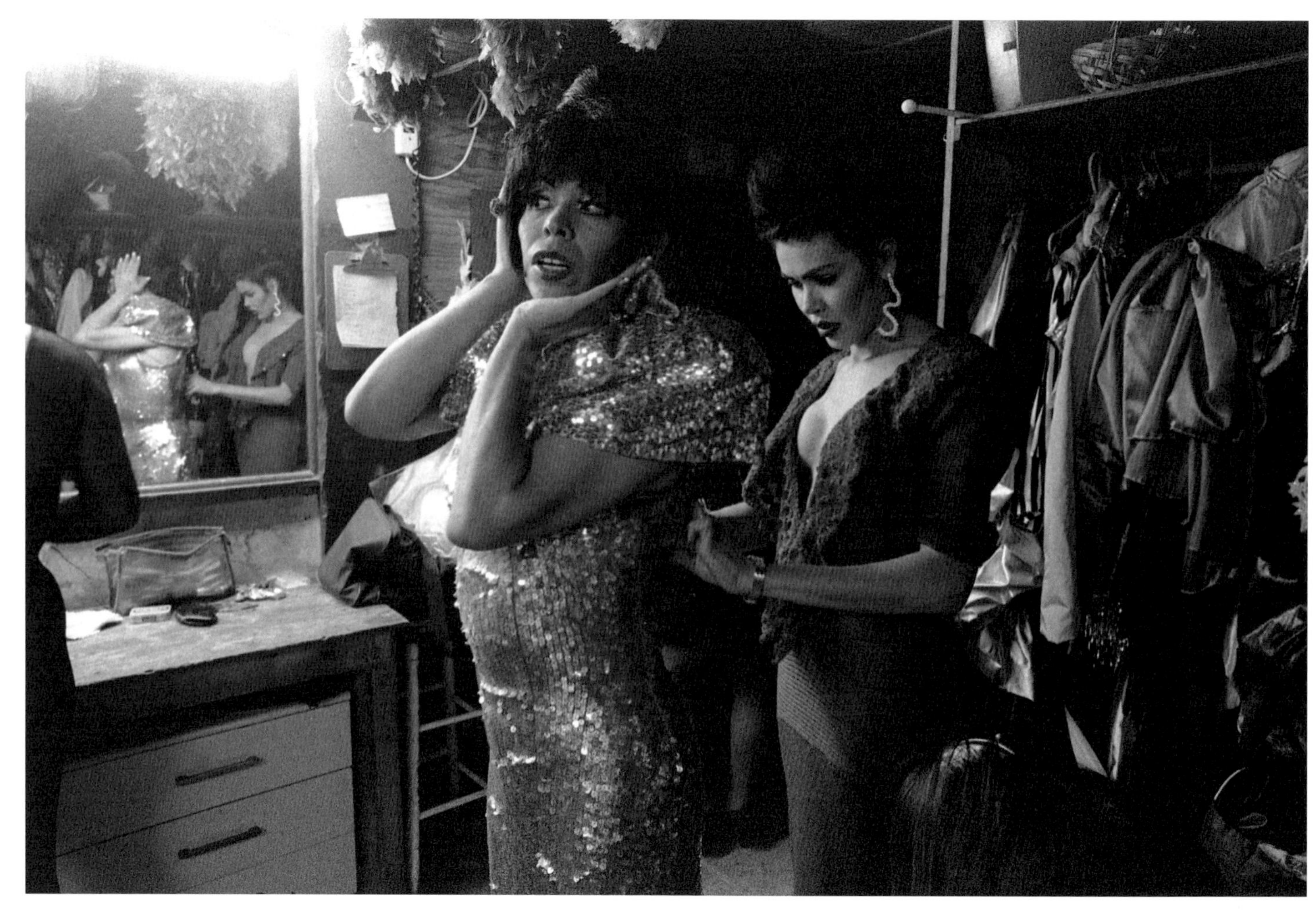

Melissa and Angela, La Plaza (1994)

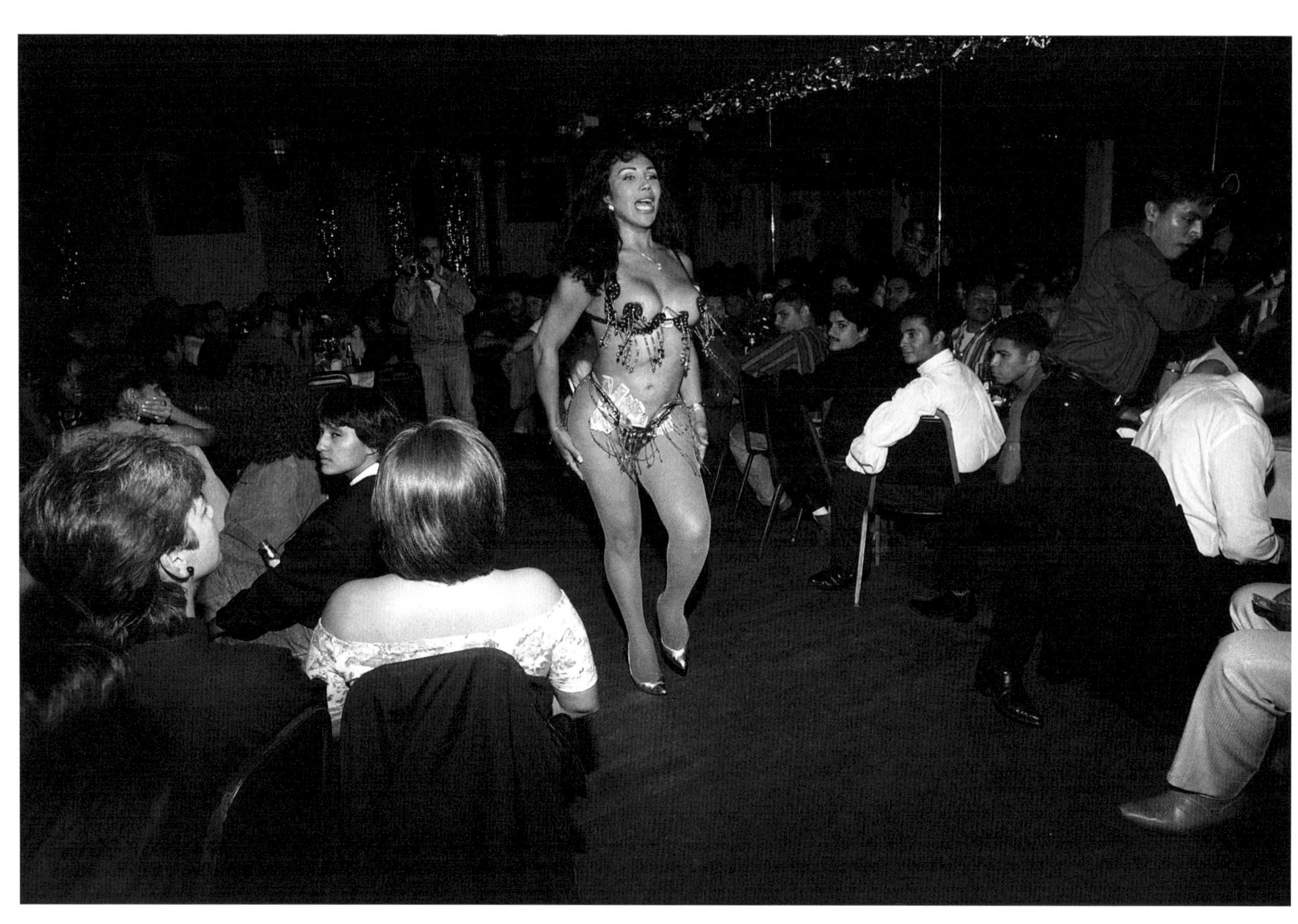

Laura, La Plaza (1995)

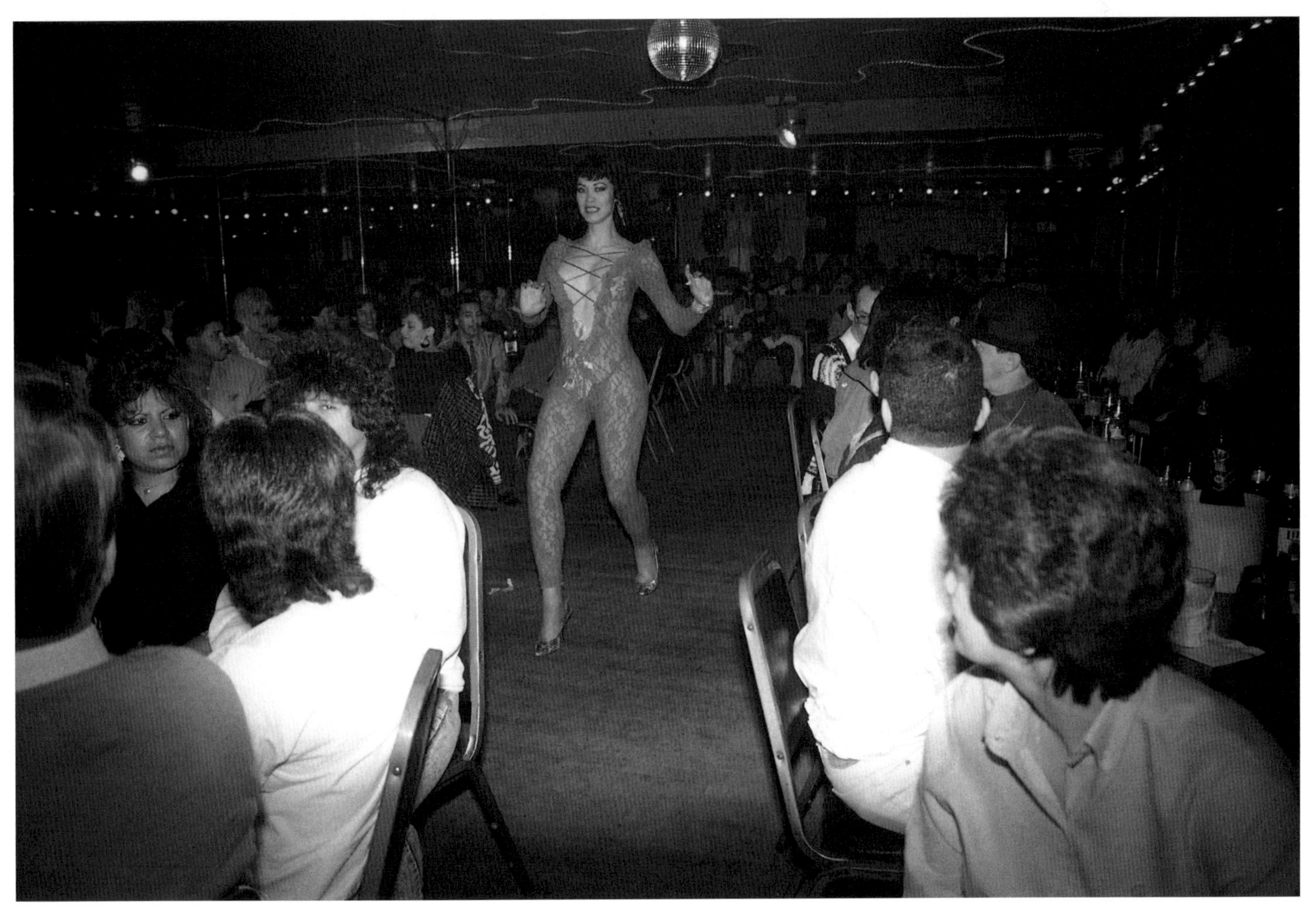

Miss Alex, La Plaza (1990)

La Plaza (1997)

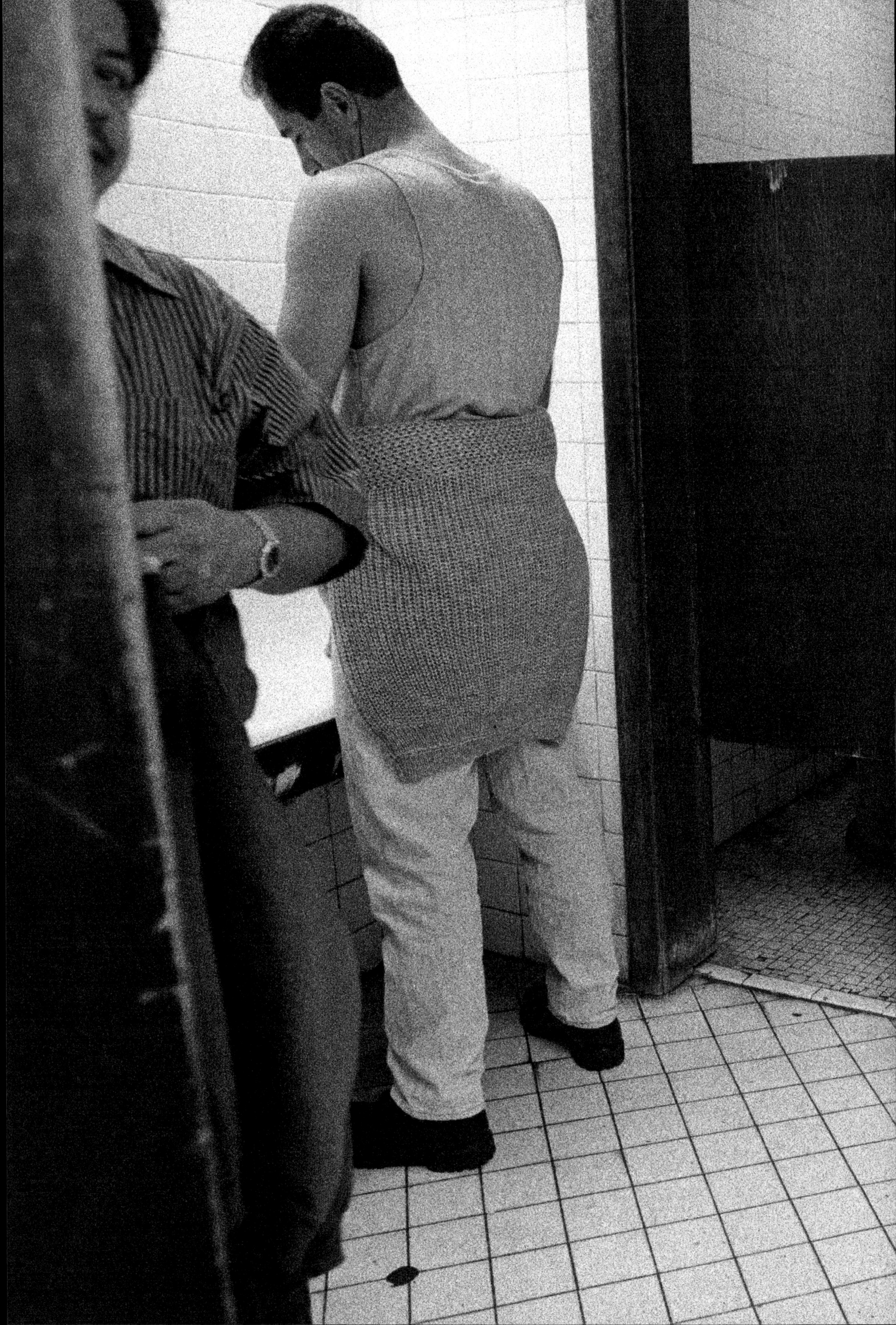

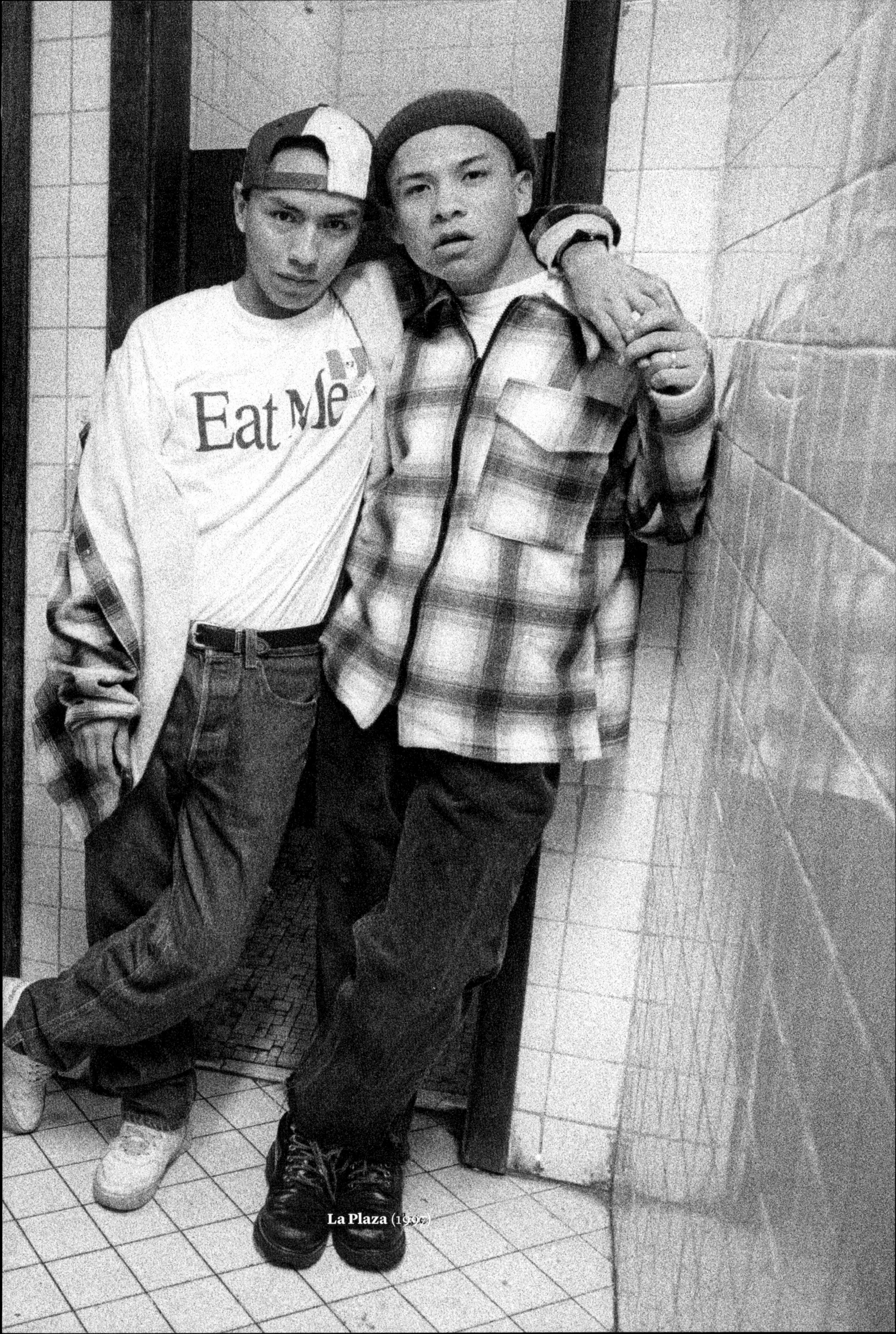

La Plaza (1997)

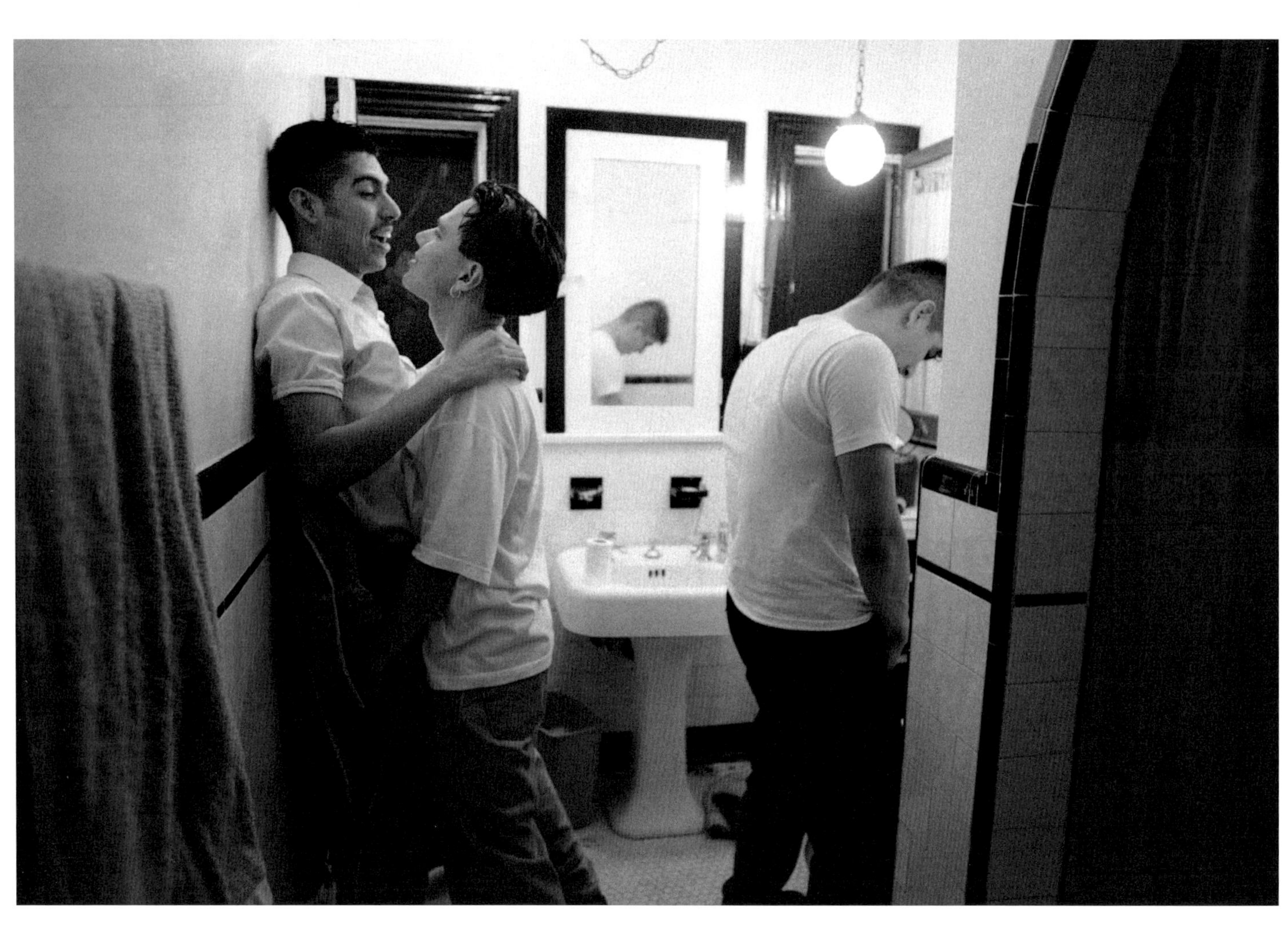

Richard Villegas Jr., friend, and Enrique,
Miracle Mile (1996)

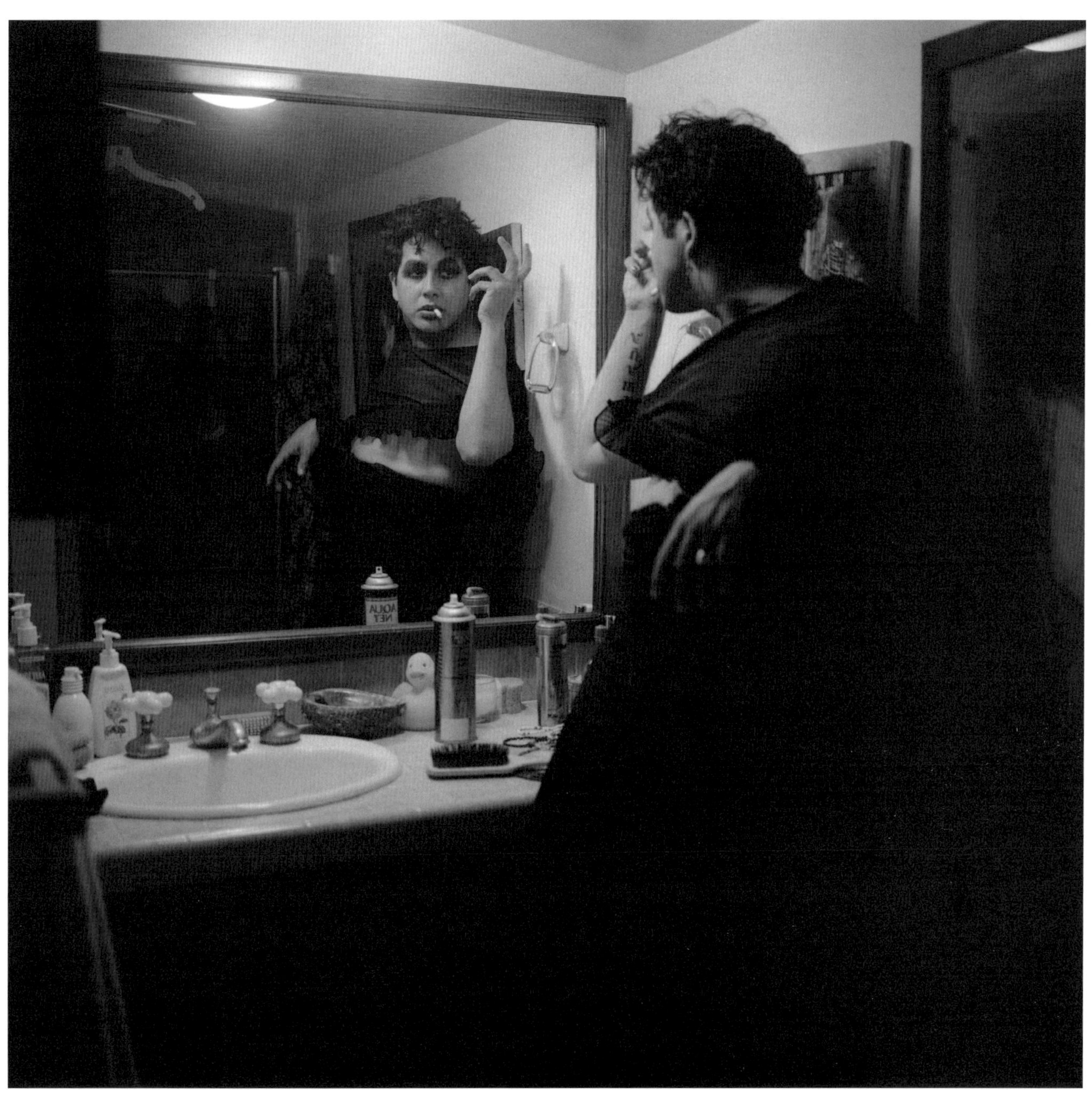

Marcus Kuiland-Nazario, Silverlake (1996)

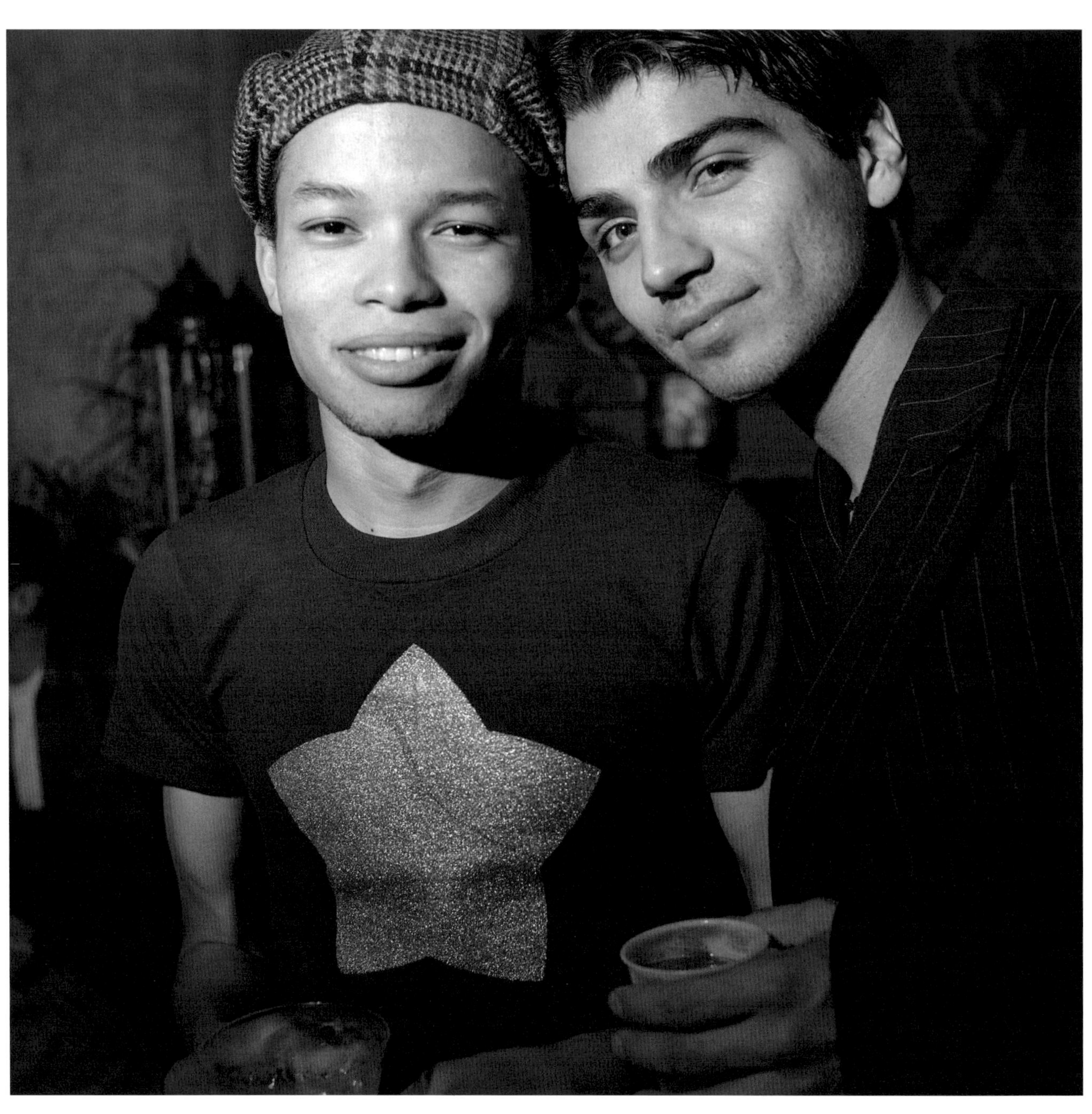

Michael Queenland and Christopher Arellano (1993)

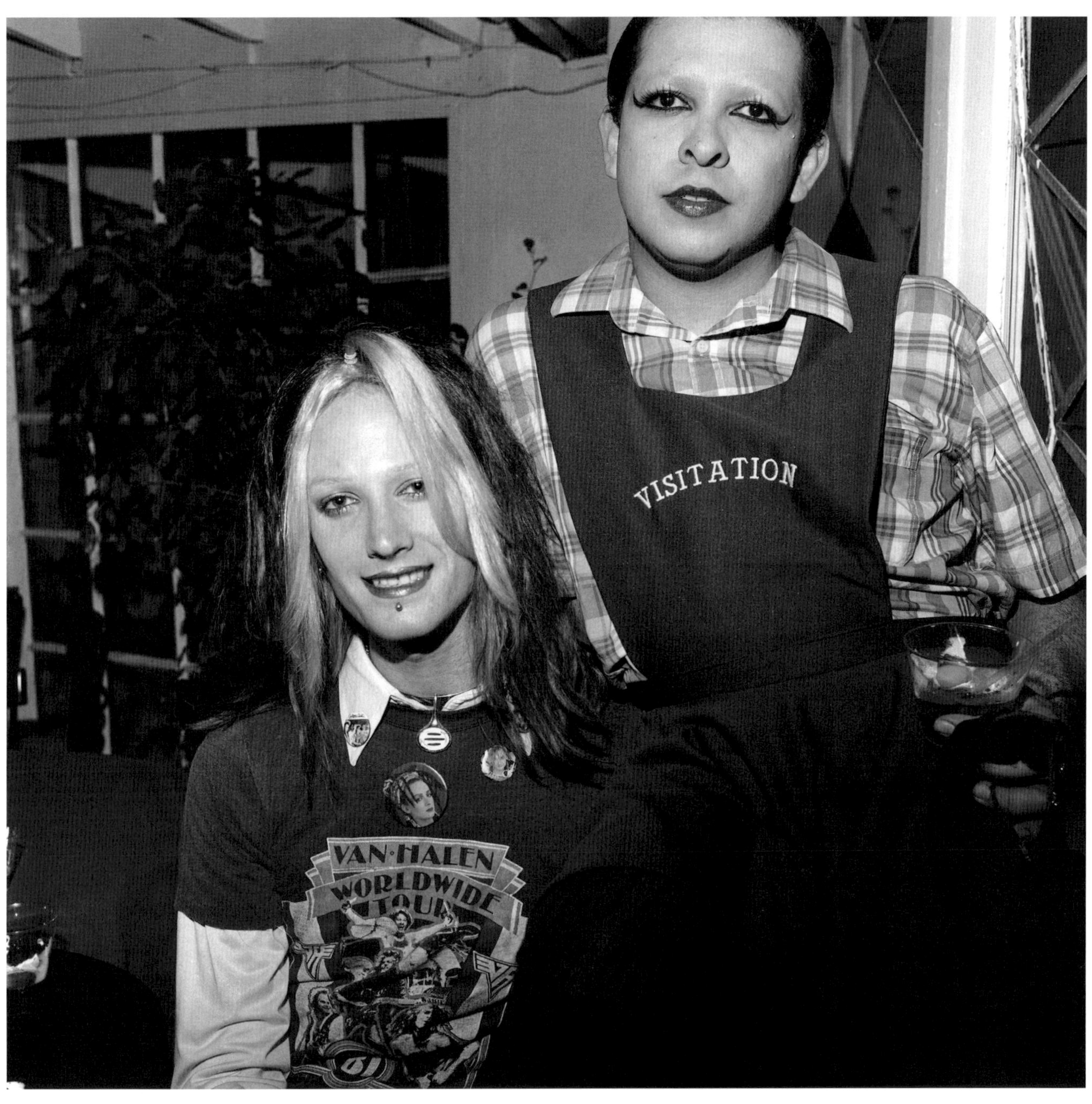

Grant Krajecki and Tommy Chiffon, Hollywood (1993)

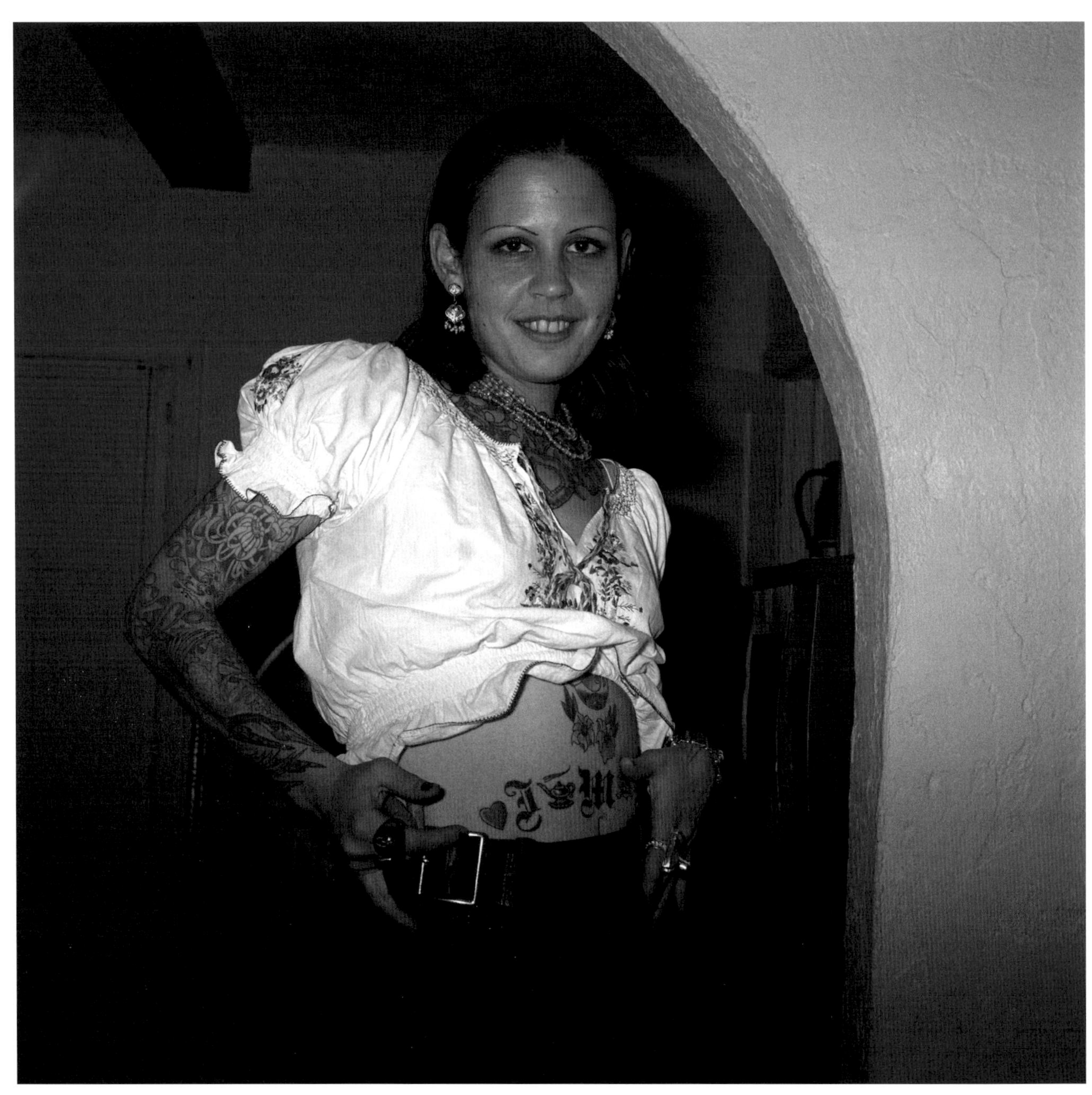

Judy Pokonosky, Echo Park (1989)

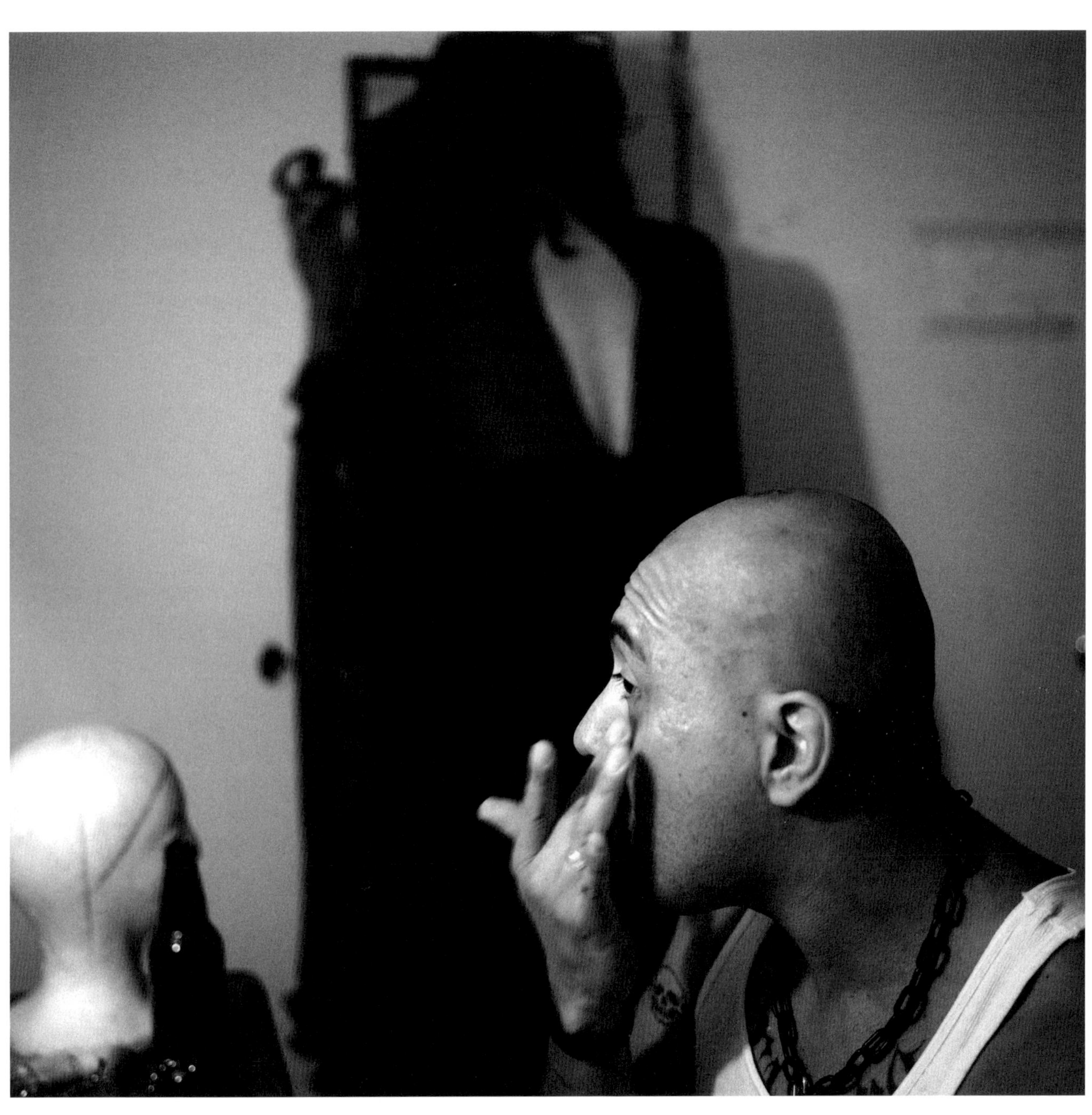

Luis Bauz, Miracle Mile (1996)

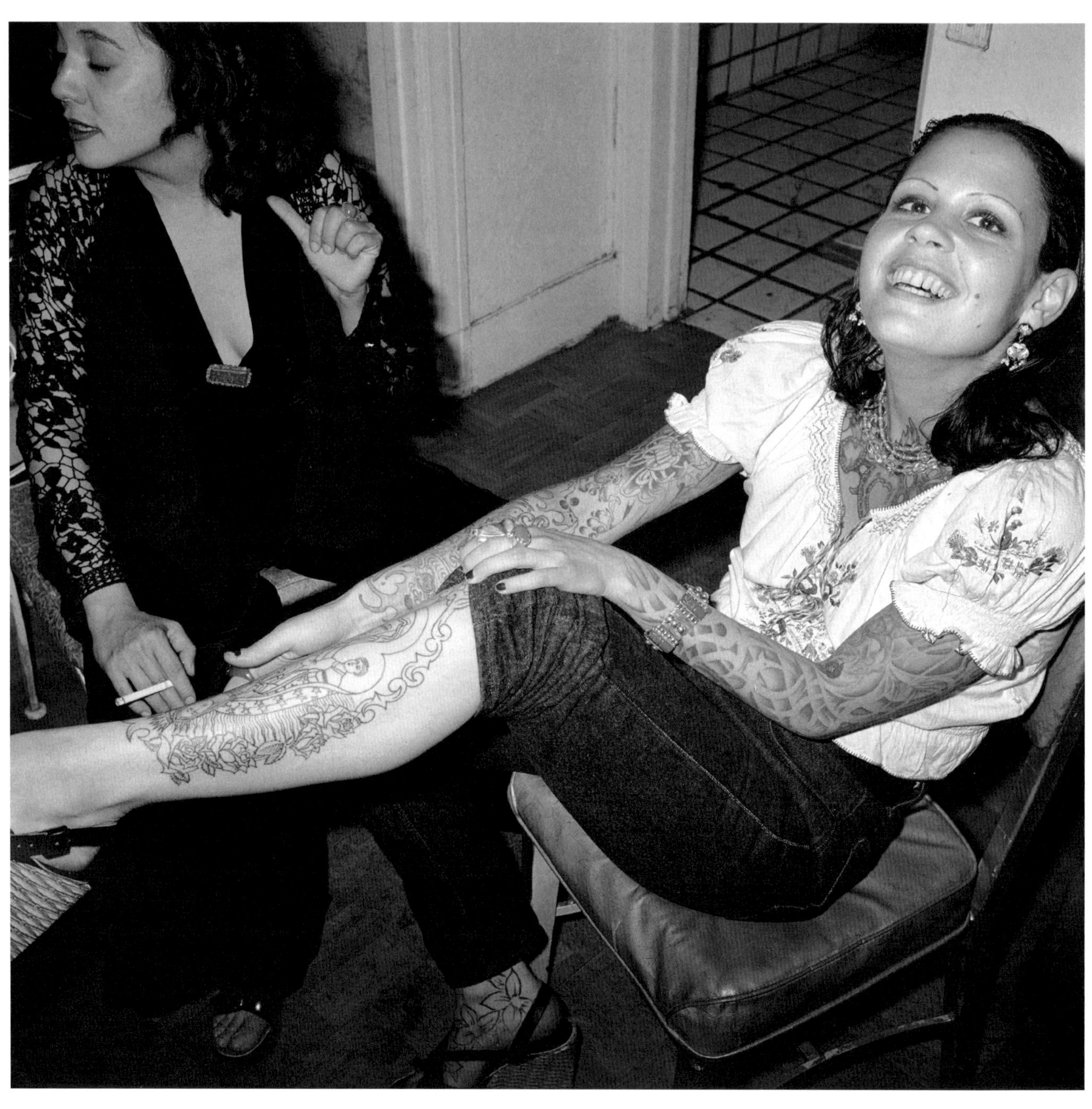

Anna LaCazio and Judy Pokonosky, Echo Park (1989)

EXTRA

A. WEEKLY

ASHION A LA MEXICANA

See Pag

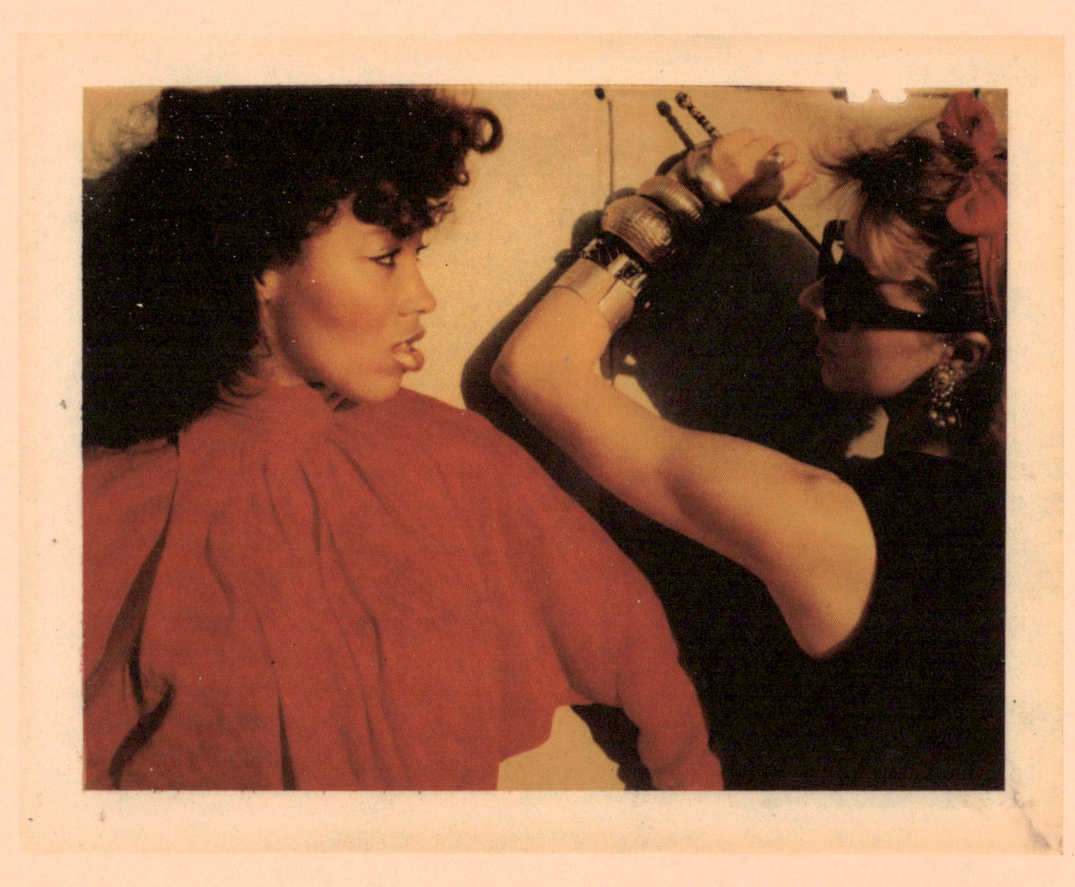

p.77 **Herminia Rivera (sister)**, *LA Weekly* Extra (1985)
Lisa Mapps and Myriam Sorigue (1985)

Los Angeles
by Reynaldo Rivera

I'm sitting here in the middle of a rainstorm trying to figure out what to write, about this city of angels. I am no writer by any stretch of the imagination. Should I write about the clubs, the Masque, Radio Club, Jewel's Catch One or The Vex and Gino's, legendary by our standard. Gino's and The Vex were predominantly latino venues; The Vex was punk rock; Gino's was new wavy and disco. Or to write about the not so legendary, like The Study, Cuffs, and the Black Lite. Or the violence of the '80s brought on by the mental hospitals closing down due to governor Ronald Reagan, the Marielitos, and war criminals coming as refugees from Nicaragua and Guatemala. The Rampart area and MacArthur park were considered the most dangerous places in the U.S but don't quote me, you can fact check later. Or all the sex leftover from the sexual revolution of the '60s and '70s, there was so much of this going on. Some neighborhoods had no cruising signs letting you know it was forbidden to drive around the block more than once. I remember Griffith Park blvd and Myra ave had such signs, and Myra even had a song to memorialize it, called *Planet Myra* by some homo called David Rostamo. This was early in the AIDS epidemic or, should I call it by its first name, Gay Cancer. It's amazing how one can be blind to something right in front of his face if he is not looking for it. I lived right in front of the bridge on Myra and Sunset also, in front of Echo Park lake on Laguna ave. I had a view of the infamous Echo Park lake bathrooms and never did I notice all the sex going on, and I lived there for years. Someone asked me if I brought any of these men home and I was like, what? So I went to look for myself. The rest, well that will be for another book—but I will say this; the sex flowed freely and frequently, these mos did not stop for anything. You could be getting stabbed or drowning in the lake; they just kept on sucking. I once crashed on my bike after running over a duck; I was riding my bike around Echo Park Lake at midnight and I scared a flock of ducks. While running back to the lake, I rode over one and went flying in the air landing on my head in a puddle of water not before skidding for about 10 feet and ending on that puddle (the duck was fine). I wasn't that lucky. I was moaning and groaning, thinking and hoping these fags would slow their roll and come help me. I could see their glaring eyes as the moonlight bounced off their corneas. But no such luck, I had to call the boyfriend I had just gotten into a fight with to come and get me. I ended up with a fractured jaw and ribs....I still laugh at this. In the morning, the joggers and strollers would take over the same space; it seemed separated by an invisible curtain that closed at 5 am. This park is so different now, so well lit, clean, and safe. You can eat your sandwich without wondering if you will get pregnant by sitting there. Echo Park lake is across the street from the apartments my mother lived in in 1970. Those were the apartments where my mother plotted my father's murder. She went over every detail: how she would dismember his body in the tub, and put it in plastic bags and throw it away in different trash cans. She had told herself if he came home that evening and abused her, she would wait for him to fall asleep and slice his throat. Is there irony in my eye, being sliced in half in an apt across the street from where she lived? Oh the good ole days of sex drugs and violence. I was from this generation that thought cocaine was the safe drug, and probably the last one to do drugs with such abandon. I remember going to Bullocks on Wilshire with my cousin Patricia for brunch and pouring the cocaine on the table and snorting lines there as the models selling the garments walked around us. She ended up killing herself at the turn of the Century. She took to heart the old saying, die young stay pretty. She drowned herself in a pool. I don't think she would have been able to deal with getting old; I don't think she knew how to do old and ugly. I think of her often and wonder what she would be like had she not offed herself.

I loved my cousin Tricia. I still remember the first time I saw her riding a bike through my village after being found by the detectives her mother had sent to Mexico to look for her. This was 1971-ish. She had long hair with blond streaks and wore a beanie, she must have been a teenager and I was around 8. I thought she was sooo cool and wild. She scandalized my village, wearing pants and smoking pot—behavior that was unheard of in my village at the time. Women didn't even wear pants; it was my cousin who was the first to do so there. She loved me because she said I looked like David Bowie. I didn't know

who that was at the time but was happy to be liked by someone so
scandalous. Years later we would meet again, after she had just come
back from London. This was 1977 at my sister's Quinceañera and
again, she scandalized my friends and family then living in Santa Ana.

I was 13 then. I saw her once again in 1980; by then I was in my
teens and in Los Angeles. She was stunning; everywhere we went
people would just stare at her. Men would constantly hit on her and
she never dropped a beat. She would stick her thumb out and in
seconds we had a ride. I was doing drugs already, but it was through
her that the level of drugs went up considerably. She had a sugar
daddy and this allowed her to do amazing amounts of speed and coke,
well pretty much anything available. She was the one to give me my
first hit of acid—did I mention that I miss her? Her candle burned at

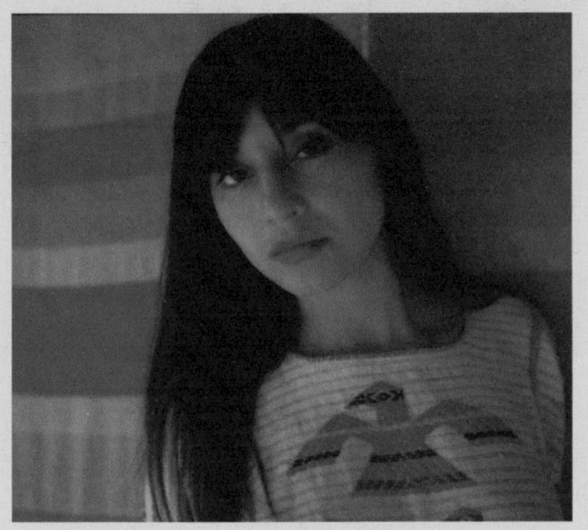

both ends. It didn't last the night but oh
what a lovely light! Speed, coke, and heroin
were the drugs of choice I think for most. It
started with coke and graduated to speed
with a heroin chaser and eventually the
chaser became it. That's when everyone
got strung out, had nervous breakdowns or
ended up in rehab.

I was 18 and taking it all in. I had
gotten a job as a janitor at the *LA Weekly*
through a friend Rae Stang who worked in
the art department. I made good friends
there, some of which I'm still friends with like Gloria Ohland who
took me in after I lost my apartment. I lived with her off and on for
years. She was an editor at the weekly and would have me do photos
for her. Also Craig Lee who was the music editor, most of the music
photos I did were for his column. Yes I dated him for a bit and no he
didn't give me AIDS. We paid $600 for a 4 bedroom house in Silver
Lake across from the triangle building that used to be Mabel Normand
studios, built for her by Mack Sennett. Remember when Silver Lake
was cheap? It's hard to believe—even for me and I lived through all
that. I used to know a speed freak who lived on Silver Lake blvd in
front of the reservoir in the '90s and only paid $700 and something.
I remember the Suki Suki club on Echo Park blvd and Scott—they
served murder like margys on tap. It was in that tall building across
from the gas station that used to be called Magic Gas. All the people
in these photos lived in these neighborhoods that are now considered

Patricia Arellano (cousin) (1978)

81

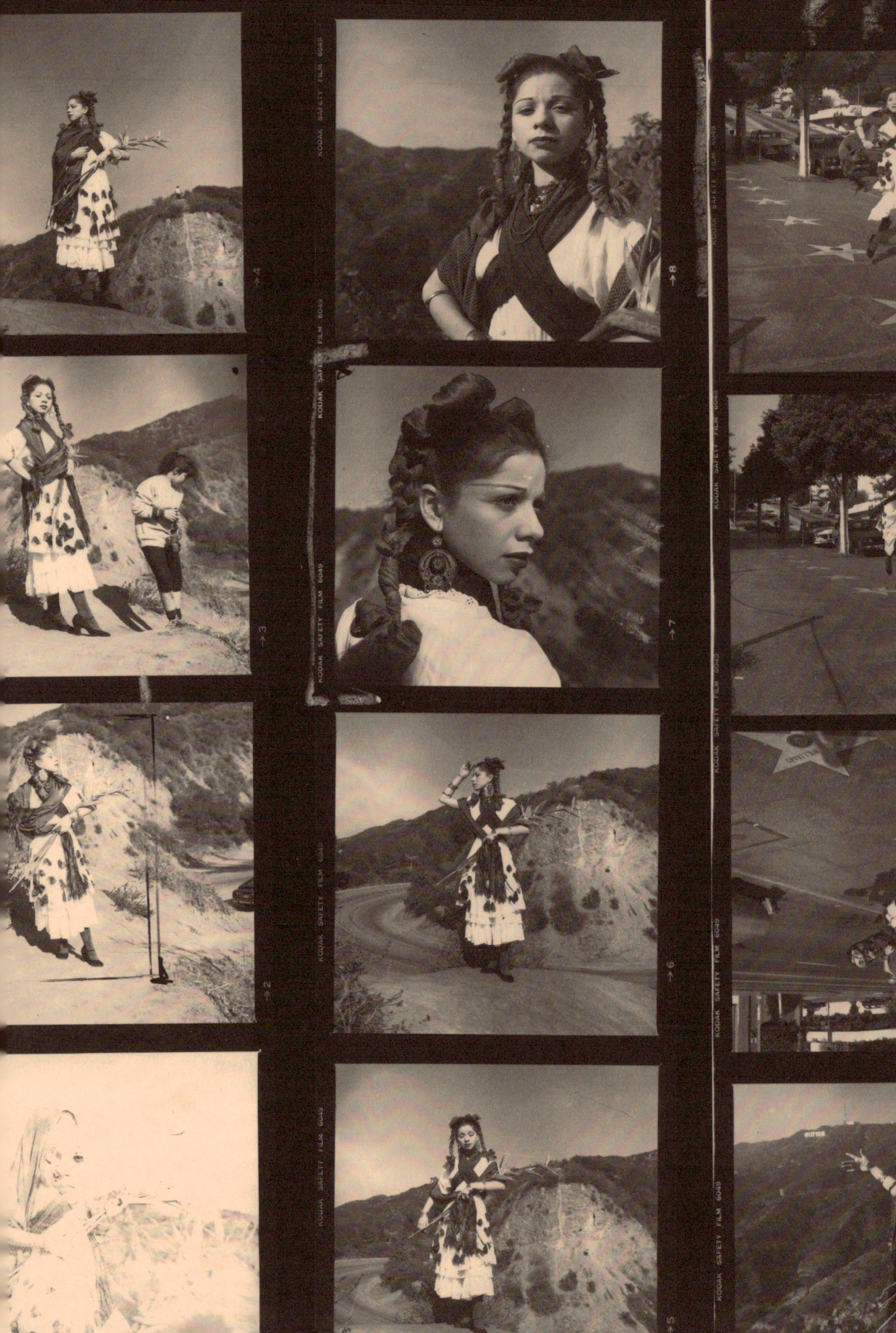

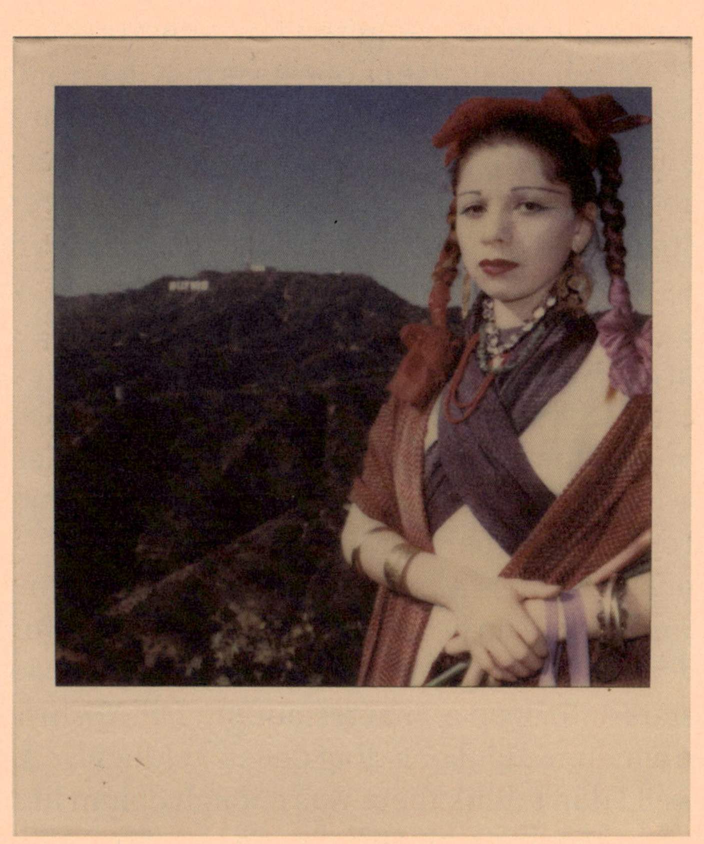

Herminia Rivera (sister) (1987)

trendy, chic, and expensive. It wasn't that long ago but it might as
well be. In a city that reinvents itself with every new generation, one
has to leave breadcrumbs to be able to find the way back. For coming
back home is not something one can do in a city that dumps all the
architectural markers one has when going back to a city like New York
or San Francisco. You can look for that brownstone in New York but
here in Los Angeles you might just find a parking lot, but this also
allows for creating a truly new city without all the baggage of the past.
You go to New York to become a New Yorker you come to Los Angeles
to reinvent yourself.

And it seems that there are quite a few New Yorkers in need of
reinvention, if we believe statistics of who is moving from where
—New Yorkers are the biggest number, next are the Texans. I don't
seem to have an issue with the Texans since I haven't been hearing
for decades about how they are culturally superior. I never was one of
those people that loved to bag on LA; I seemed to always find myself
defending this city that I thought was unjustly criticized. We were all
thought to be superficial. We were never seen as a multicultural city,
it seemed that everyone that came here or critiqued the city always
did by the west side or the white folk they met without acknowledging
that the majority of the city was not white and was not here to be a star
or to be in the industry, the majority of us were either born into this
dream world or ended up here for other reasons.

I was thinking of Miss Alex chasing her body-building lover from
Mexico City and ending up here smoking crack and performing at La
Plaza. I wonder if all those performers at Mugy's came to Hollywood
to be movie stars or to open a Thai restaurant. Did Yoshi San think he
was gonna be a matinee idol or a drag queen at Mugy's? And the girls
at La Plaza, well I don't think there was enough opium in Afghanistan
for that dream. When living in Berlin in the late '80s, it was the food
I missed most from Los Angeles; falafels didn't quite cut it. I was used
to having Thai, Chinese, Japanese, Mexican, Ethiopian, Salvadorian,
Armenian, and Greek food at any given time. Canter's or Chuan Chim
at 3 am—it was with these same people whom we shared the space
and experience of Los Angeles. I've lived in Highland Park, Glassell
Park, Pasadena, Echo Park, Silver Lake, Lincoln Heights, with a small
stint in Hollywood. I considered myself an Angelino and not just from
a specific neighborhood; we used to go to the movies in Westwood
and shopping to Vinyl Fetish or Poseur on Melrose or get pizza on
Hollywood blvd or cruising on Whittier blvd. I remember visiting my

cousins in East LA with a German friend back in '89, and at one point my friend was showing them photos of pyramids from our trip to Mexico. My cousin turned to her and said, "Wow you guys went to Egypt?" My friend turned to her and said, "EGYPT? These are from your people!" My cousin then said, "MY people? There's no pyramids in East LA!!!!"

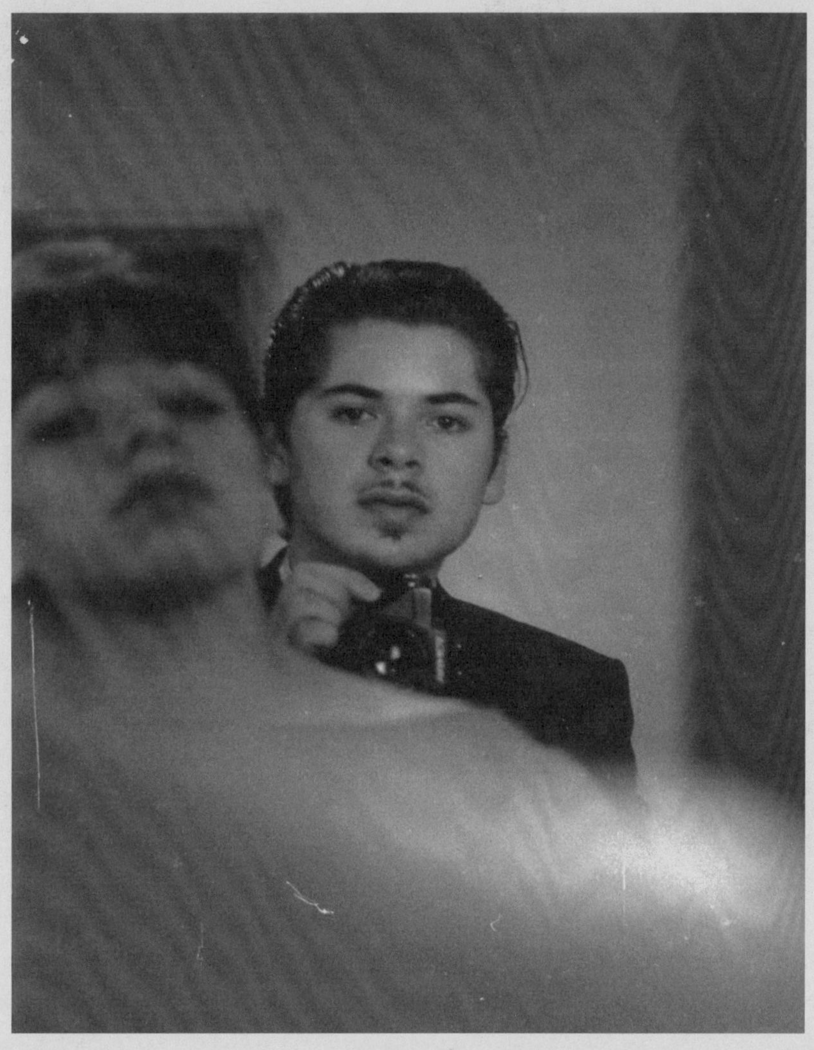

Herminia and Reynaldo Rivera (1981)

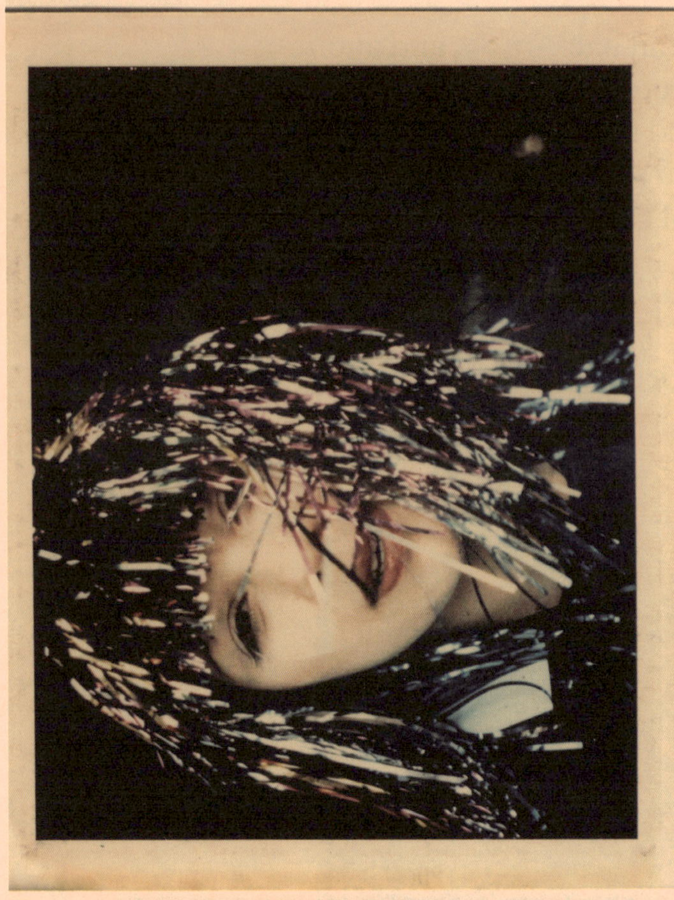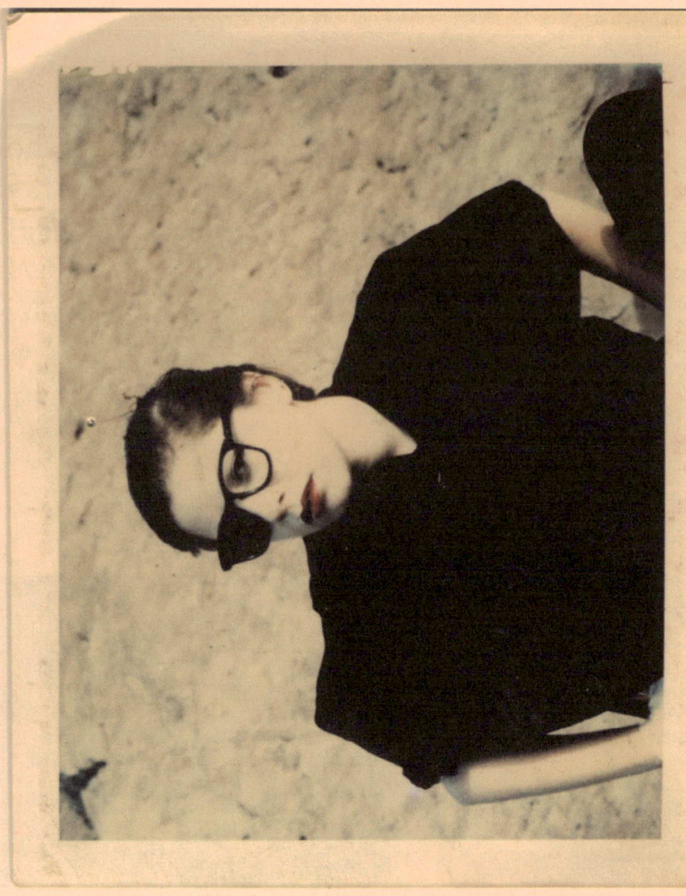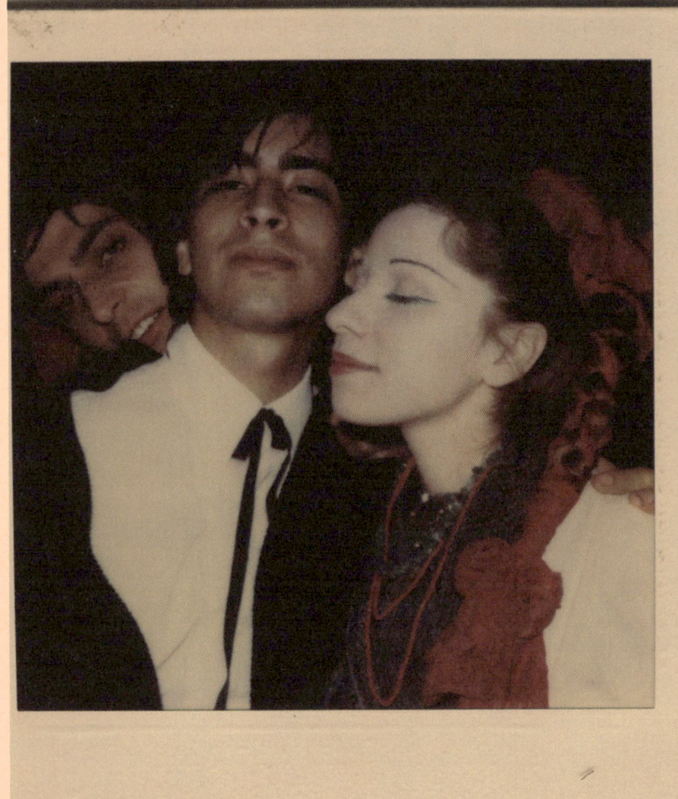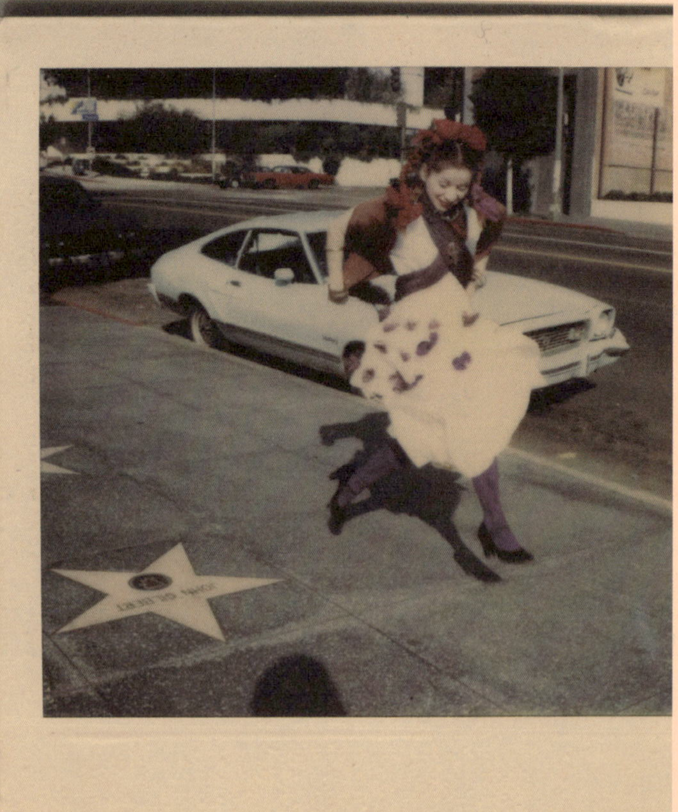

Polaroids (1983–87)

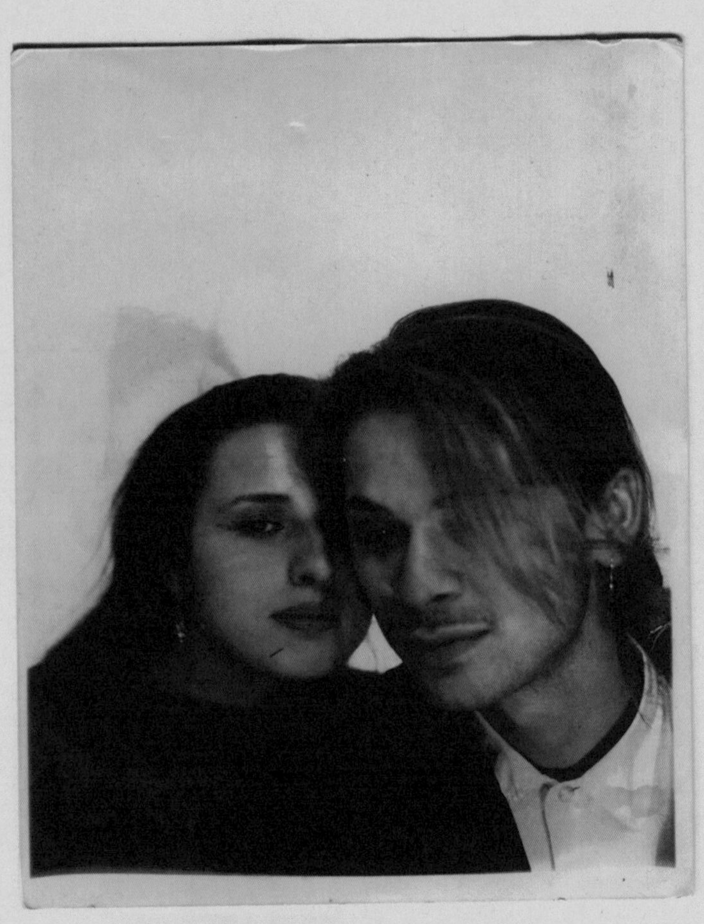

Tatiana and Reynaldo, Spain (1985)

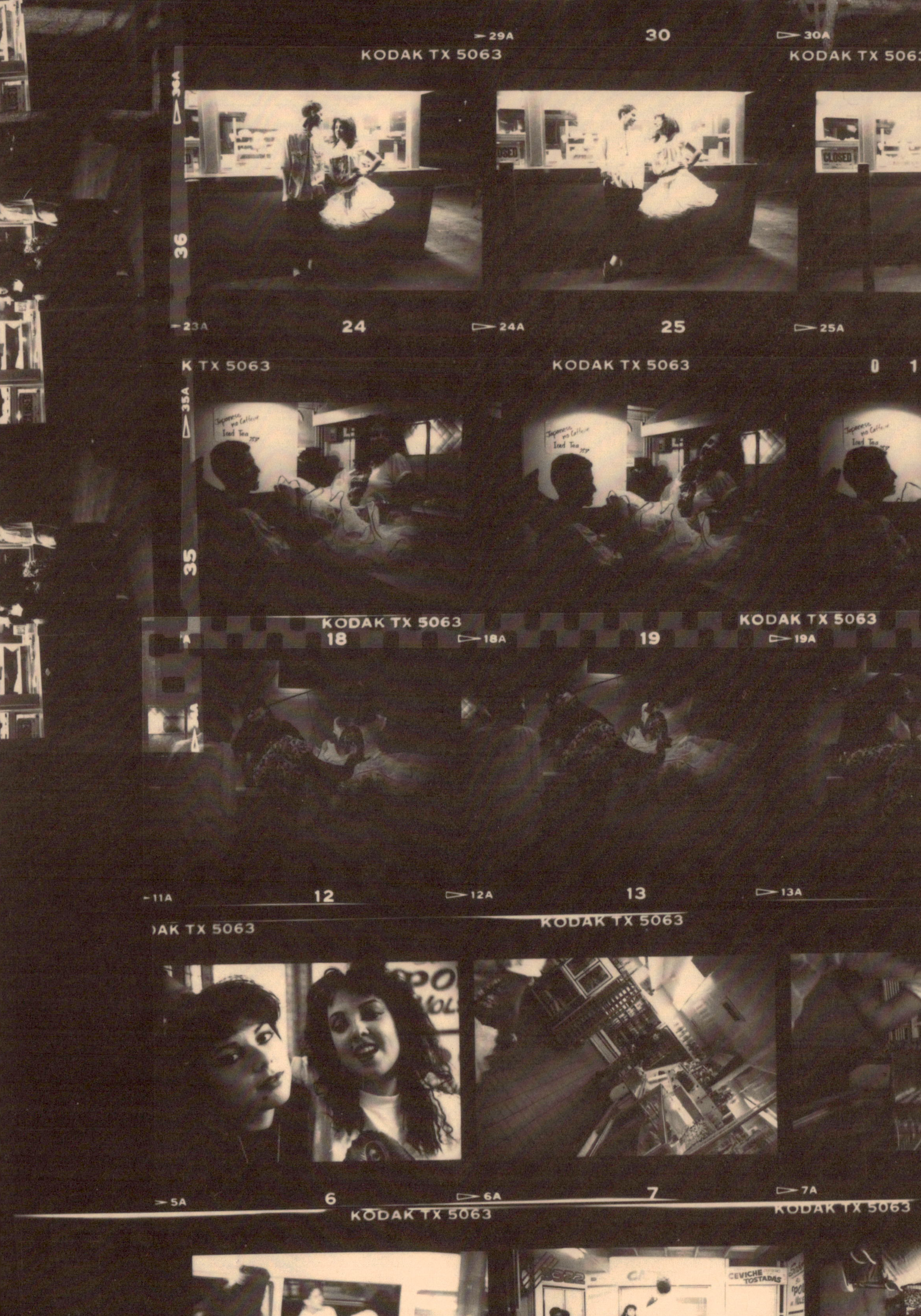

29A
30
30A
KODAK TX 5063
KODAK TX 5063
23A
24
24A
25
25A
K TX 5063
KODAK TX 5063
0 1
KODAK TX 5063
KODAK TX 5063
18
18A
19
19A
11A
12
12A
13
13A
DAK TX 5063
KODAK TX 5063
5A
6
6A
7
7A
KODAK TX 5063
KODAK TX 5063

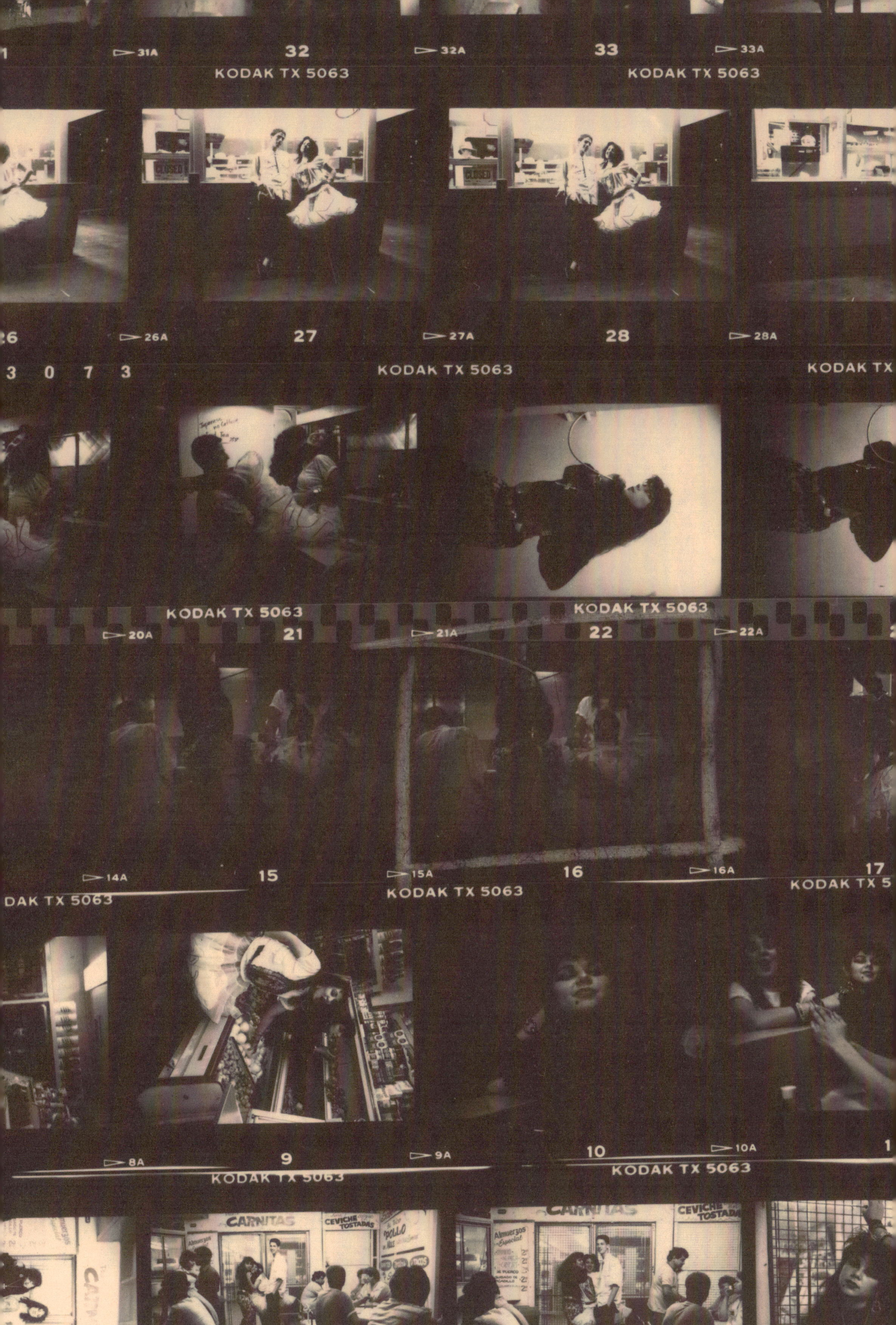

House Party
417 PARK VIEW ST. Los Angeles Ca.
brought to you in part by a Grant from the Rivera Foundation ©89.
All Donations go to The Might be Homeless!!

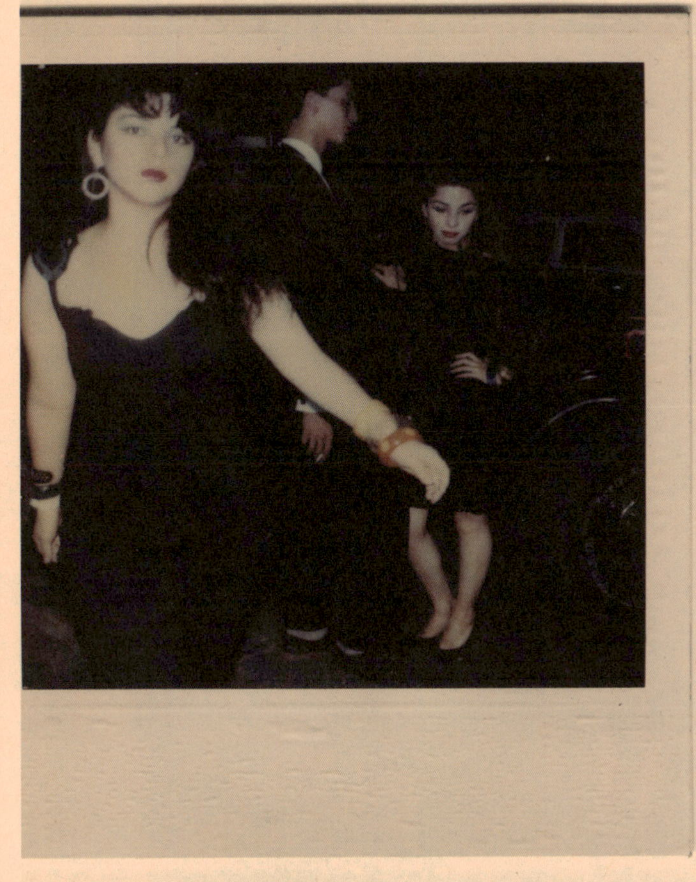

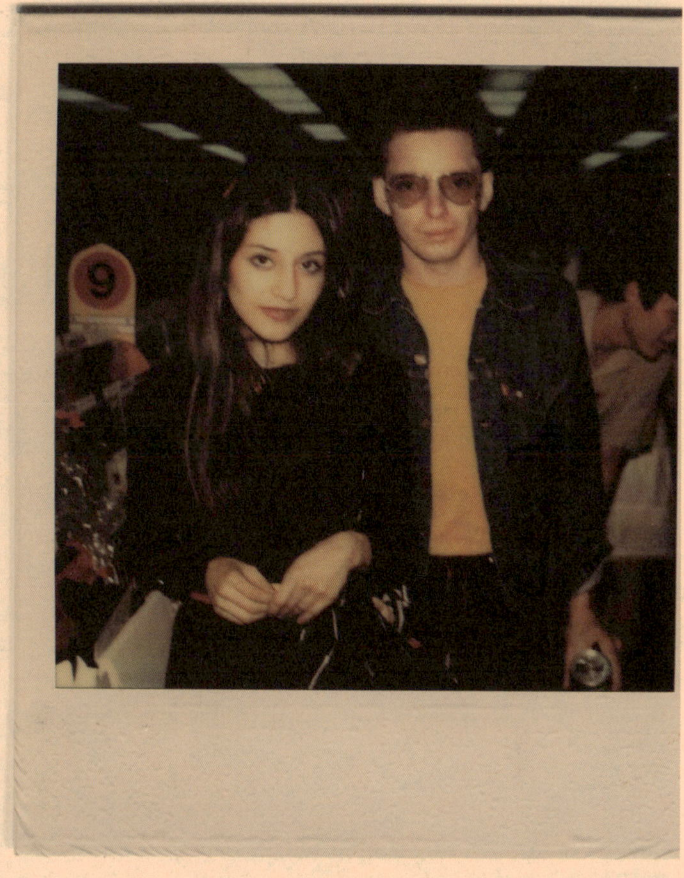

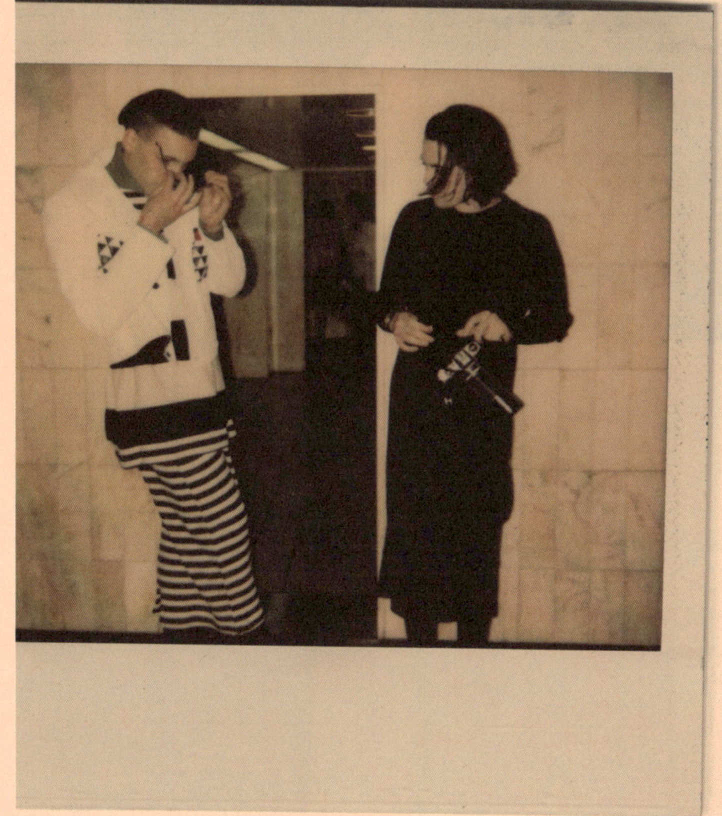

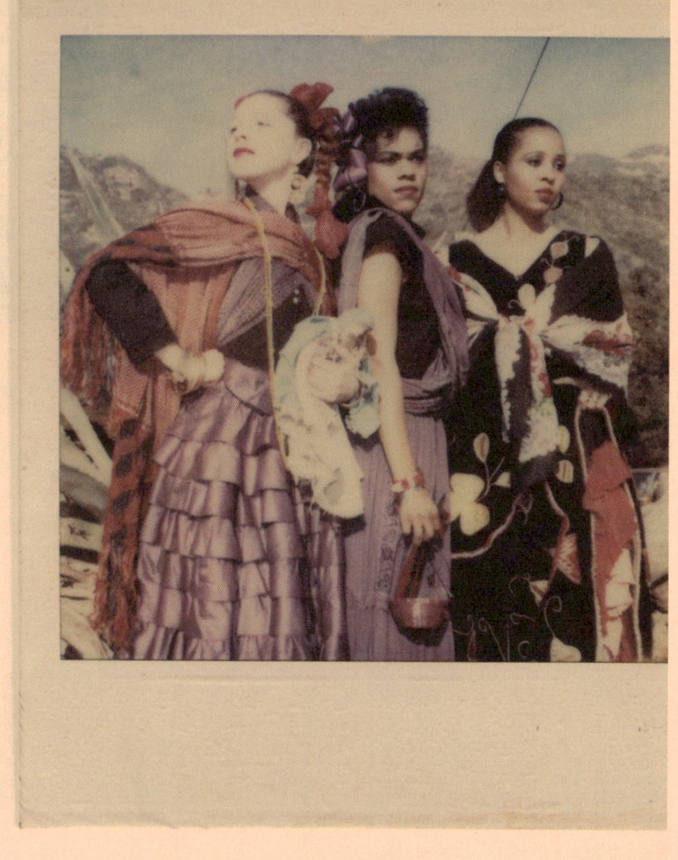

Polaroids (1979–88)

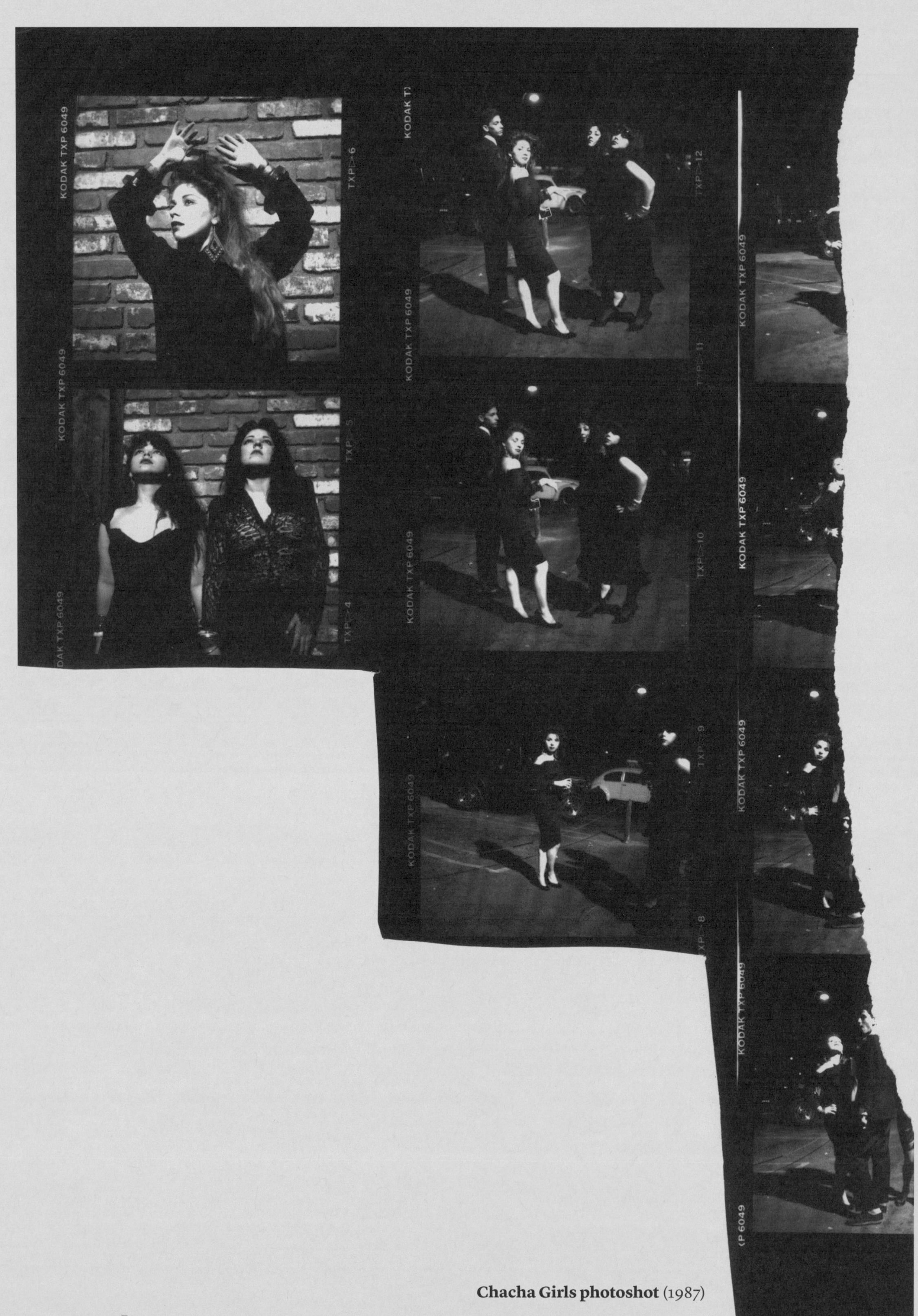

Chacha Girls photoshot (1987)

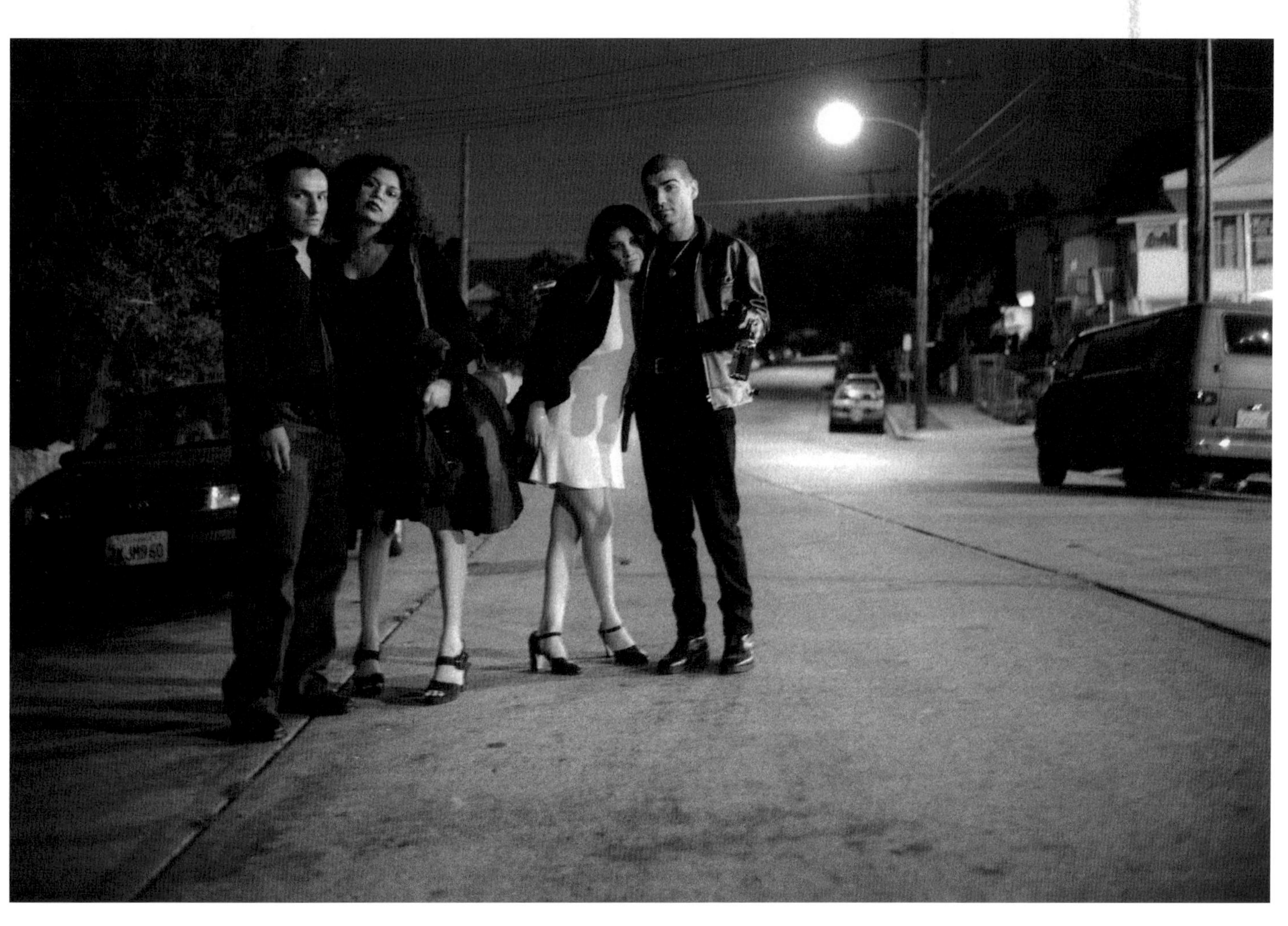

**Ramón García, Monica Canales, Annette, and
Christopher Arellano**, Echo Park (1995)

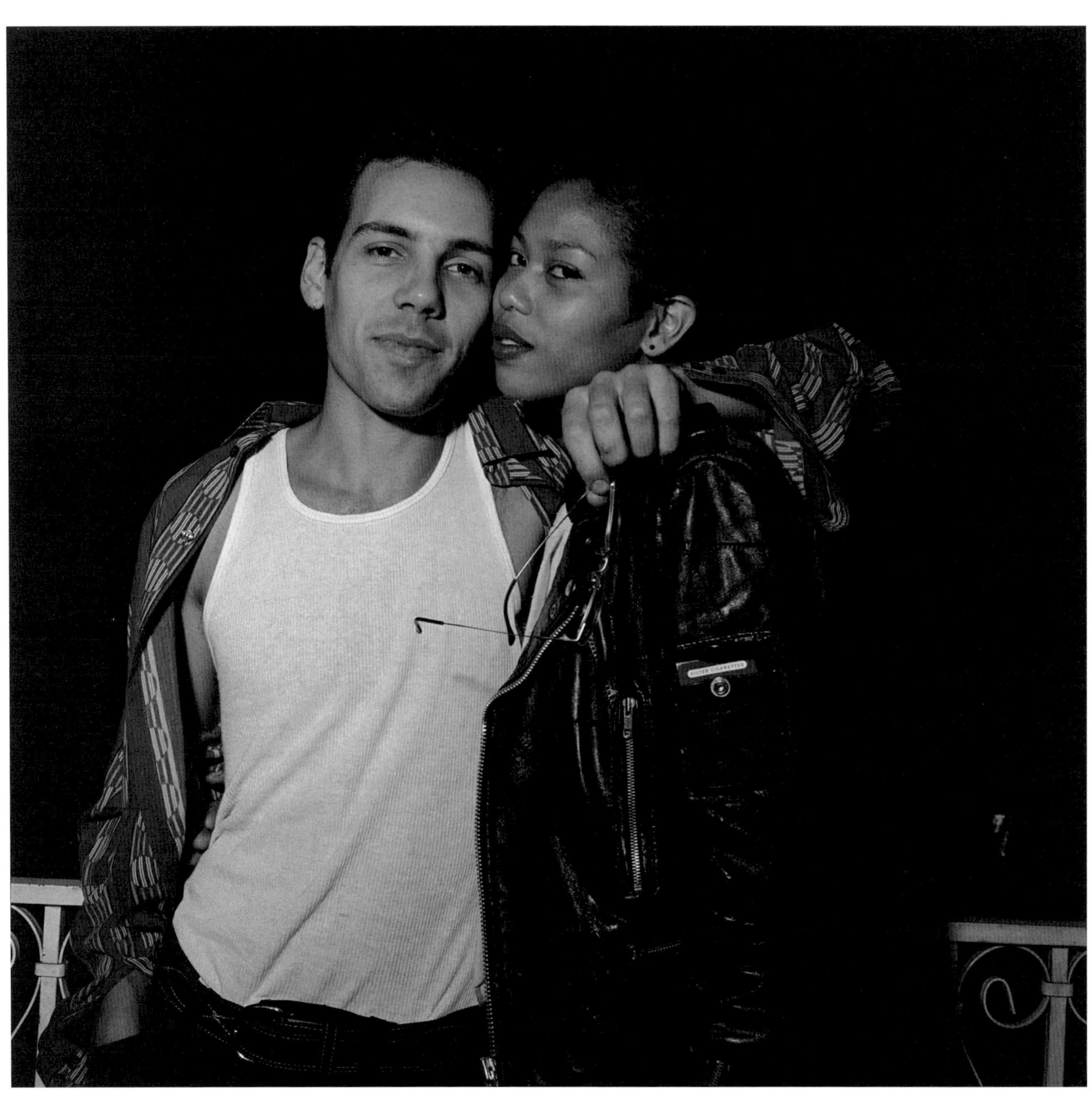

Ivan Morley and Pauletta Pierce, Echo Park (1995)

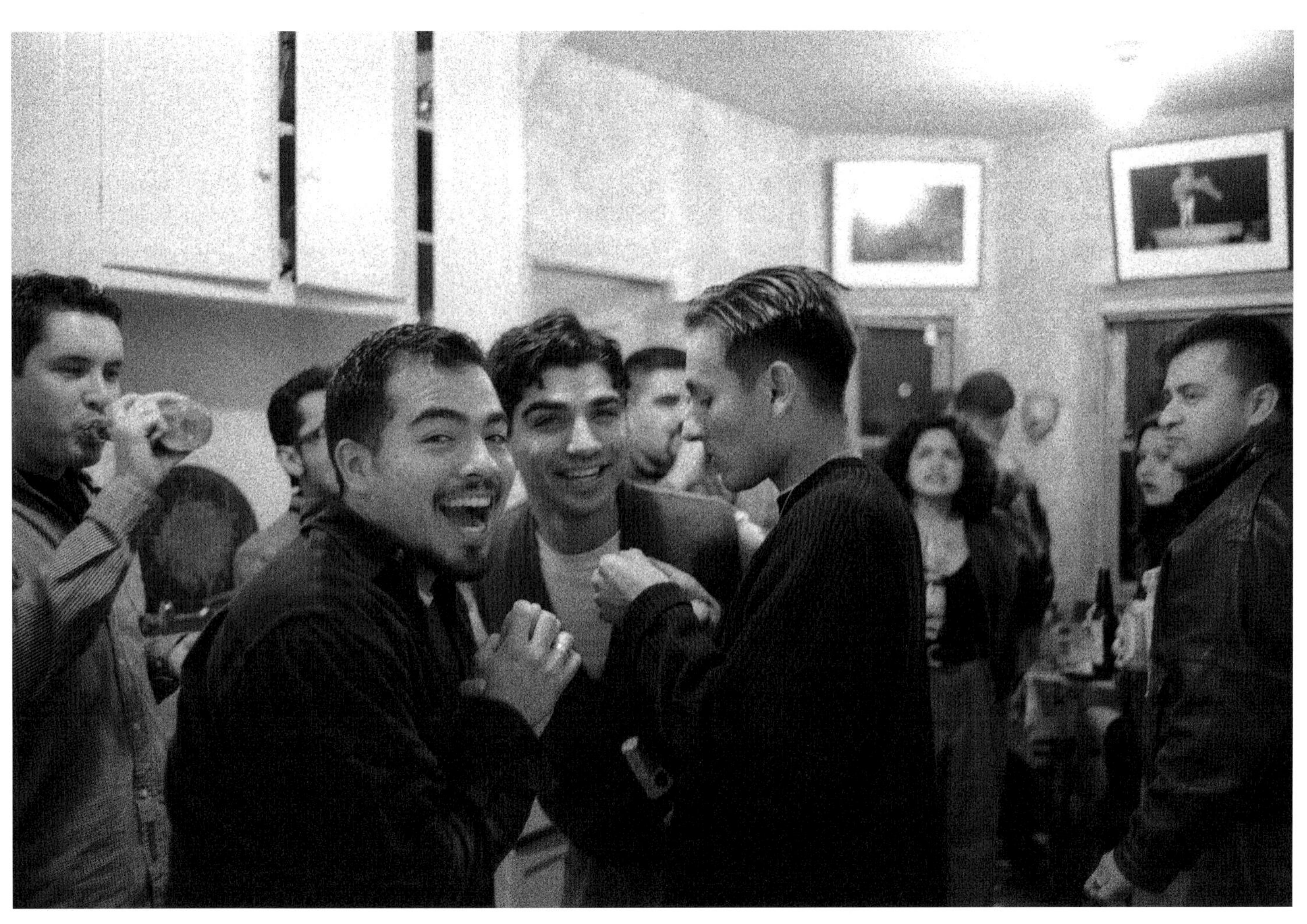

Miguel, Jerry, Christopher, and Ramón,
Echo Park (1995)

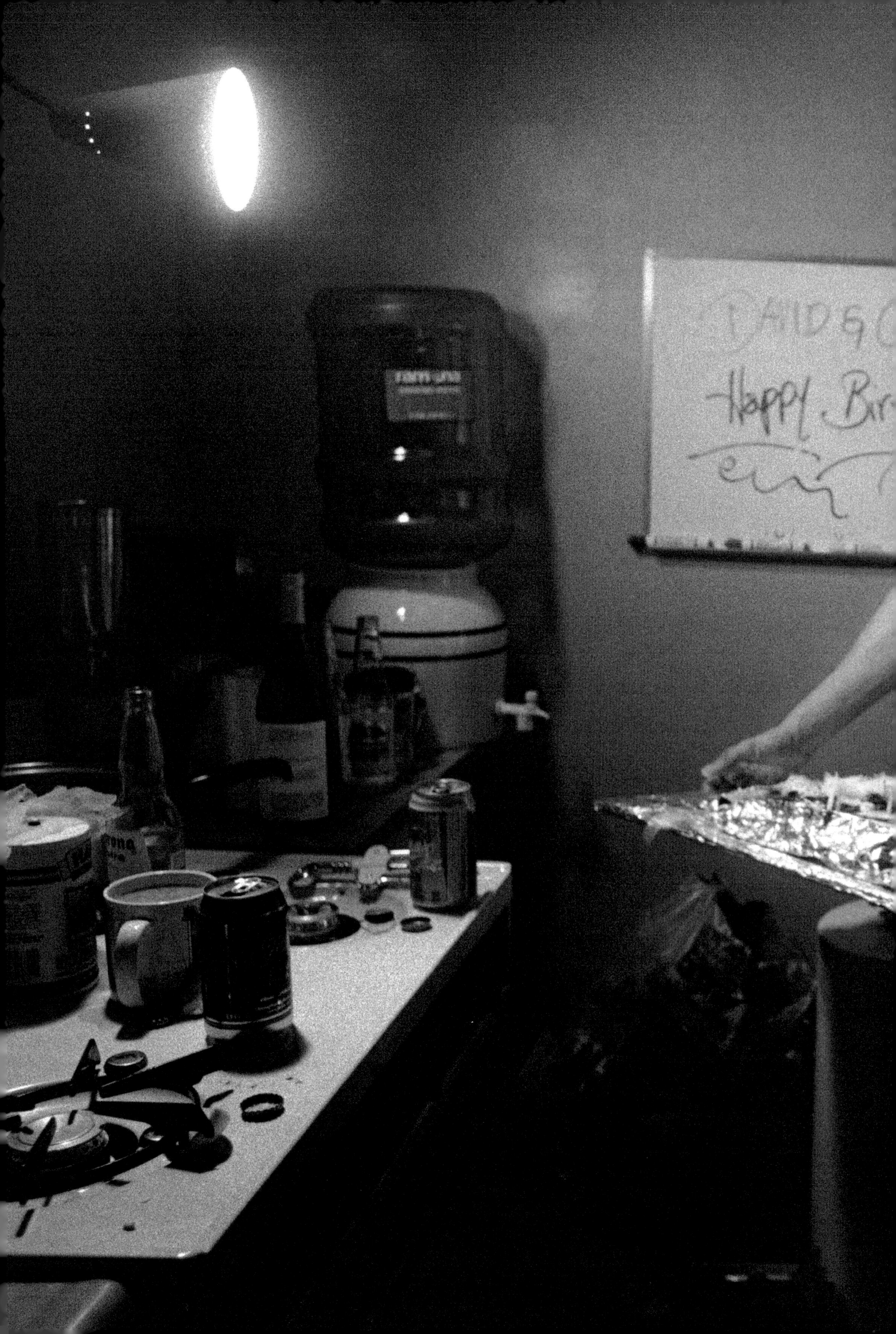
Happy Bir

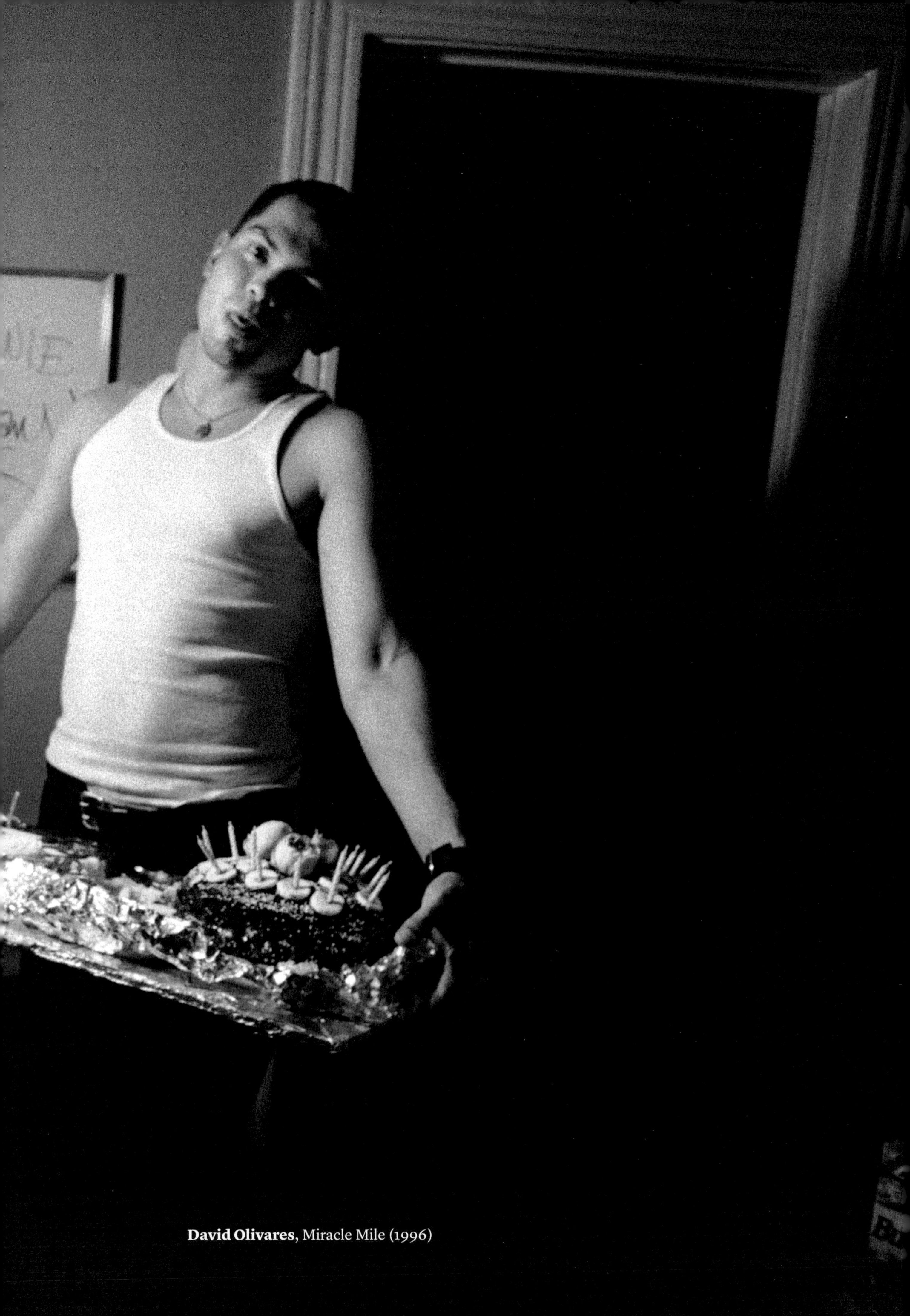

David Olivares, Miracle Mile (1996)

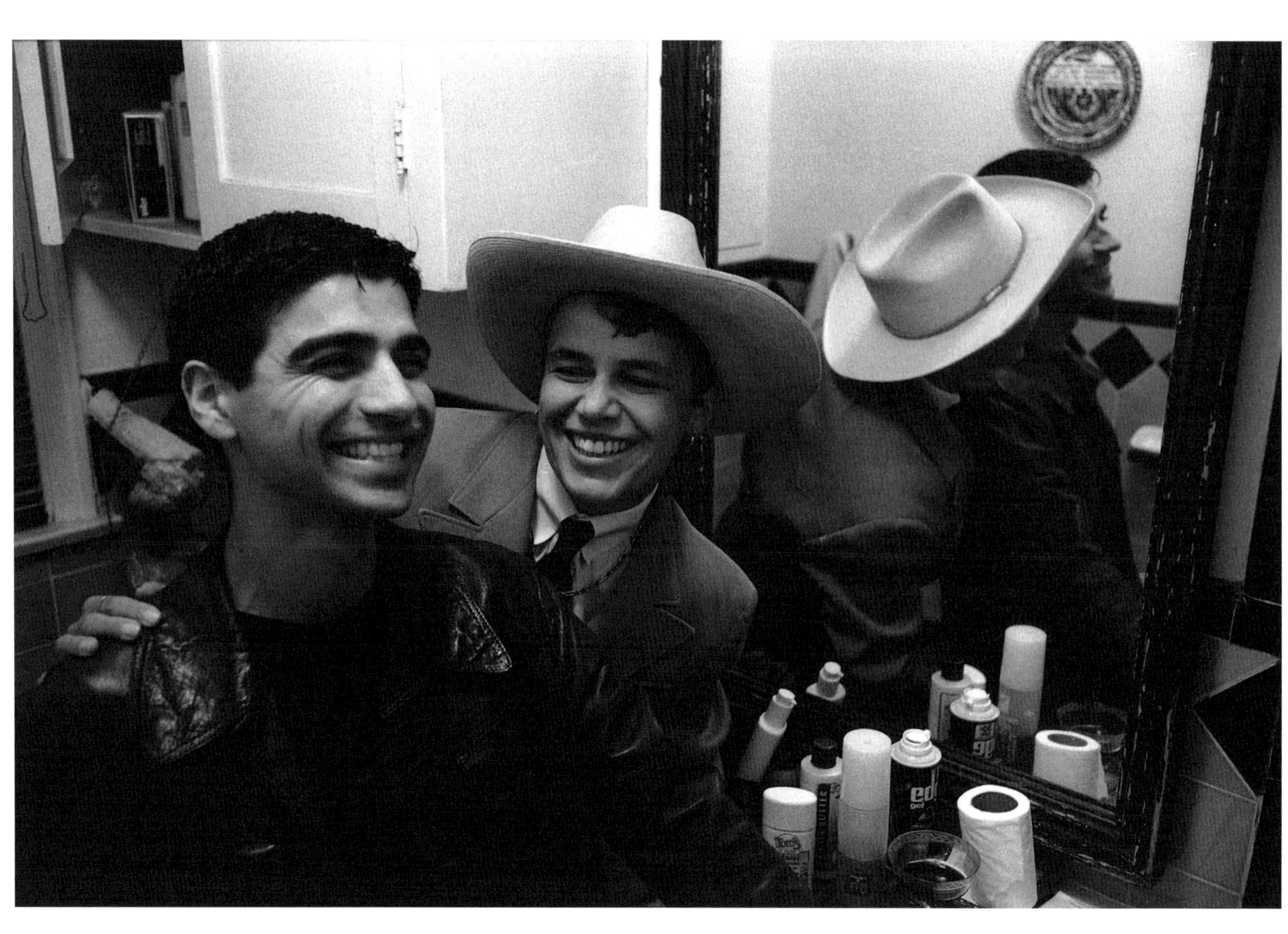

Christopher Arellano and Annette Weber,
Echo Park (1999)

98

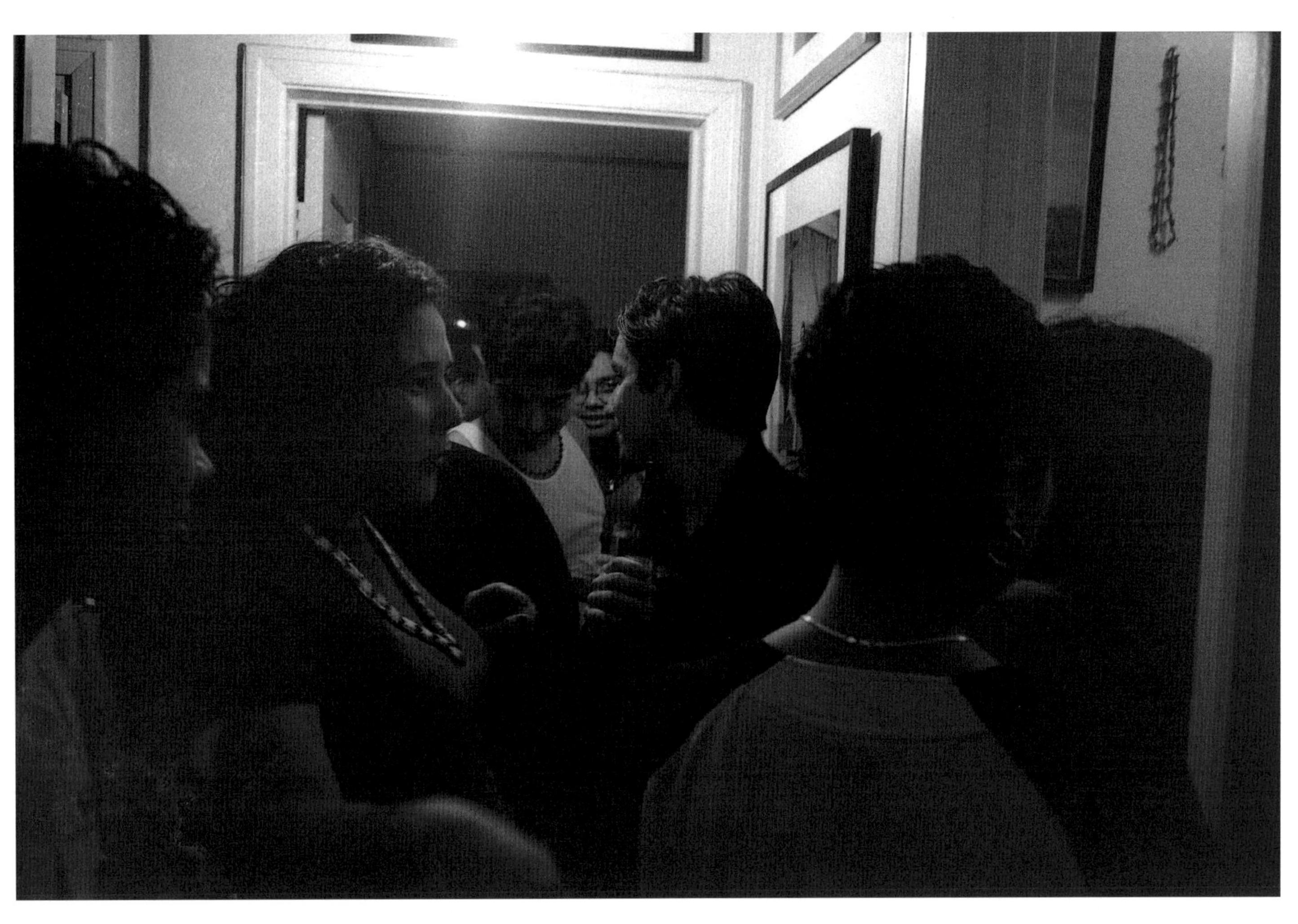

Party, Echo Park (1995)

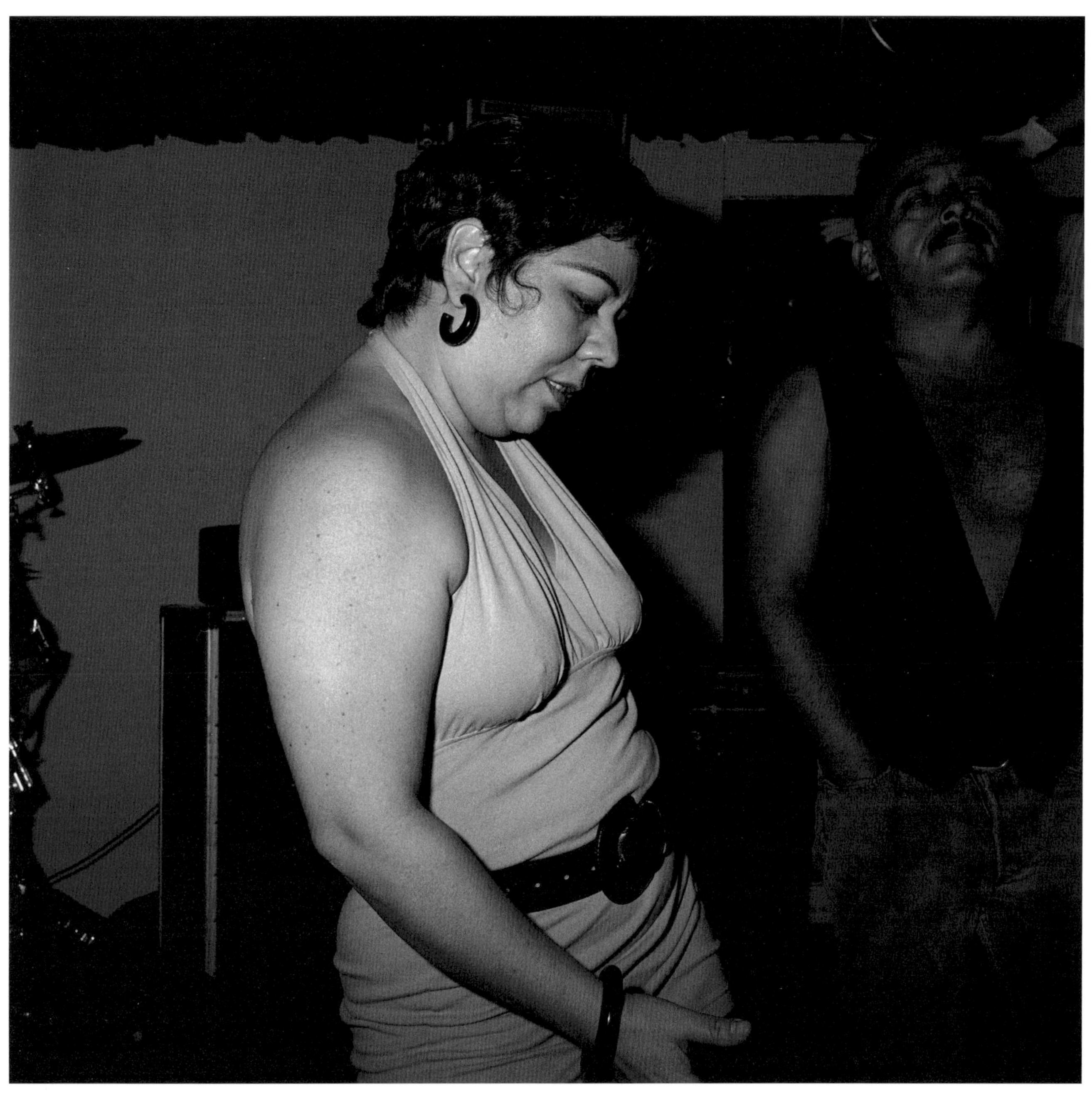

Cunt Club (1992)

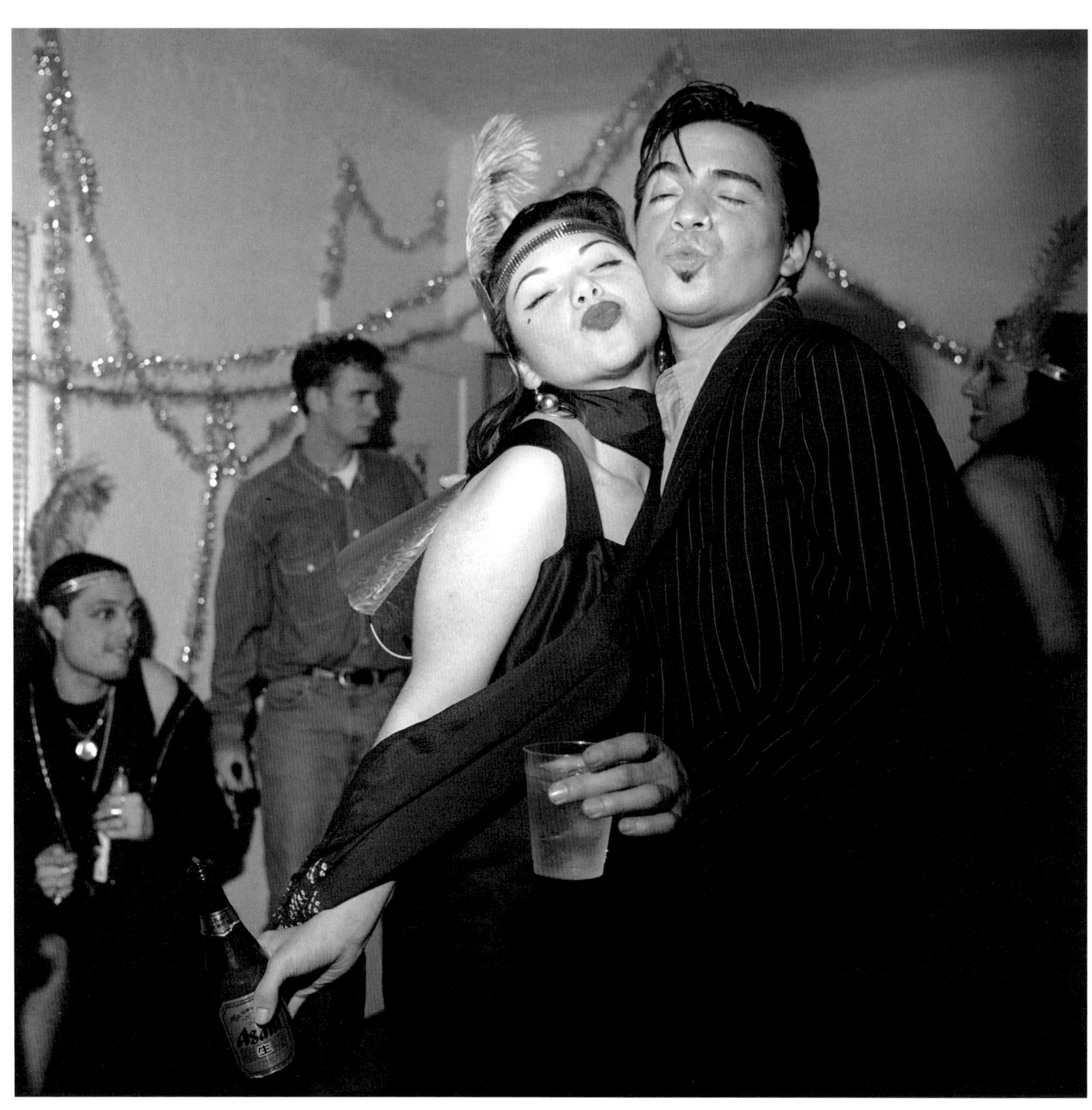

Connie Rivera and Mario Calvano, Echo Park (1990)

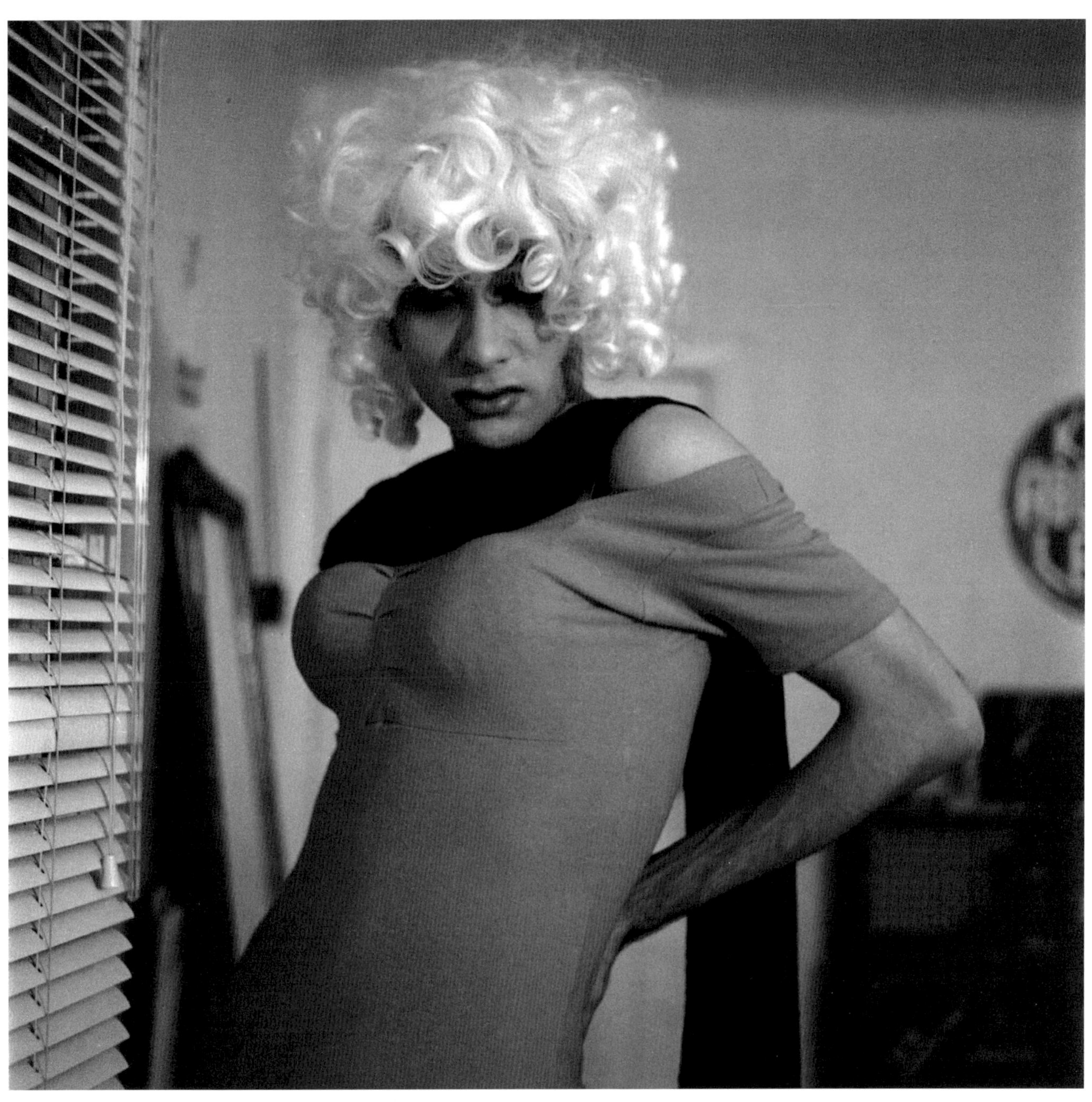

Untitled, Echo Park (1991)

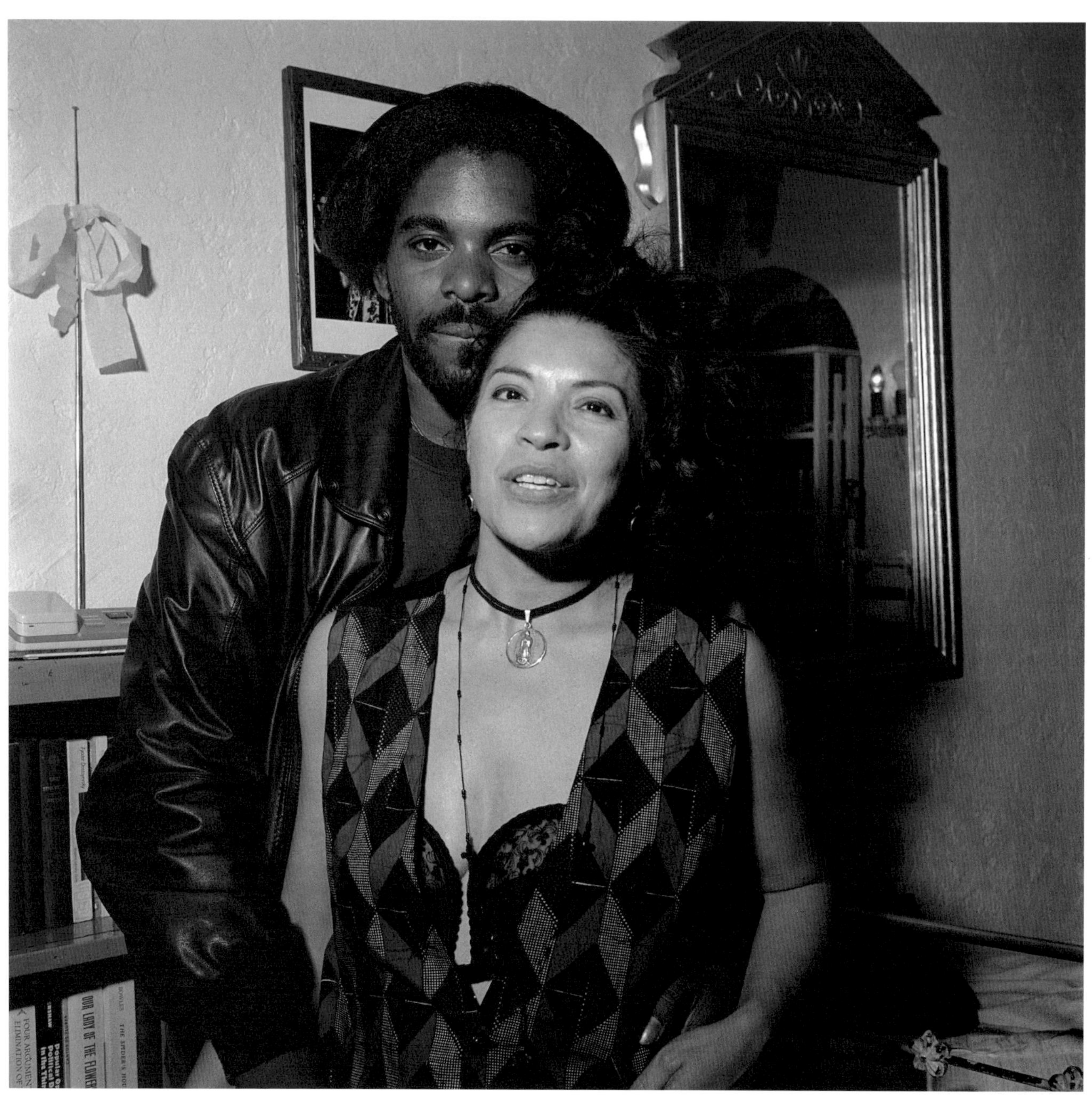

Bobby and Sandra Ramirez, Echo Park (1993)

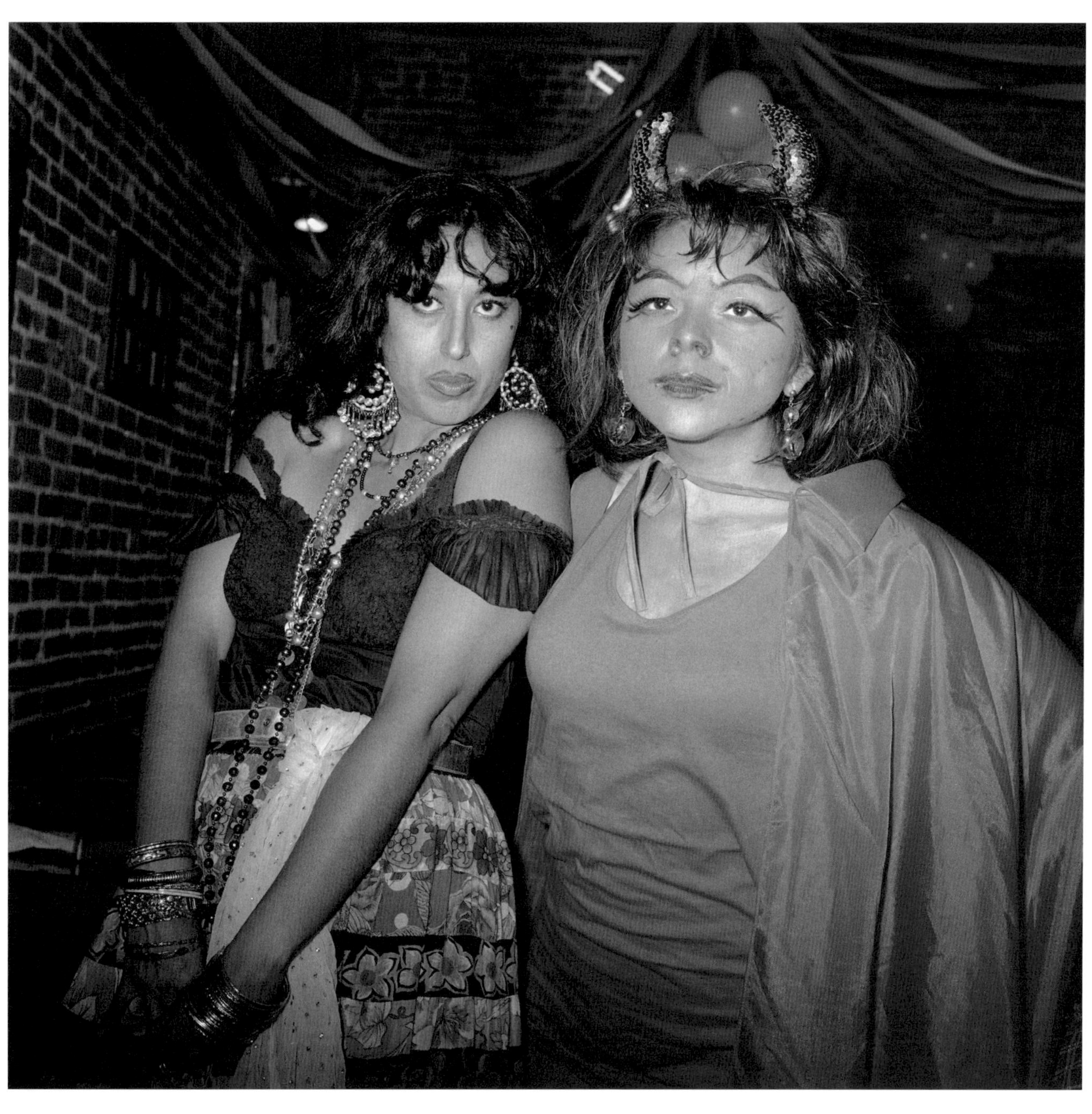

**Alicia Armendariz (Alice Bag) and
Connie Rivera**, Hollywood (1989)

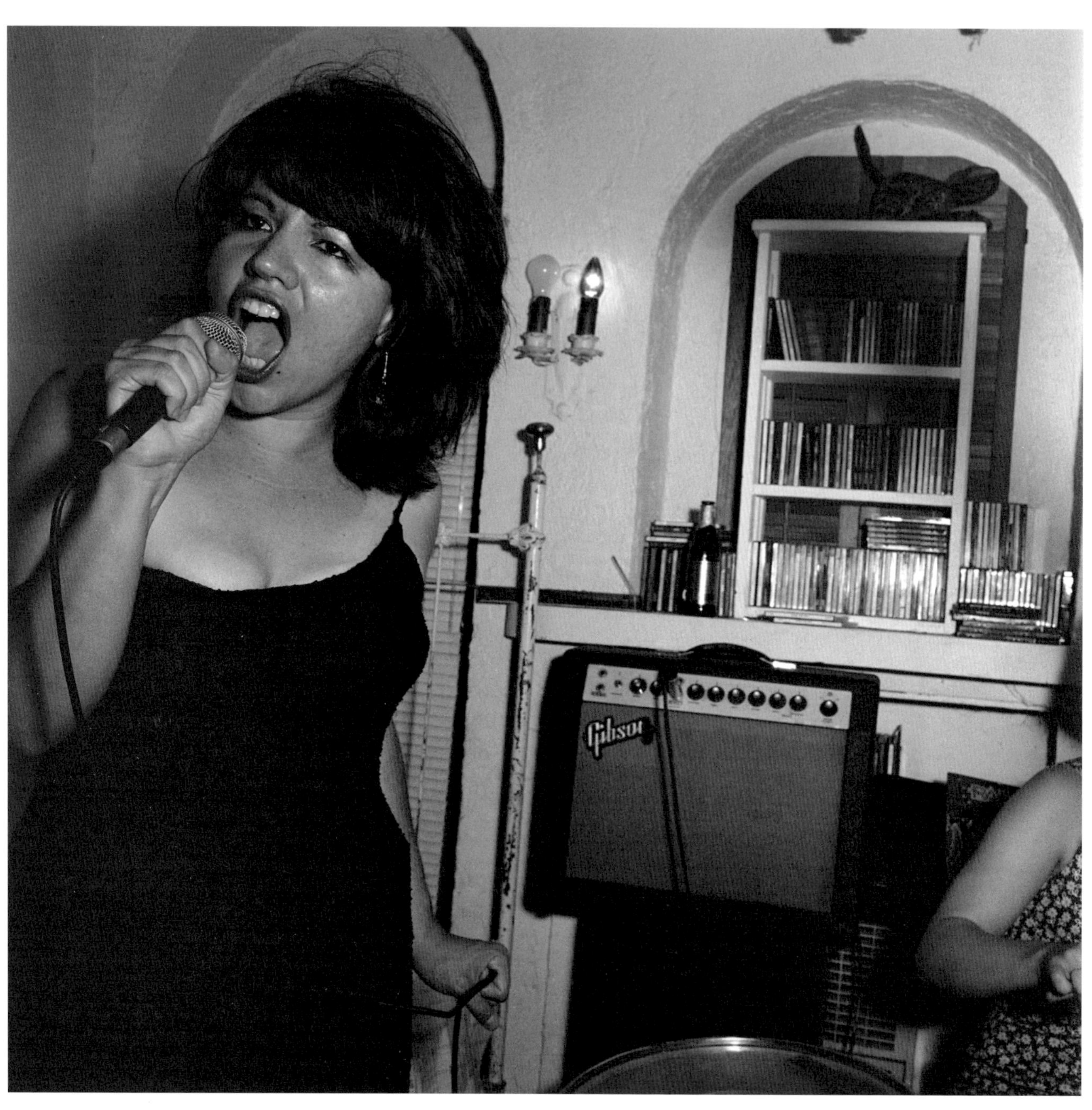

Cindy Gomez, Echo Park (1992)

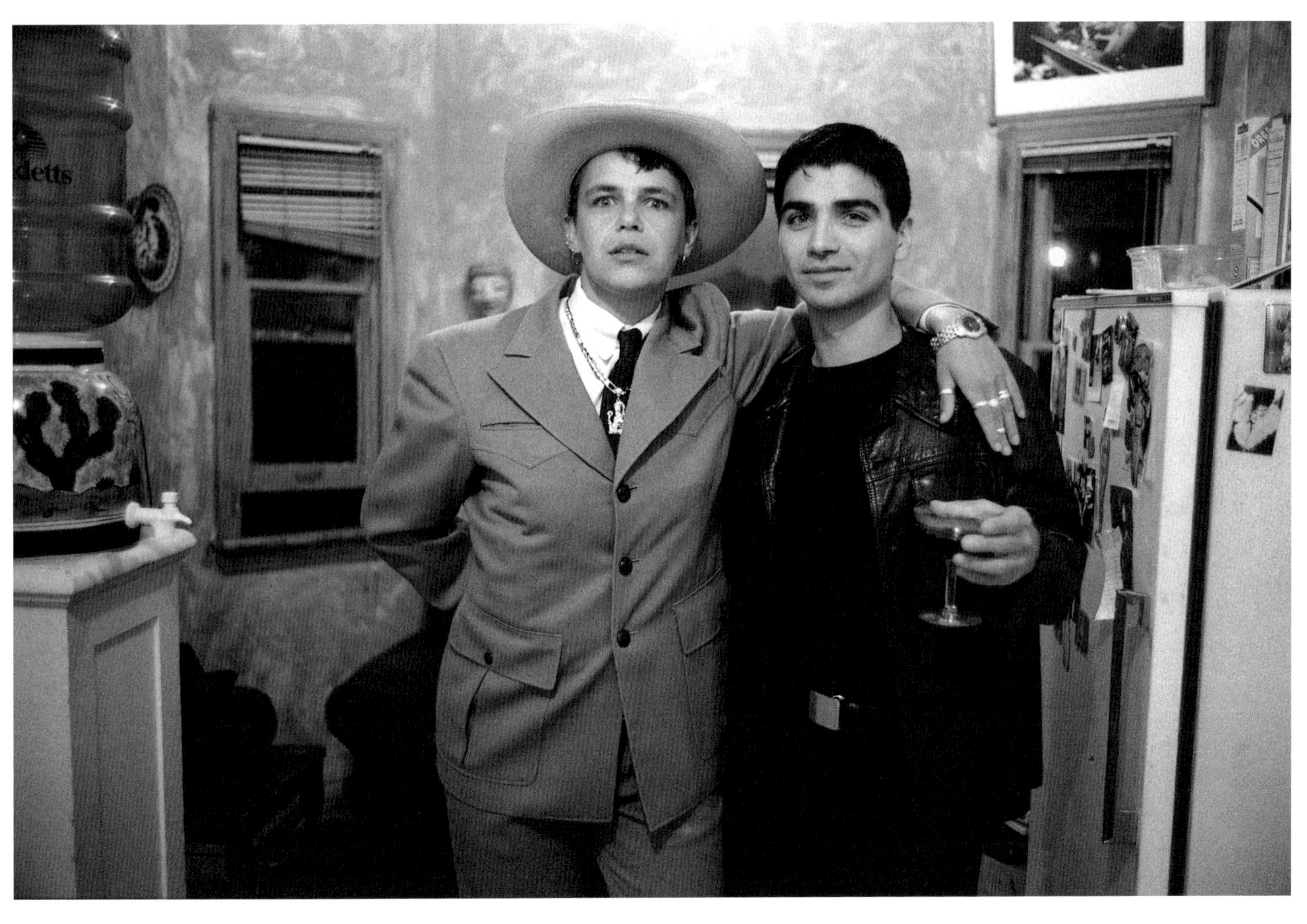

Annette Weber and Christopher Arellano,
Echo Park (1999)

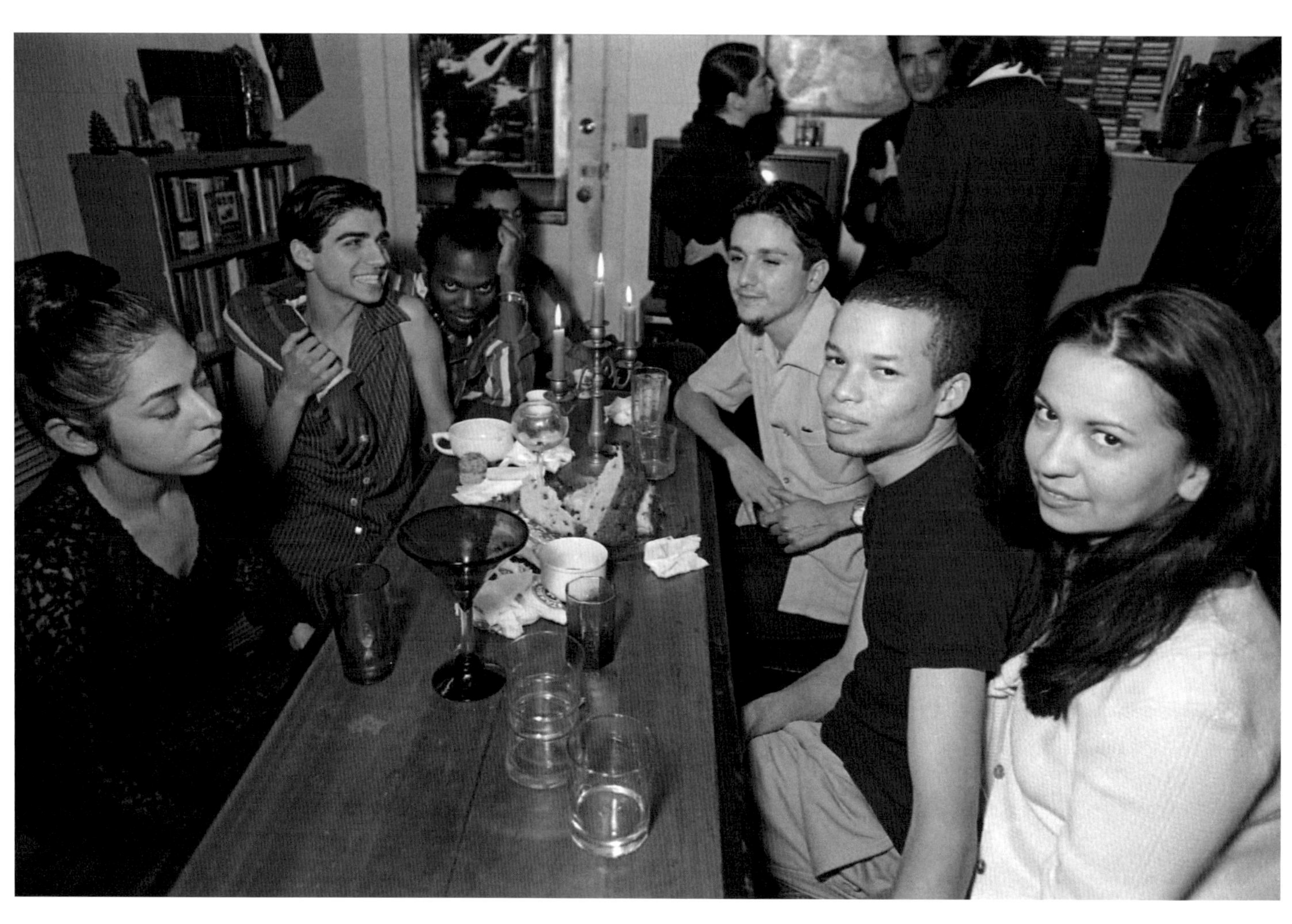

Arlene, Christopher Arellano, Wes Cuttler, Henry, Michael Queenland, and Renée, Echo Park (1992)

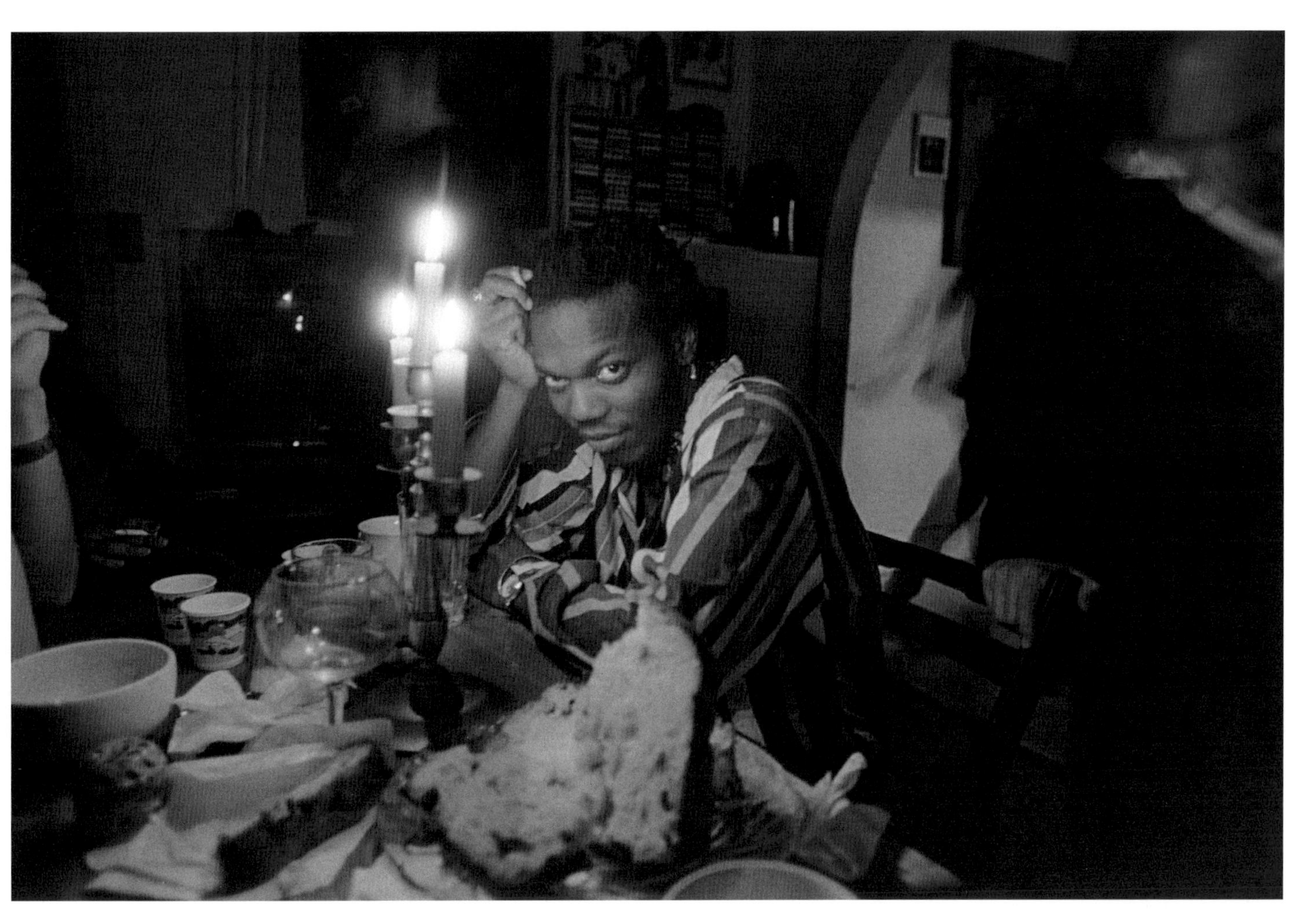

Wes Cuttler, Echo Park (1992)

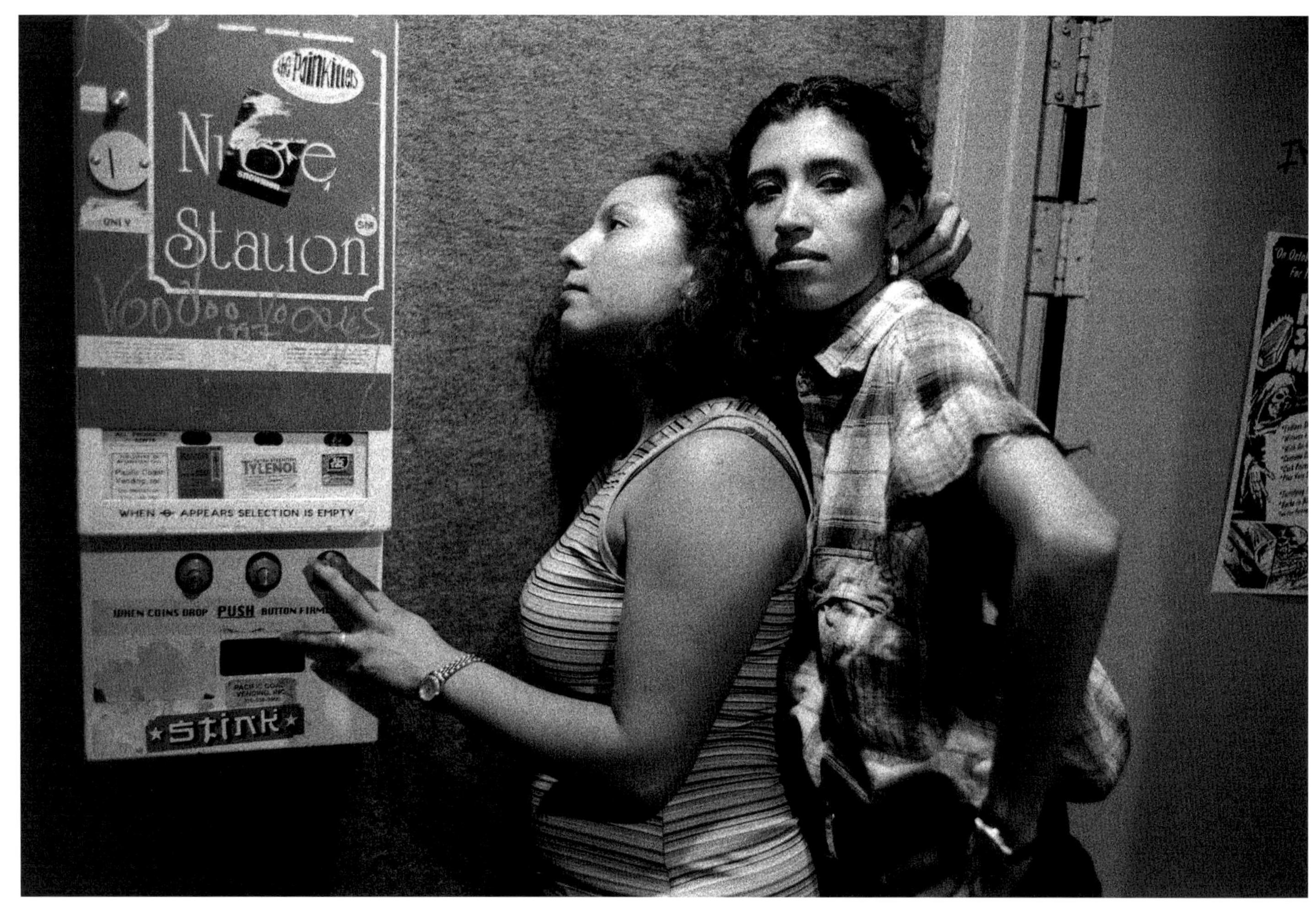

Ramona Ortega and Gia Hernandez, Dreams (1995)

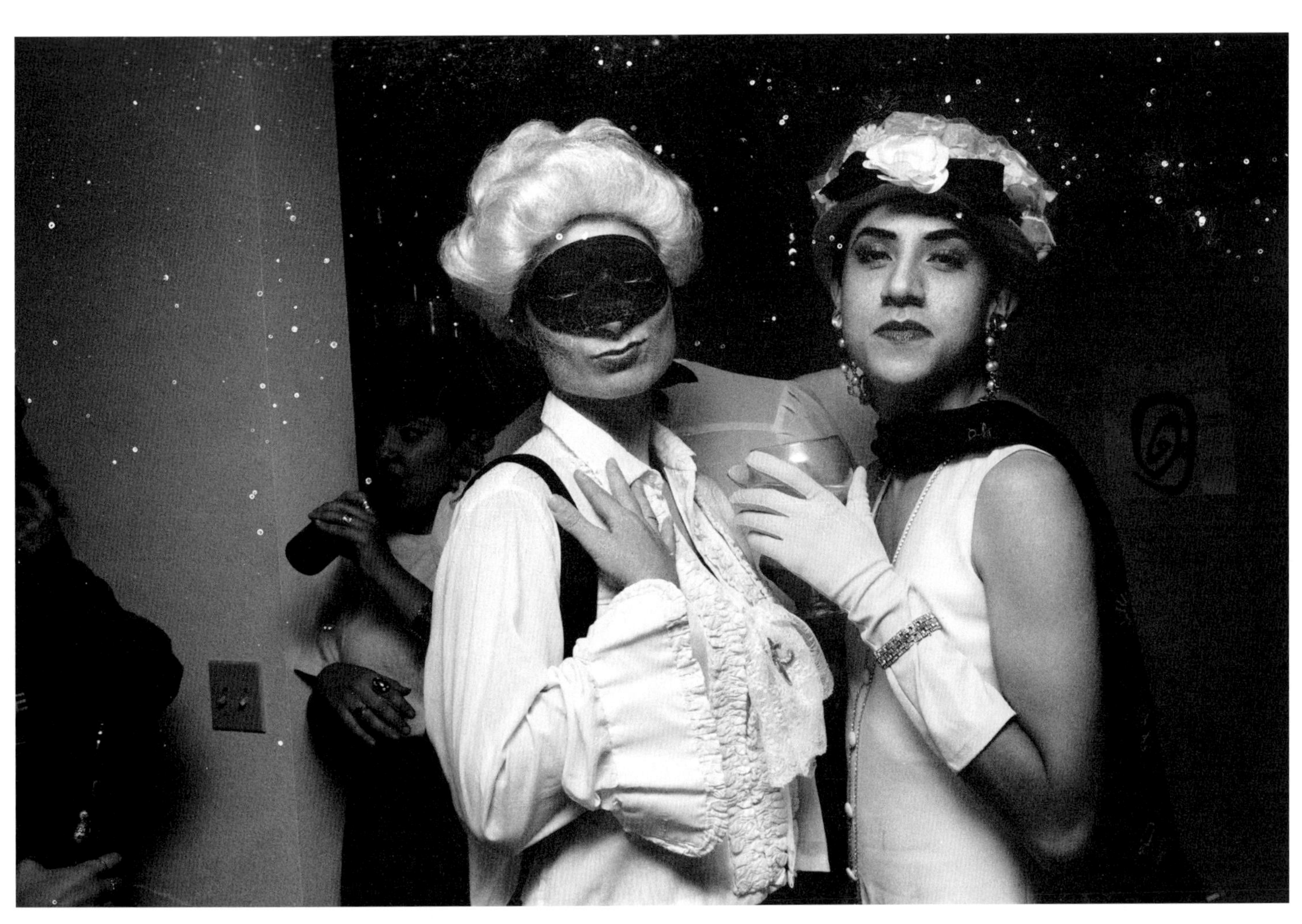

Elyse Regehr and Javier Orosco, Downtown LA (1989)

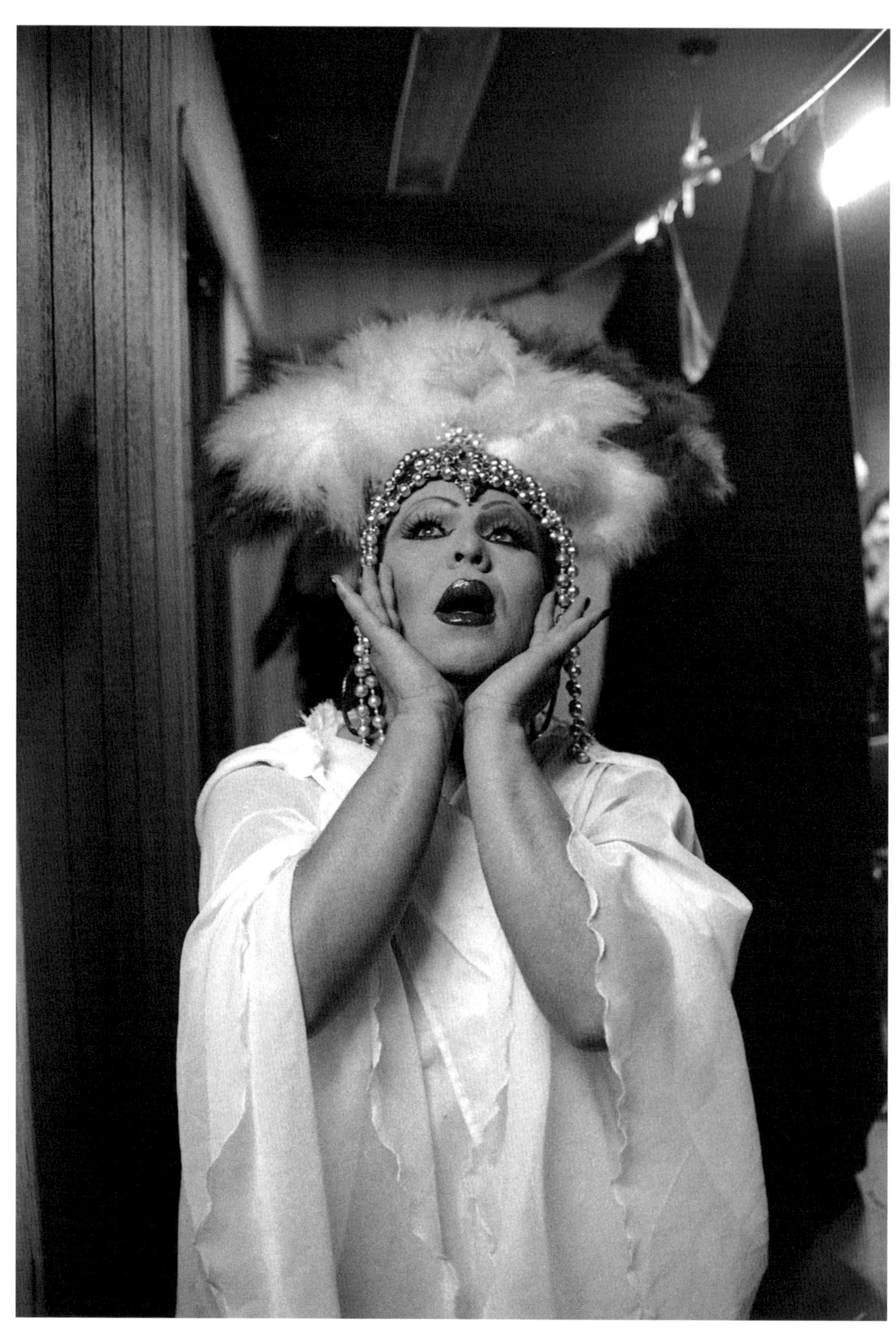

Olga, Silverlake Lounge (1995)

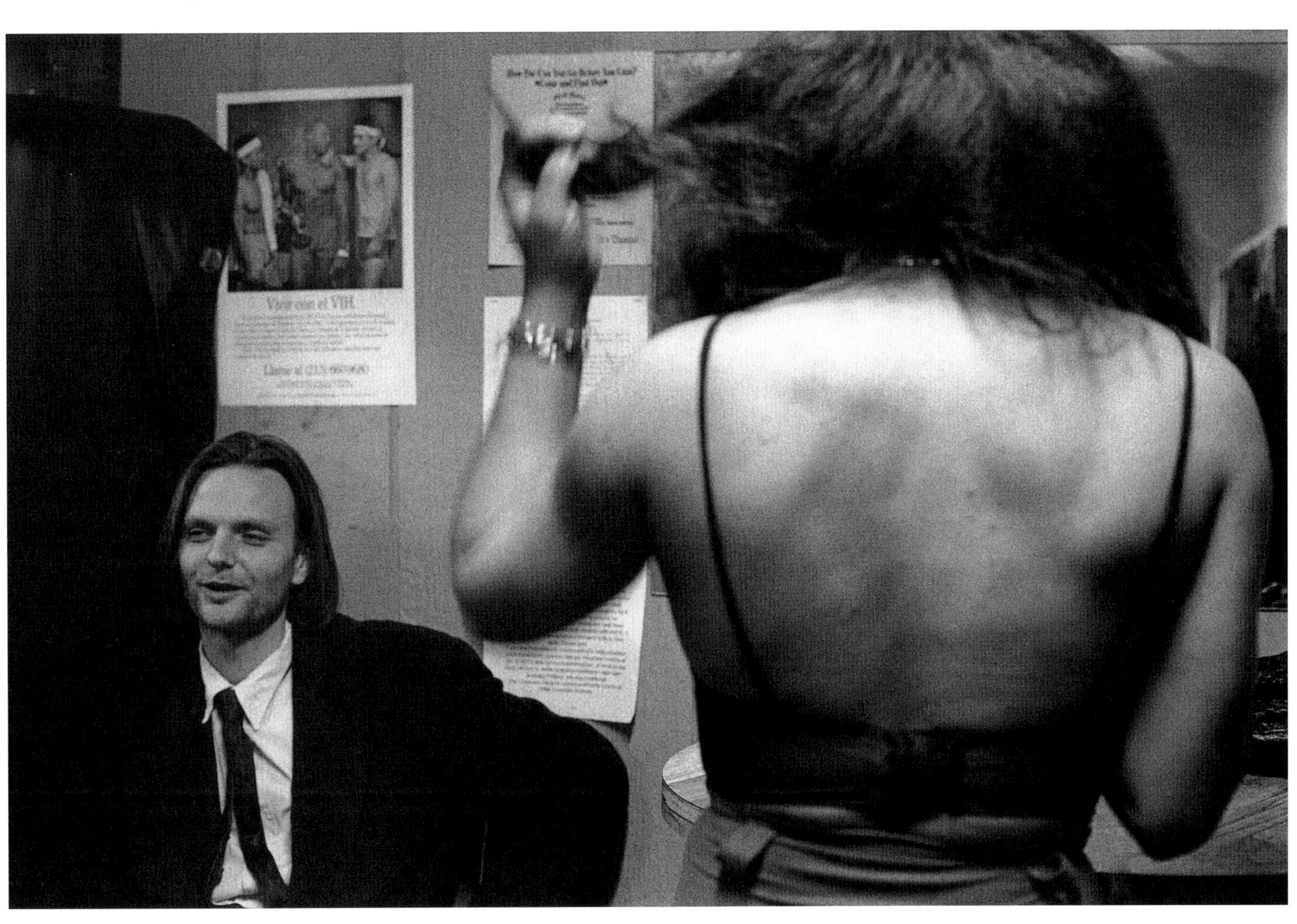

Thomas and performer, Silverlake Lounge (1995)

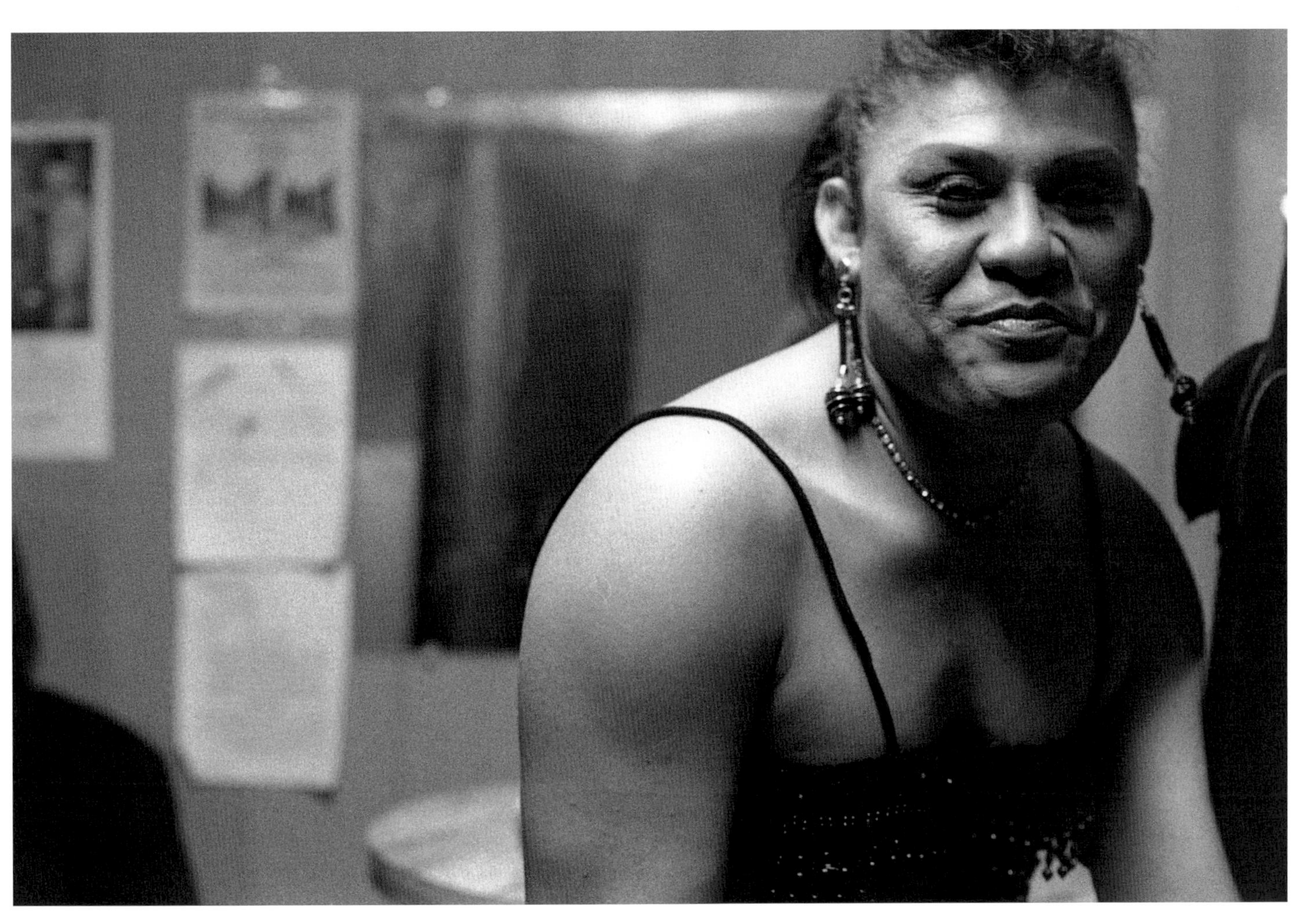

Performer, Silverlake Lounge (1995)

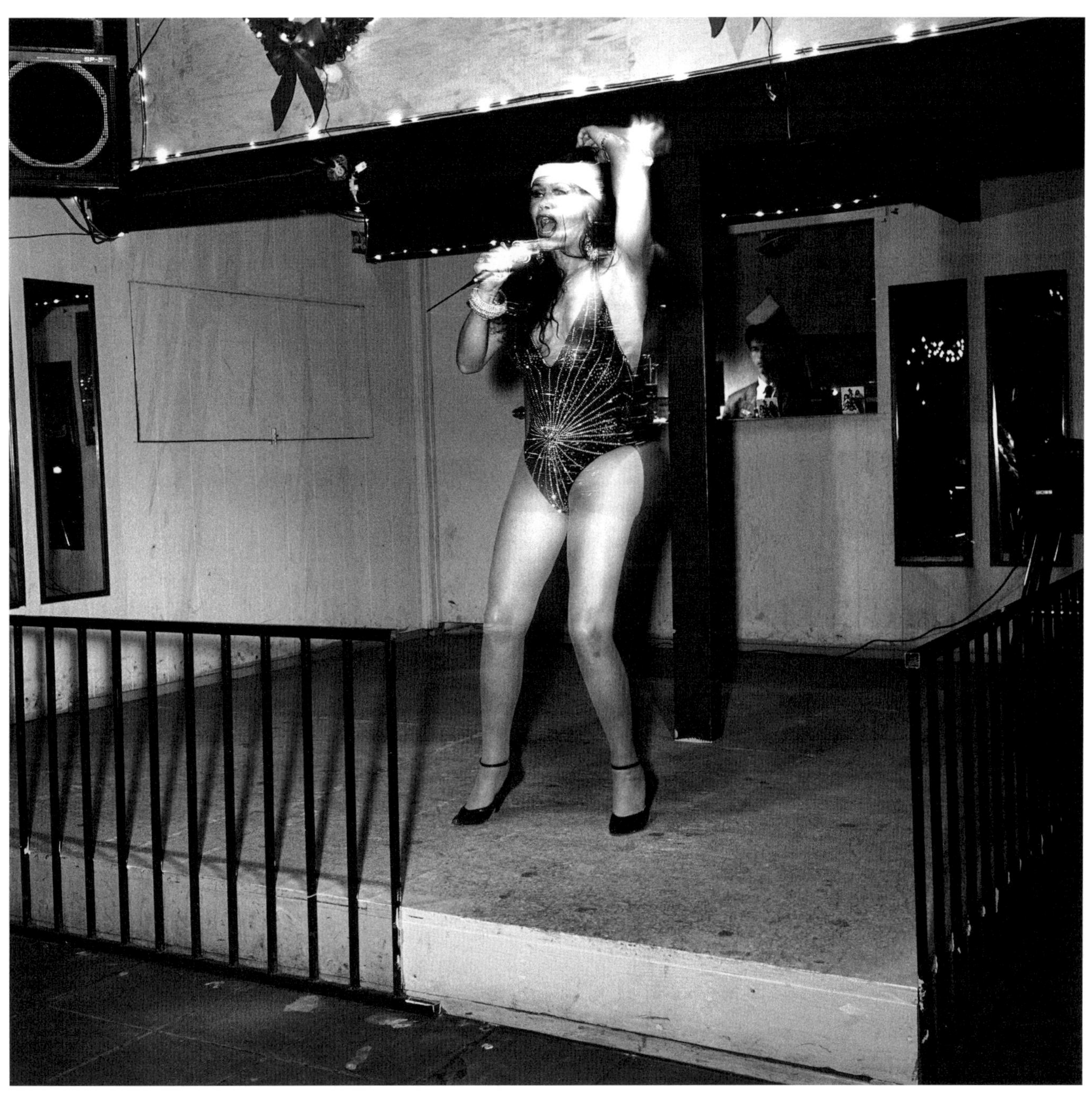

Tatiana Volty, Silverlake Lounge (1986)

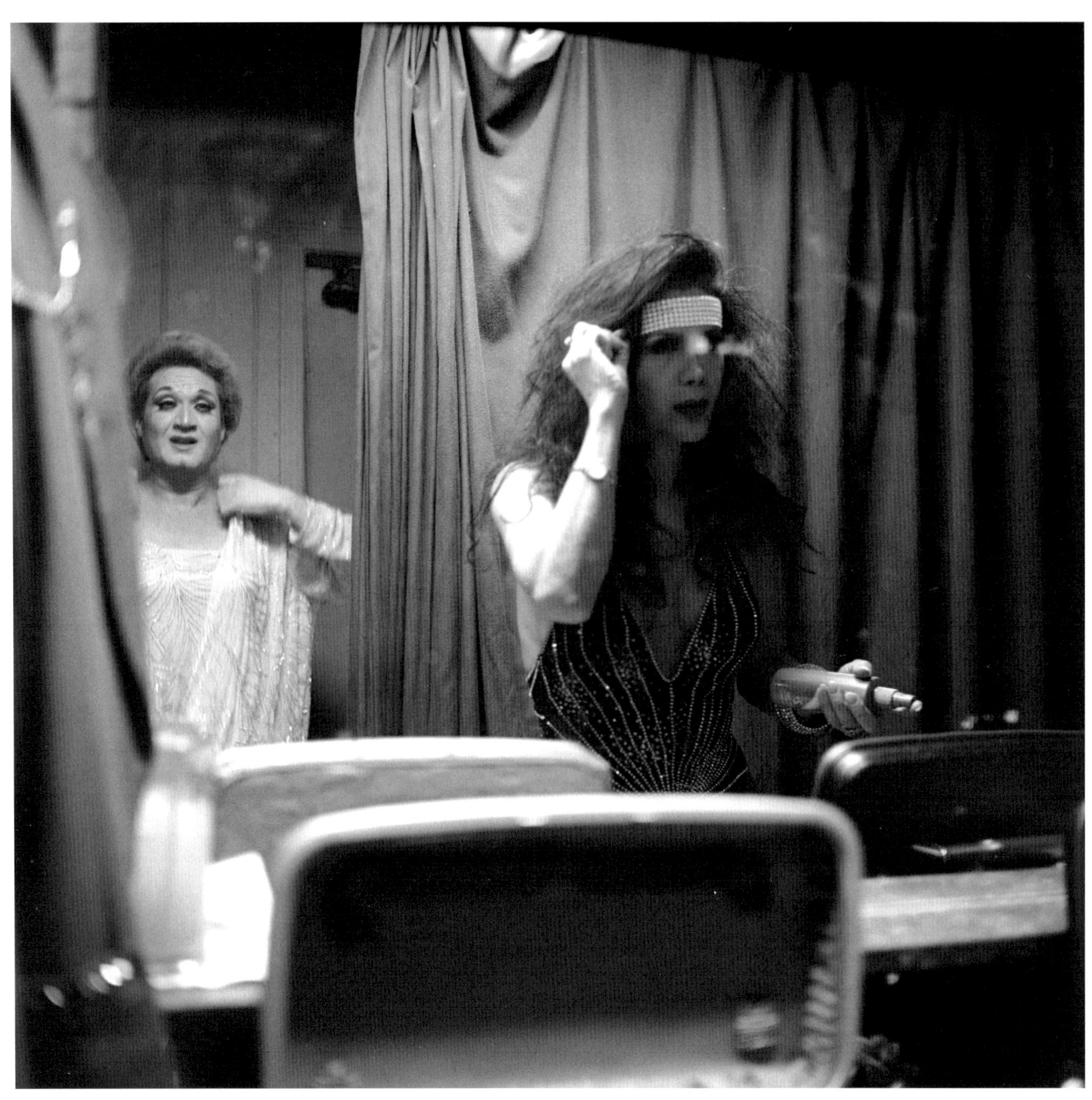

Montenegro, Tatiana Volty, Silverlake Lounge (1996)

Tatiana
by Luis Bauz

In her memory and to Chris and Rey who inspired this writing.

It was a gray Sunday afternoon in 1995, clouds pregnant with rain. I liked walking to La Plaza on my days off. As if by spiritual force, I felt myself drawn to one of the bars there, almost empty on that particular Sunday. At one table sat four butch lesbians and at another, a woman next to a fancy Latino man, sporting a huge moustache, a red carnation on the right edge of his coat, and wearing expensive cologne we could all smell. I sat down at a sticky table and ordered the promotional offering: *2 MARGARITAS FOR THE PRICE OF ONE.*

The show was about to begin. Someone in the DJ booth announced: "Ladies and gentlemen, the one and only, Tatiana Volty!" Flipping around in my seat, I ran my tongue all around the salt-rimmed glass, thinking there was no way it could be true. There was a momentary pause as the lights illuminated an empty stage, but then a female voice from an unseen person echoed through the speakers: "You should be clapping for me, stupids!" And I clapped, laughing, wanting to scream for such an encounter, as she appeared.

Tatiana had been one of the main attractions at a gay bar called El Deval that I passed every morning on my way to high school in Colonia Condesa in Mexico City in the '80s. She had also been a legend at the Gallery Bar in Acapulco in the late '70s. That rainy afternoon, Tatiana sang *Piel Morena* and I realized how much time had passed since I had last seen her. She couldn't have been past her late 20s, and now she was in her late 50s, but it didn't matter. She moved across space in a flamboyant white dress with a huge satin tail, calling out to me with her *AURA!*

When the show was over, she exited the dressing room and I approached her, explaining my own story, spilling my memories of her. I told her how influential she had been to my novel *The Woman With The Hair of Fire*, written while she was working at the Deval. I remembered the owner, Martha Valdespino, who lived in the same building as my family and whose lover was the chief of police.

We always saw him coming in and out and knew that their relationship was the only reason the club hadn't been shut down. Tatiana was
moved by my recitations, and I told her I wanted to know the tale of
her whole life. She began by leaning her body close and telling me
a secret: "Darling, El Deval always hid *kilos* of cocaine."

I yearned to know more from Tatiana so we exchanged numbers
and I promised that I would write about her life. From that moment,
her stories never ceased, and we embarked on a friendship that would
play a constant role in my life for years to come.

When we spoke next, I learned about boyhood Tatiana, and
how he knew early on that the body he'd been born into was the
wrong one. He was forcefully beaten by his father for dressing and
undressing his sisters′ dolls. Amidst a childhood of black eyes and
schoolyard bullying, the only refuge was the closeness of a pillow
held tight, dreams of being on another planet, or sometimes dreams
of never waking up at all. As soon as he turned fifteen he fled from
his home to Mexico City. He did all sorts of jobs, anything for enough
money to enroll in the International Amalia Mendoza Ballet, which
he ultimately did. Still going through day-to-day life in his biologically
male form, dancing was one of his only sources of liberation. One day,
a female dancer in the company got sick, and when her replacement
was tragically unavailable, Tatiana offered to take her place. As she
recounted the story, I could almost imagine all of the dancers' faces,
shocked and doubtful. But Amalia resigned and decided to give him
a chance.

"You have no idea what that meant to me," Tatiana explained,
"at rehearsal they were fascinated that I knew all the steps, but at
home I practiced the women's routines more than the men's. That
night was turning point, a hit. I became somebody else.

"In mid-sixties Mexico City, being a drag queen was worse than
being a thief," she continued, "but I baptized my balls and declared
them ovaries. There were so many great underground parties for
transvestites, yet they were haunted by a constant fear of police and
the drunk violent machos that lingered on the streets. We formed a
community—people that wanted to participate in all the hidden
happenings of the city together—and we'd revel in the fucked up
reactions of men as they would try to grab our pussies, only to receive
a special surprise."

Tatiana's next moment in the spotlight came in the form of an
impromptu meeting. During one of her late nights, she came across

Diana Mariscal, an alternative actress who always wore black and loved Jack Kerouac. Diana invited a group of transvestites to her home and introduced them to Alejandro Jodorowsky, who was in the middle of casting his new film *Fando y Lis*, in 1967.

"I knew about Jodorowsky's alarming reputation," Tatiana said, "in magazines and newspapers, there were photos of him setting pianos on fire during his events, people dancing naked all around, crucified cats on the wall. But by the end of our exchange, Alejandro kissed Diana on the cheek and told her, *They are exactly what I need, and the star transvestite is her!* And he pointed at me. The way he chose the word "her" made me believe in the Virgin of Guadalupe more than any church service ever had before. The dates were set, my excitement began to build, and thank the fucking Lord, I was finally a woman."

Being a film star, though, did not live up to Tatiana's expectations. Every day, the crew would pick her up in a rancid van and take her to a remote location, where hours were spent under relentless summer sun.

"We didn't have anything to drink," she said. "We would try desperately to produce enough saliva just to say our lines."

Filming concluded the moment Alejandro declared that he had gotten enough footage. It was the middle of the day, and the crew instantly packed up and mounted their fancy cars, leaving all the girls behind.

"We never saw them again. My only pay was the dress and umbrella I wore in the movie. We tried to hitch a ride back but everyone was scared of us, until a man hauling chickens stopped and motioned for us to hop in. He told us to sit on top of the cages and hold on, because he was already late for his delivery, and I grabbed my umbrella tightly, claiming it as my lucky charm."

Tatiana went back to Mexico City and tried to make ends meet by waitressing.

"But the city was so repressive and cruel," she explained "prejudiced and tainted by uppity Catholic morality. I dreaded the moments when someone would find out I was a man in women's clothes. I saved money like crazy, telling myself that each cent put me a step closer to becoming my true self, my complete self. Finally, in 1977, I got a US Visa and went to San Francisco, falling into the world of cheap hotels and drag queens. I prostituted myself, dressing as a woman, and soon I learned that men loved my in-betweenness—

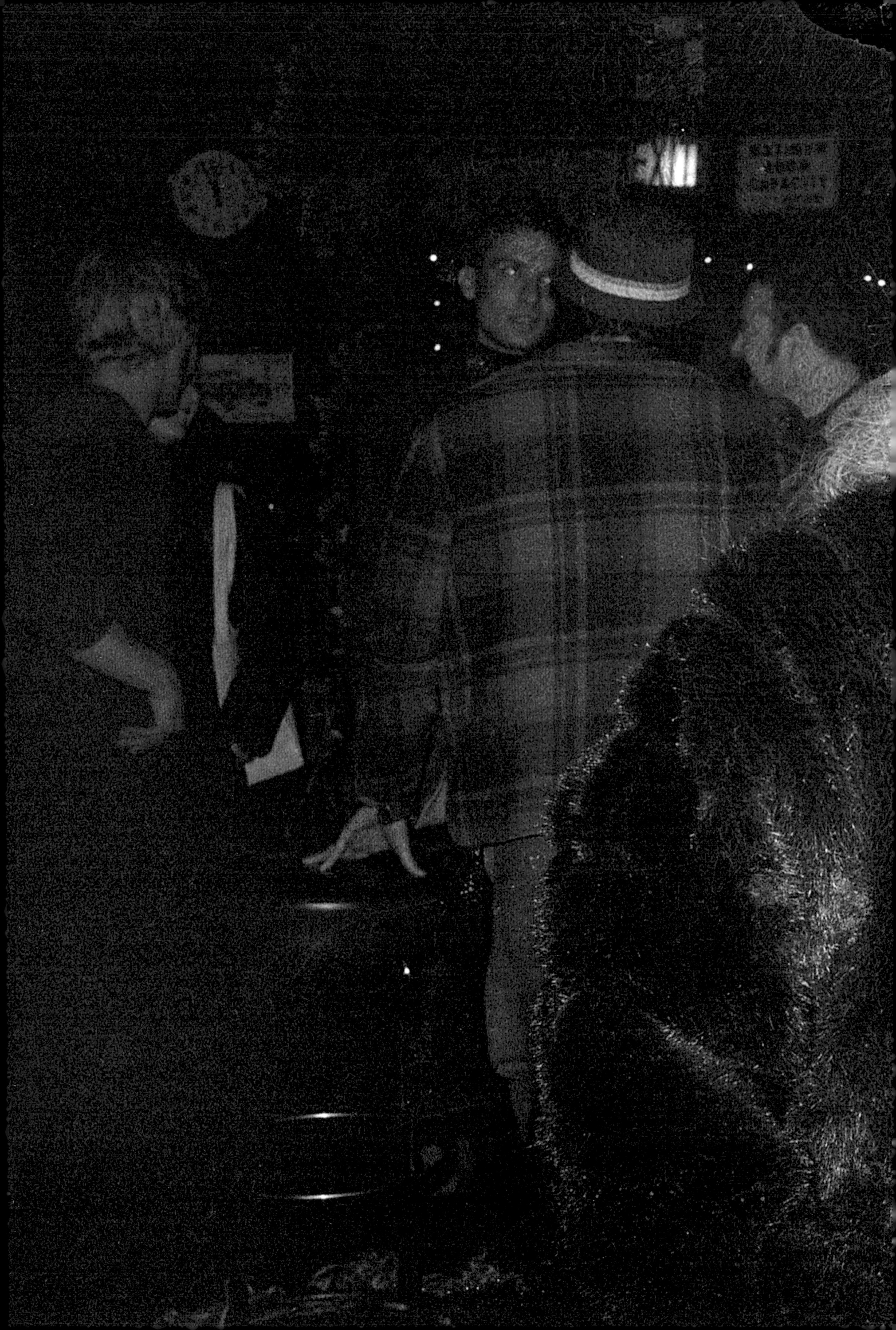

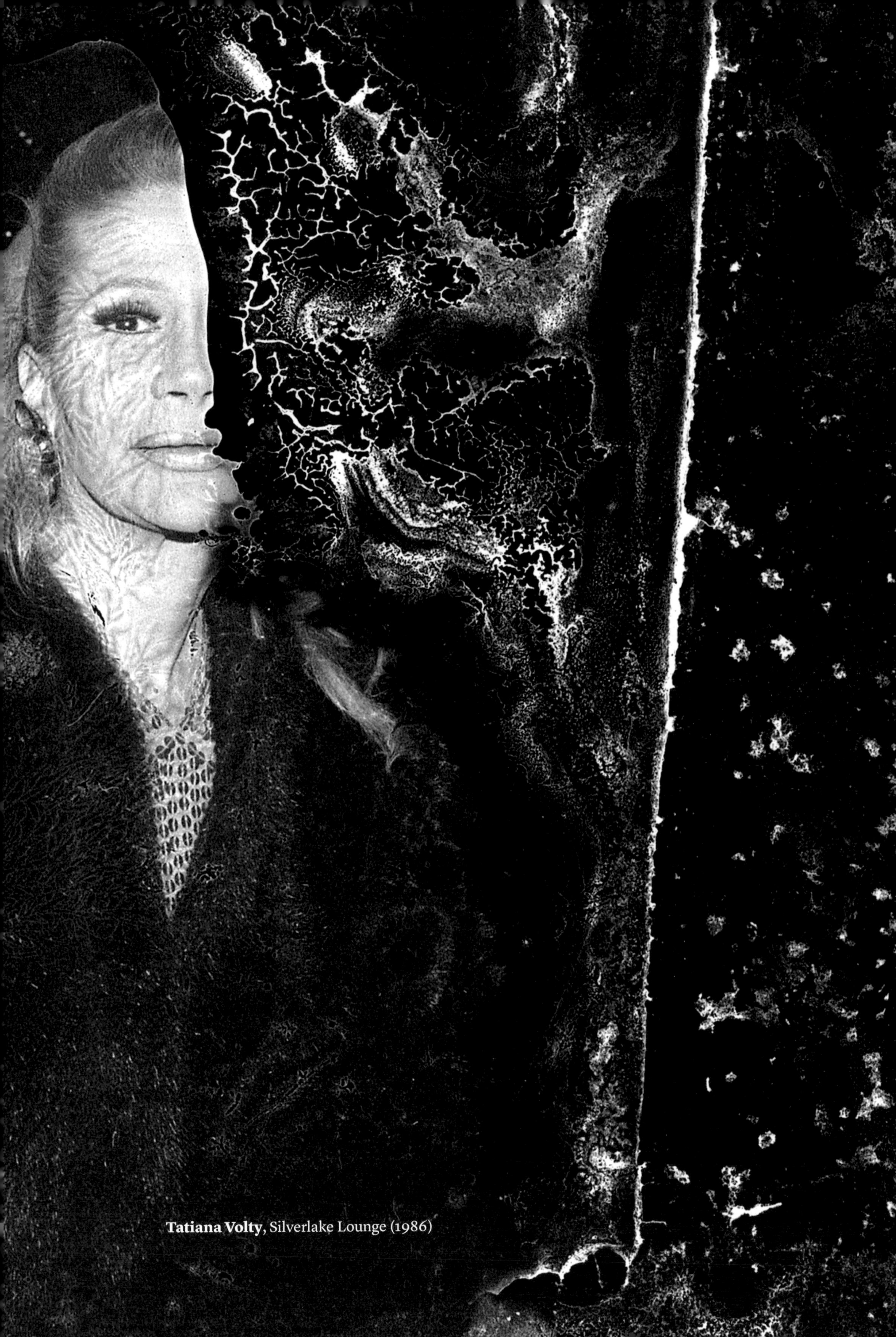

Tatiana Volty, Silverlake Lounge (1986)

I have a big dick," Tatiana said, laughing. This was before her surgery.
"It's close to ten inches, but what do I need it for? Just to go pee,
I guess. But men love it. And I started to notice a pattern, routinely
finding men who loved to sit on my huge pecker while watching a girl
rub herself, lick her tits. I was being paid well. The '70s were almost
over, but I was doing alright—I had become a famous trans prostitute."

Tatiana's stories from the 1980s all take place in Los Angeles.
She moved there on the first of January, 1980, after a split-second
decision was made while throwing an empty champagne bottle out of
the window. Despite the risk, LA clubs proved to be friendly sites
for her.

"I would get offers from La Plaza, Los Barrilitos, and Circus—
the premiere LA disco. I knew my rates and was always treated with
respect, even when I told managers or club owners that I wanted
things like orchids in my dressing room. LA was a blessing in my life.
And somehow my personal worth stemmed from my talents in the
bedroom—people knew about me, they wanted me. "

One of Tatiana's favorite moments to boast about was when
Italian singer Raffaella Carrà complimented her. "Raffaela was a true
diva, one of my lifelong inspirations. She saw me on stage one night
and went back to the dressing room later to congratulate me. She even
told me was jealous of my long legs. It was the best praise I ever
received."

Yet those first years in Los Angeles also tested Tatiana, ex-
hausting her to such an extent that she knew she had to make changes.

"There was so much alcohol, coke, and speed during that time...
it could have killed me," she said. "I remember this one awful
morning, I was so hungover, and I was just holding my pillows, trying
to breathe. Out of nowhere, I felt that the Virgin of Guadalupe came
to visit me—she told me that I needed to change my life. So I did."
She opened her own beauty salon and stopped performing as frequently. Most surprising of all, Tatiana got married. Her new wife was
a Colombian woman named Aurora who wanted Tatiana to focus only
on the salon.

"Her beauty was explosive," Tatiana recalled. "Aurora wanted
a green card, but I was still an illegal alien. Somehow, the fraction of
heterosexuality I had left in me kept me stuck to her. I took care of
her, she was in love with me, and we were married for over a year.
I was still performing here and there, and one night at a show, I met
Michael, a farm boy from North Carolina who confessed that he'd

fallen in love with me, watching me over the past few months.
I agreed to go out with him, and it felt beyond perfect. He treated me
like a lady. We'd drive in his car with the stereo crooning Frank Sinatra
songs. He gave me the guts to leave Aurora and be in charge of my life.
I went back to the stage, I took care of my beauty salon, and I went
to bed with Michael every night."

Michael was a fixture in Tatiana's life for a long time. That is
until one morning, years later, when our mutual friend Raul Thomas
called me.

"Tatiana just broke up with Michael. Go, please, help her. She is
ready to kill herself."

I rushed to her home in Silver Lake and rang the doorbell for
over an hour. I could see her through the windows, angrily throwing
objects across the house. Finally, she opened the door. Behind her
were mountains of shattered glass and debris, and she looked at
me with the look of someone whose heart had been completely and
utterly broken.

"He left me" she said, "for a *man*. How could he?"

In between hugs of consolation, I told her, "It's not about the
gender, it's about the soul we find."

She broke down in tears and we spent the whole day together.

Tatiana's journey from a transvestite to transgender reached
a turning point with one of her most lucrative private customers.

"He would take me to the best places in Beverly Hills and give
me gifts like Chanel perfume. As I've come to learn, the truth always
comes out, so eventually his family found out about me and we had to
stop seeing each other. On our last night together, among champagne
and fresh linen, he told me I could ask for anything I wanted.
His proposals included a house, a yacht, my own chain of salons, but
I said no to all of it. I told him I wanted him to pay for my whole sex
change. Fly me out to Sweden, where it could be done right. I told him
I wanted a real vagina, one that feels. He was confused, and told me
I had an amazing dick, but I told him *Fuck the dick*. I wanted to be
a woman. And that was it."

He paid for Tatiana's psychology sessions and all the arrange-
ments of her operation.

"Going overseas terrified me," she said. "I went to the church on
Placita Olvera to pray to the Virgin. I got on my knees, crying, begging
her: *My little brown mother, if I die in the operating room it has to be in
your name. I place my life in your hands*."

Tatiana flew to Sweden and had a successful operation.

After her sex change, she was ordered to abstain from sex for at least four months. So she waited, following the doctor's rules, and finally the time came to celebrate. She put on a mink coat and headed out to the Red Horse on Western Avenue. As she was about to walk in, she noticed a man on the sidewalk—a handsome Salvadorian, skinny and tattooed.

"You are so beautiful, mami!" he called out to her, his voice echoing on the streets. She was enticed by him and easily fell back into her performances of seduction. They went home together that night.

"I was afraid in the beginning," Tatiana admitted, "but he turned out to be a real gentleman. He was the first person after my sex change, so I guess he took my real virginity. I'll never forget him."

I have found that the most remarkable parts of Tatiana's stories are how she tells them—honestly, unapologetically, often with laughter, never holding back details.

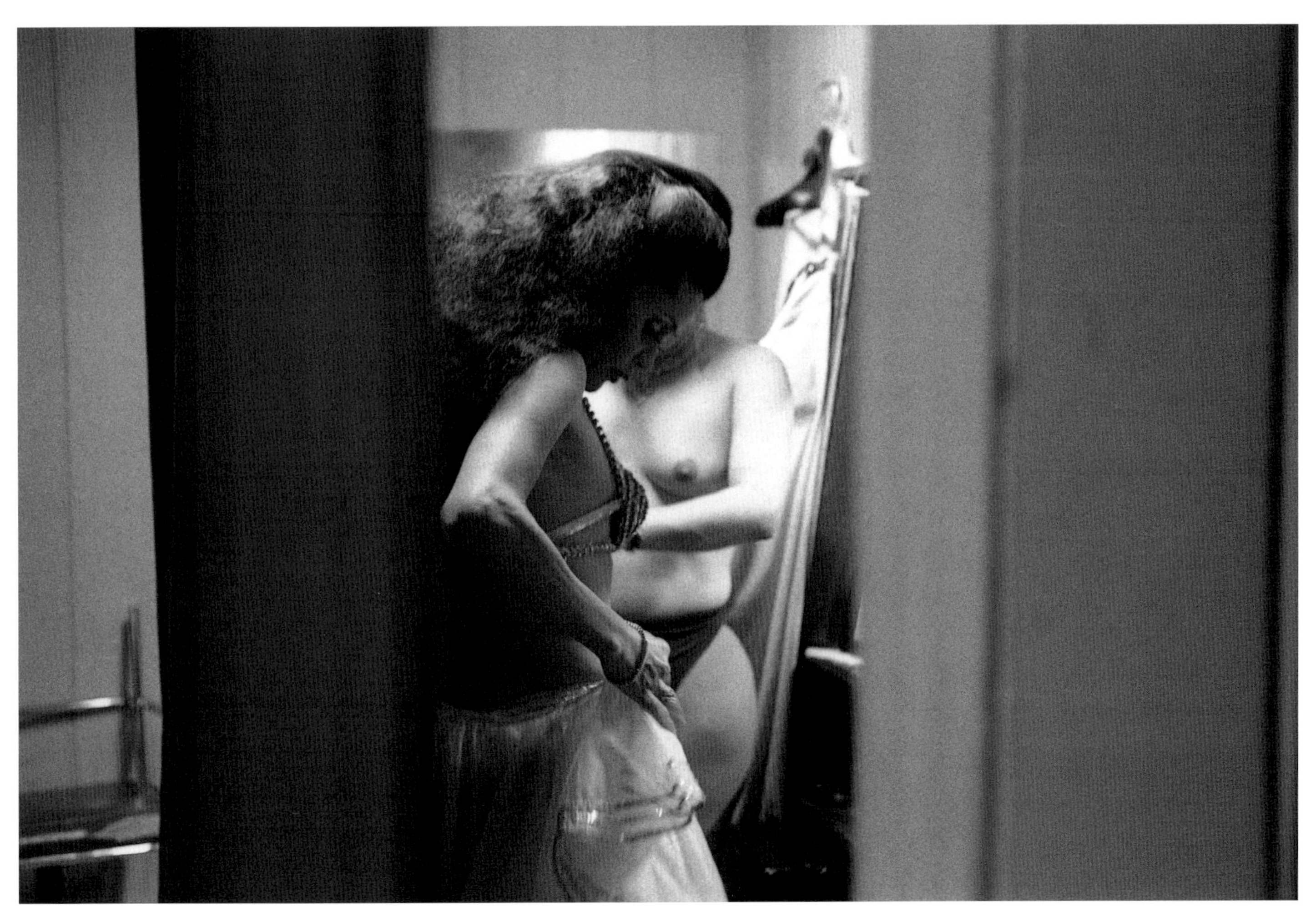

Tatiana Volty, Silverlake Lounge (1996)

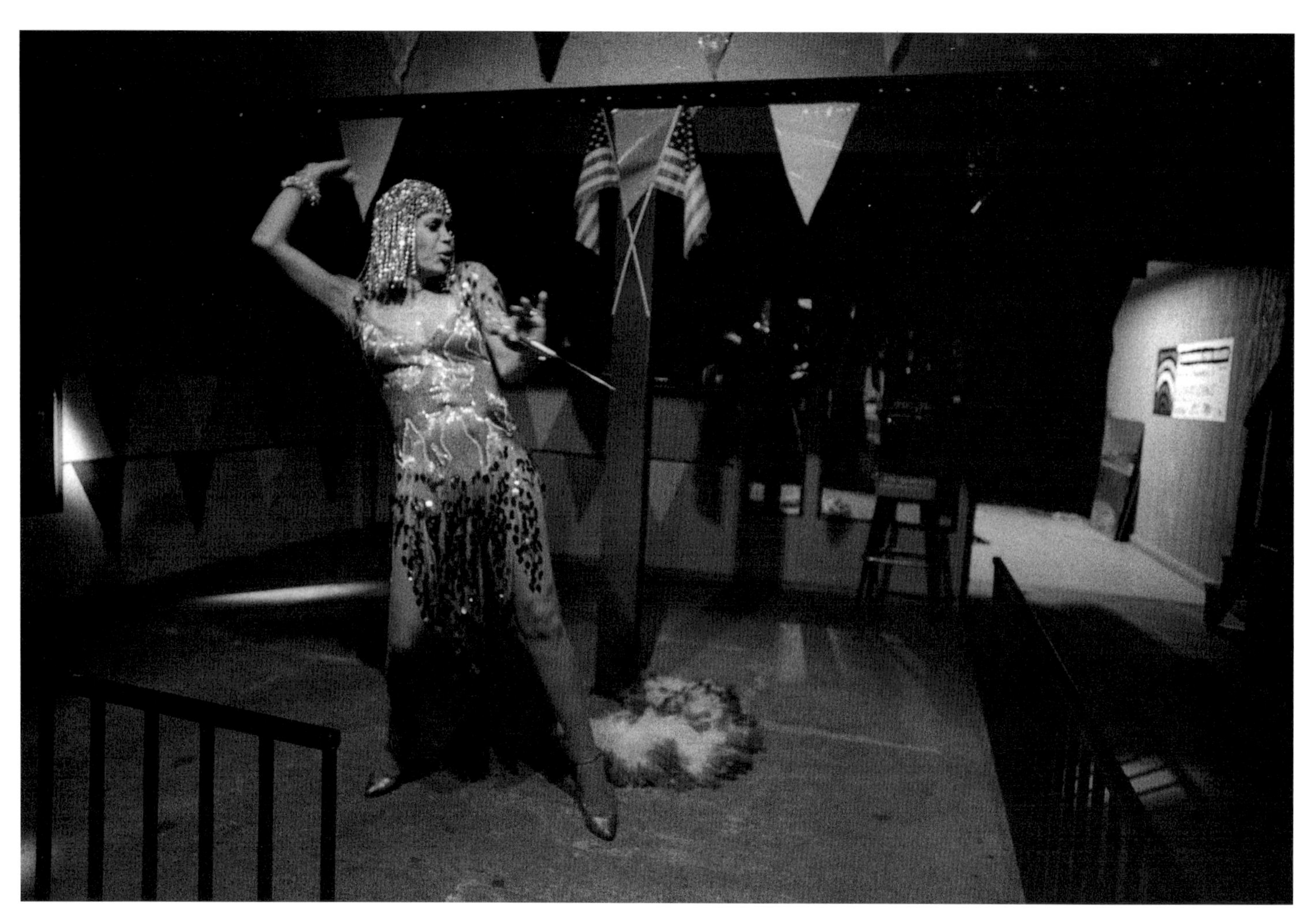

Tatiana Volty, Silverlake Lounge (1996)

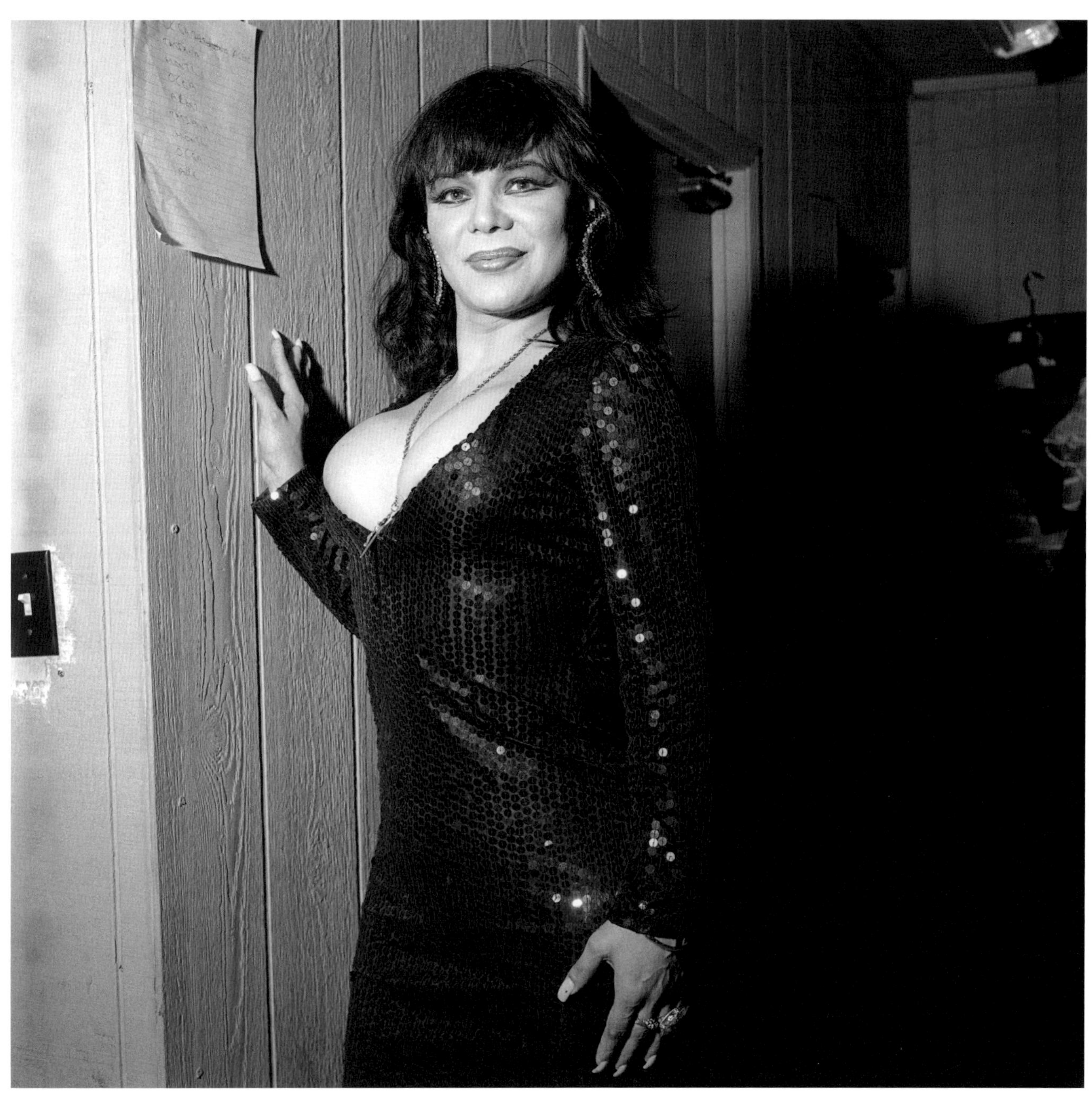

Miss Alex, Silverlake Lounge (1994)

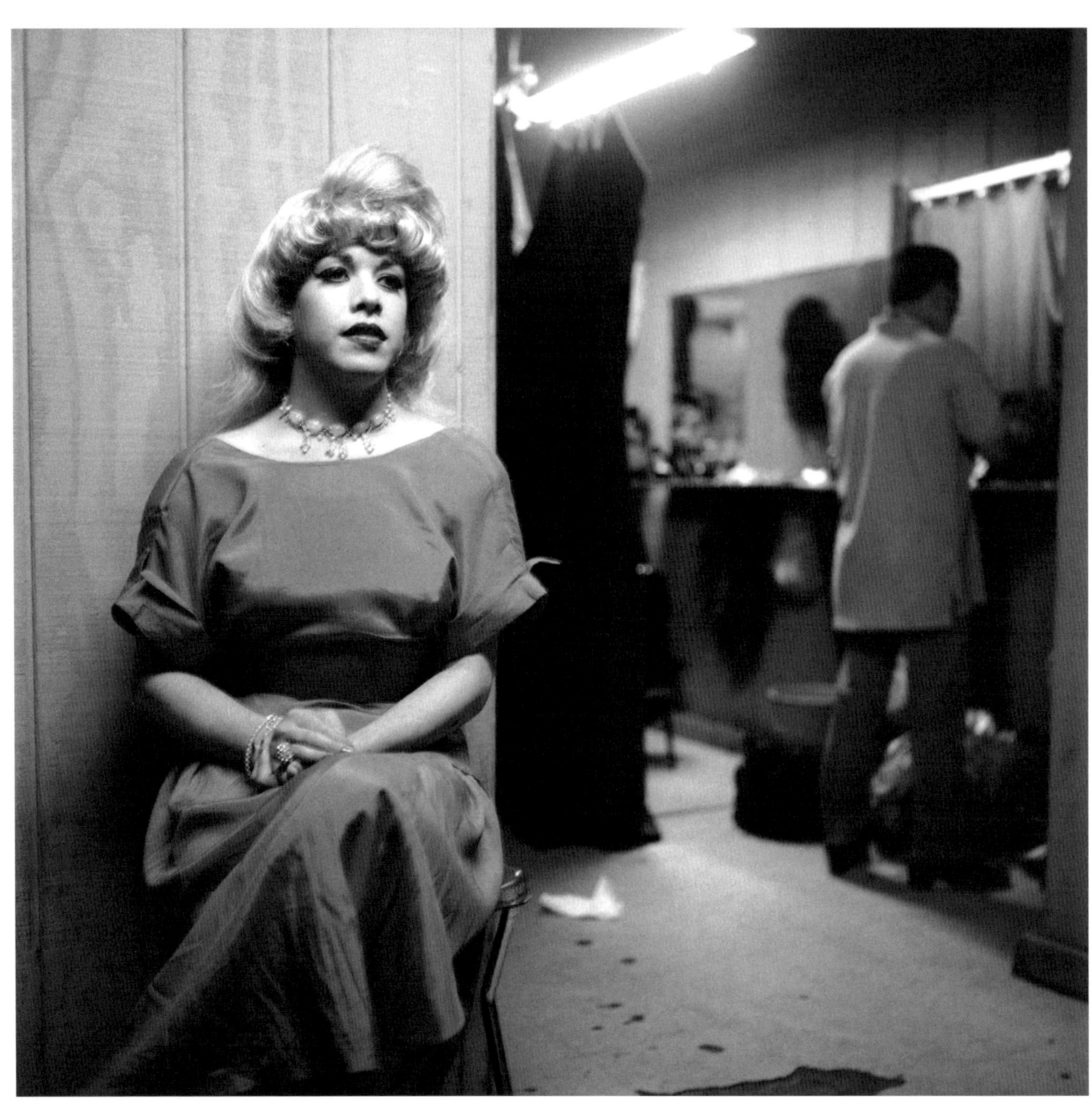

Performer, Silverlake Lounge (1995)

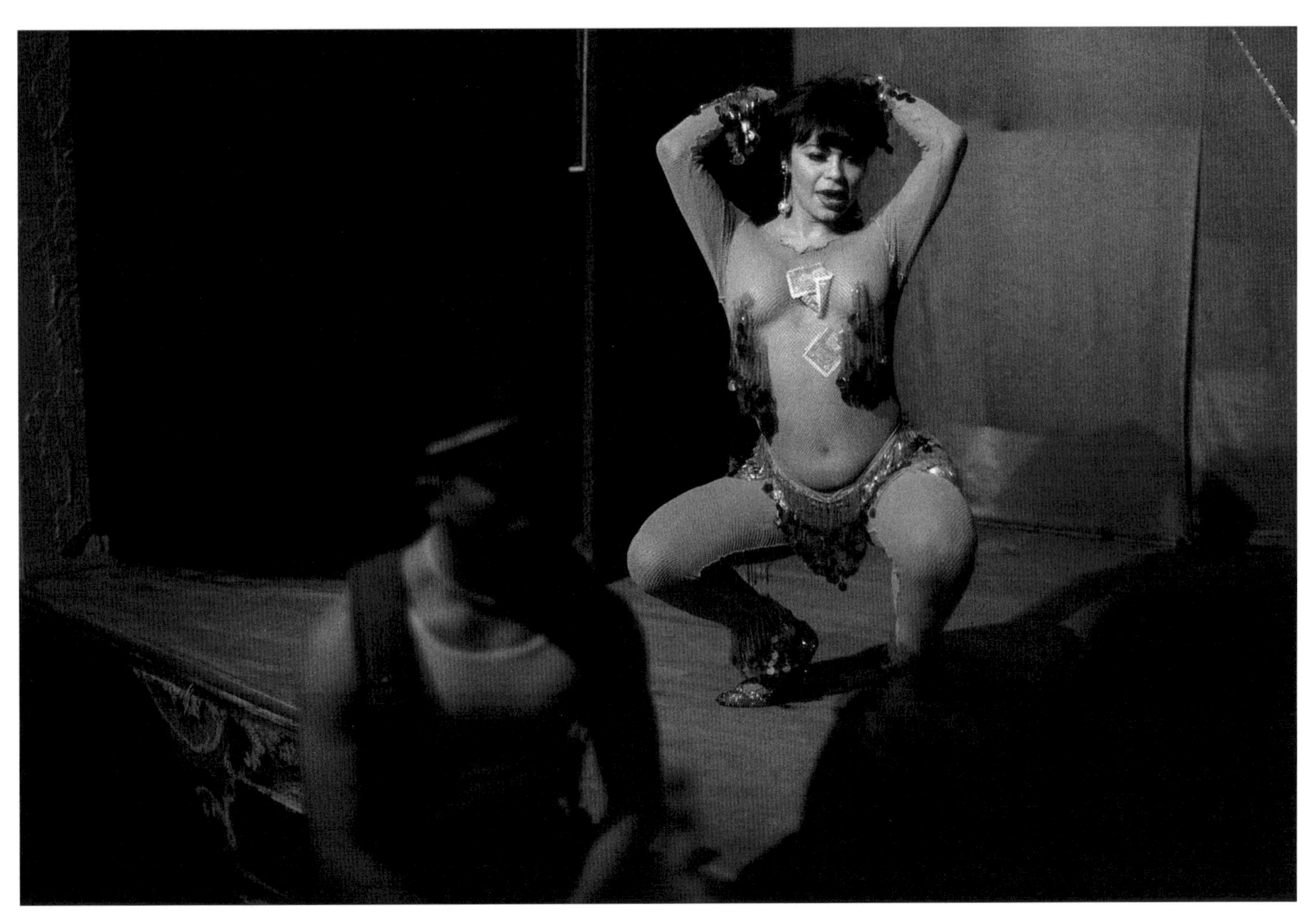

Miss Alex, Silverlake Lounge (1994)

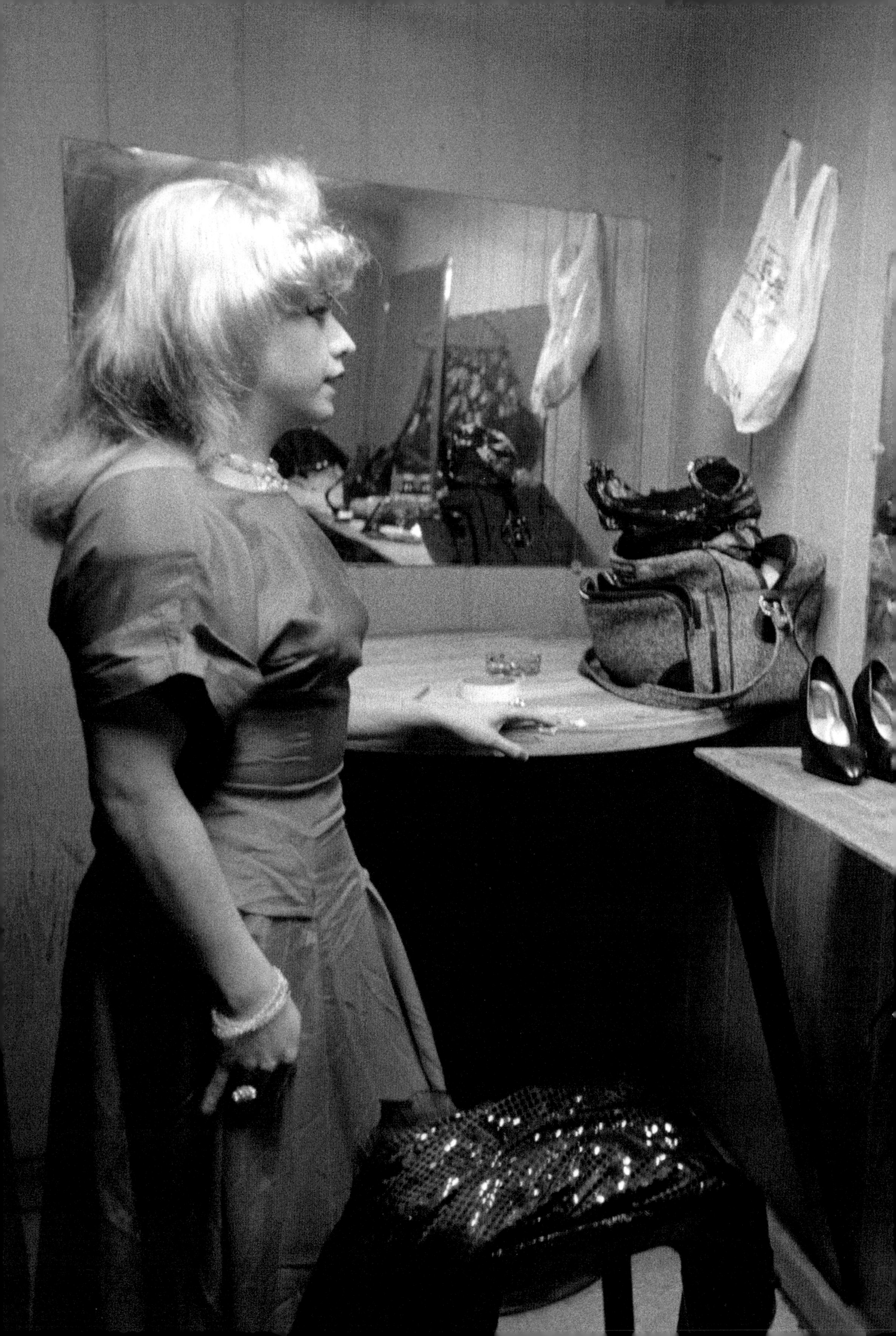

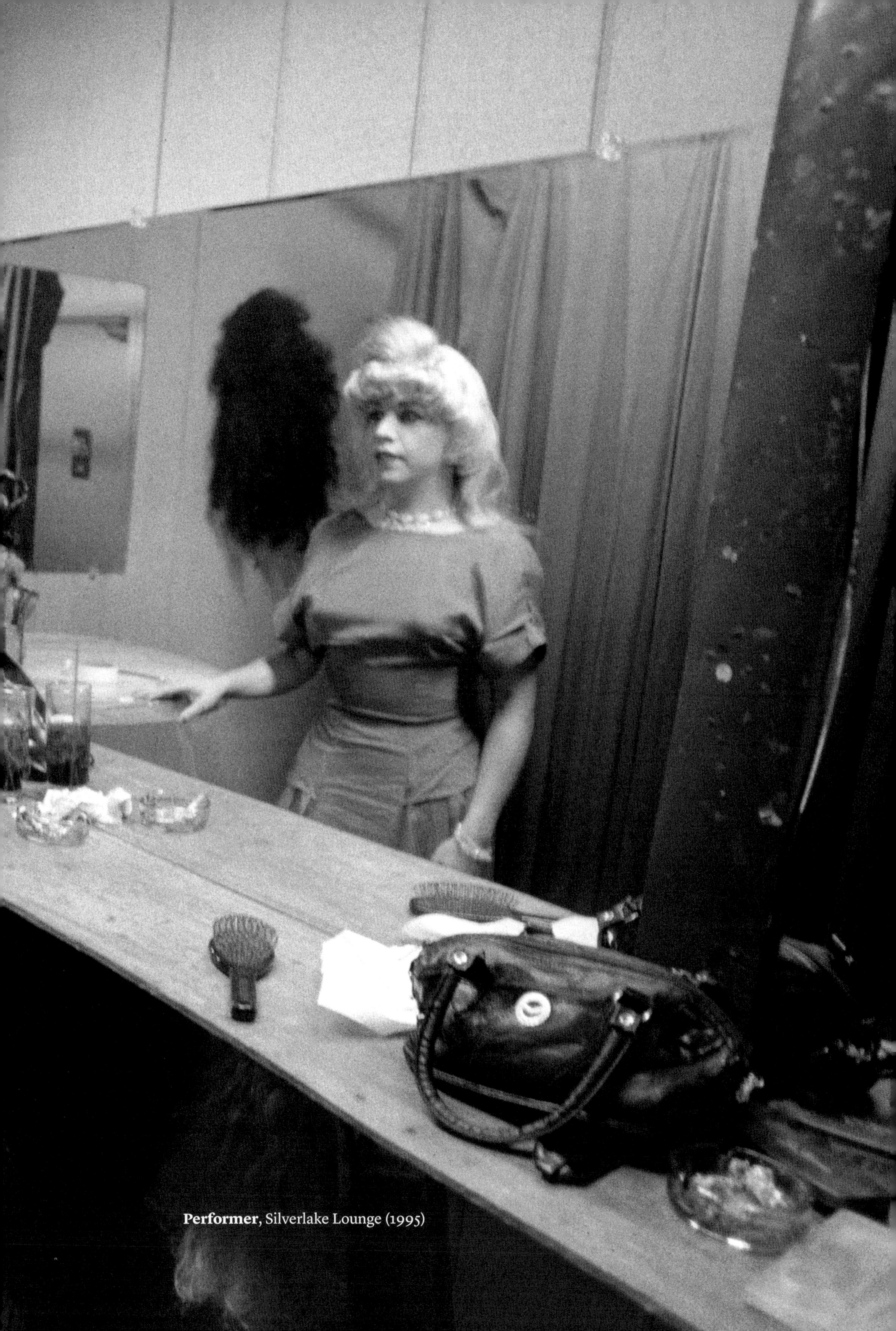

Performer, *Silverlake Lounge* (1995)

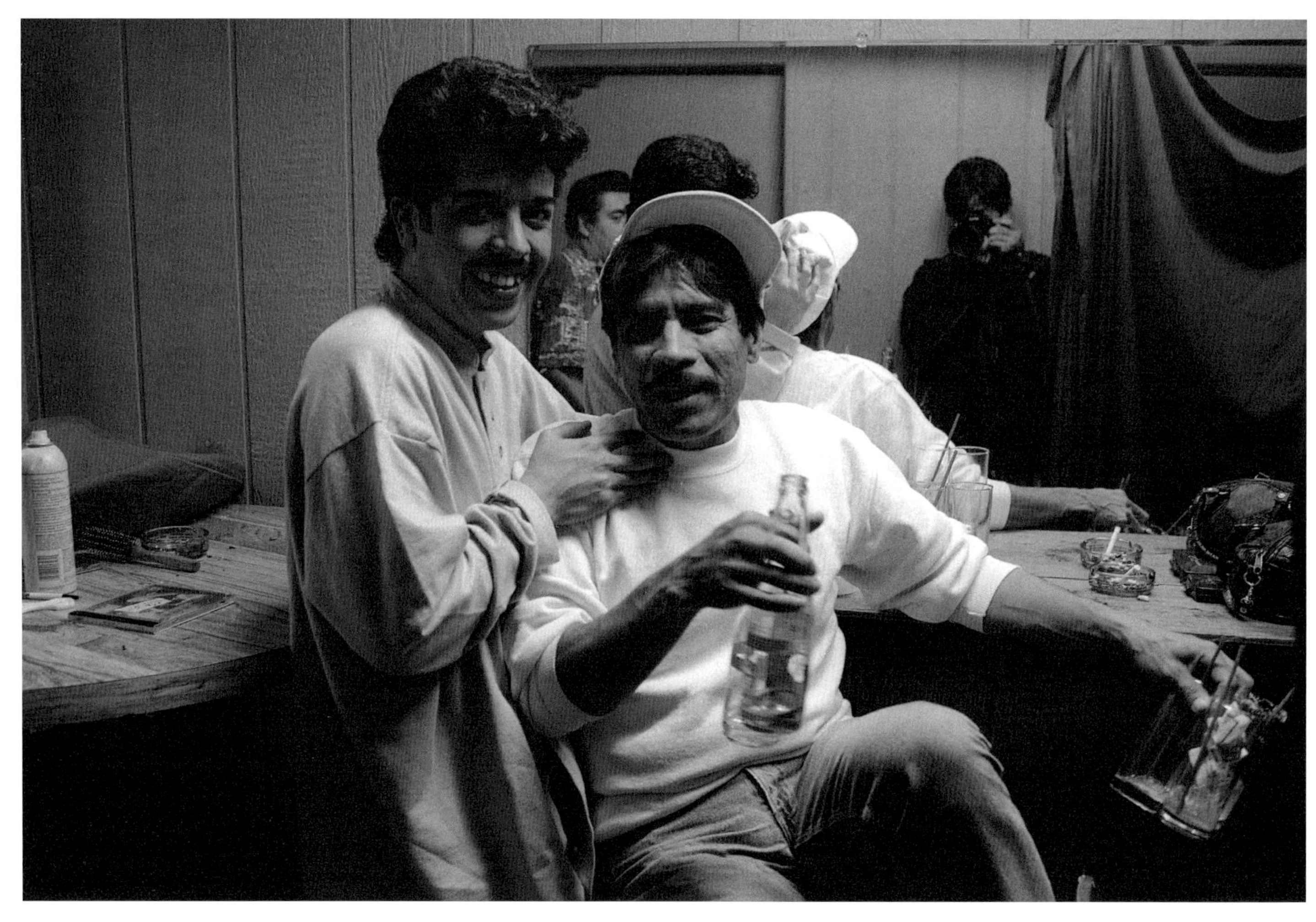

Performer and friend, Silverlake Lounge (1995)

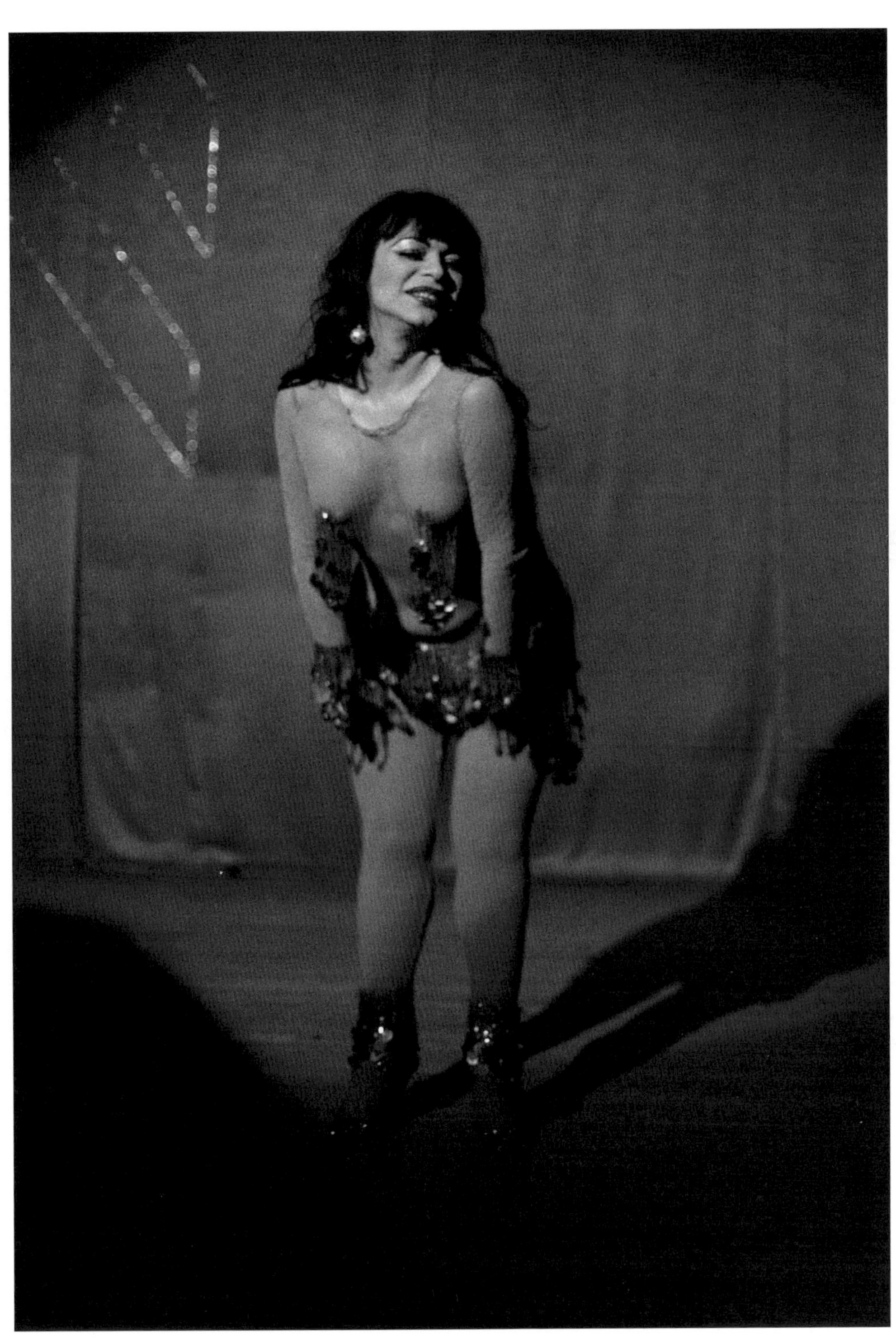

Miss Alex, Silverlake Lounge (1994)

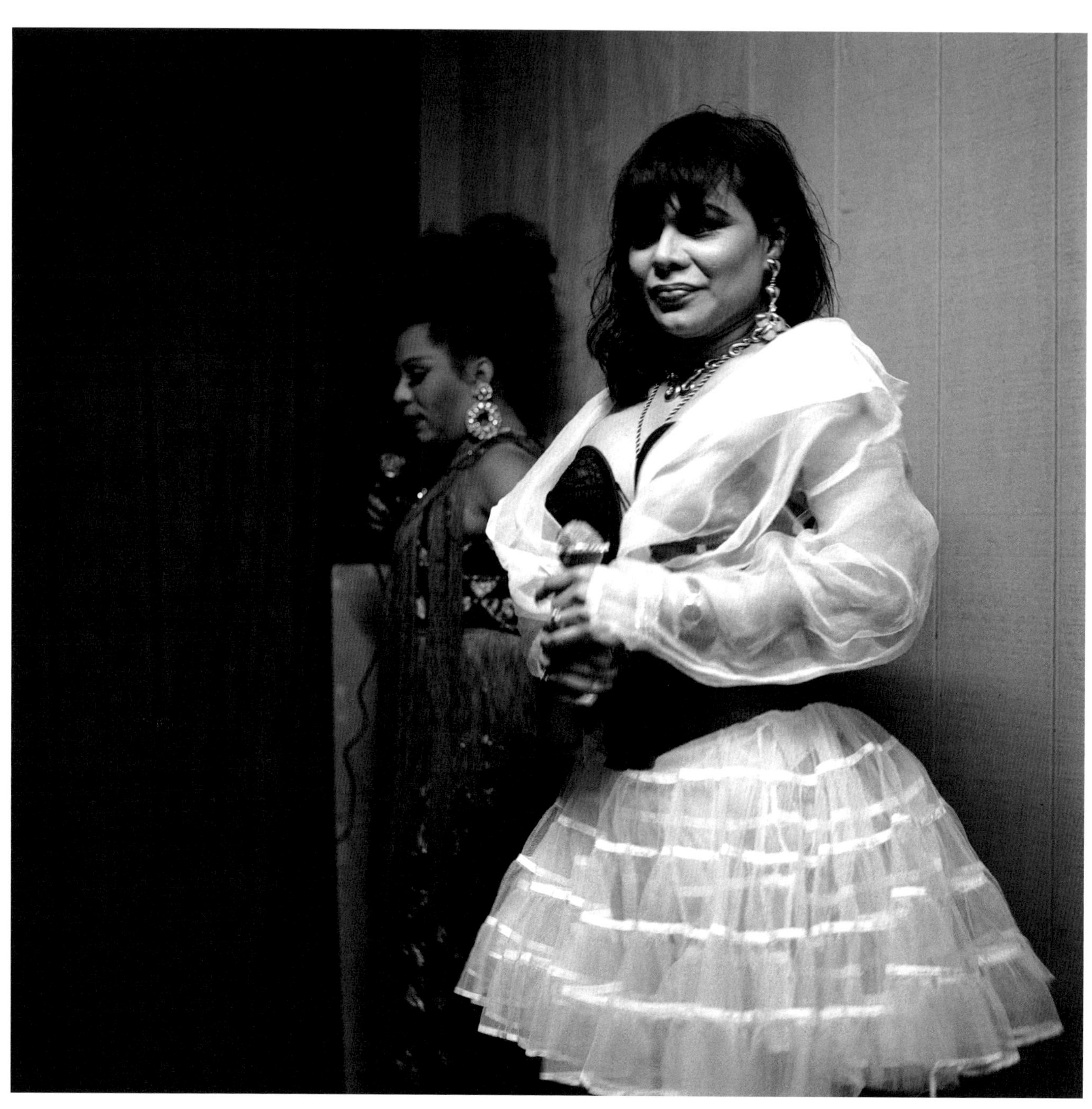

Miss Alex, Silverlake Lounge (1994)

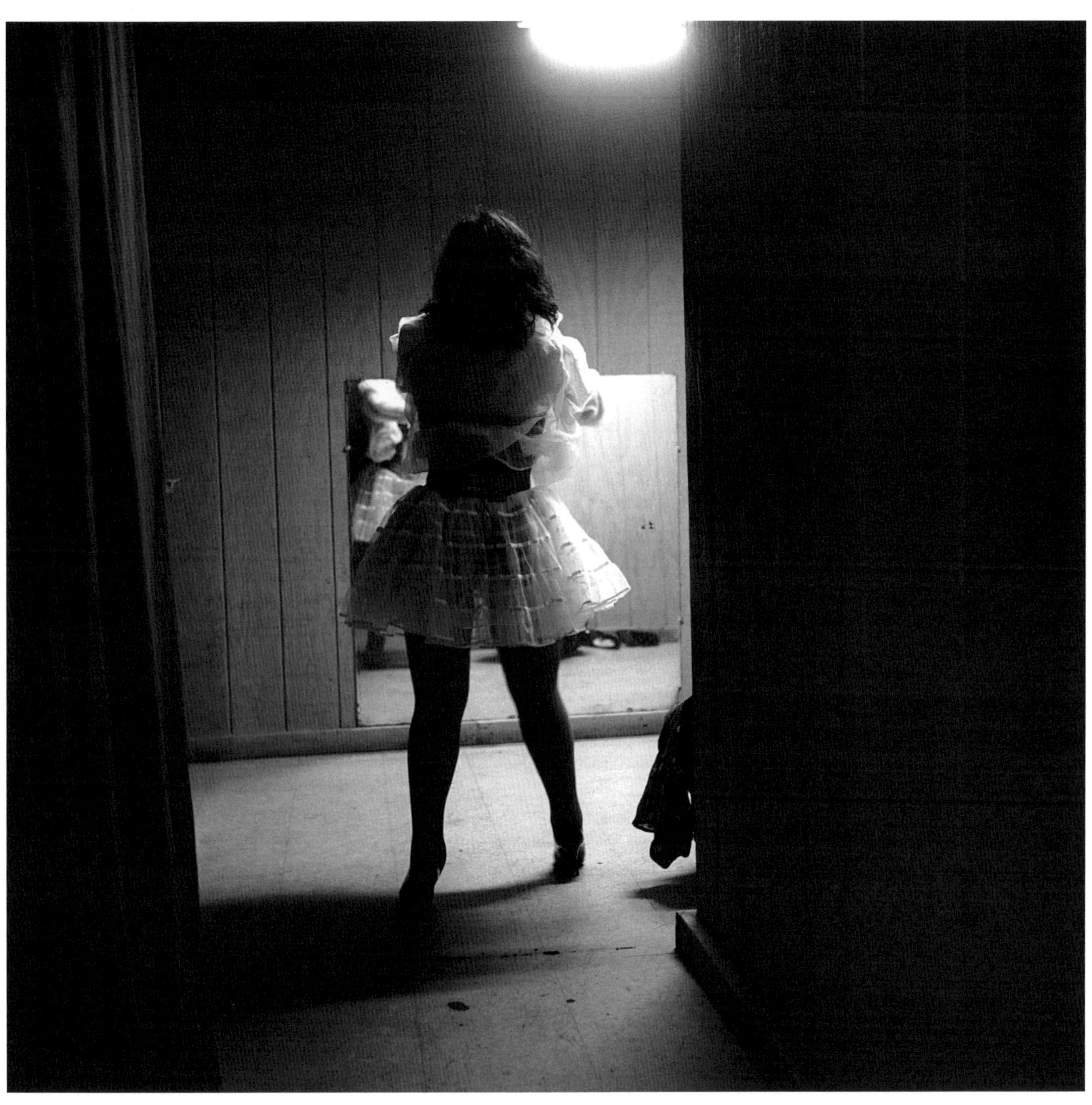

Miss Alex, Silverlake Lounge (1994)

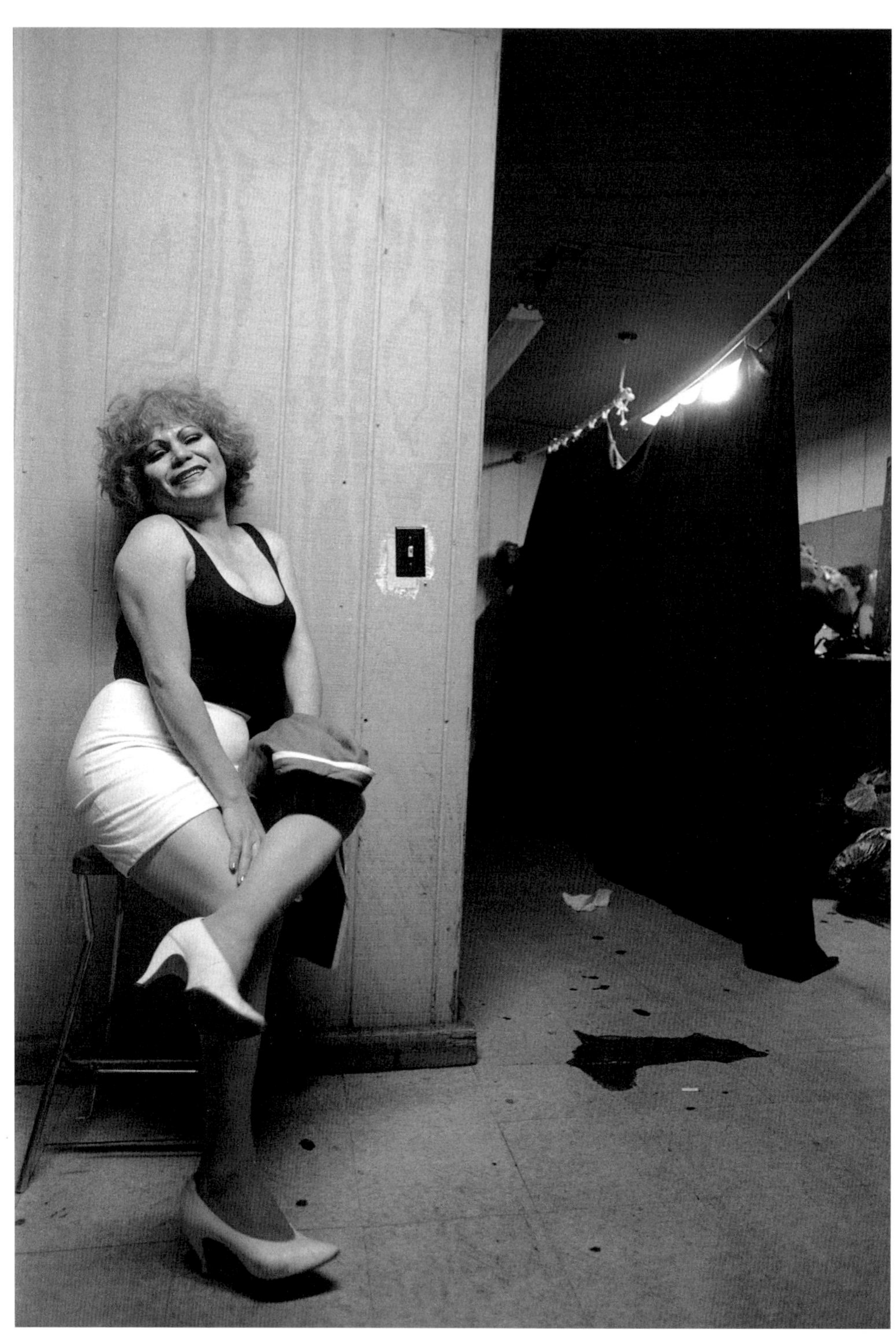

Vanessa, Silverlake Lounge (1995)

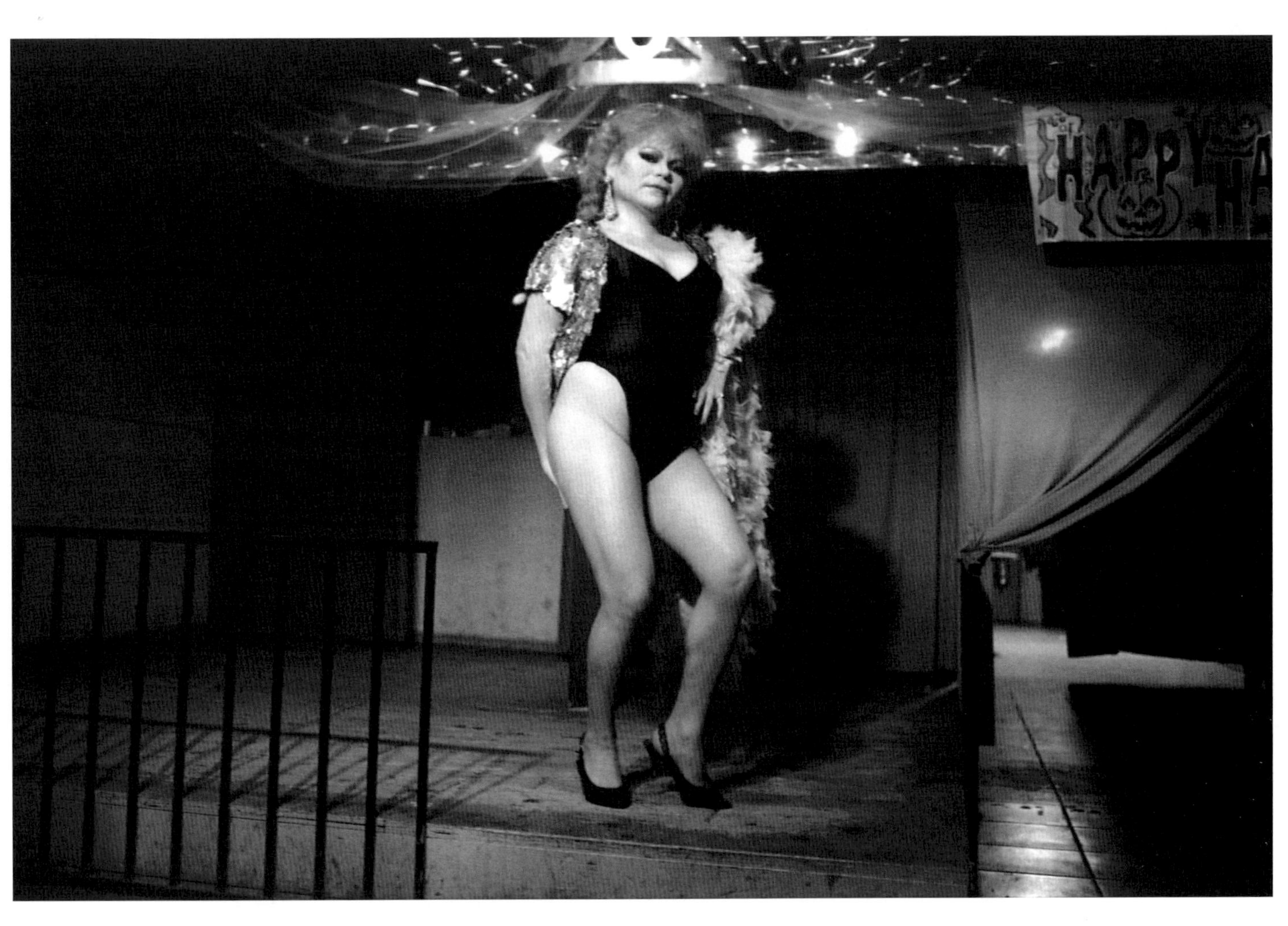

Vanessa, Silverlake Lounge (1995)

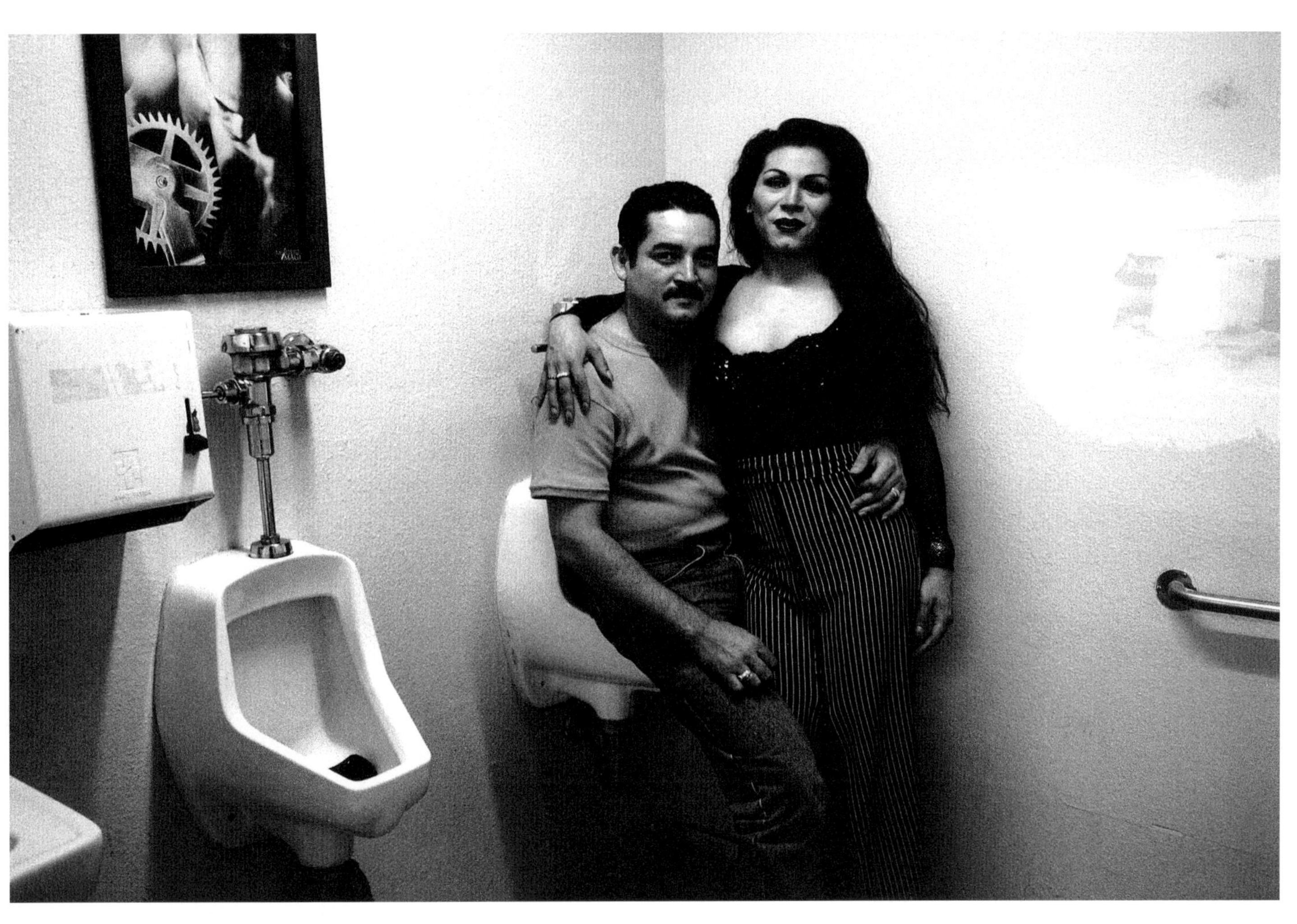

Silverlake Lounge (1995)

Silverlake Lounge (1995)

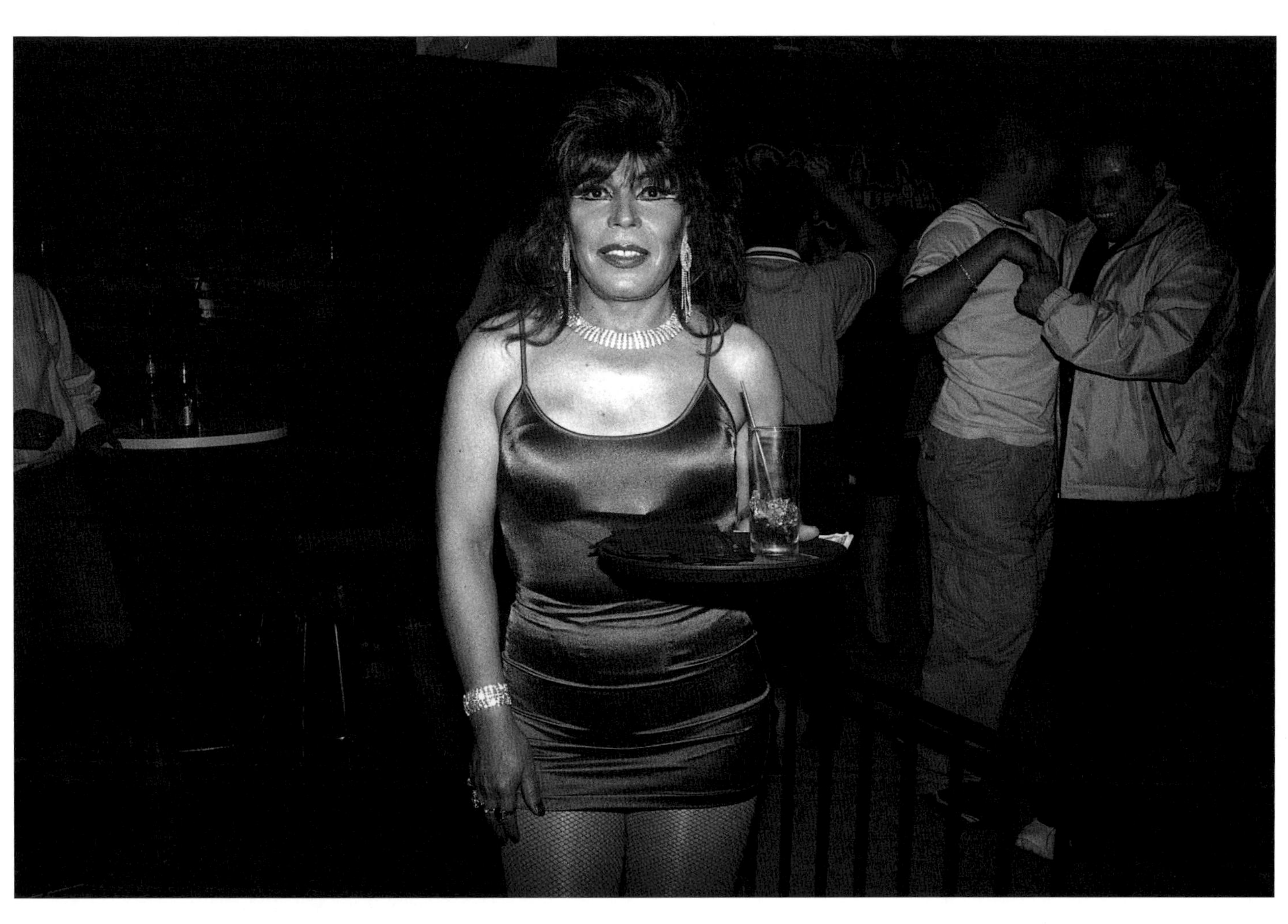

Hostess, Silverlake Lounge (1995)

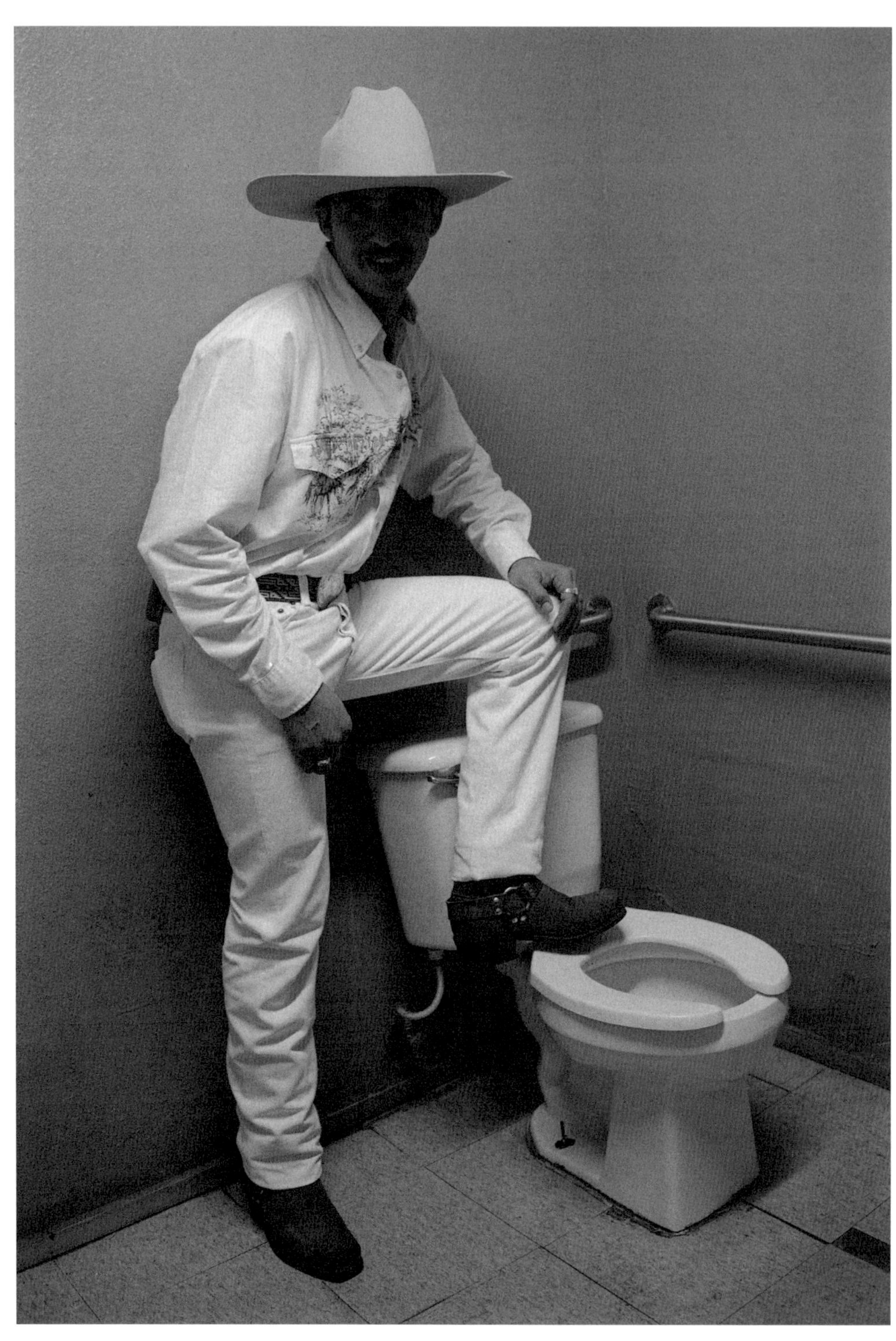

Patron, Silverlake Lounge (1995)

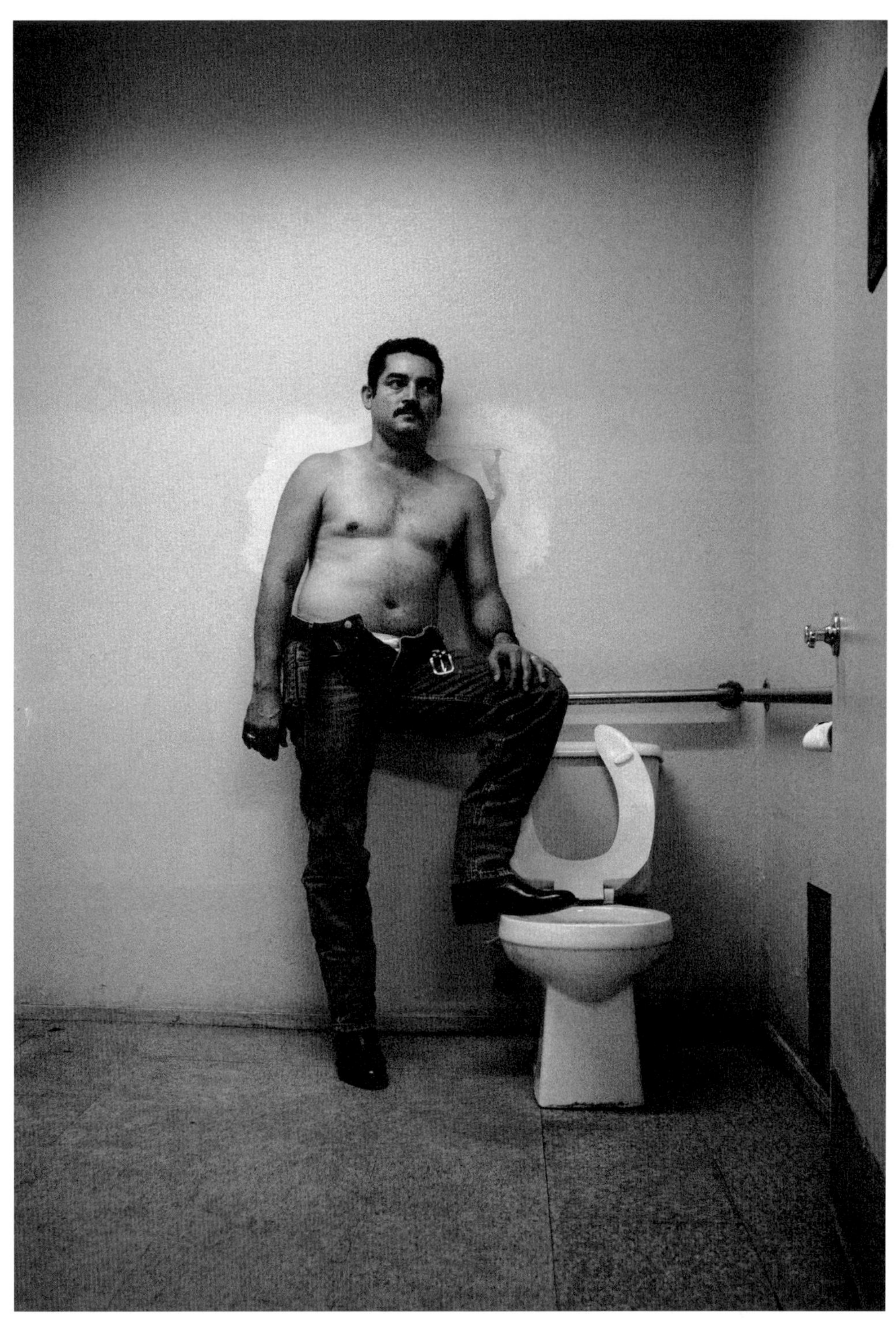

Patron, Silverlake Lounge (1995)

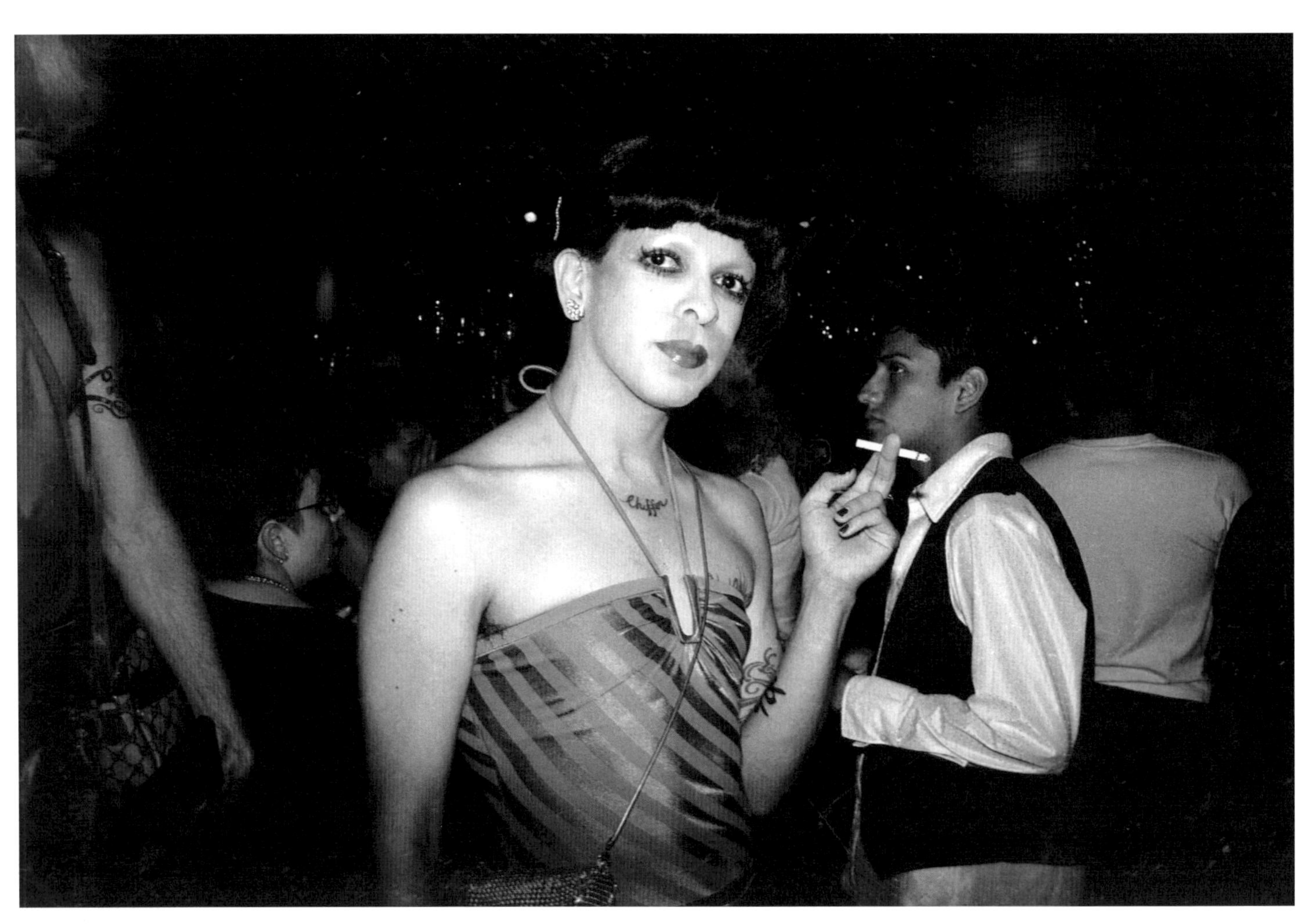

Tommy Chiffon, Silverlake Lounge (1996)

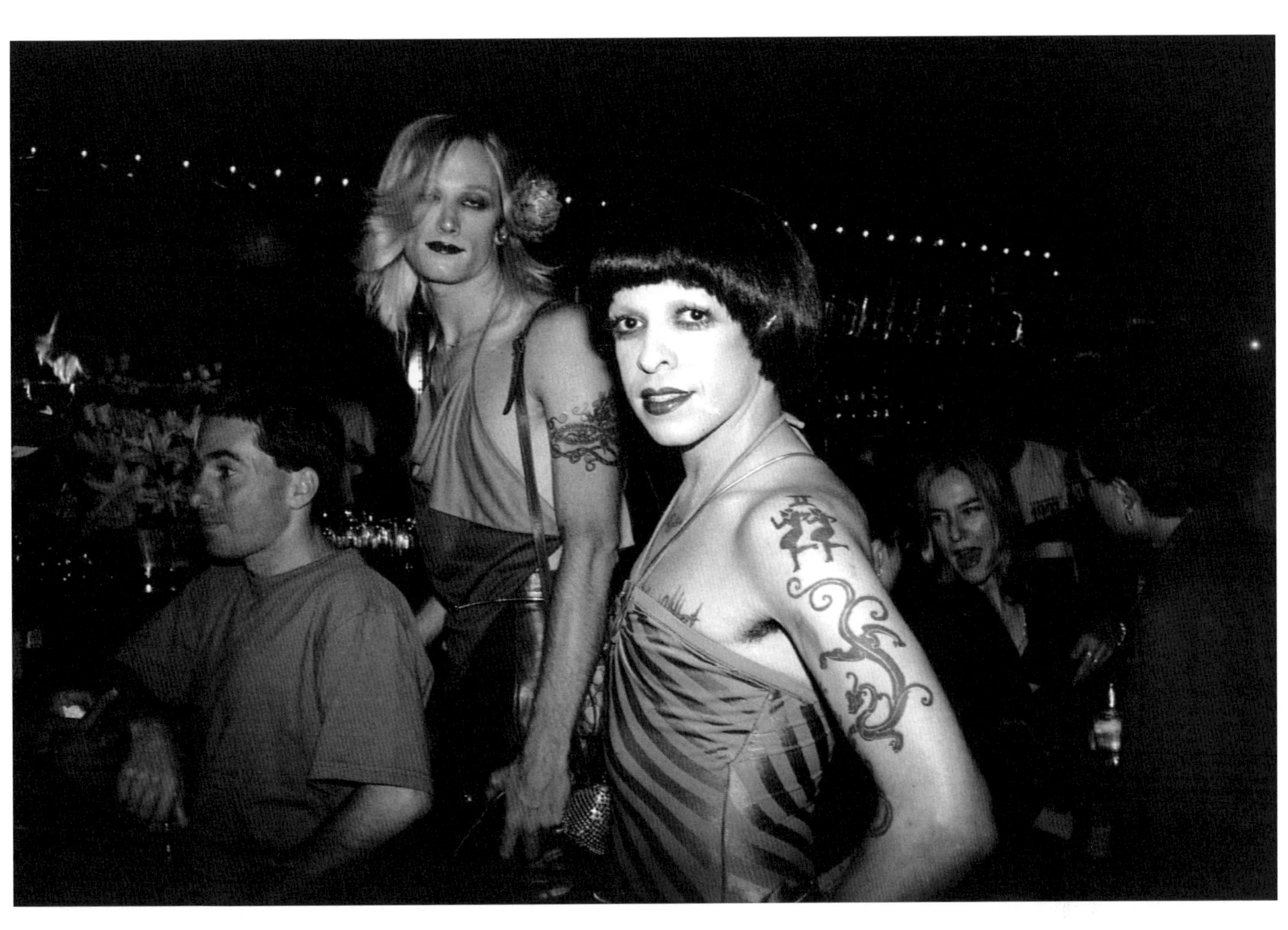

Grant Krajecki and Tommy Chiffon,
Silverlake Lounge (1996)

147

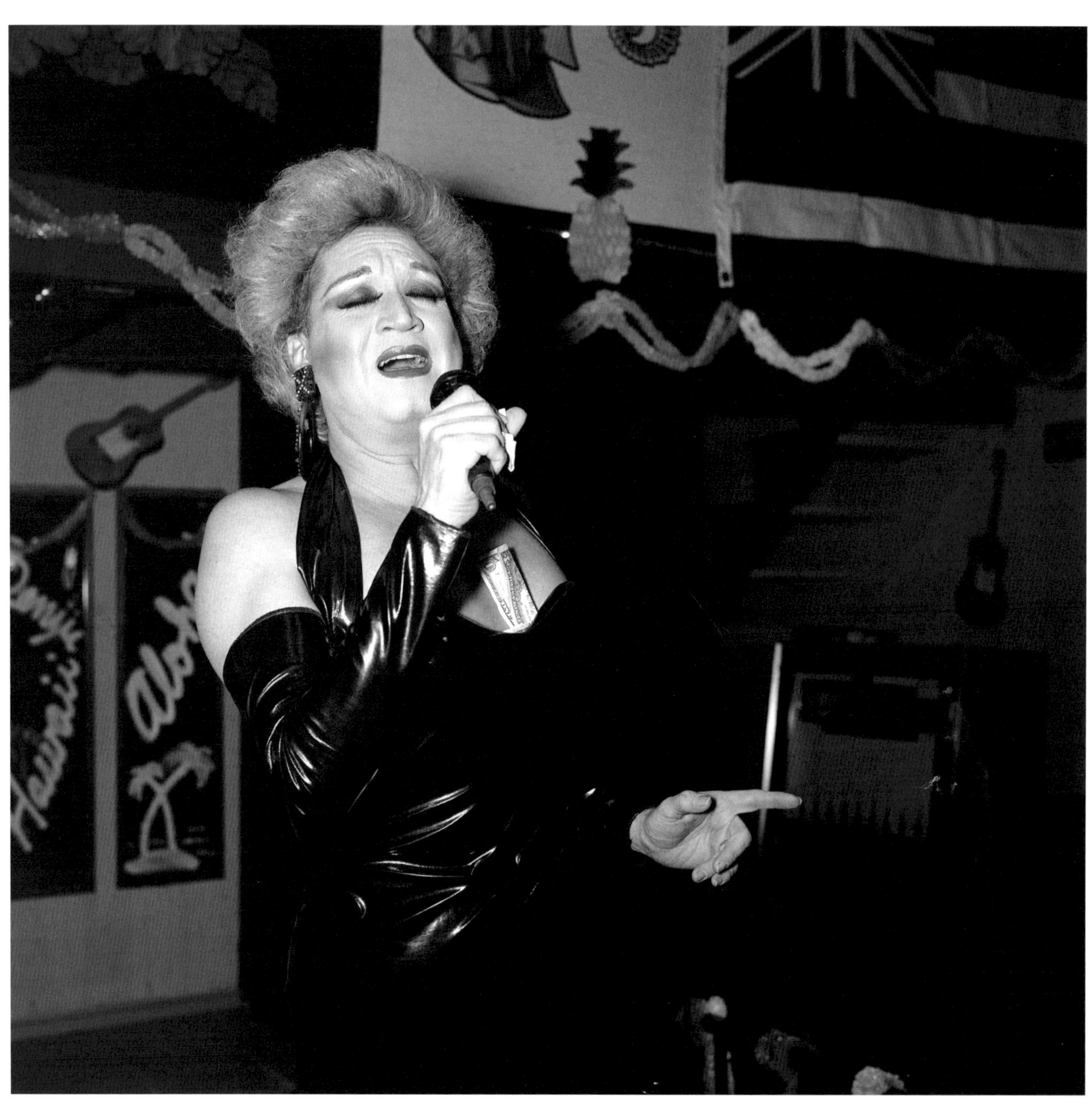

Montenegro, Silverlake Lounge (1995)

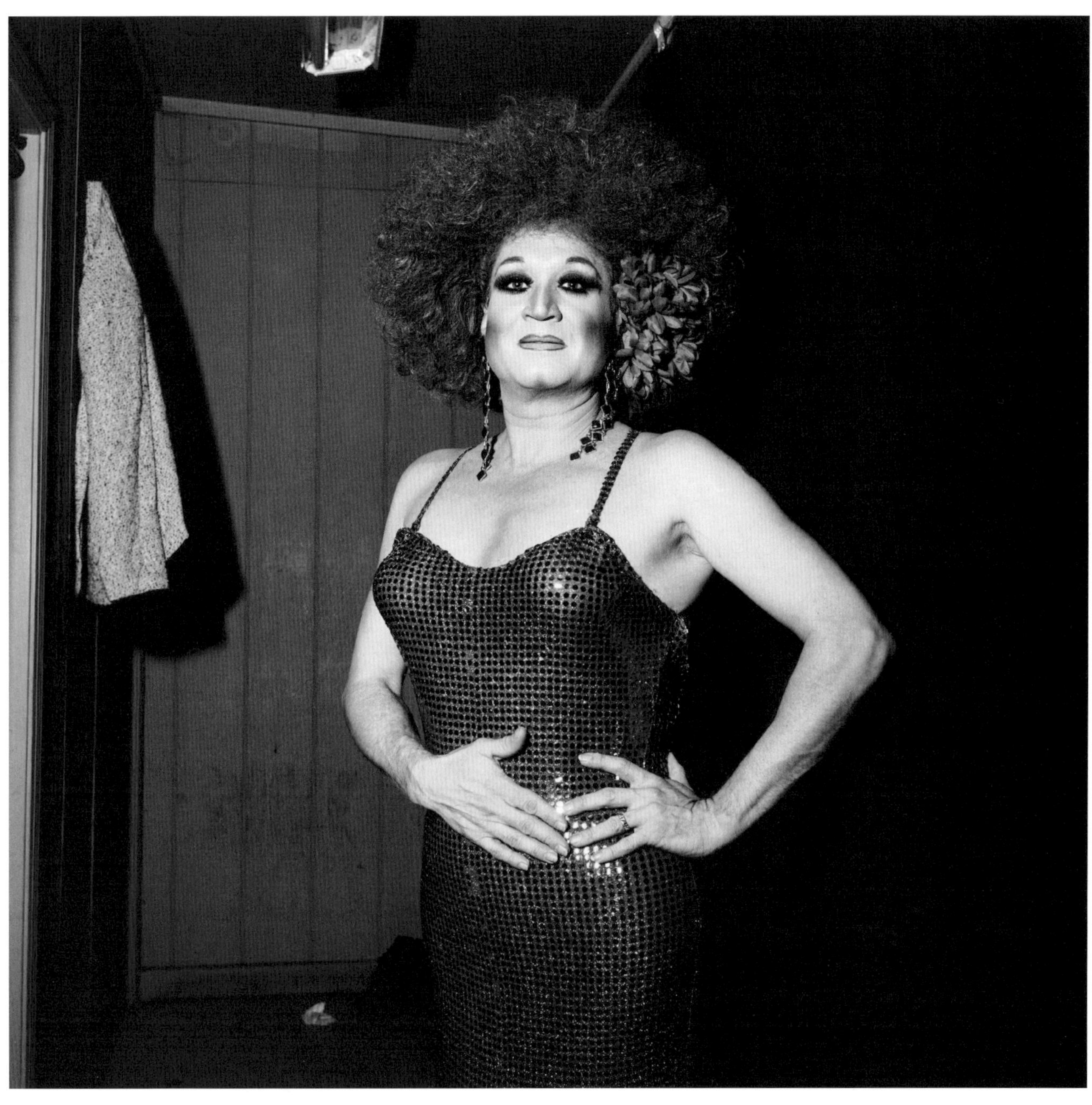

Montenegro, Silverlake Lounge (1995)

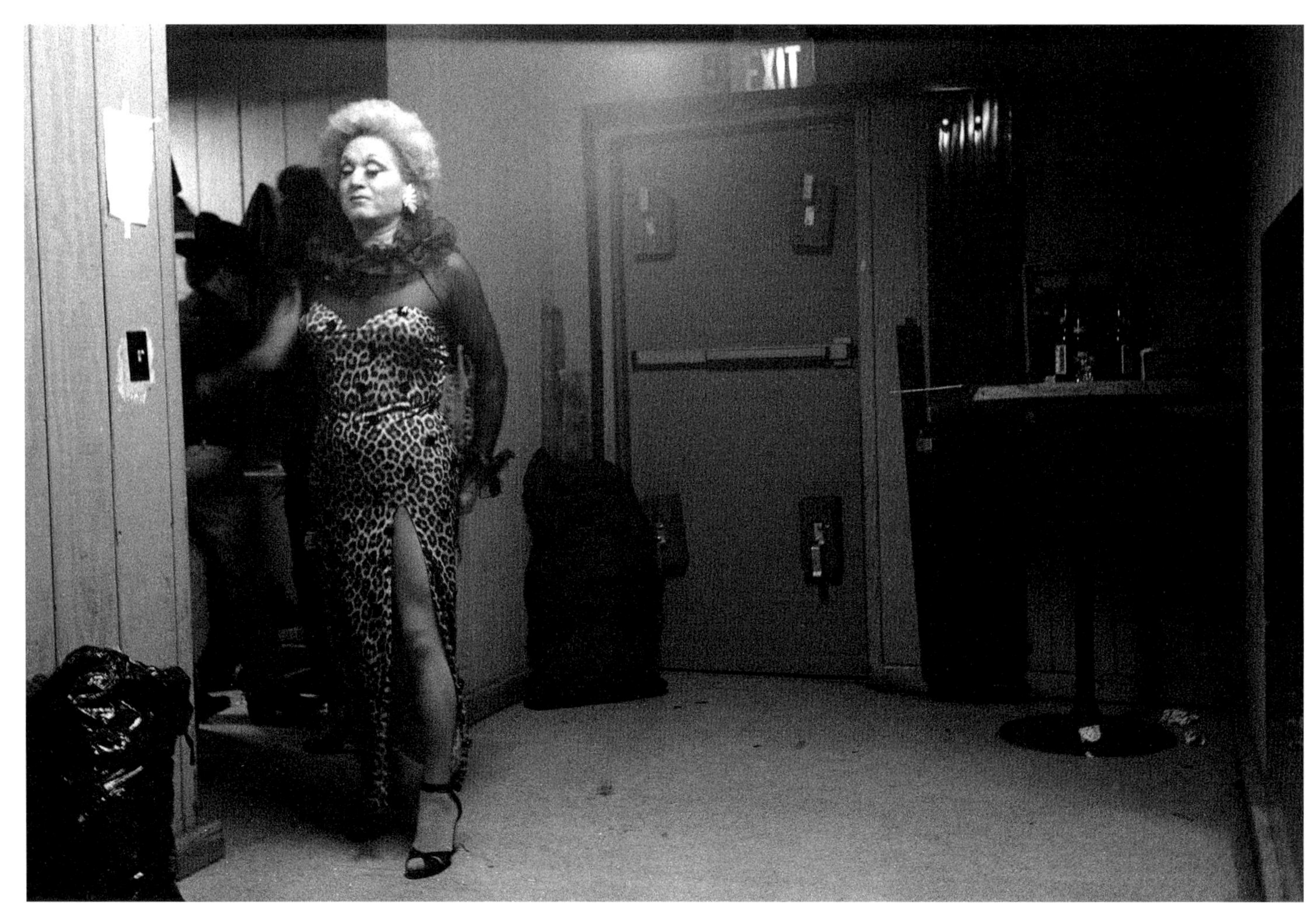

Montenegro, Silverlake Lounge (1995)

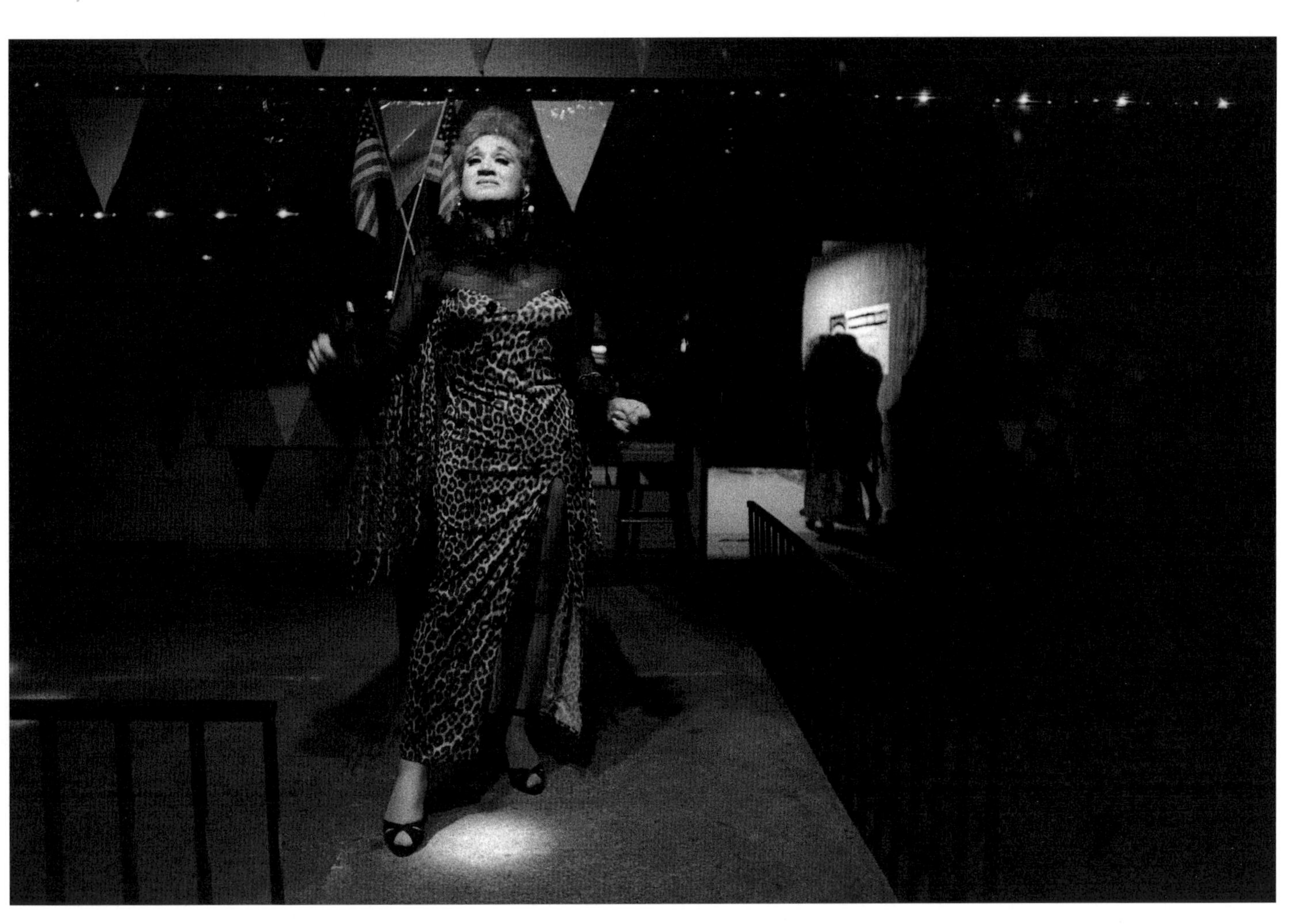

Montenegro, Silverlake Lounge (1995)

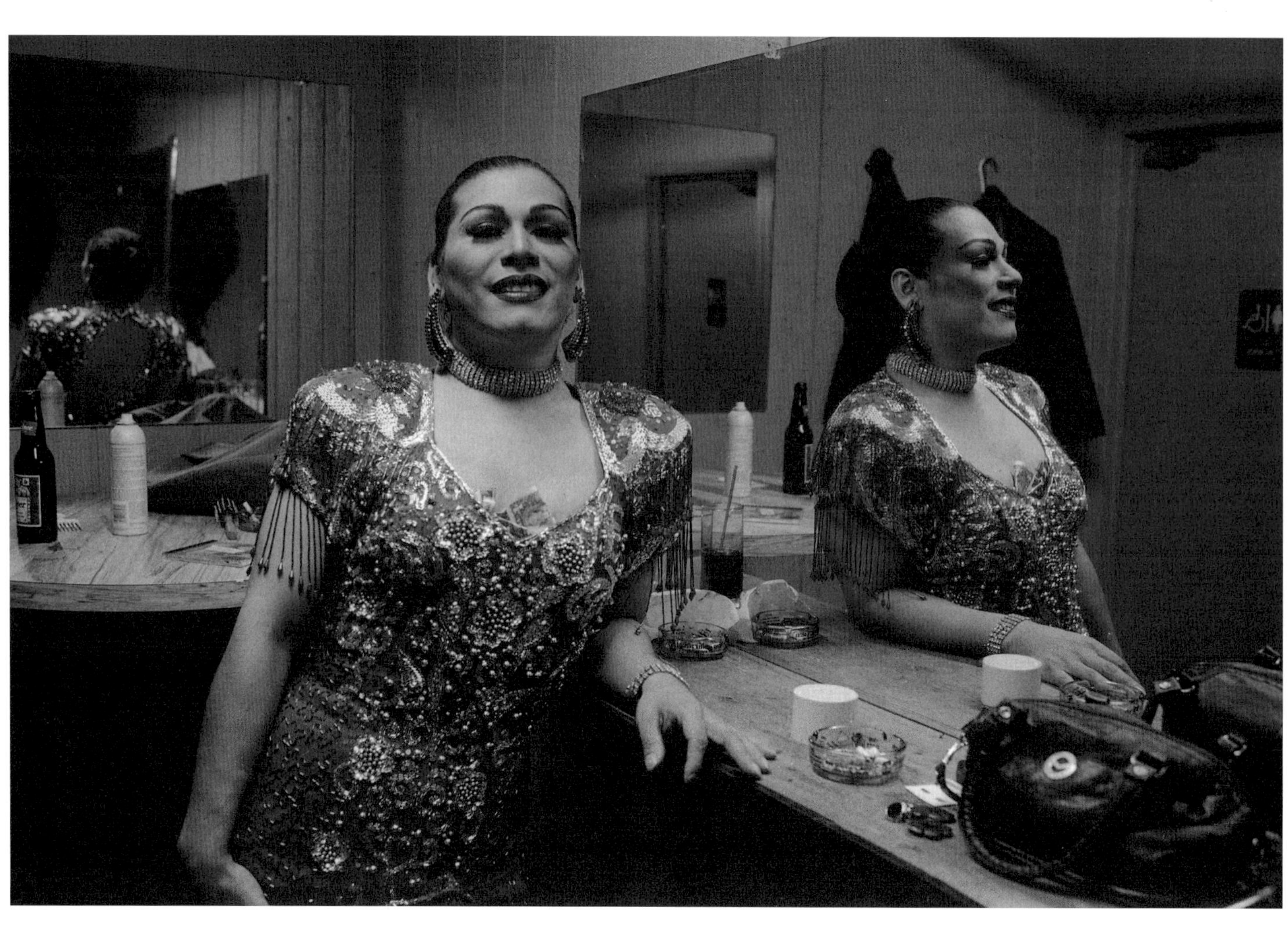

Performer, Silverlake Lounge (1995)

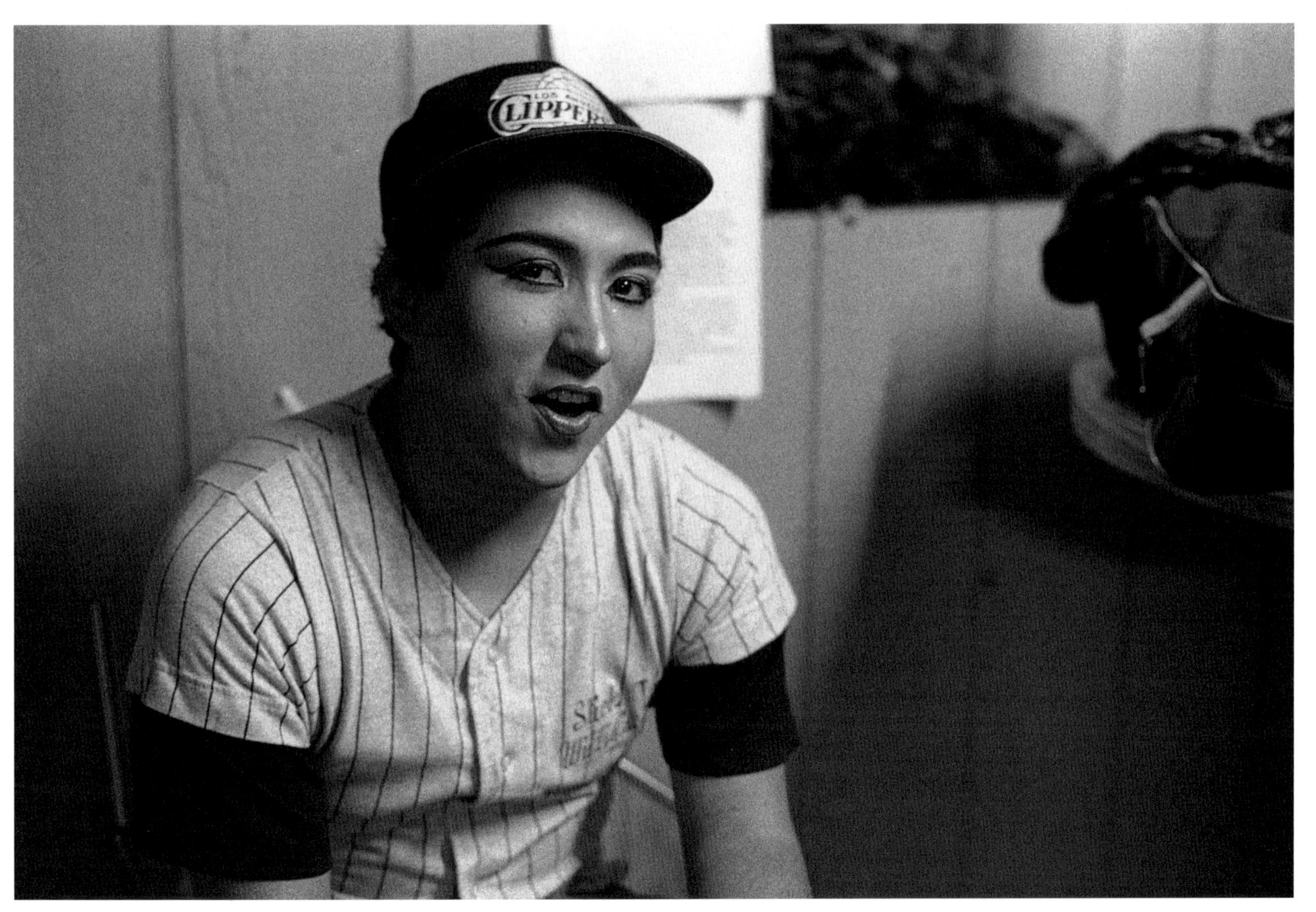

Performer, Silverlake Lounge (1995)

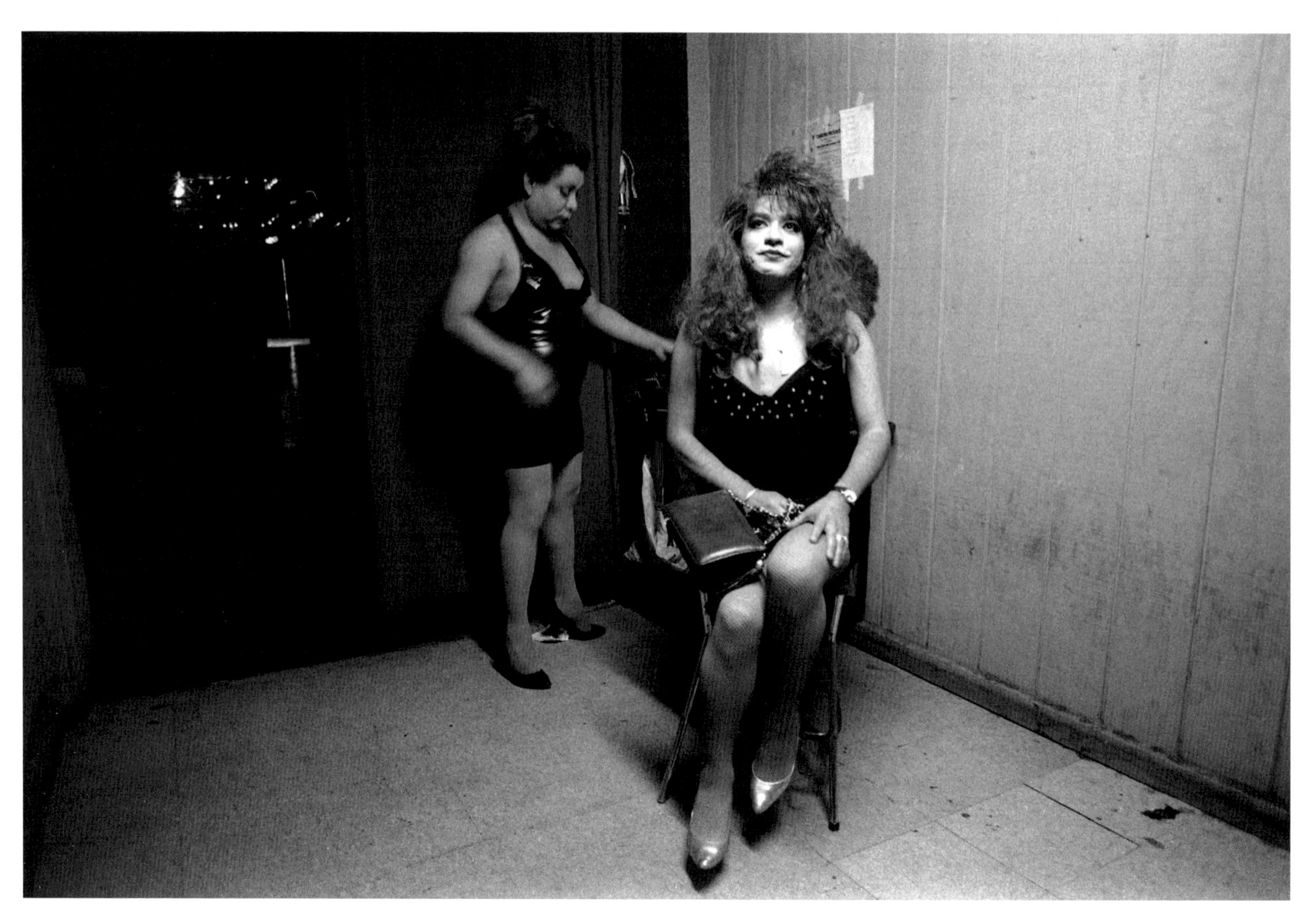

Olga and patron, Silverlake Lounge (1995)

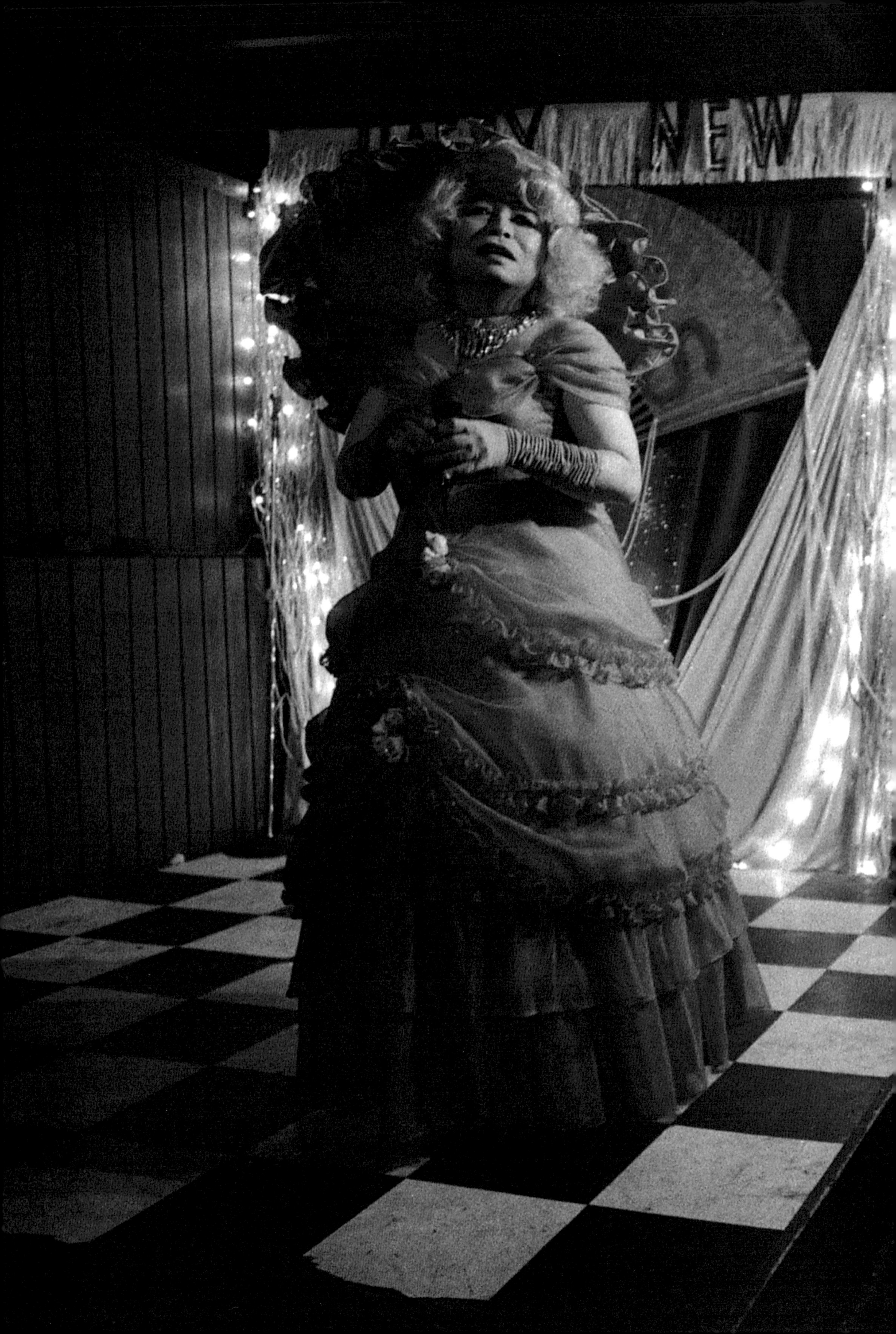
NEW

Yoshi (owner), Mugy's (1995)

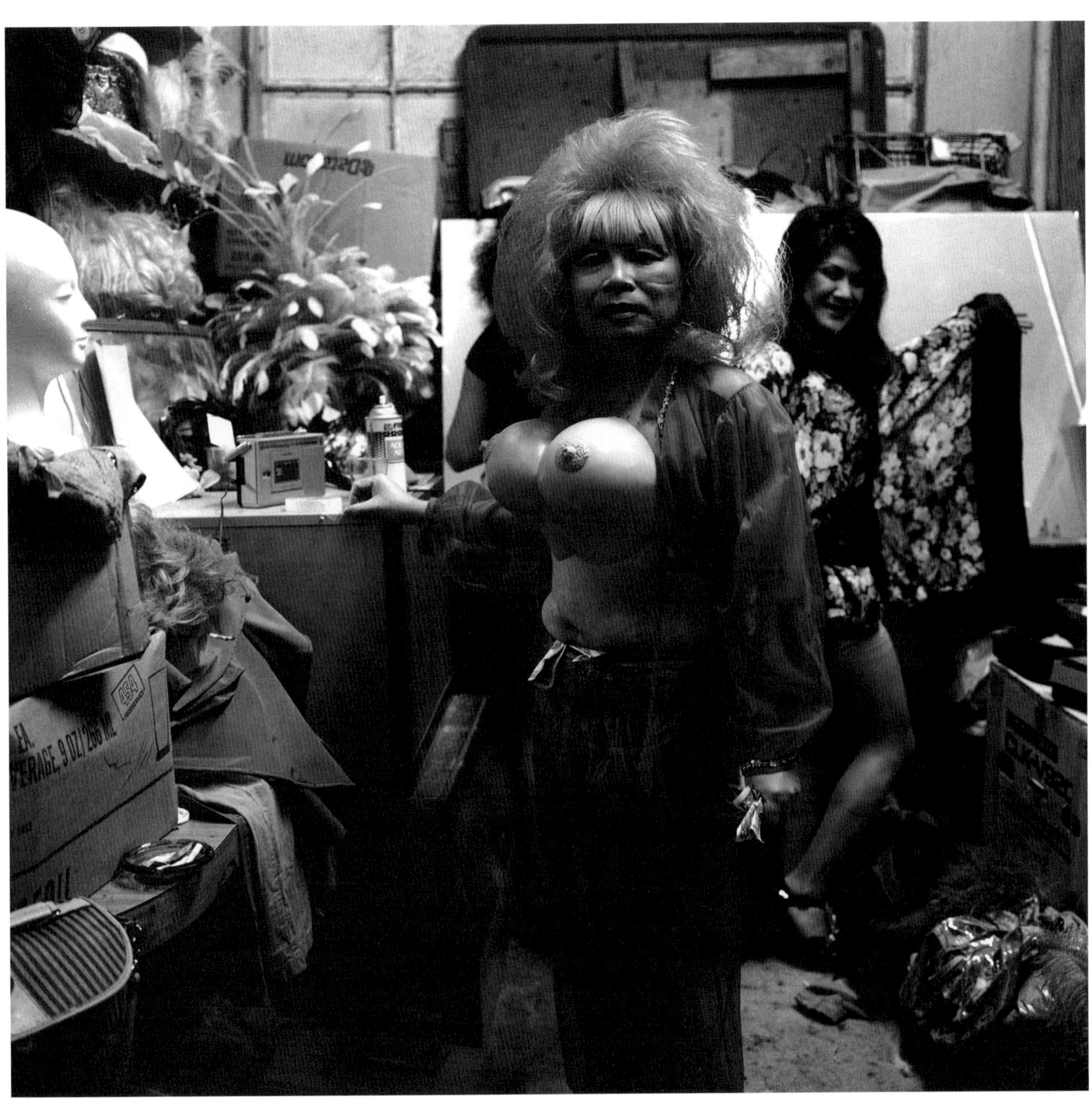

Yoshi (owner), Mugy's (1995)

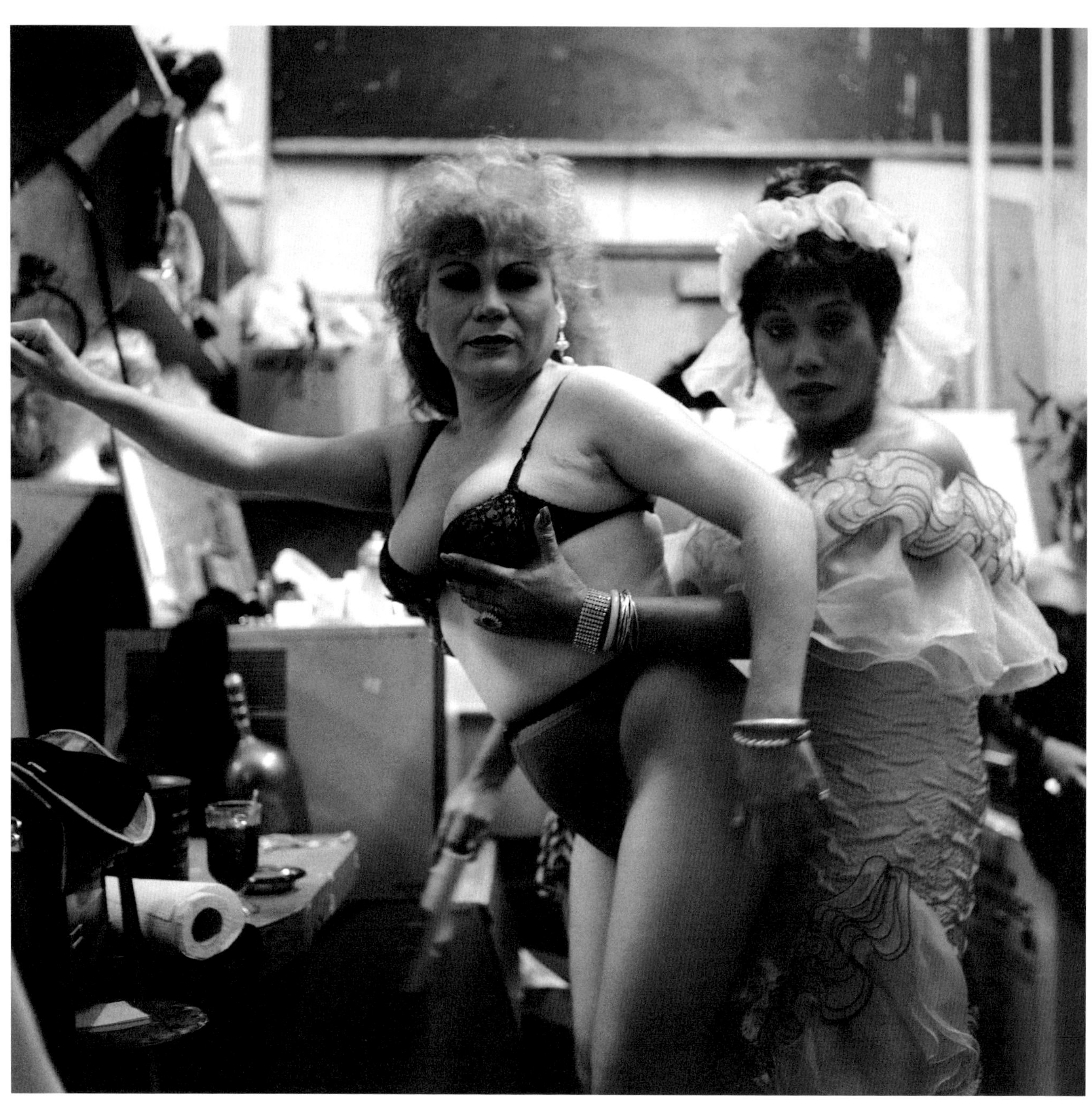

Vanessa and performer, Mugy's (1995)

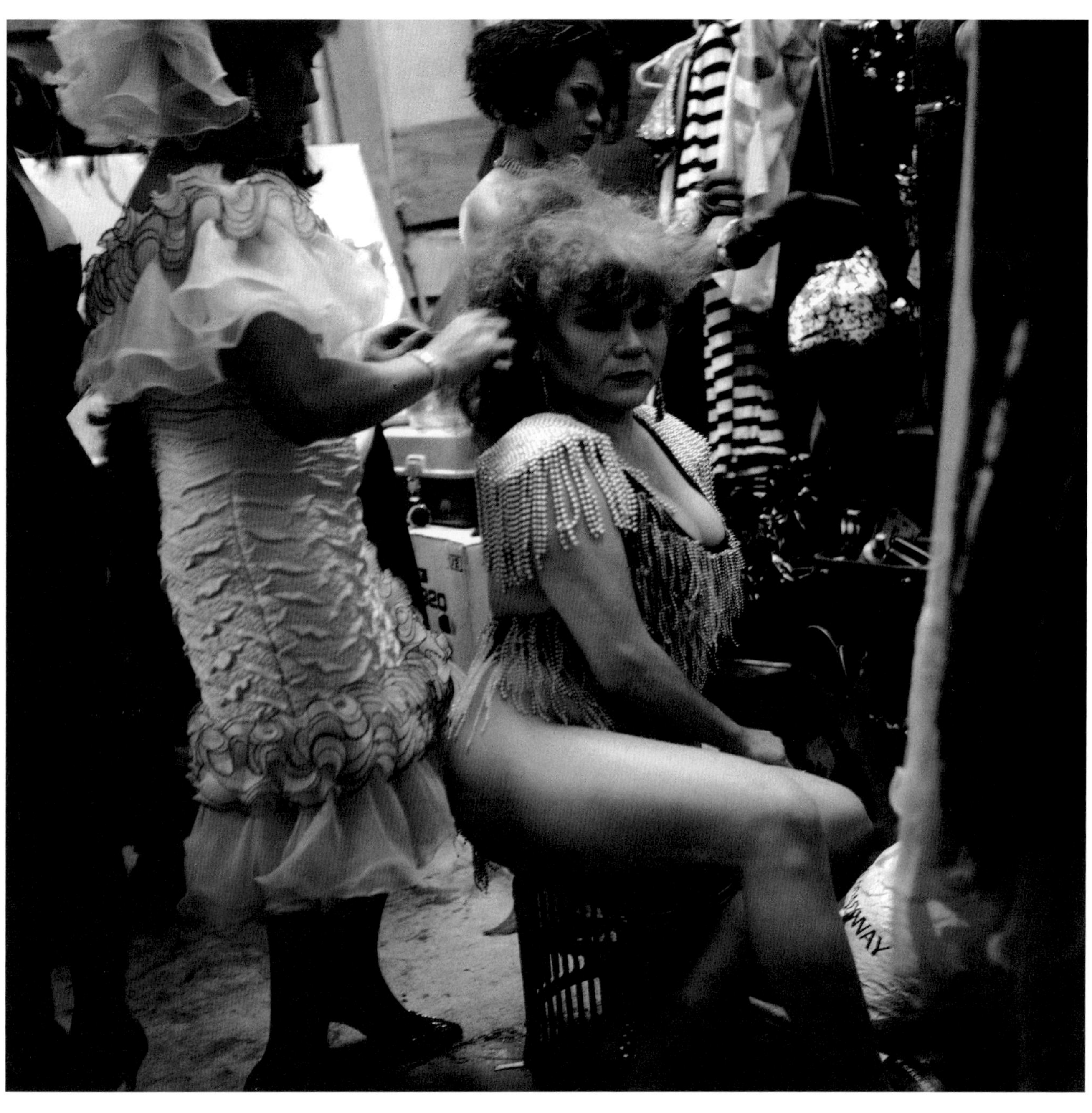

Vanessa, Mugy's (1995)

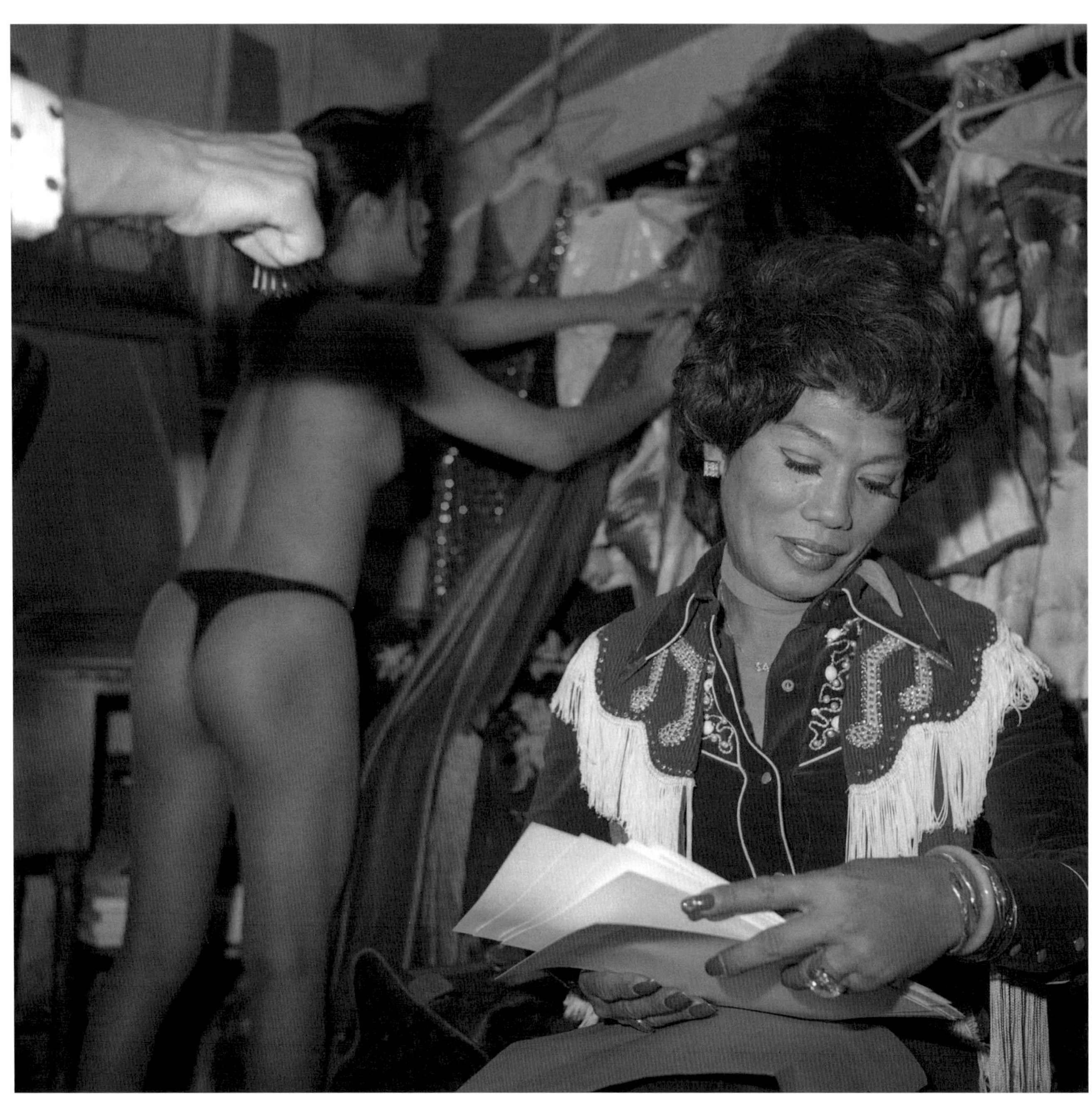

Tina and performer, Mugy's (1995)

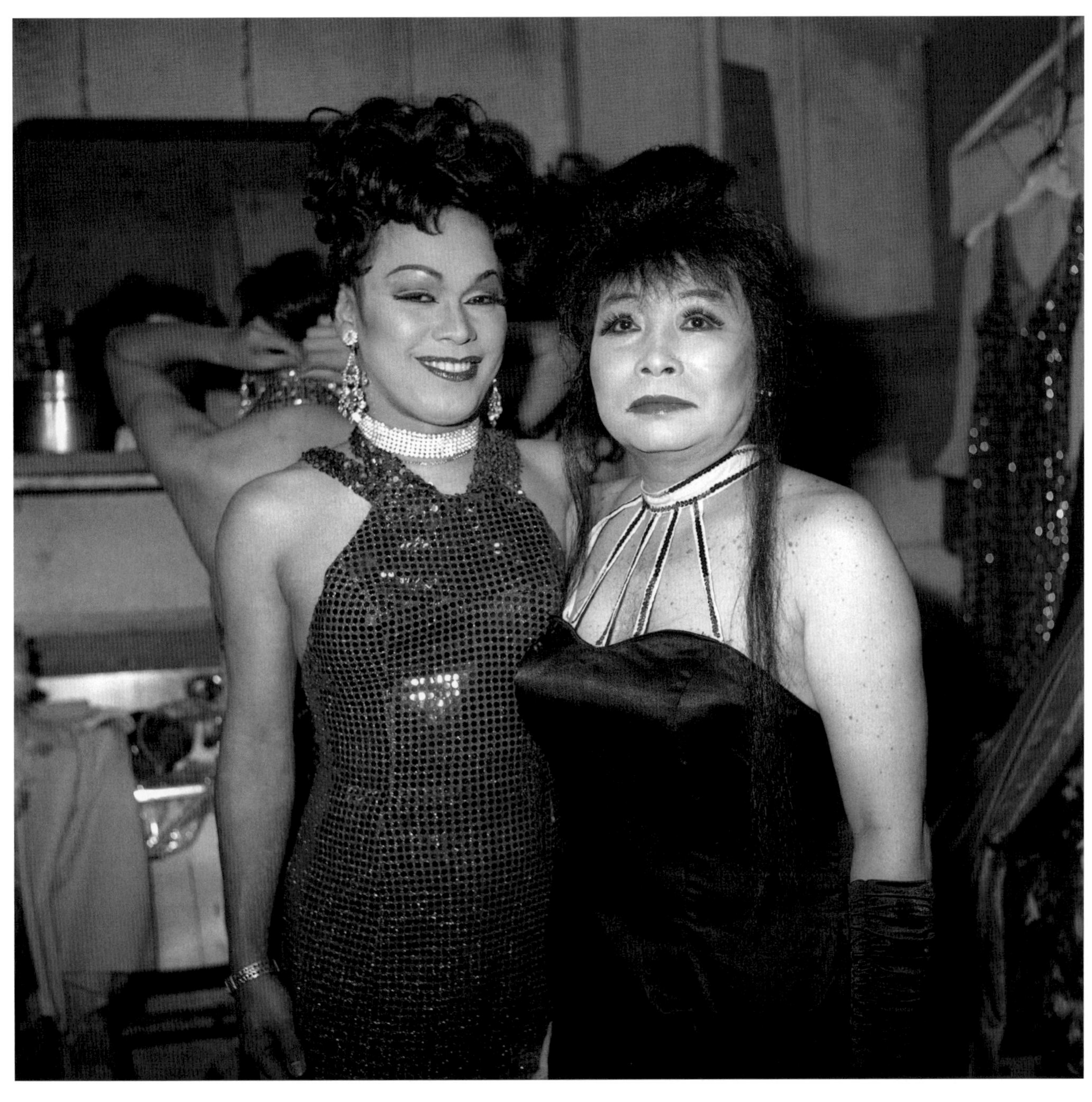

Tina and Yoshi, Mugy's (1995)

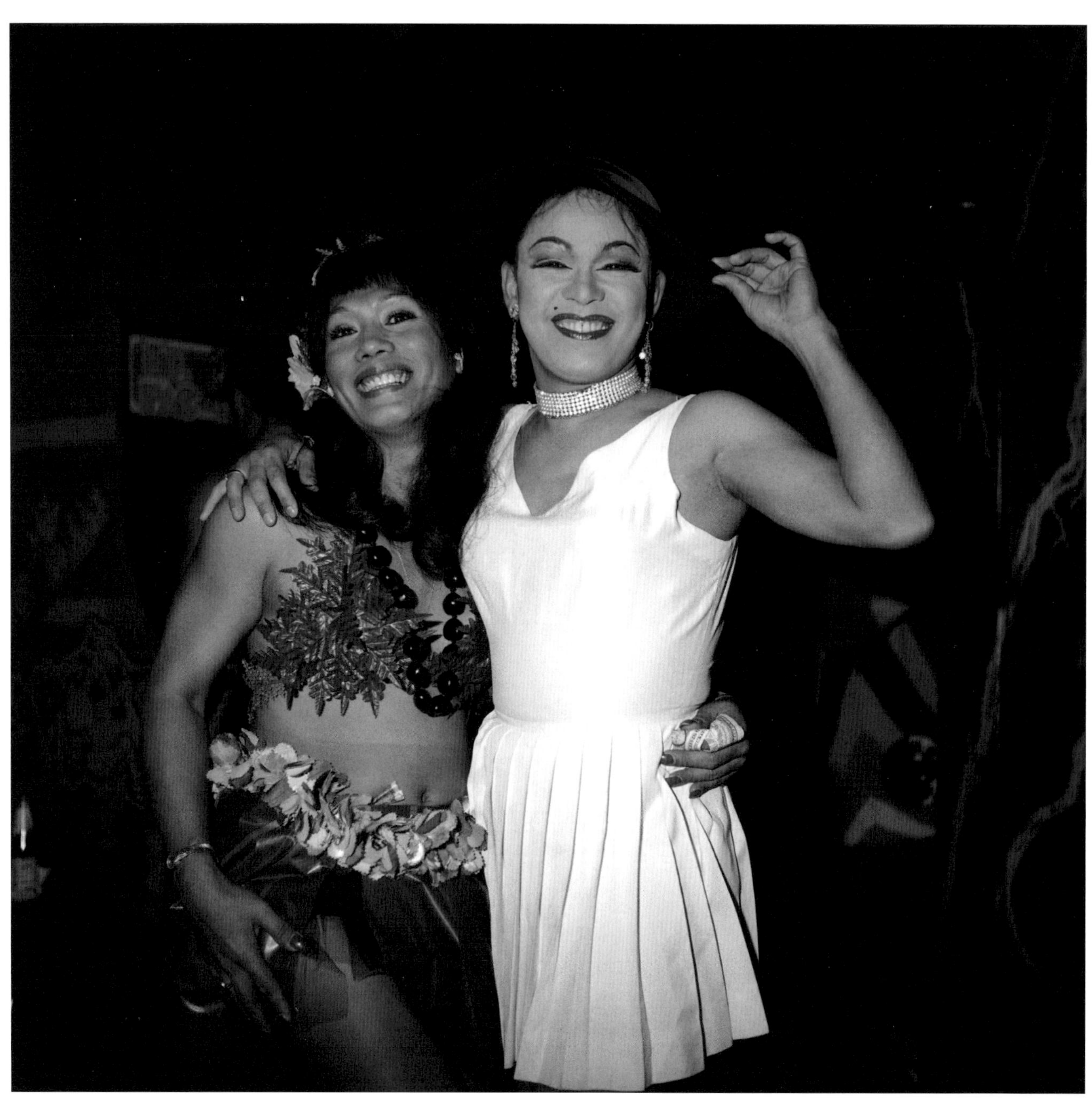

Performer and Tina, Mugy's (1995)

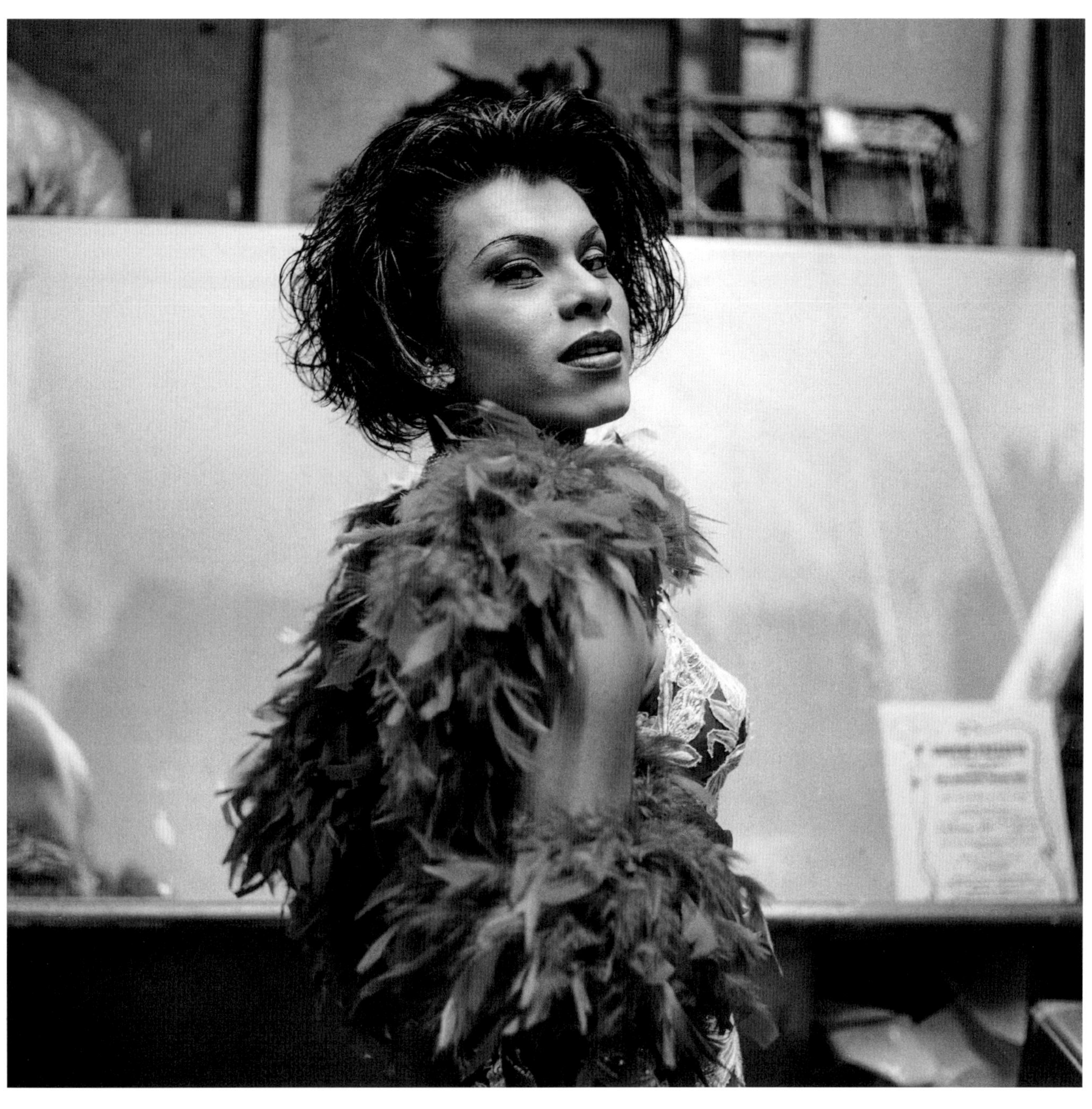

Mugy's (1995)

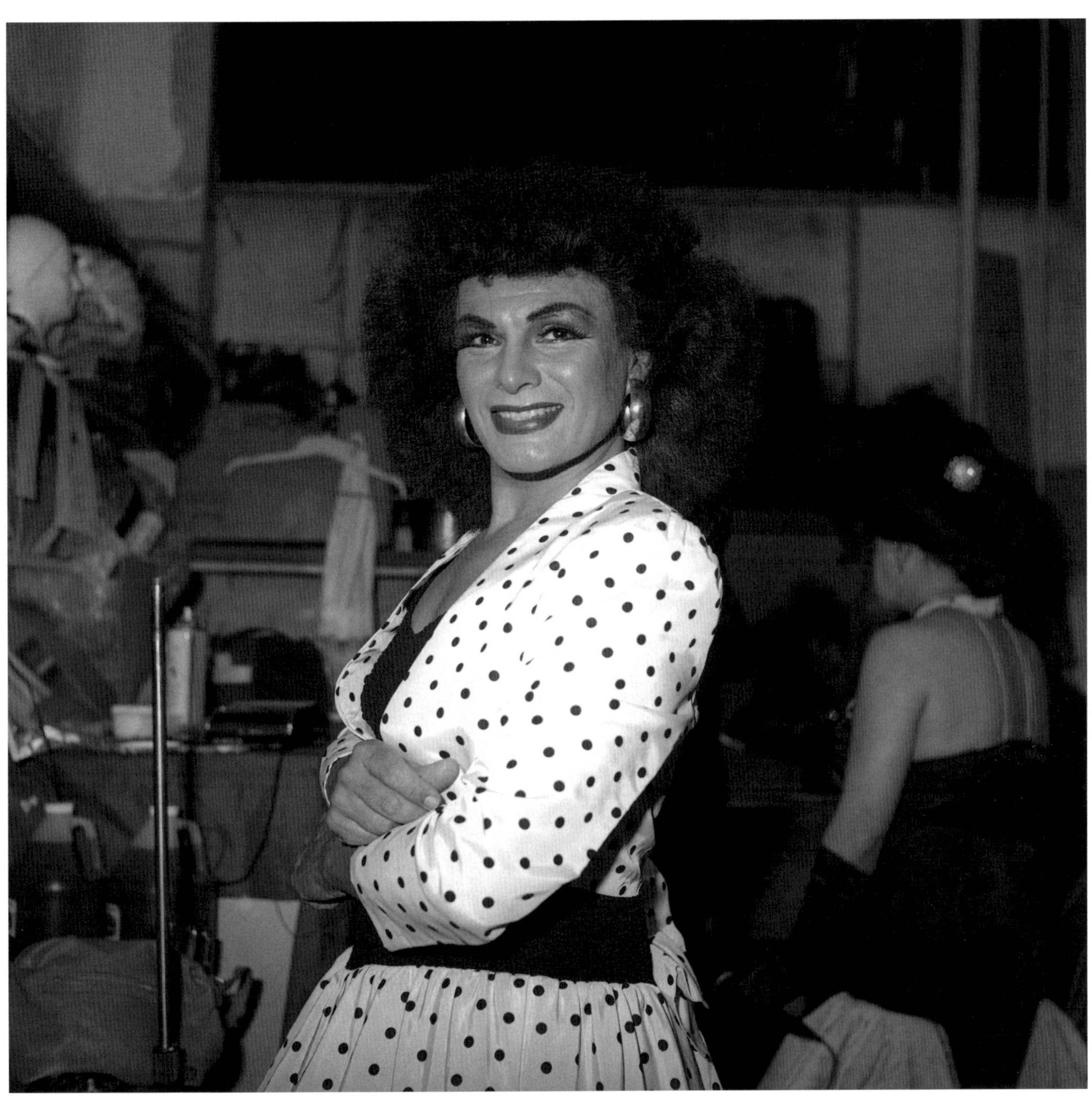

Joan Crawford, Mugy's (1995)

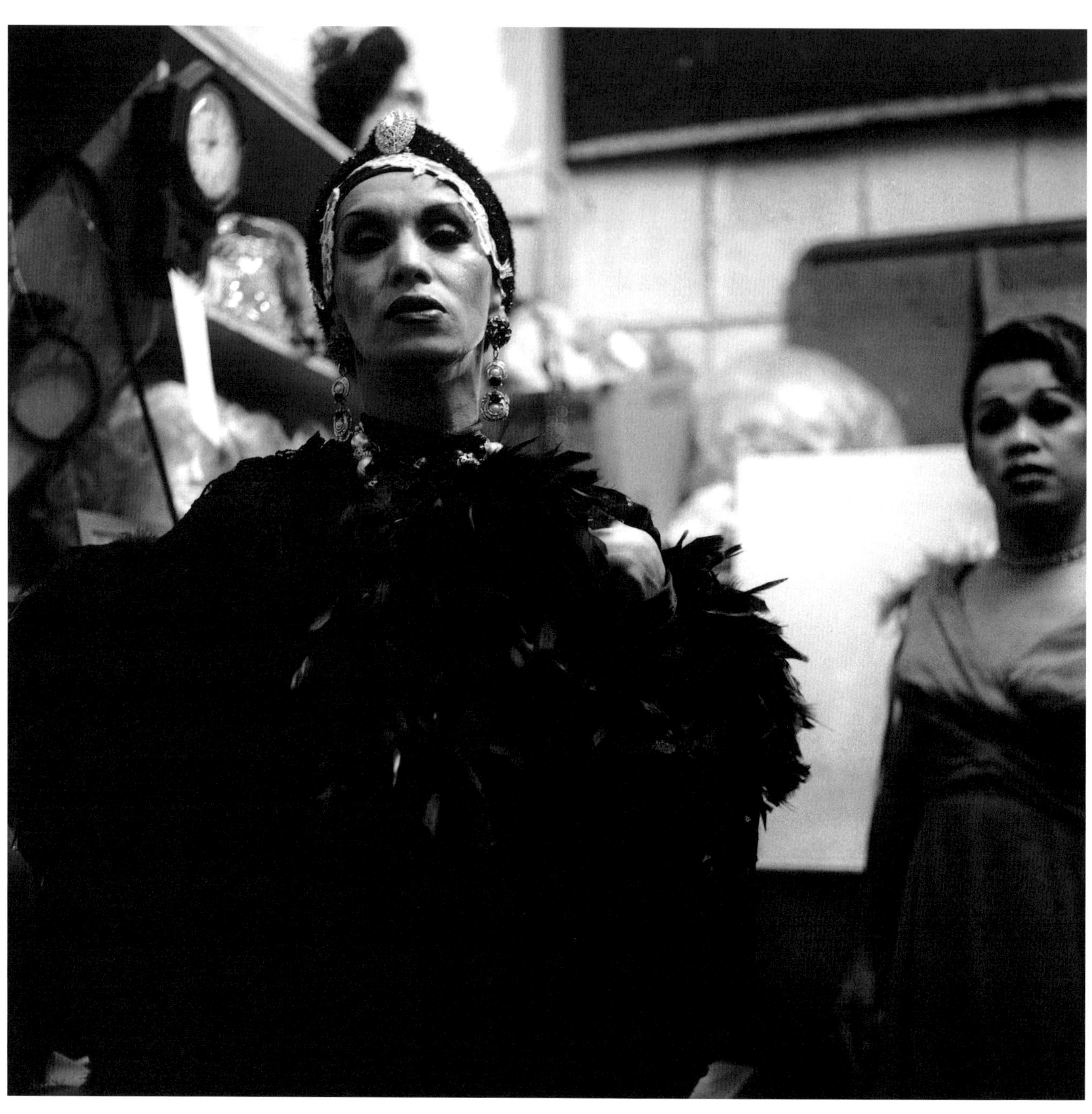

Performer, Mugy's (1995)

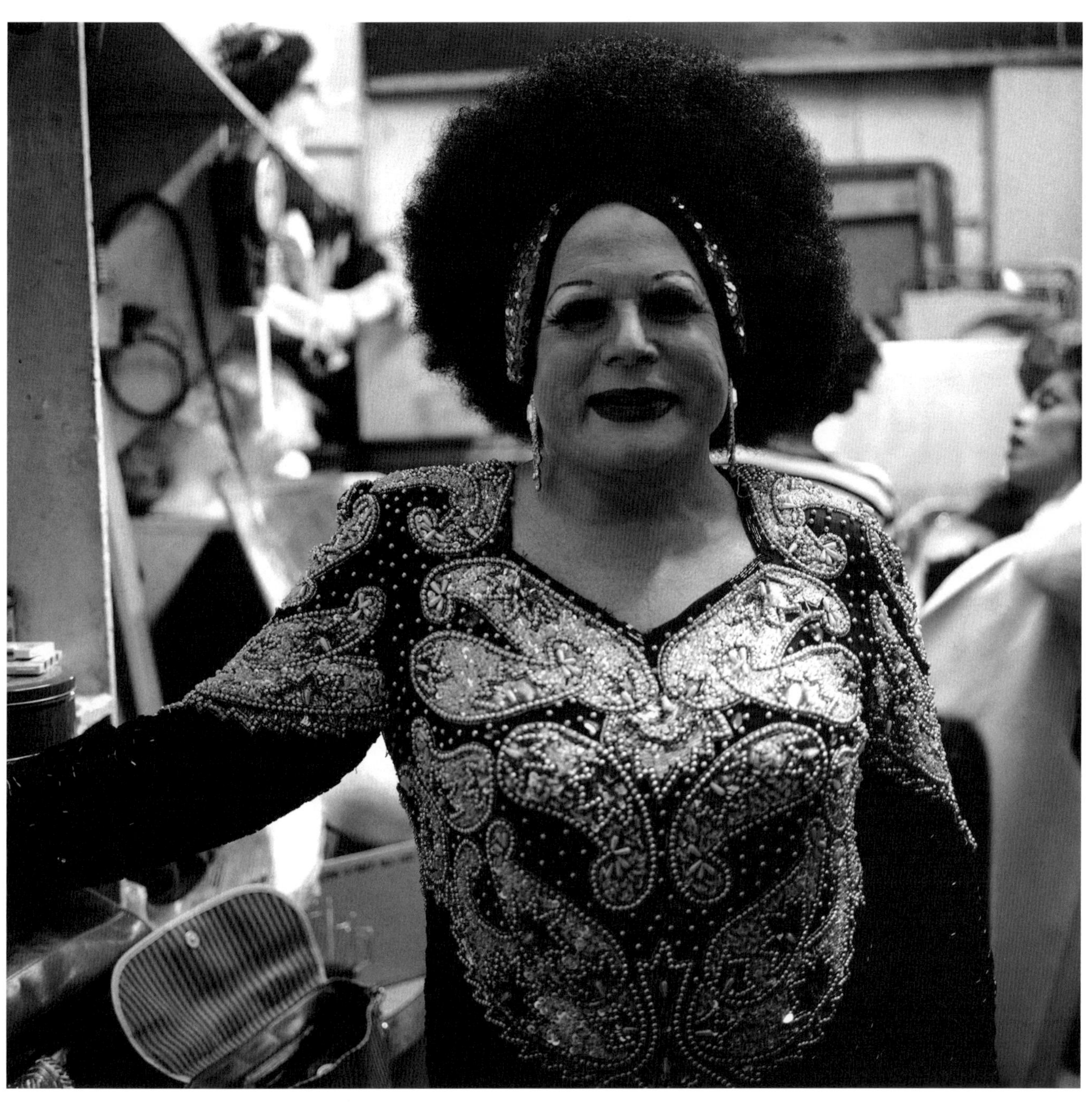

Magician, Mugy's (1995)

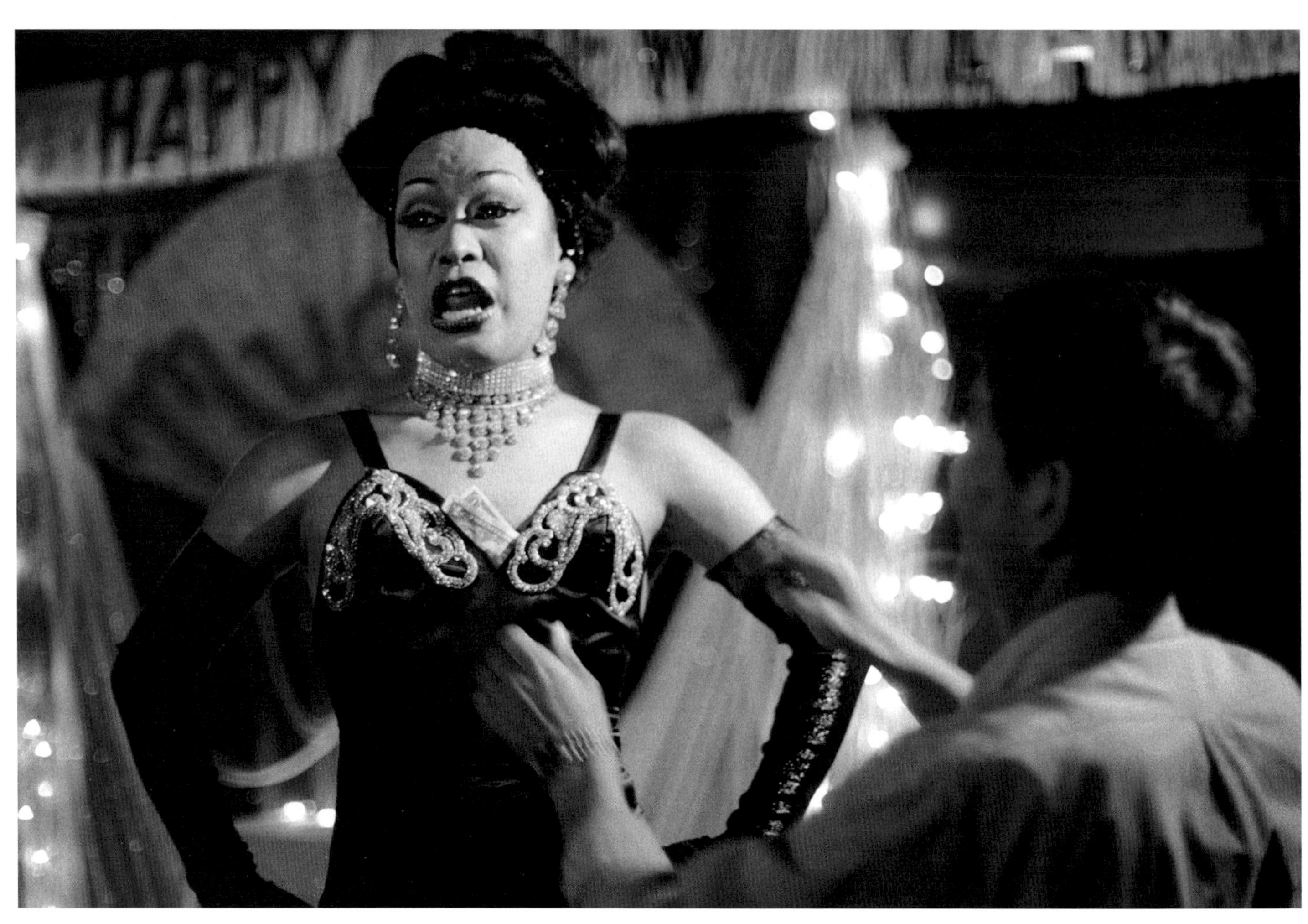

Tina, Mugy's (1995)

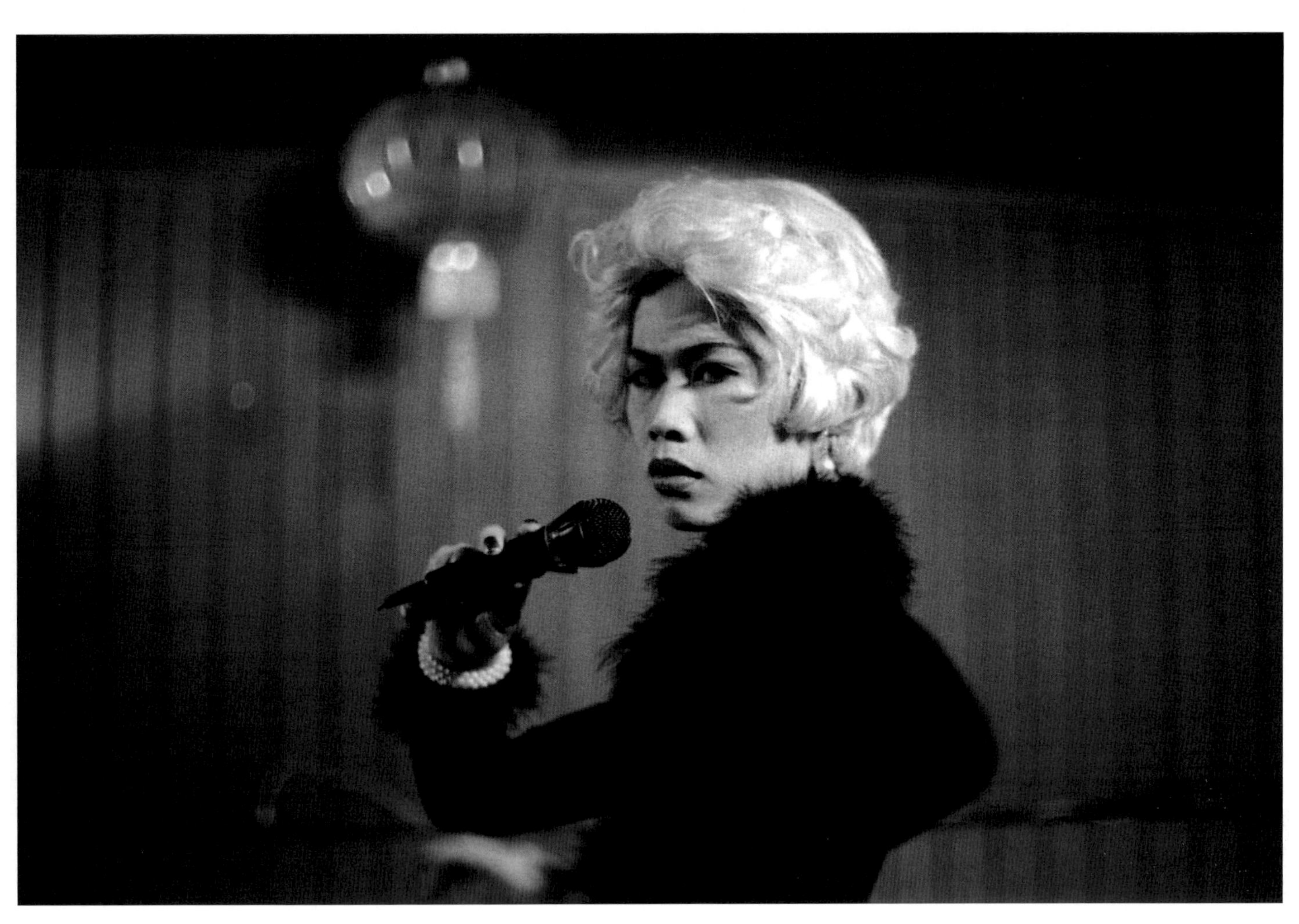

Performer, Mugy's (1995)

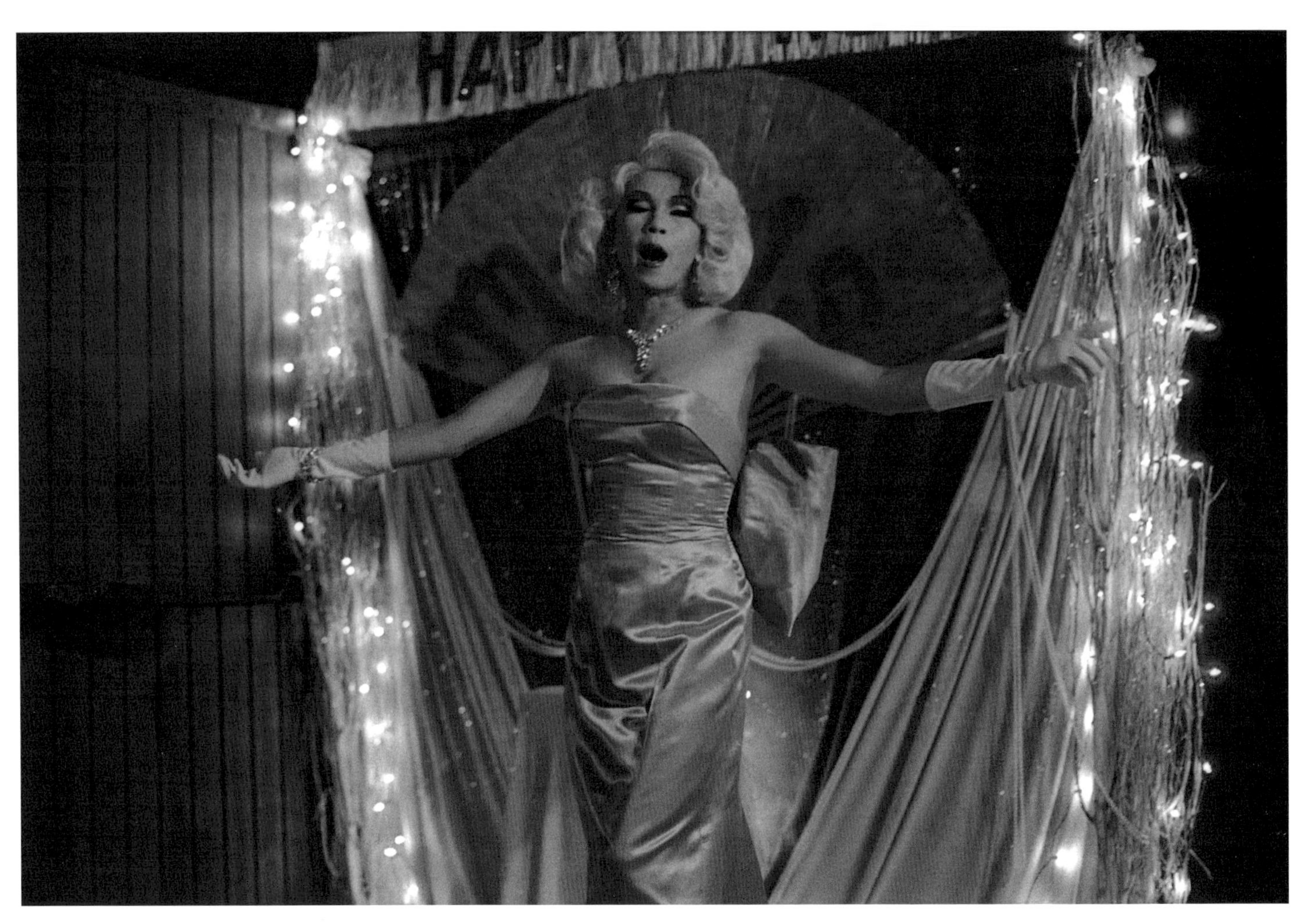

Performer, Mugy's (1995)

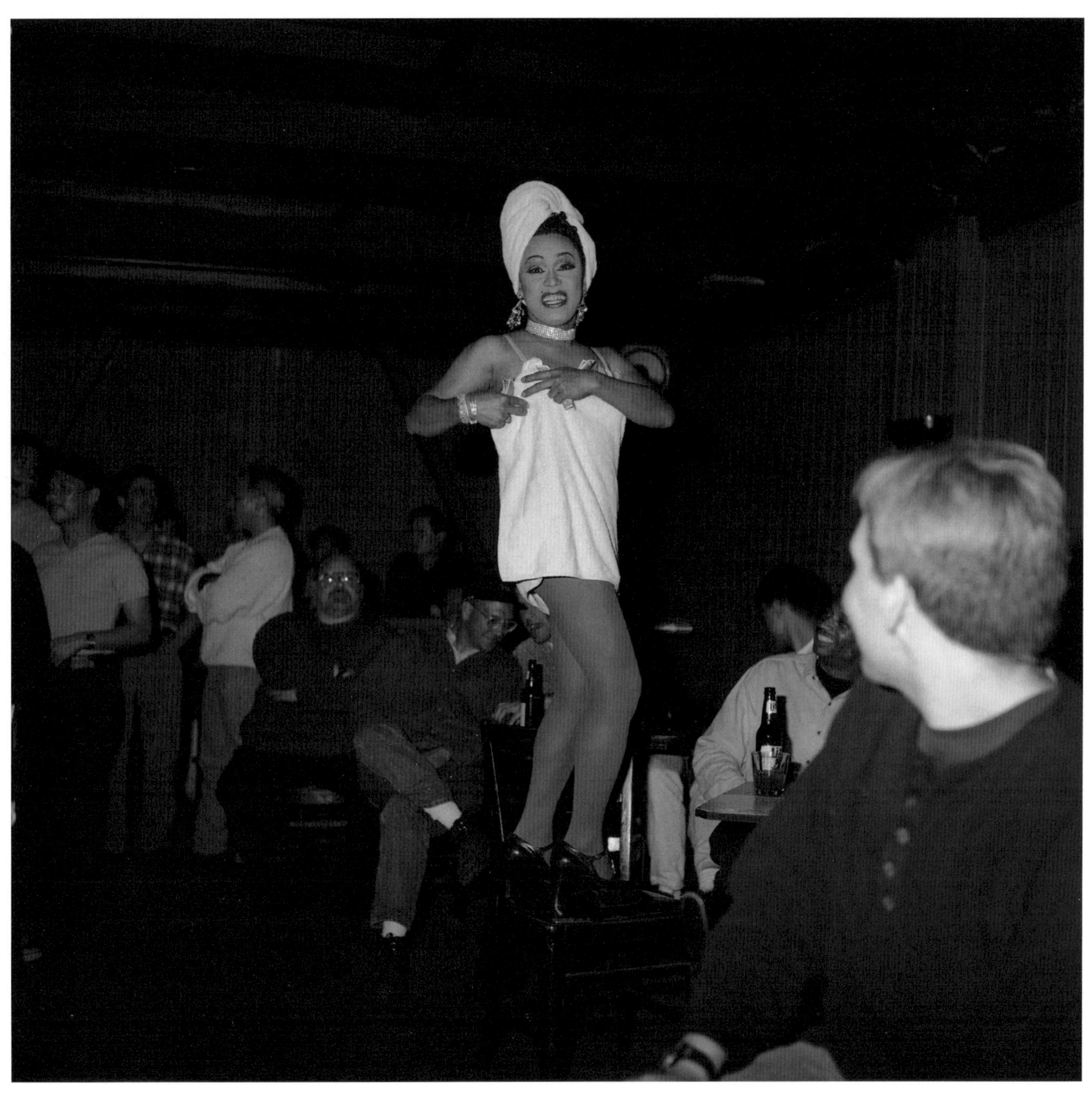

Tina, Mugy's (1995)

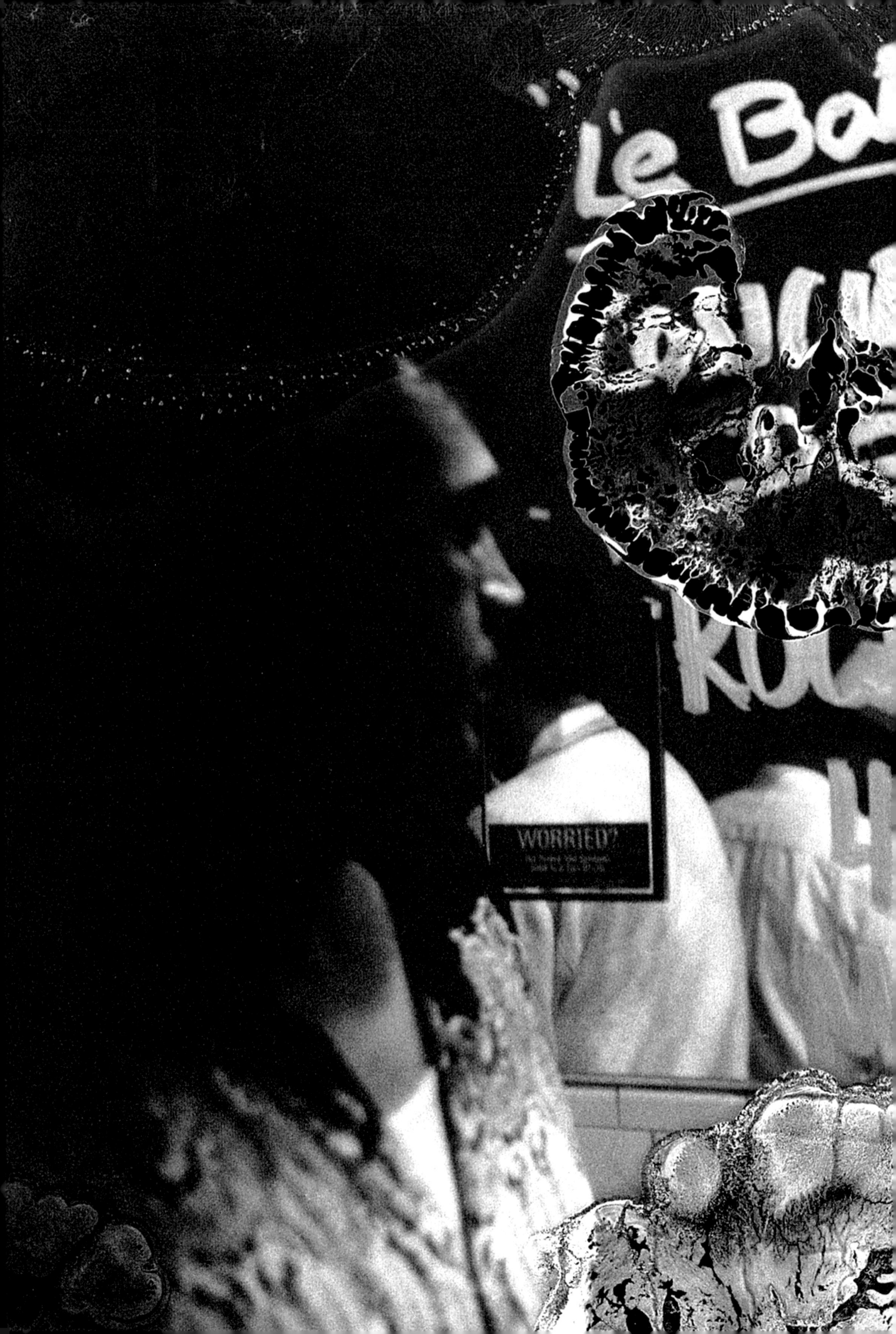

Le Ba
WORRIED?

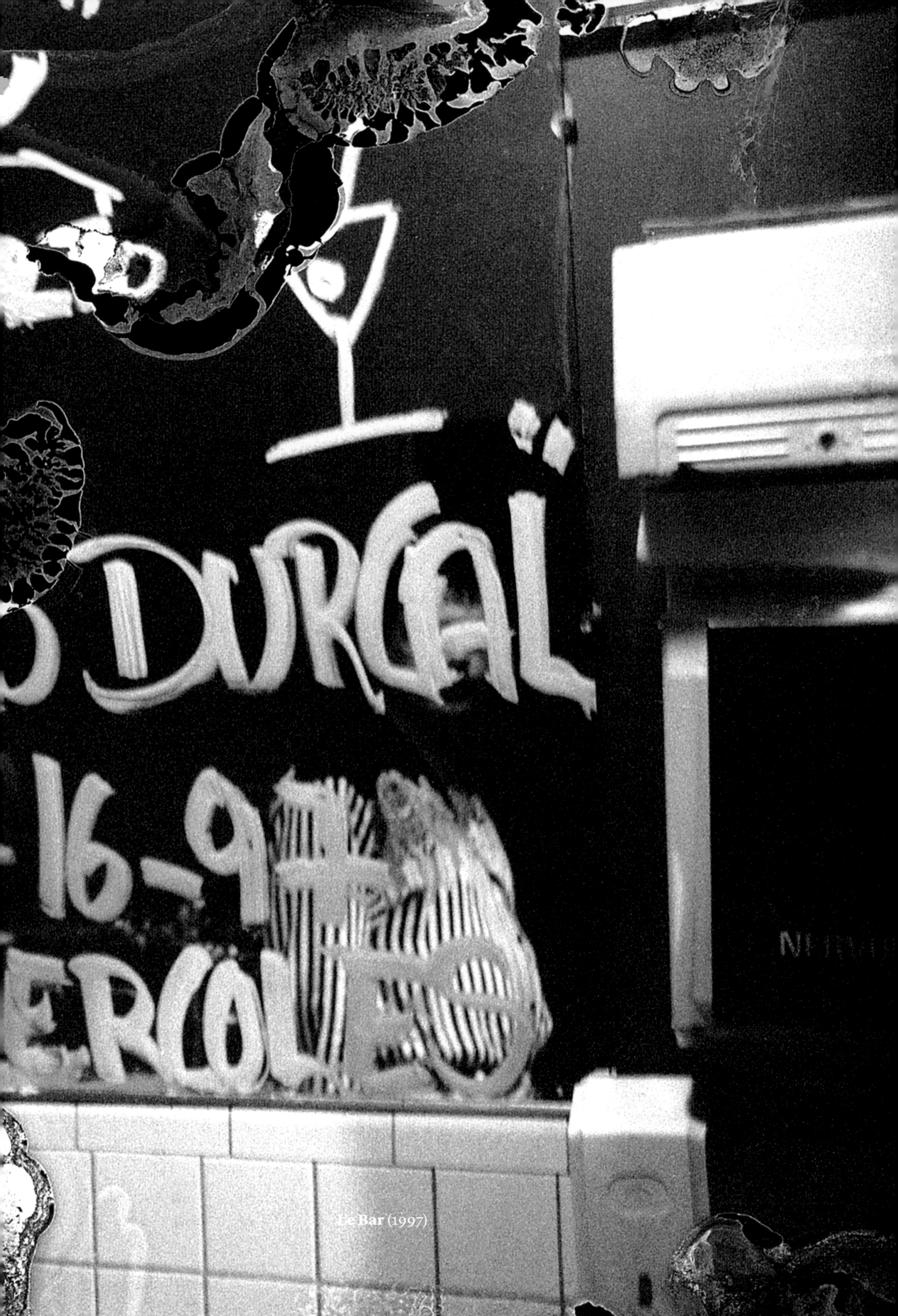

Le Bar (1997)

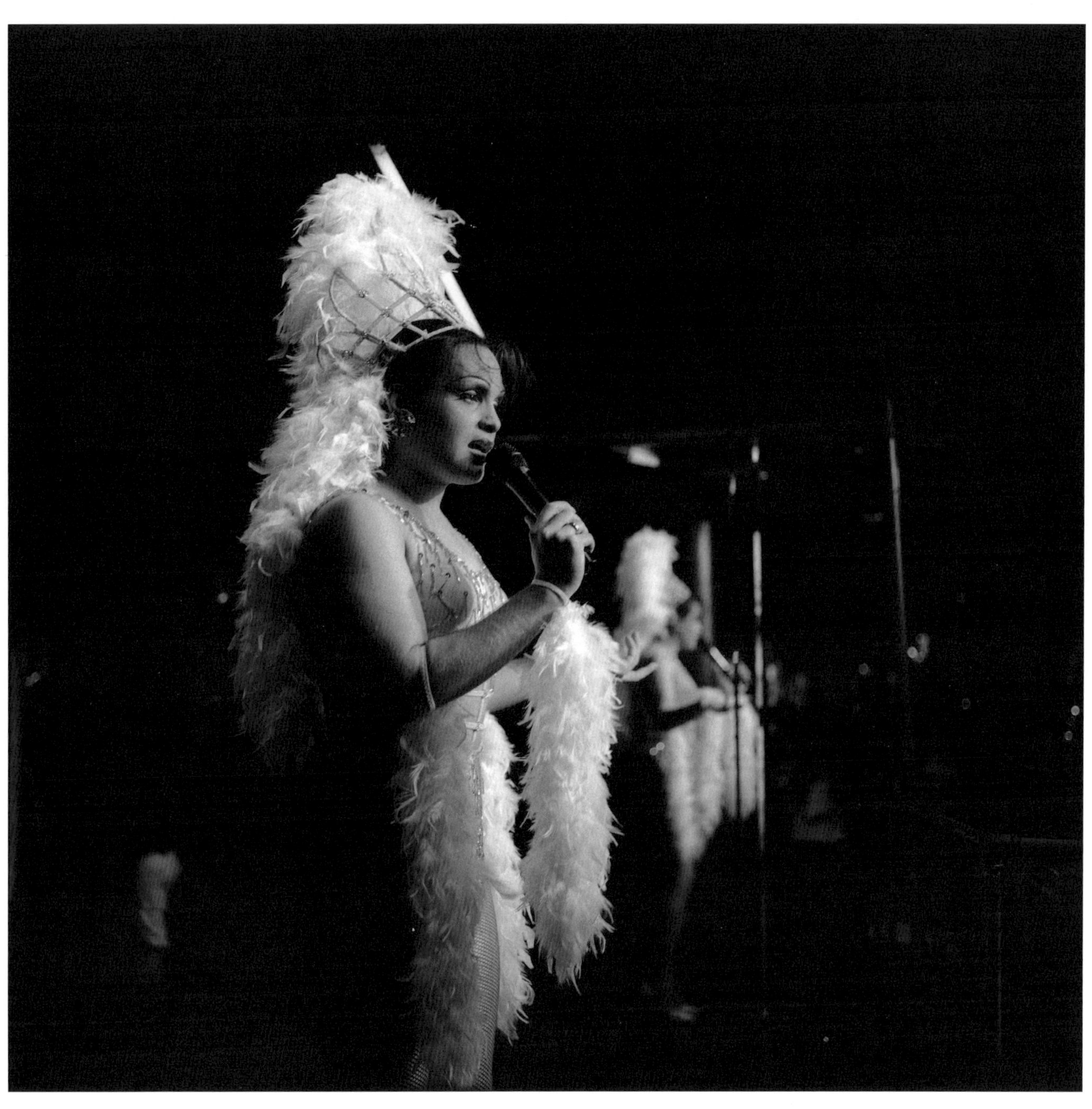

Maria Felix, Le Bar (1997)

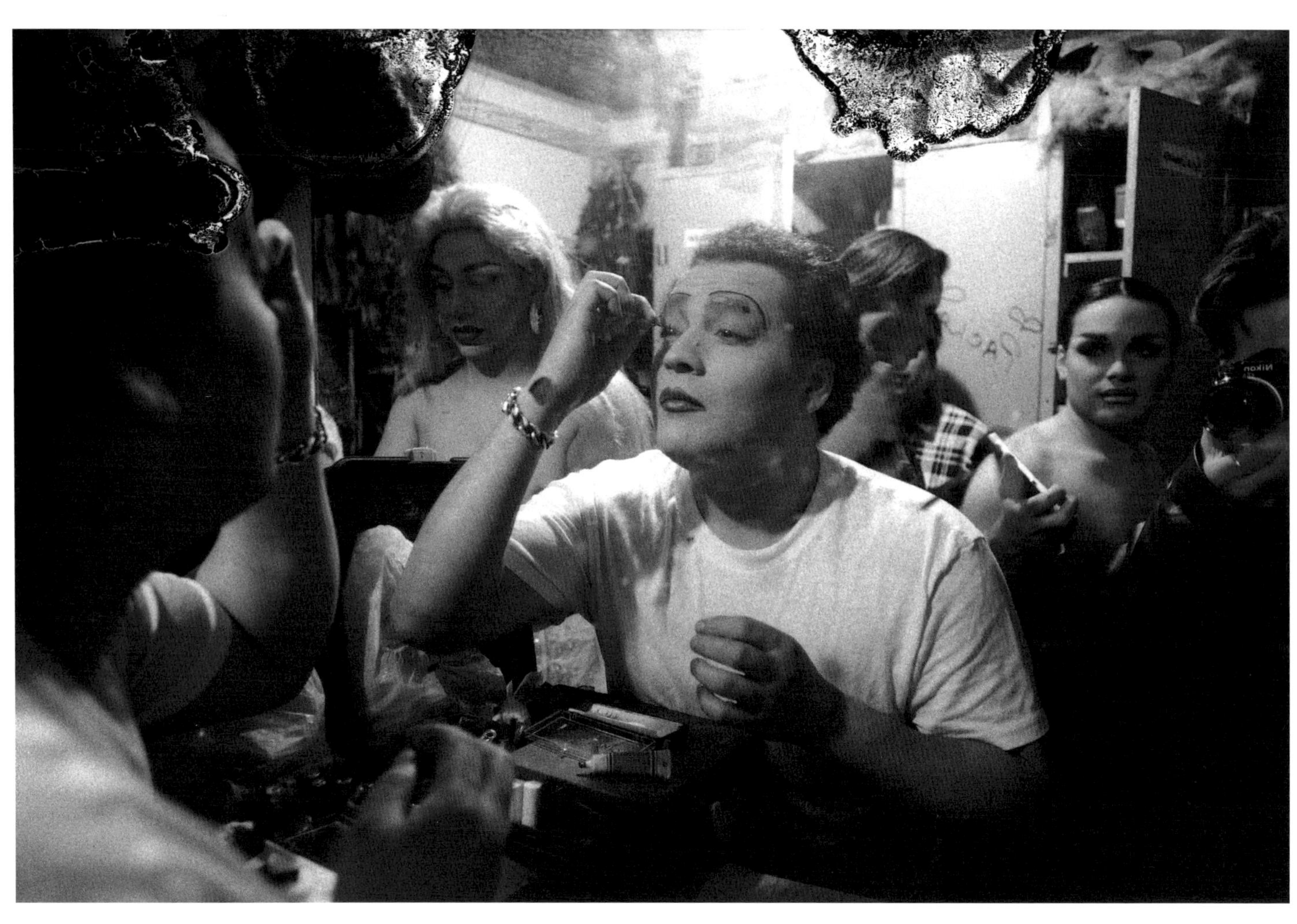

Paquita and Reynaldo, Le Bar (1997)

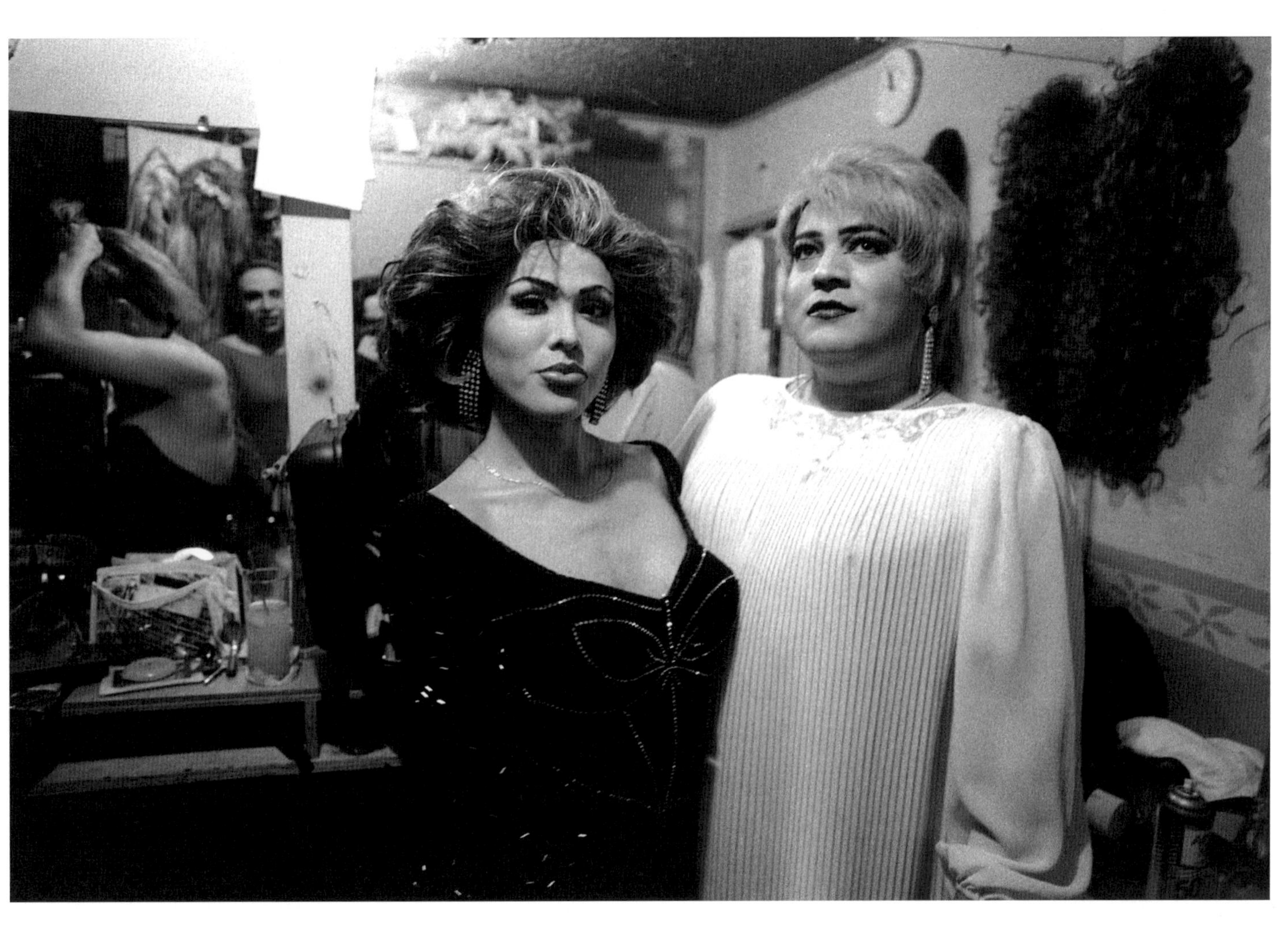

Paquita and friend, Le Bar (1997)

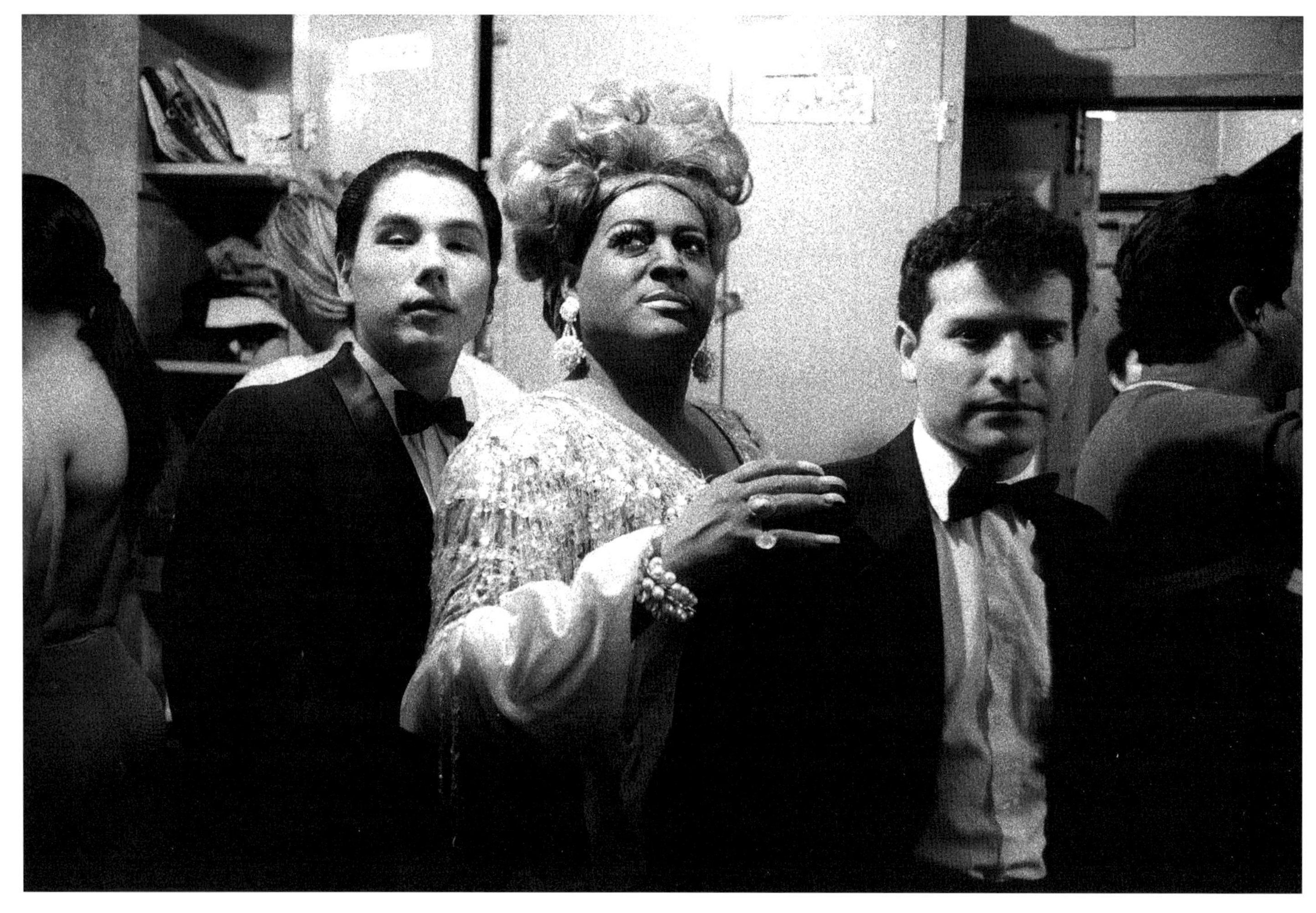

Paquita and friends, Le Bar (1997)

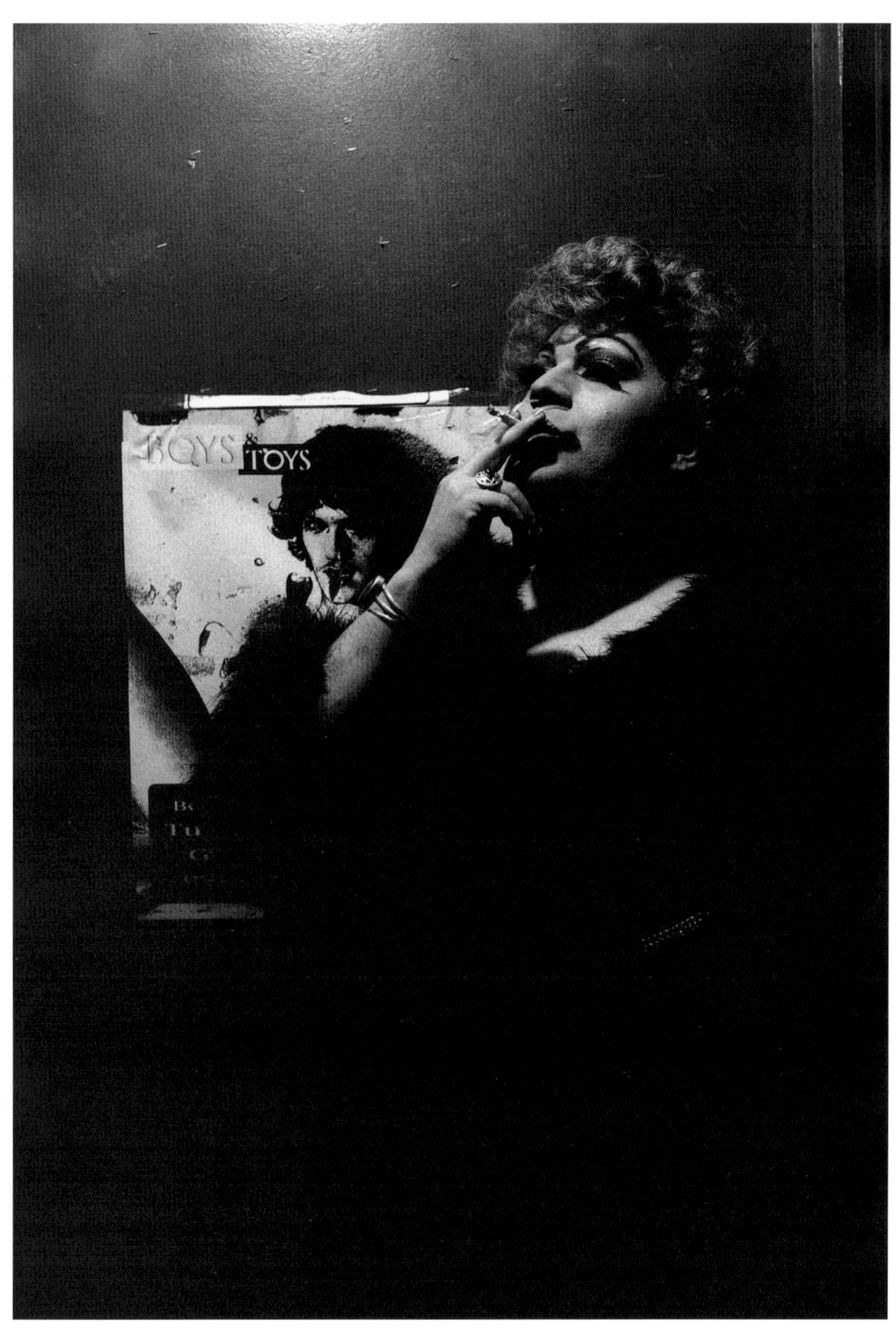

Paquita, Le Bar (1997)

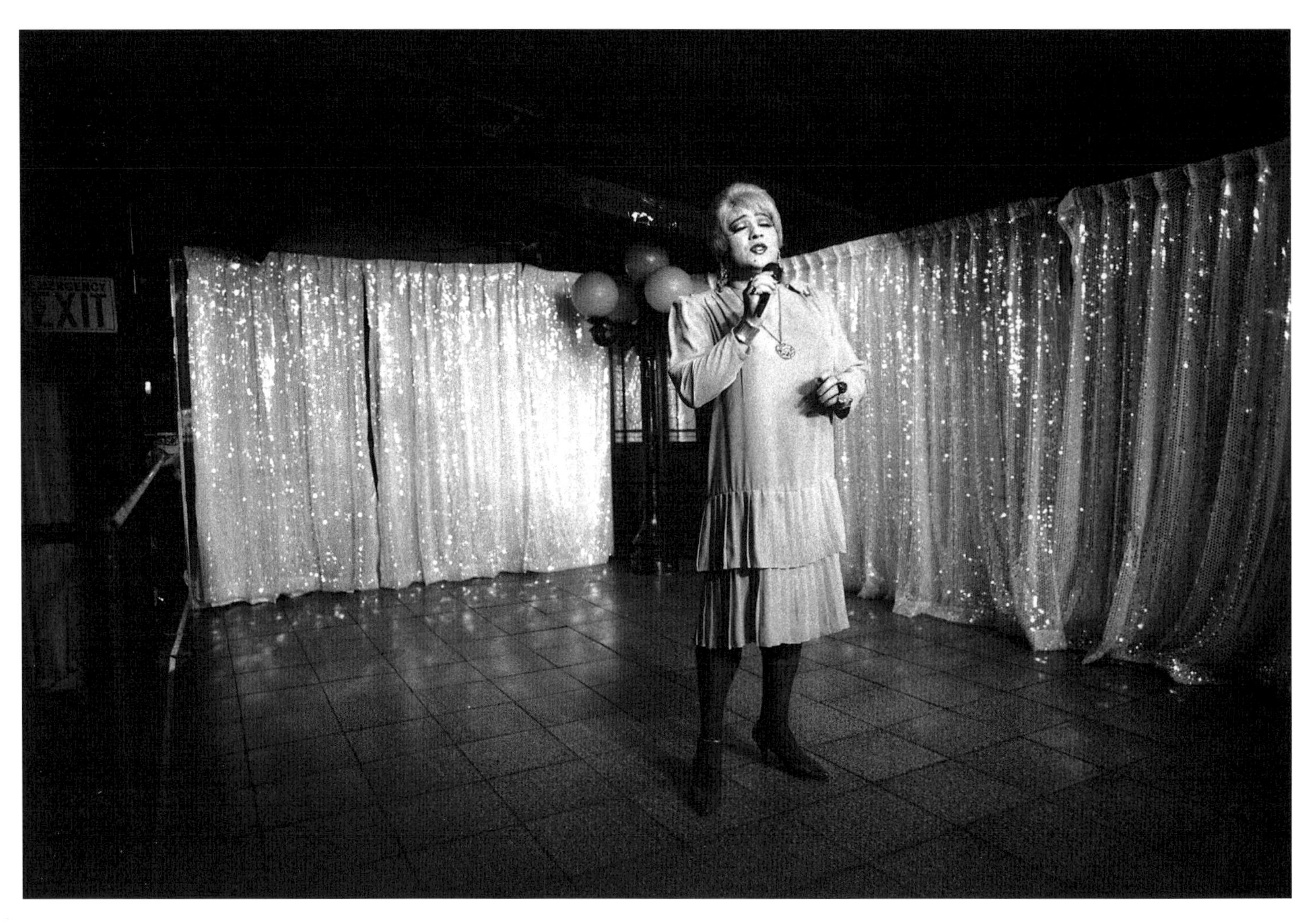

Paquita, Le Bar (1997)

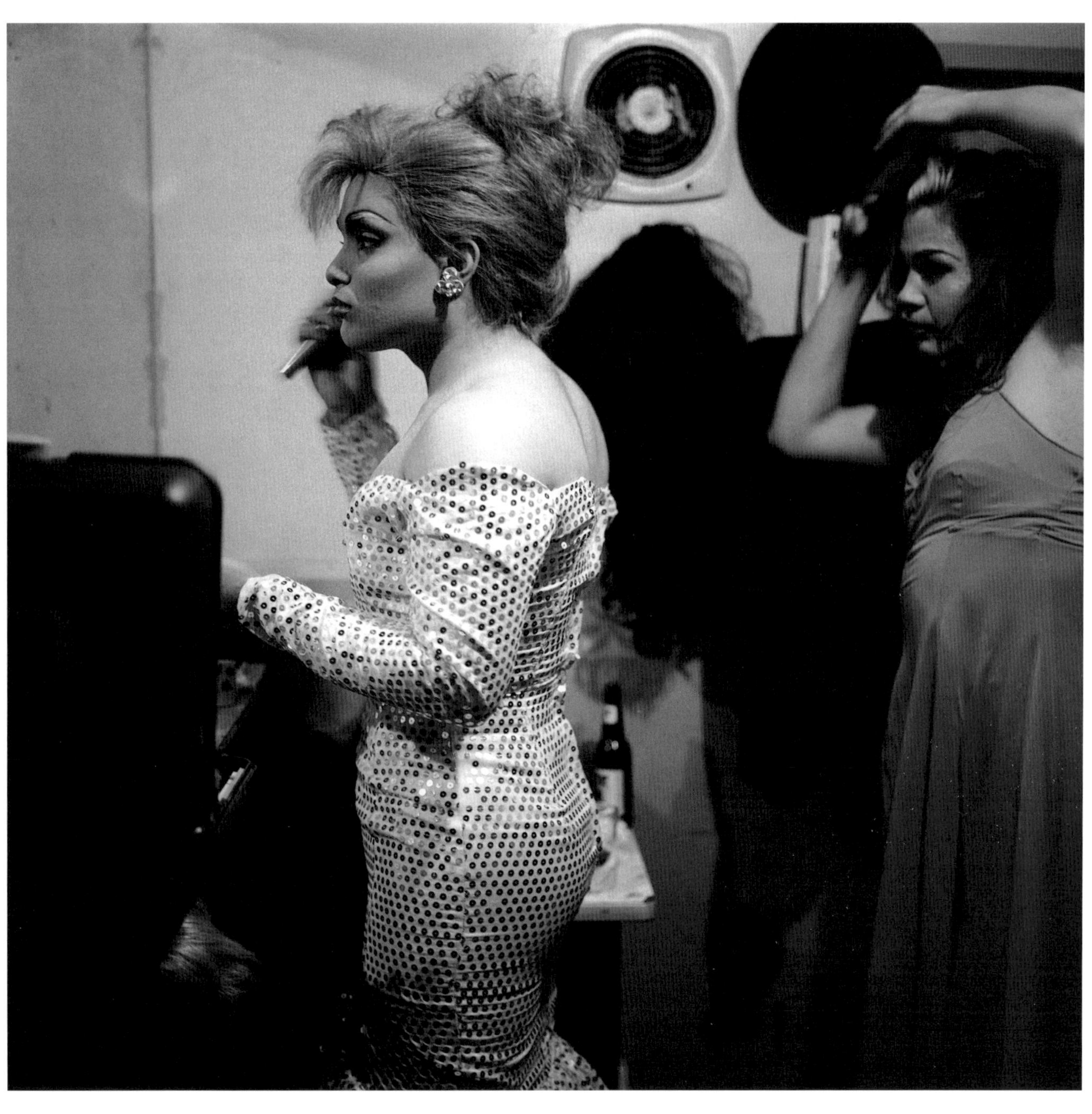

Yuri and Gloria, Le Bar (1997)

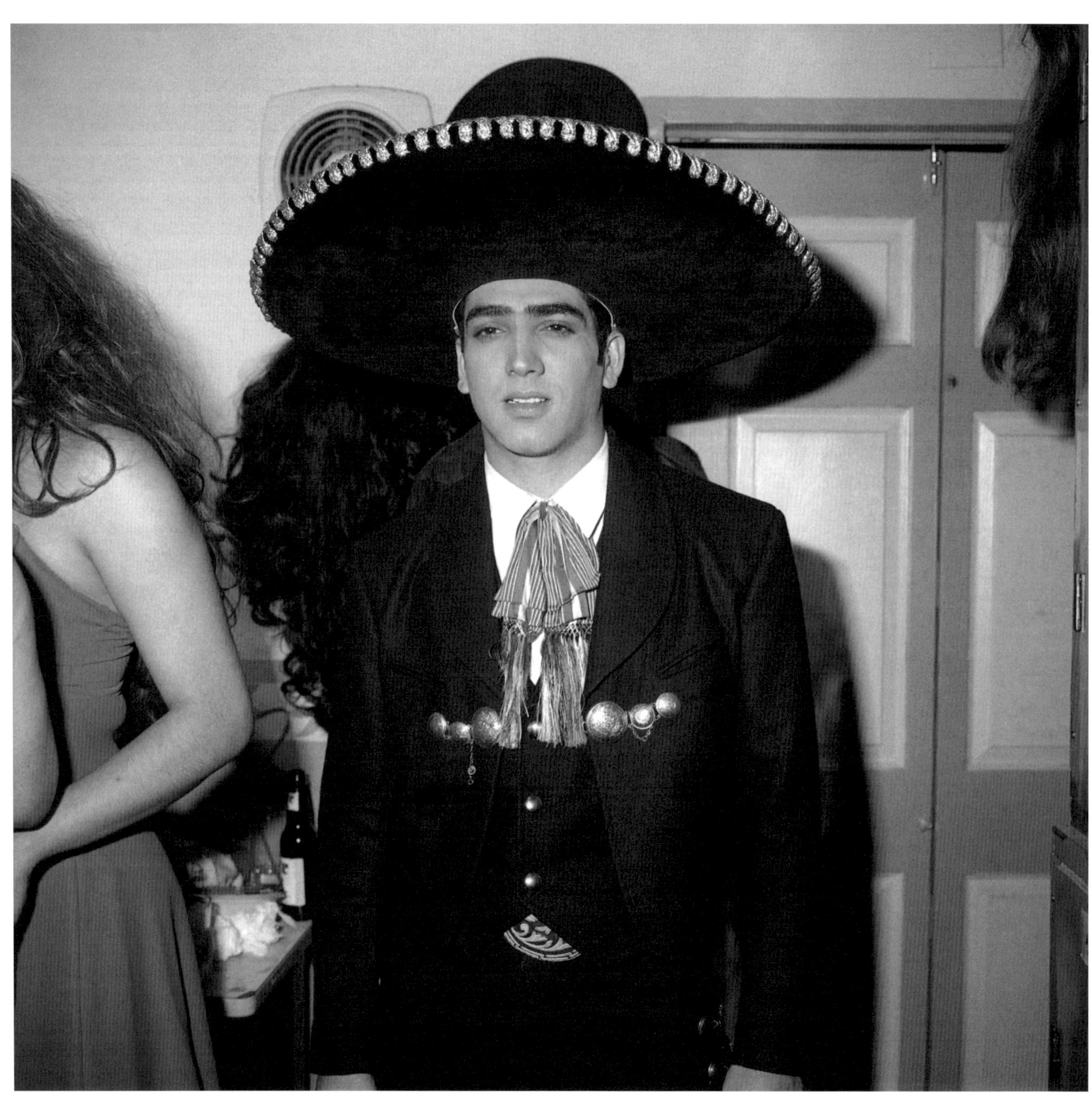

Alejandro Fernandez, Le Bar (1997)

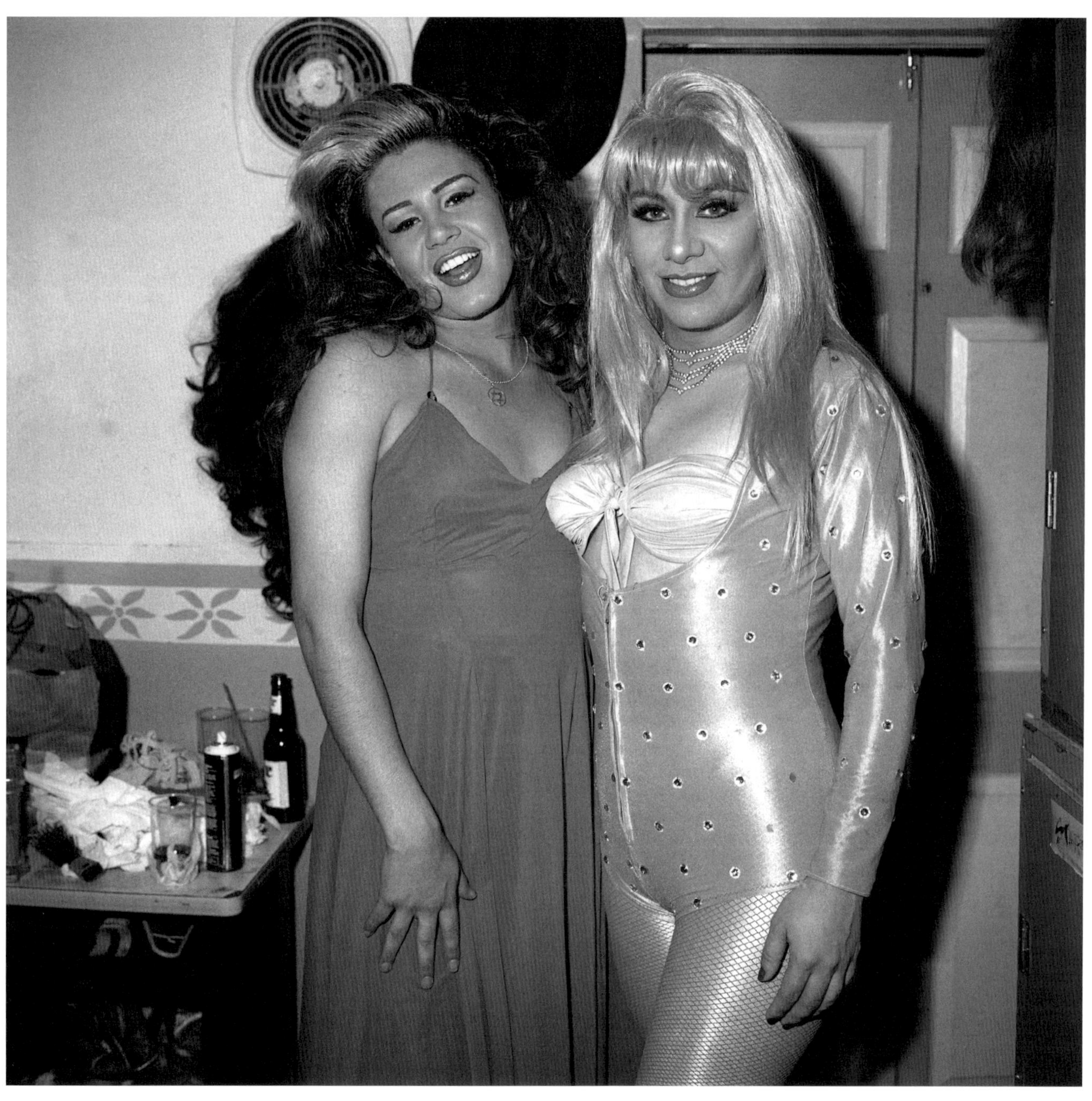

Yuri and Gloria, Le Bar (1997)

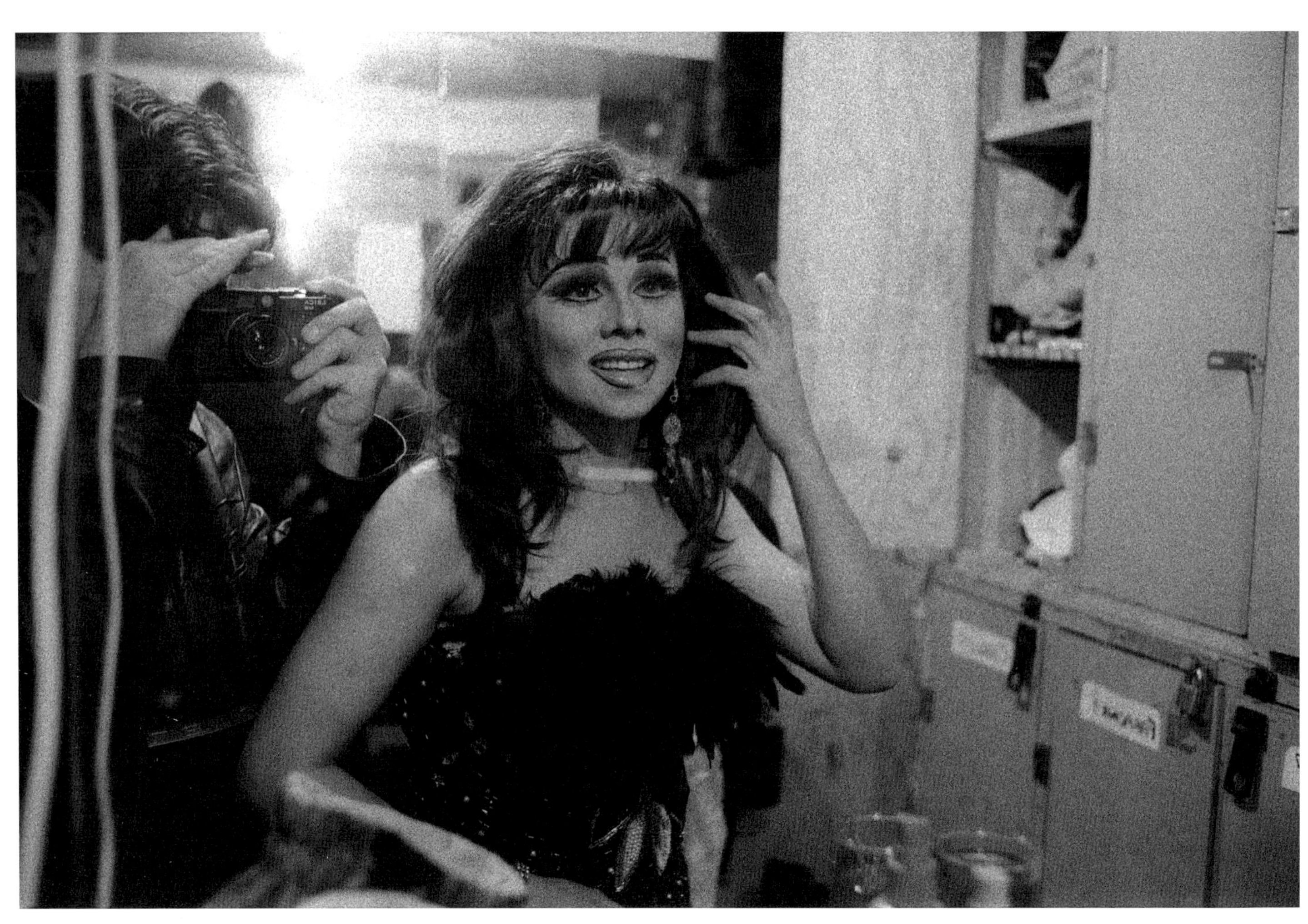

Performer, Le Bar (1997)

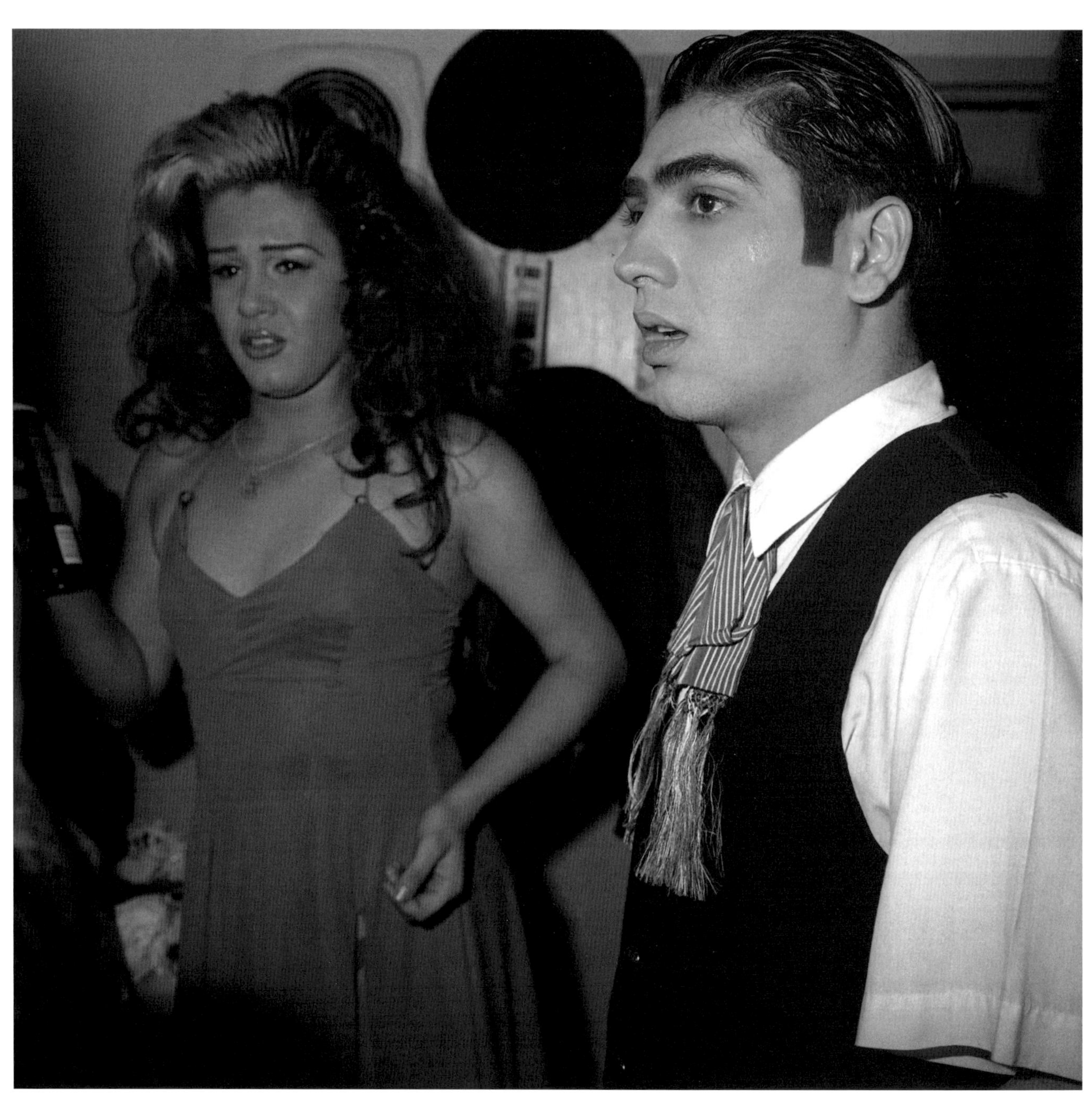

Gloria and Alejandro, Le Bar (1997)

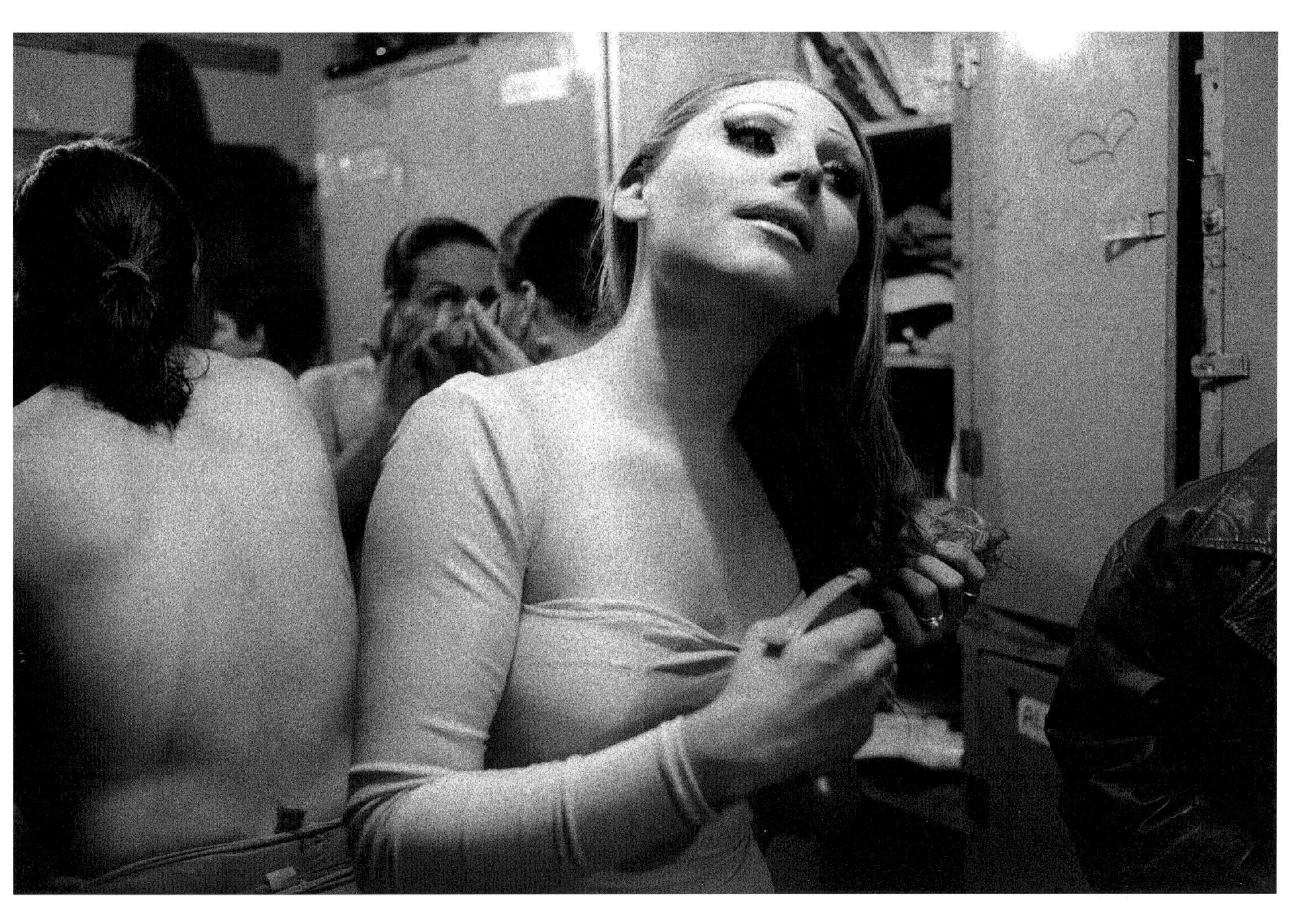

Performer, **Le Bar**, (1997)

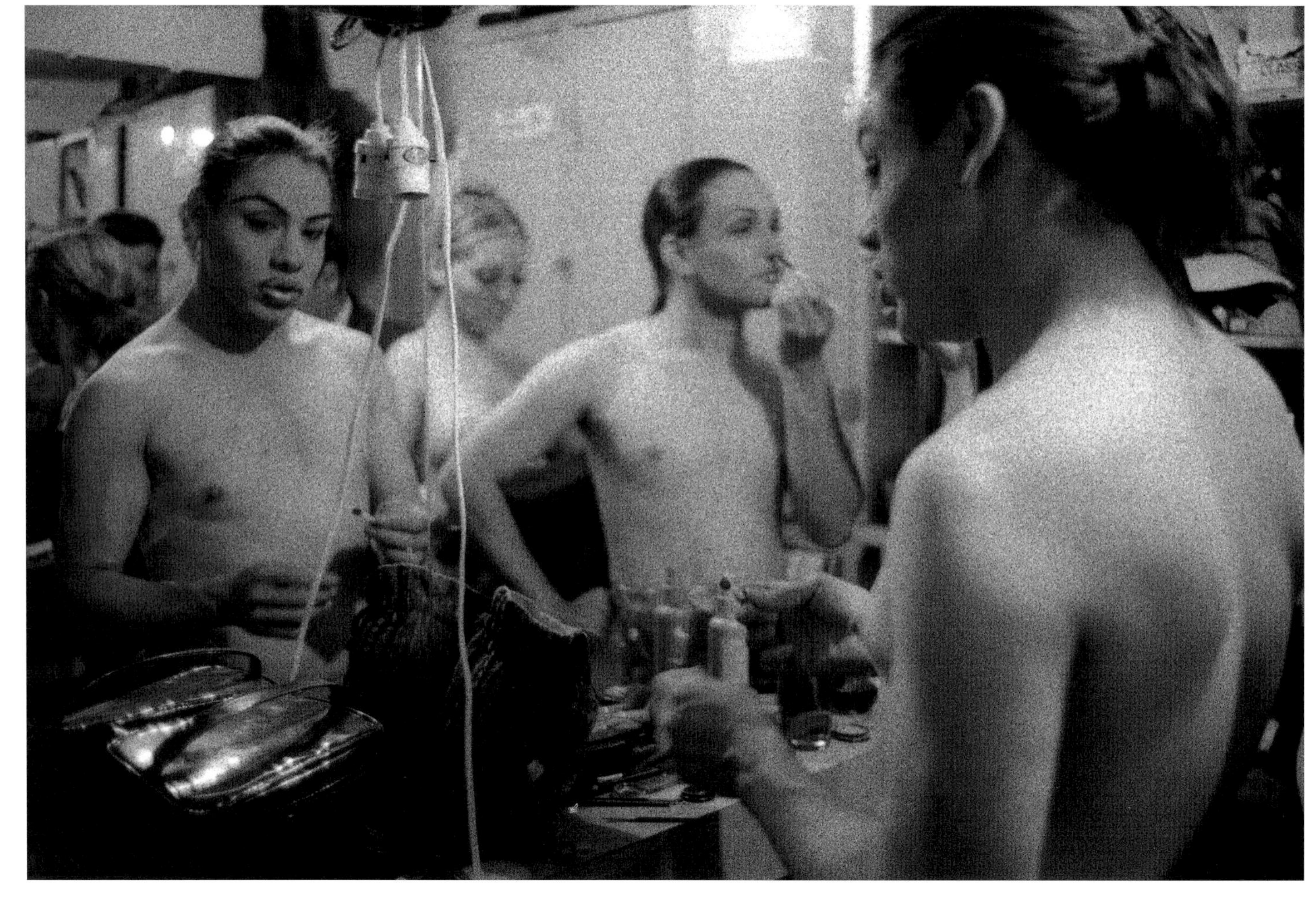

Performer, Le Bar (1997)

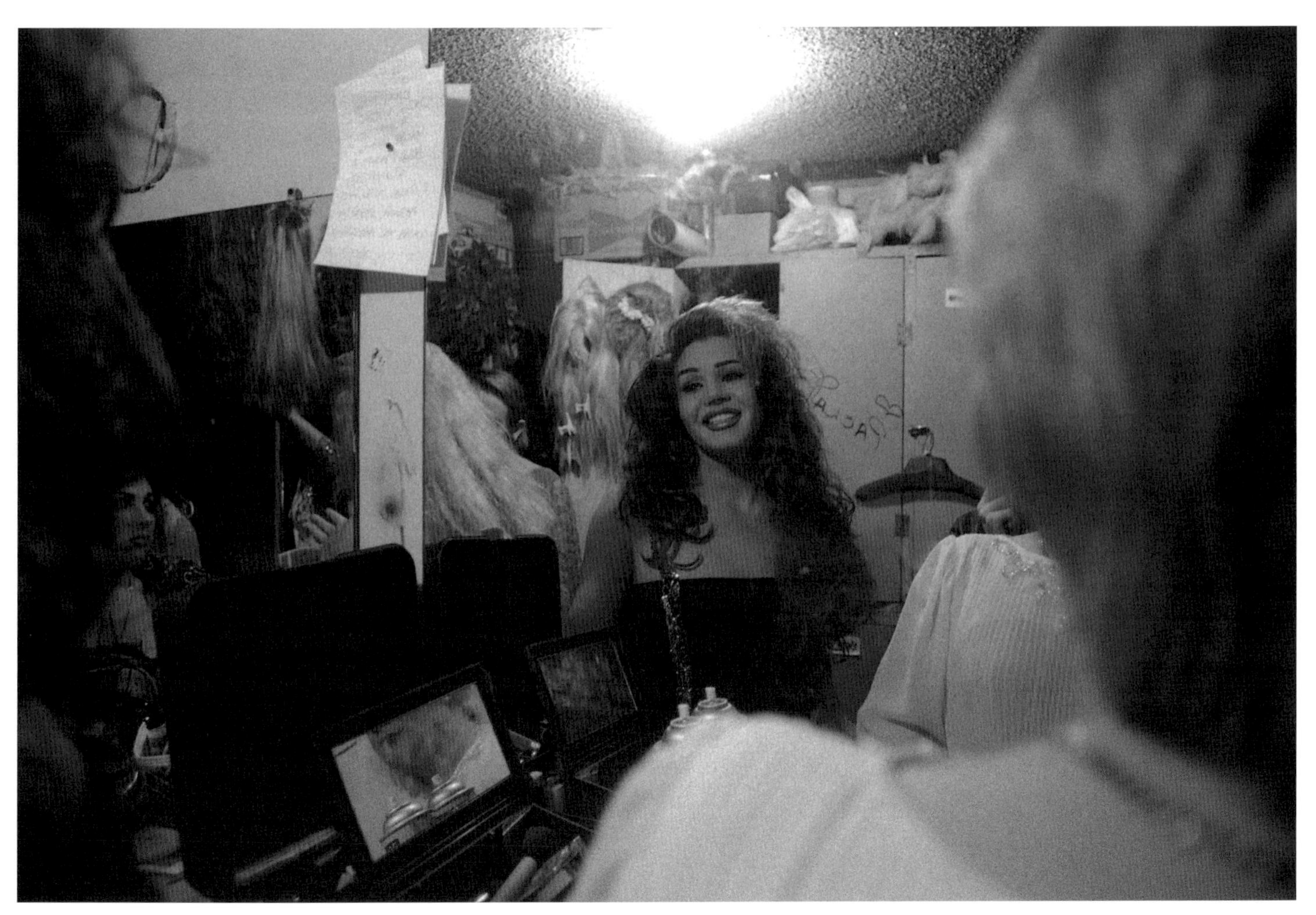

Gloria, Le Bar (1997)

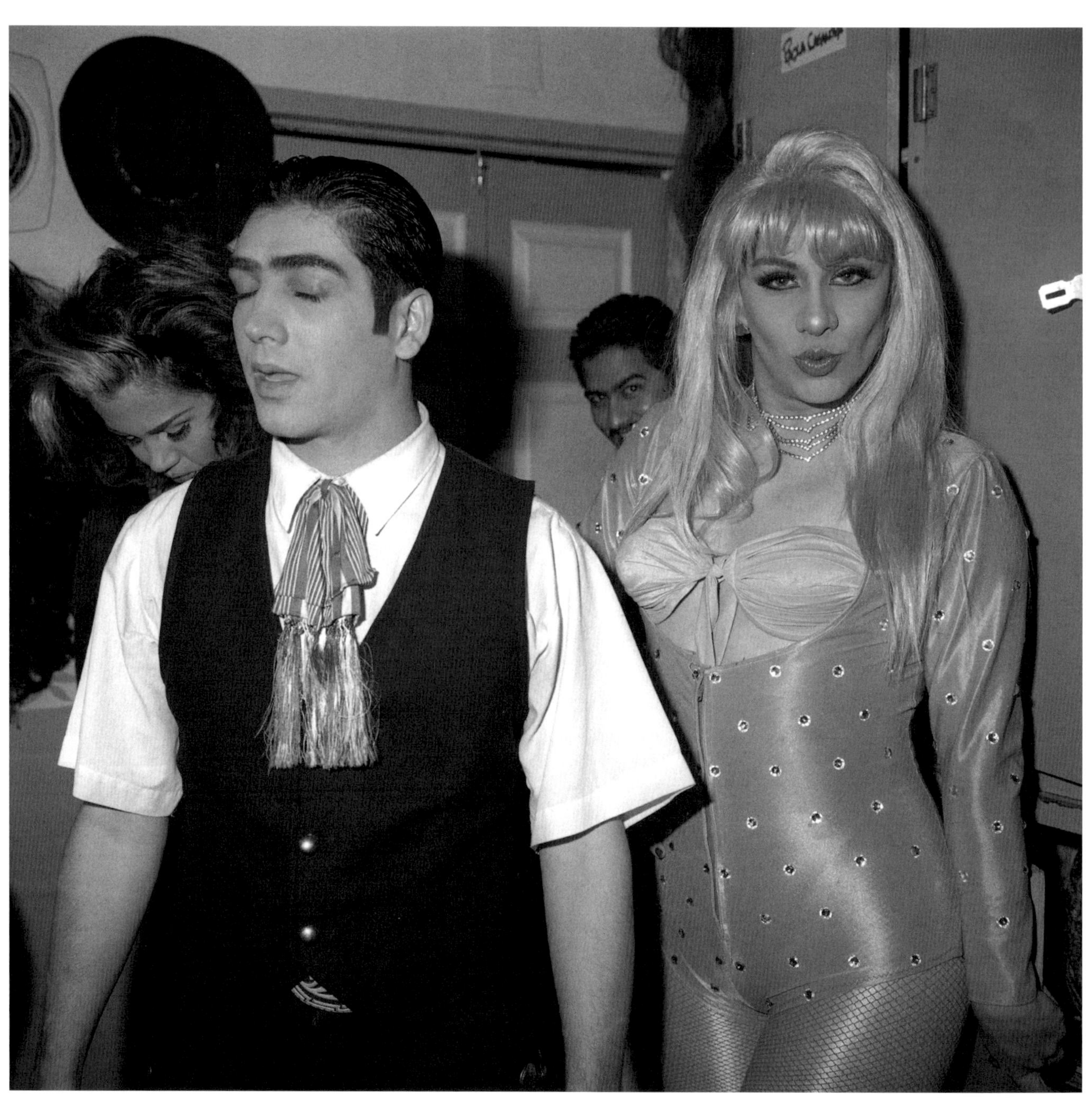

Alejandro and Yuri, Le Bar (1997)

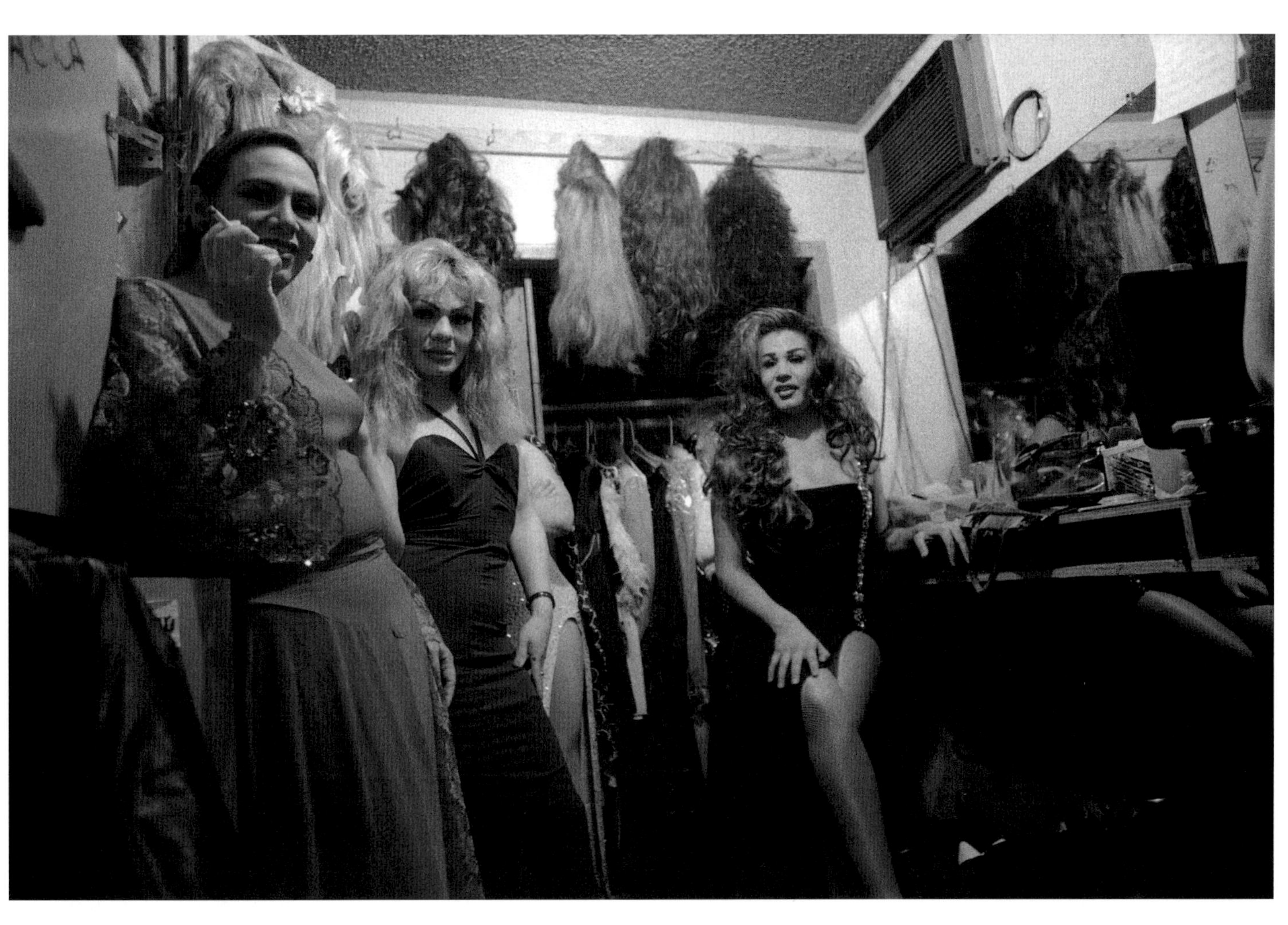

Performers and Gloria, Le Bar (1997)

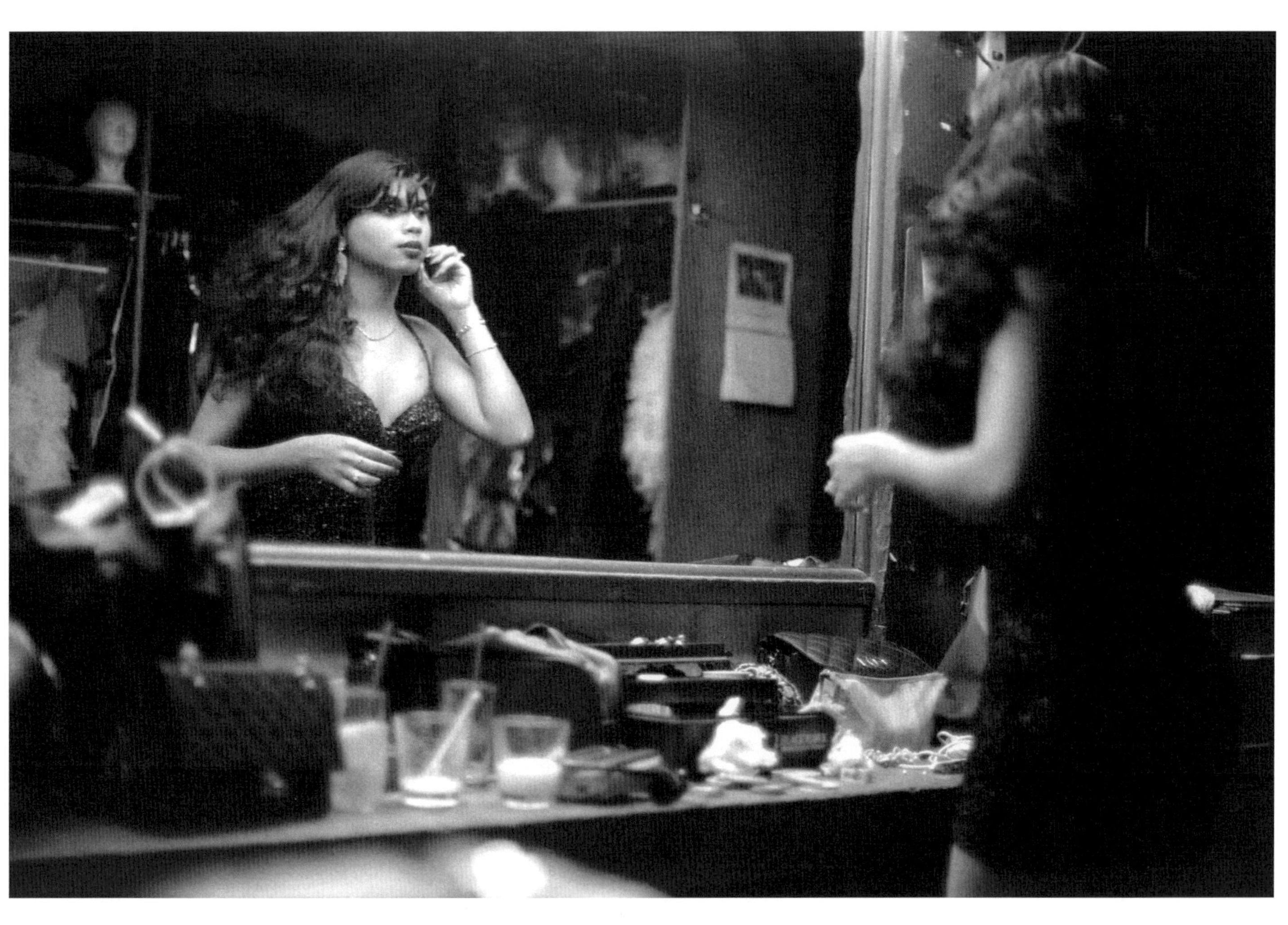

Performer, La Plaza (1997)

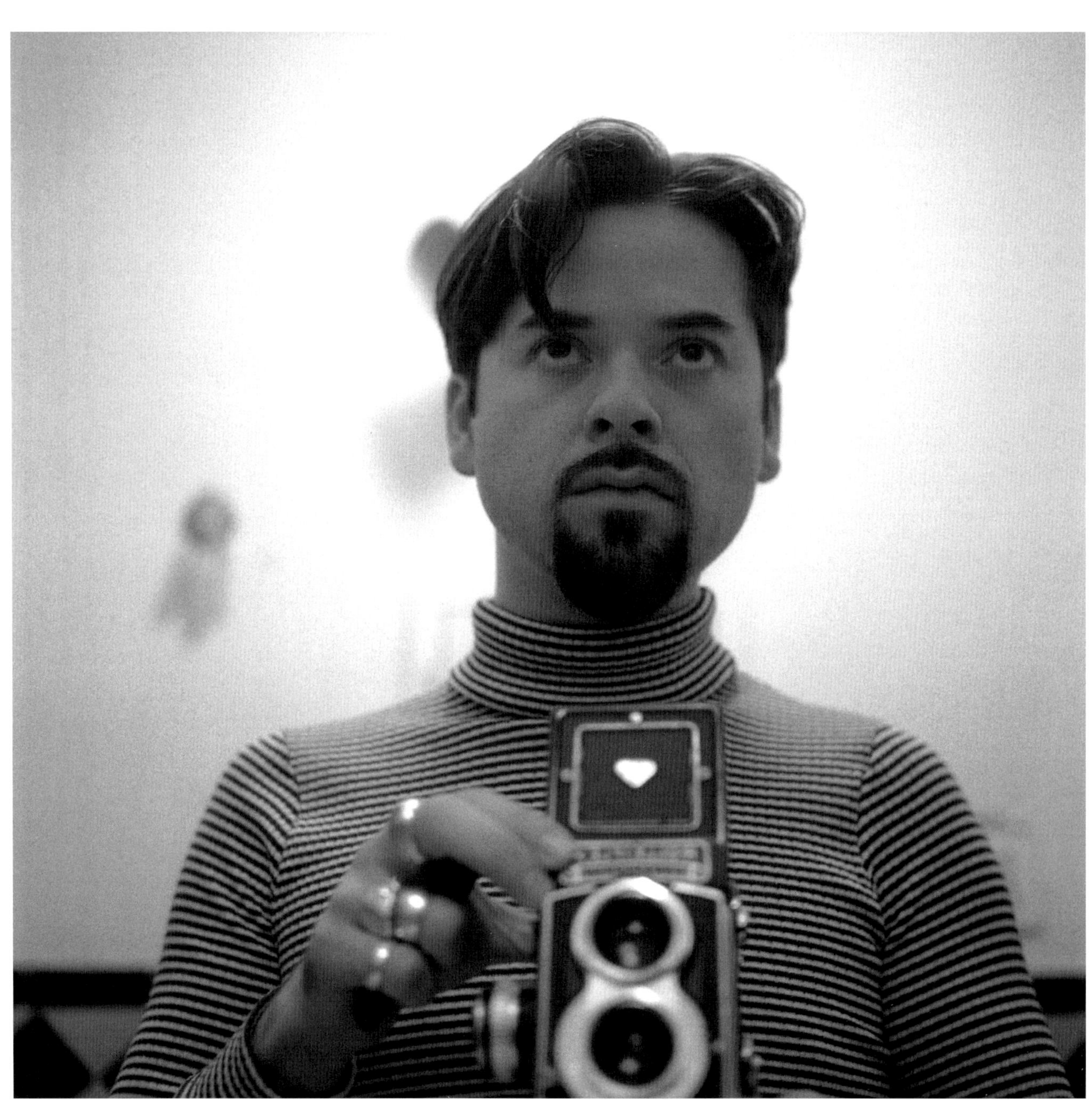

Reynaldo Rivera, Echo Park (1996)

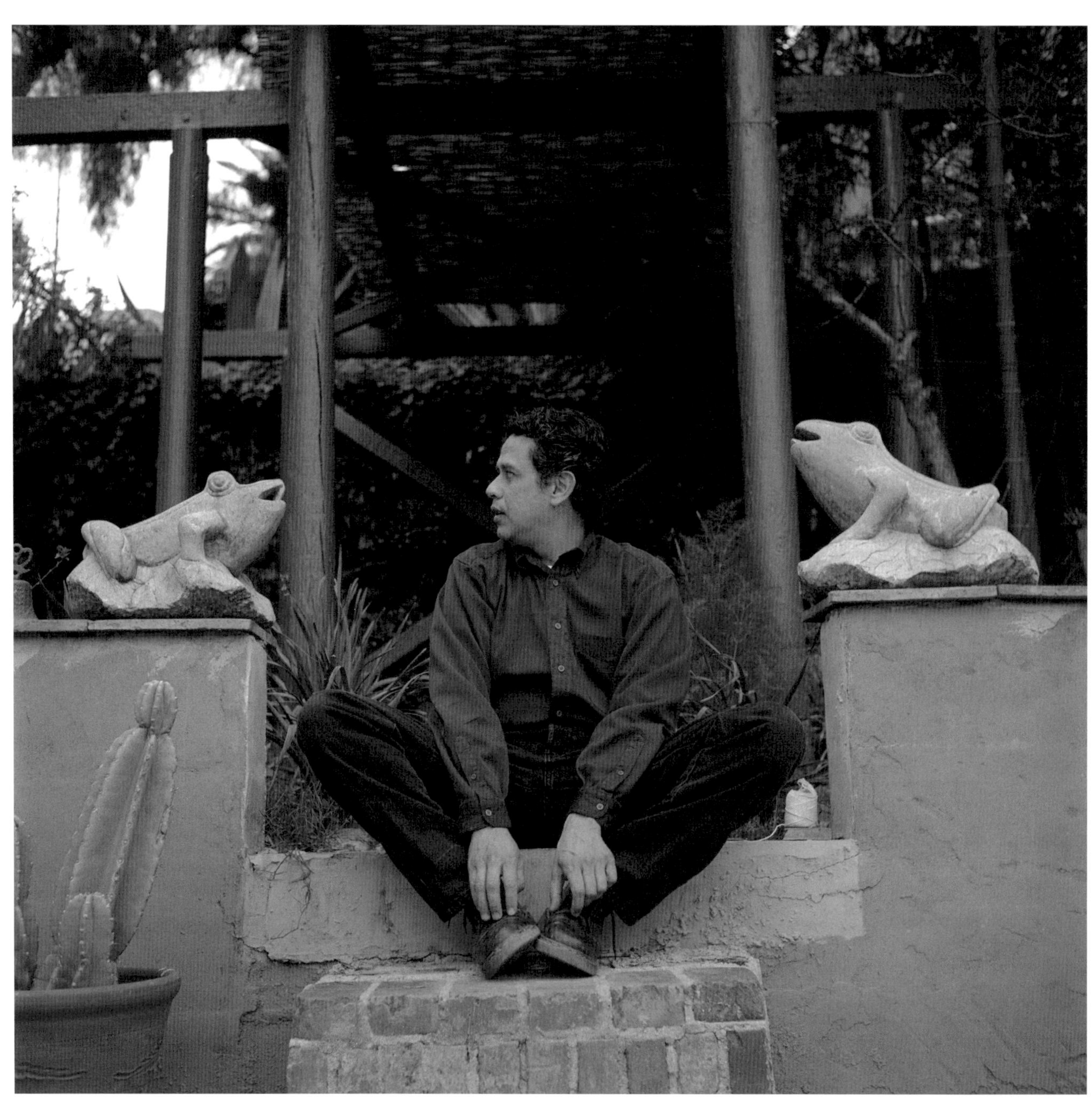

Roberto Gil de Montes, Echo Park (1995)

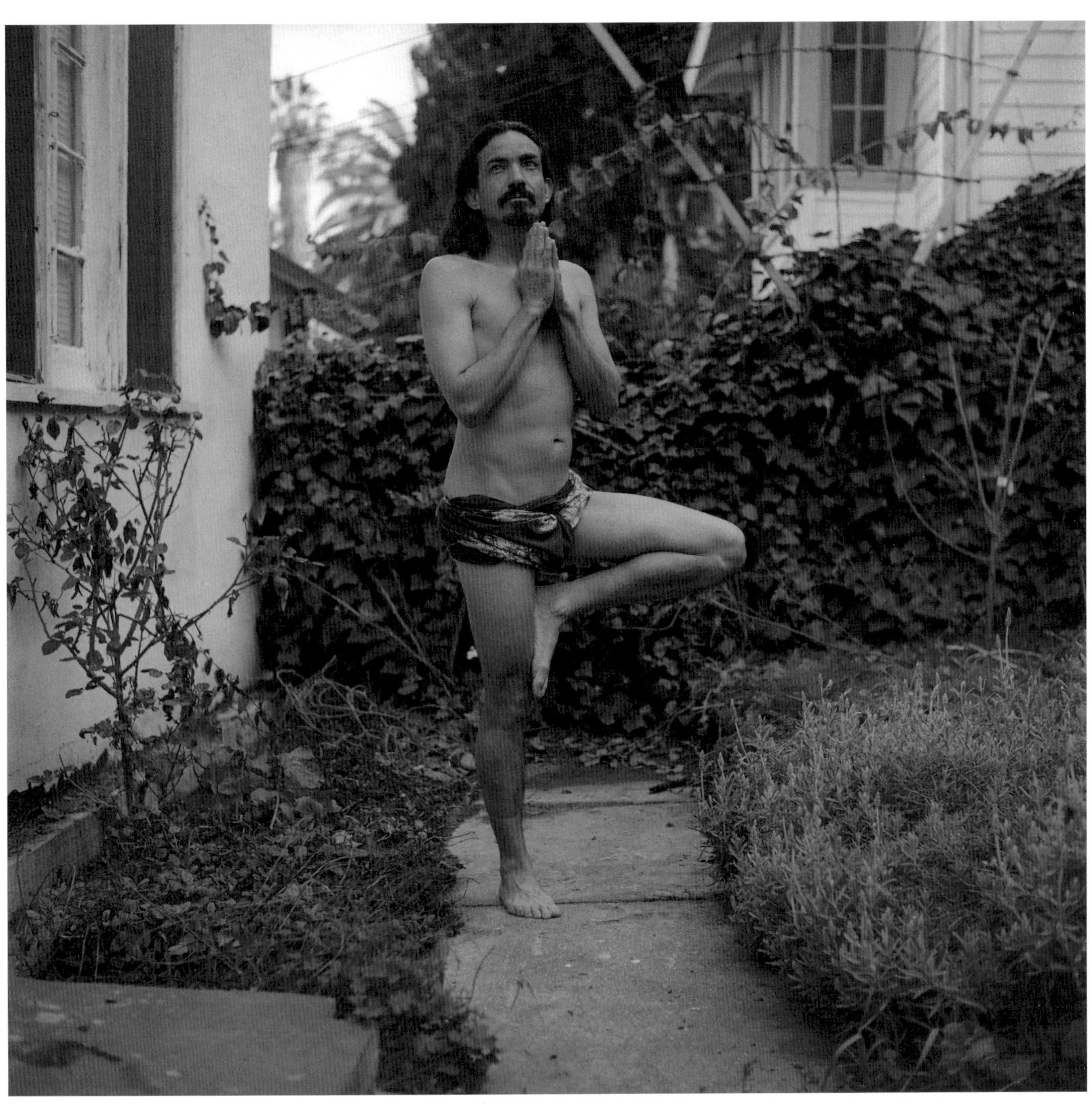

Francesco Siqueiros, Echo Park (1993)

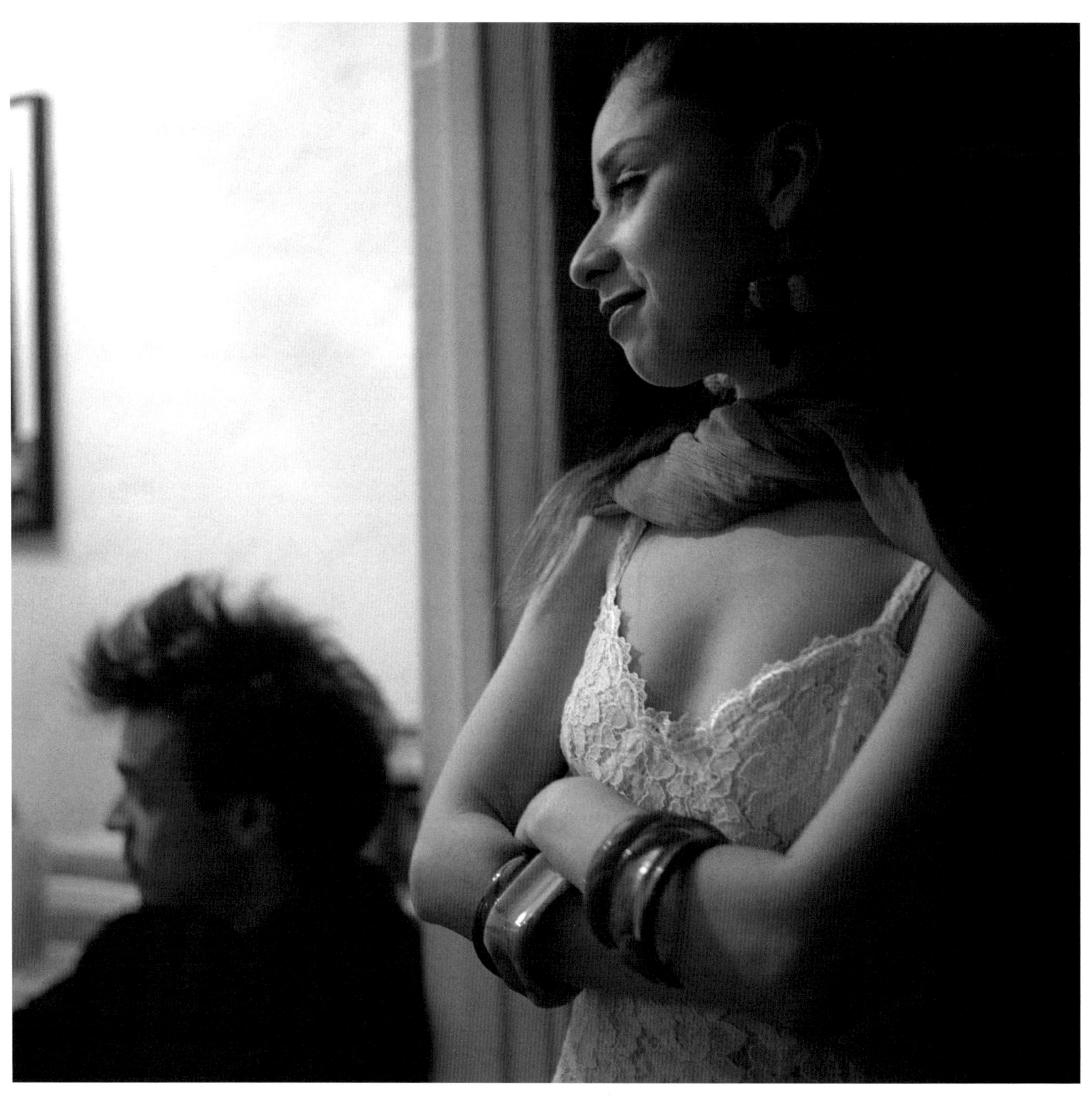

Daniel Martinez and Herminia Rivera, Echo Park (1994)

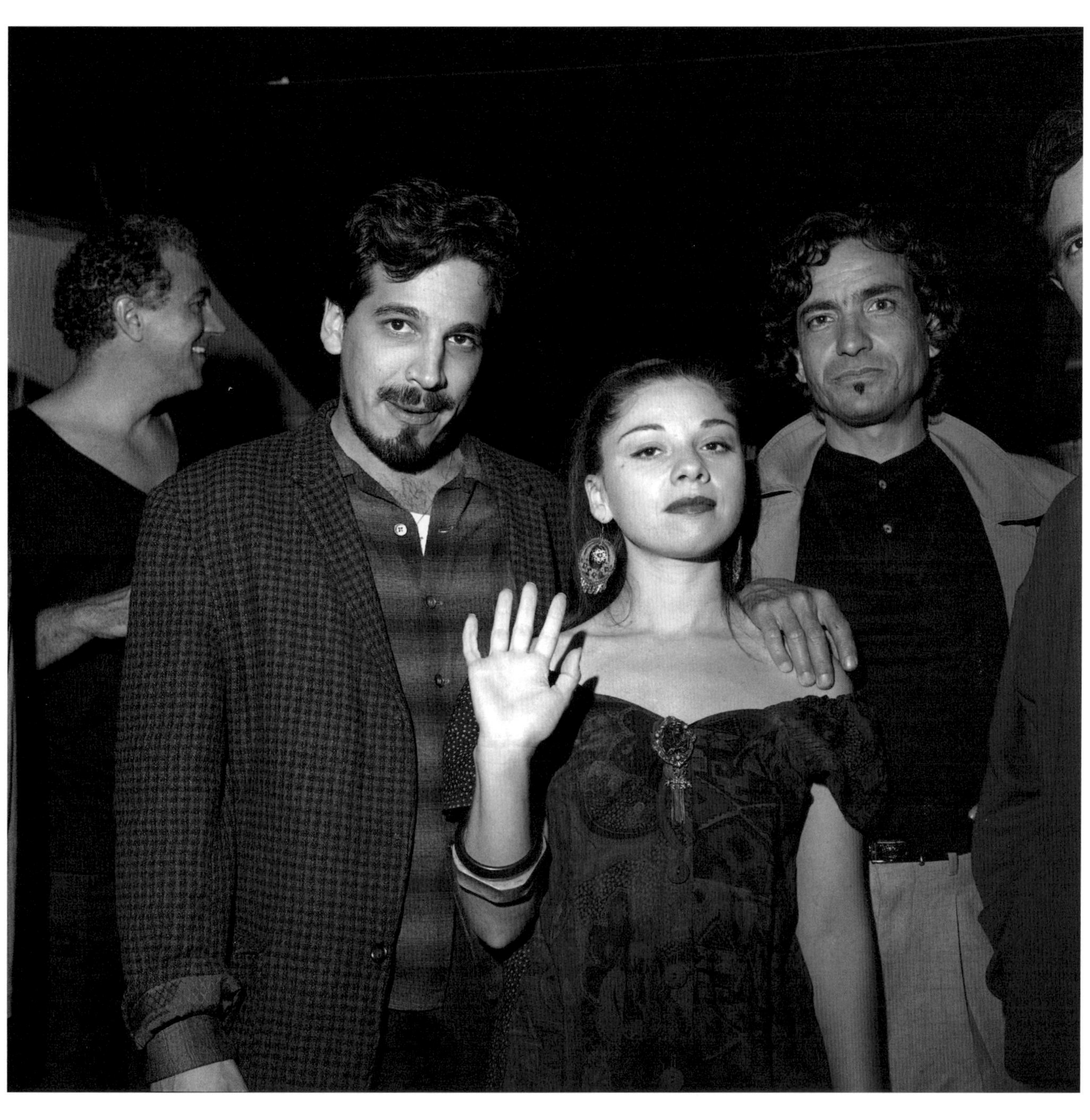

**Rubén Martínez, Herminia Rivera,
and Francesco Siqueiros**, Echo Park (1993)

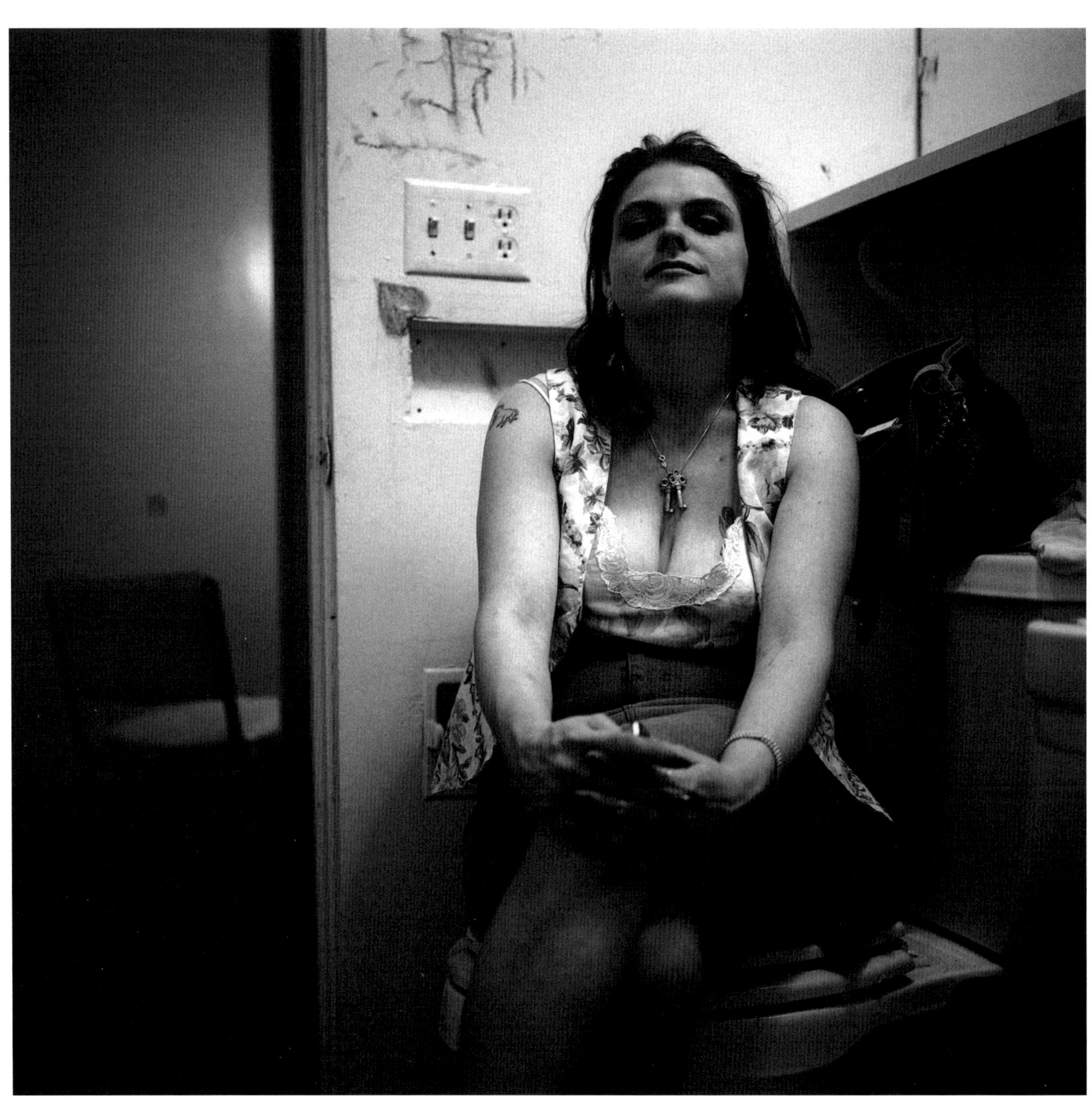

Untitled, Downtown (1996)

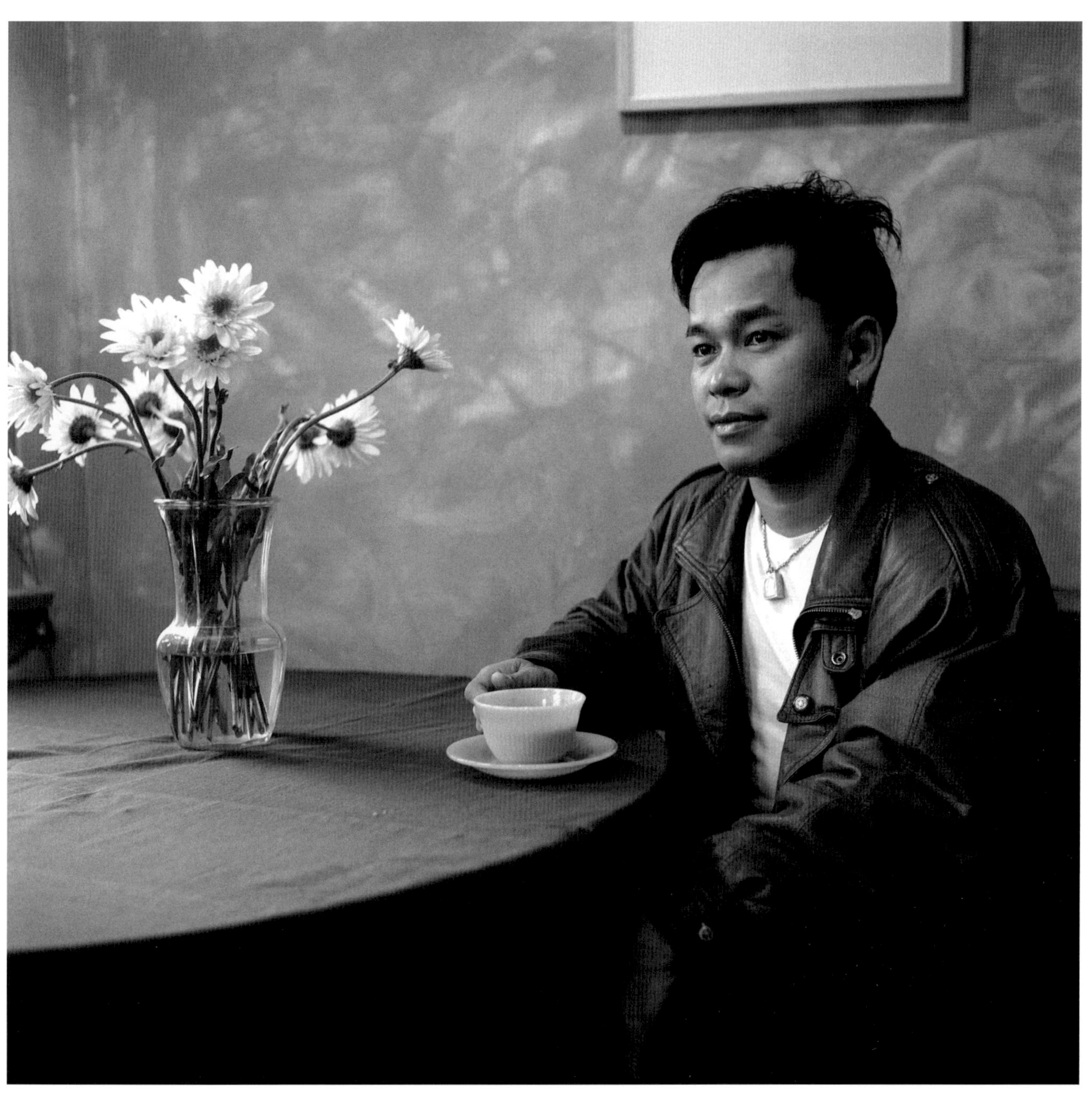

Ou, Echo Park (1995)

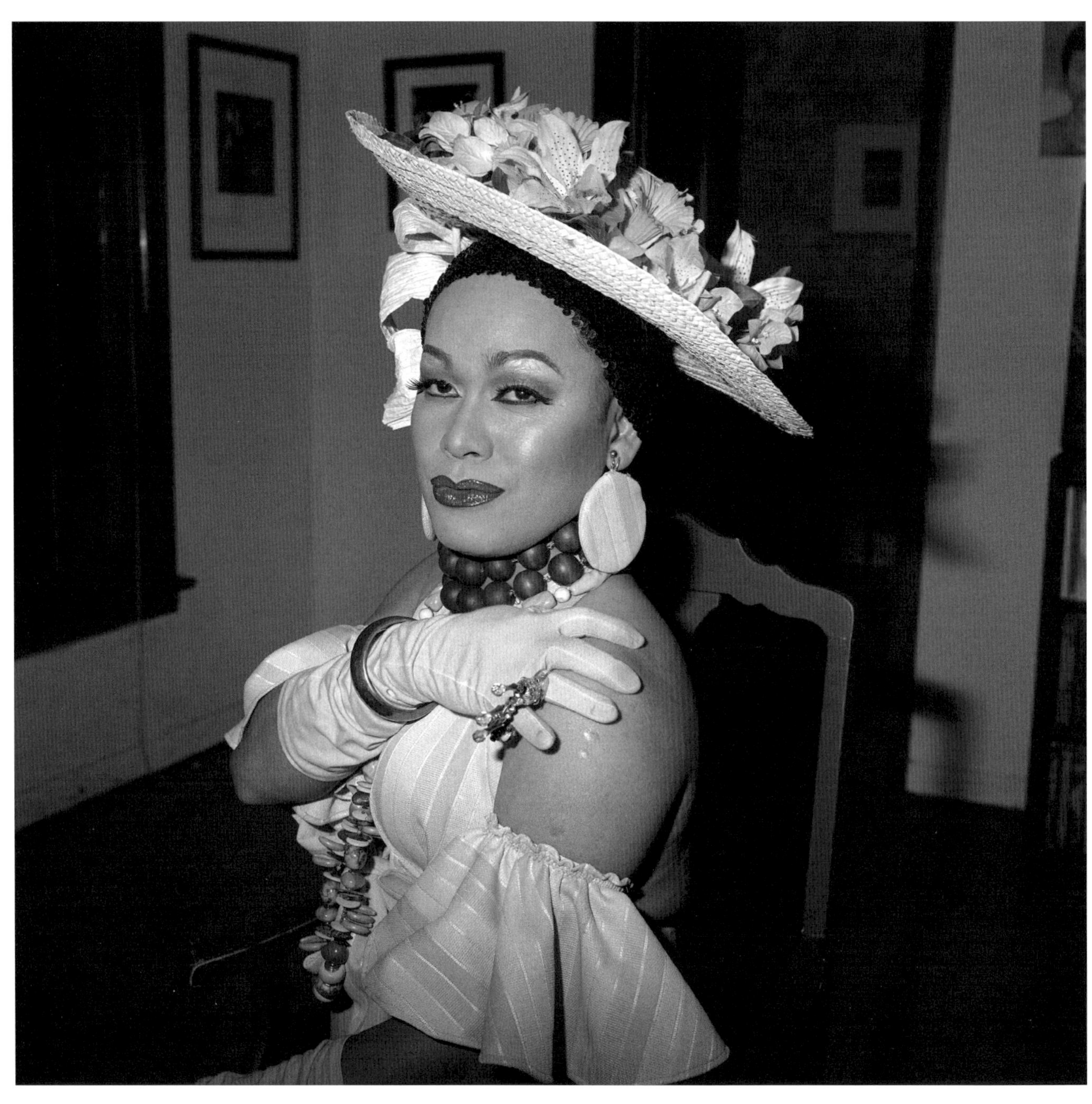

Tina, Echo Park (1995)

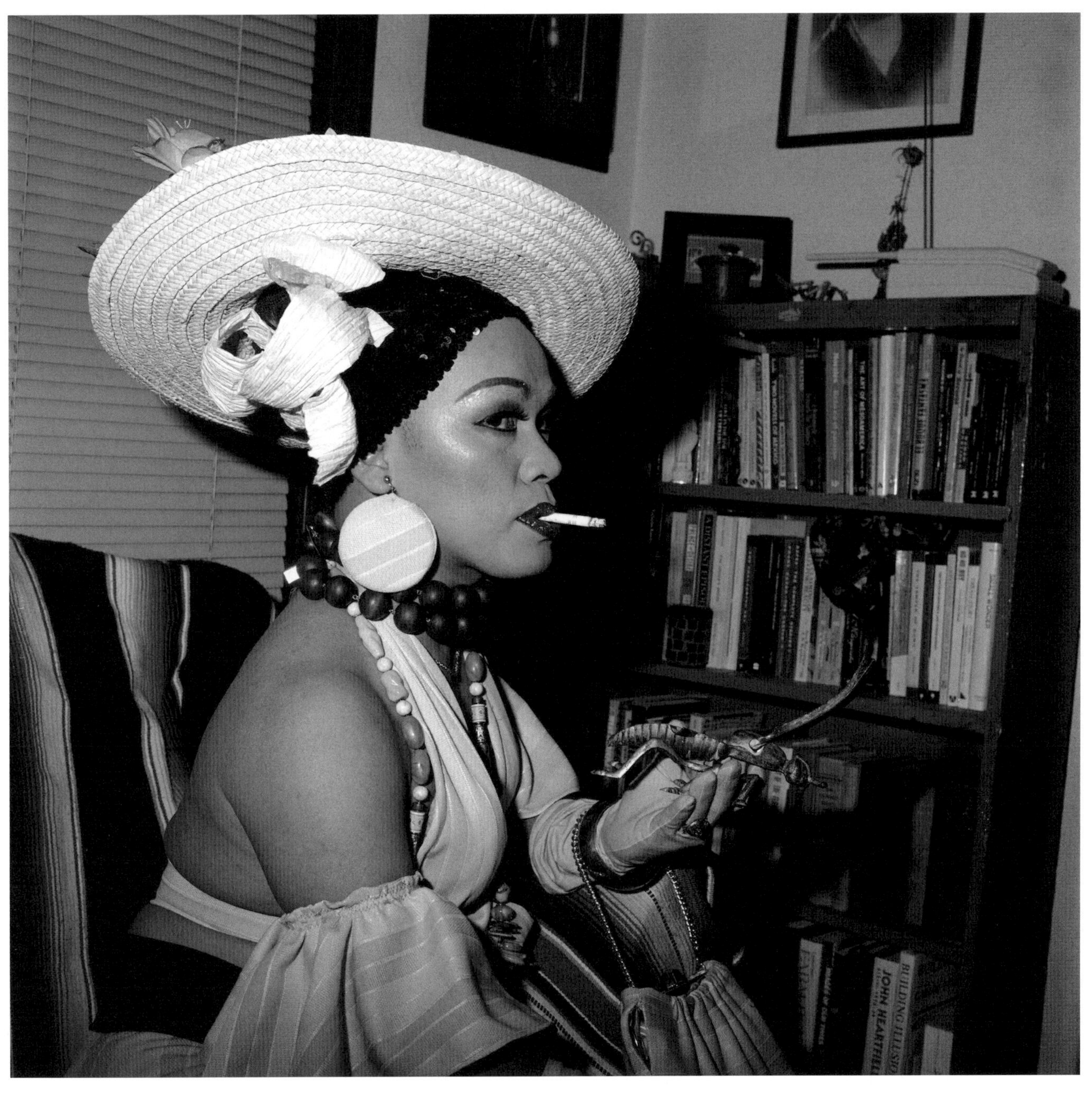

Tina, Echo Park (1995)

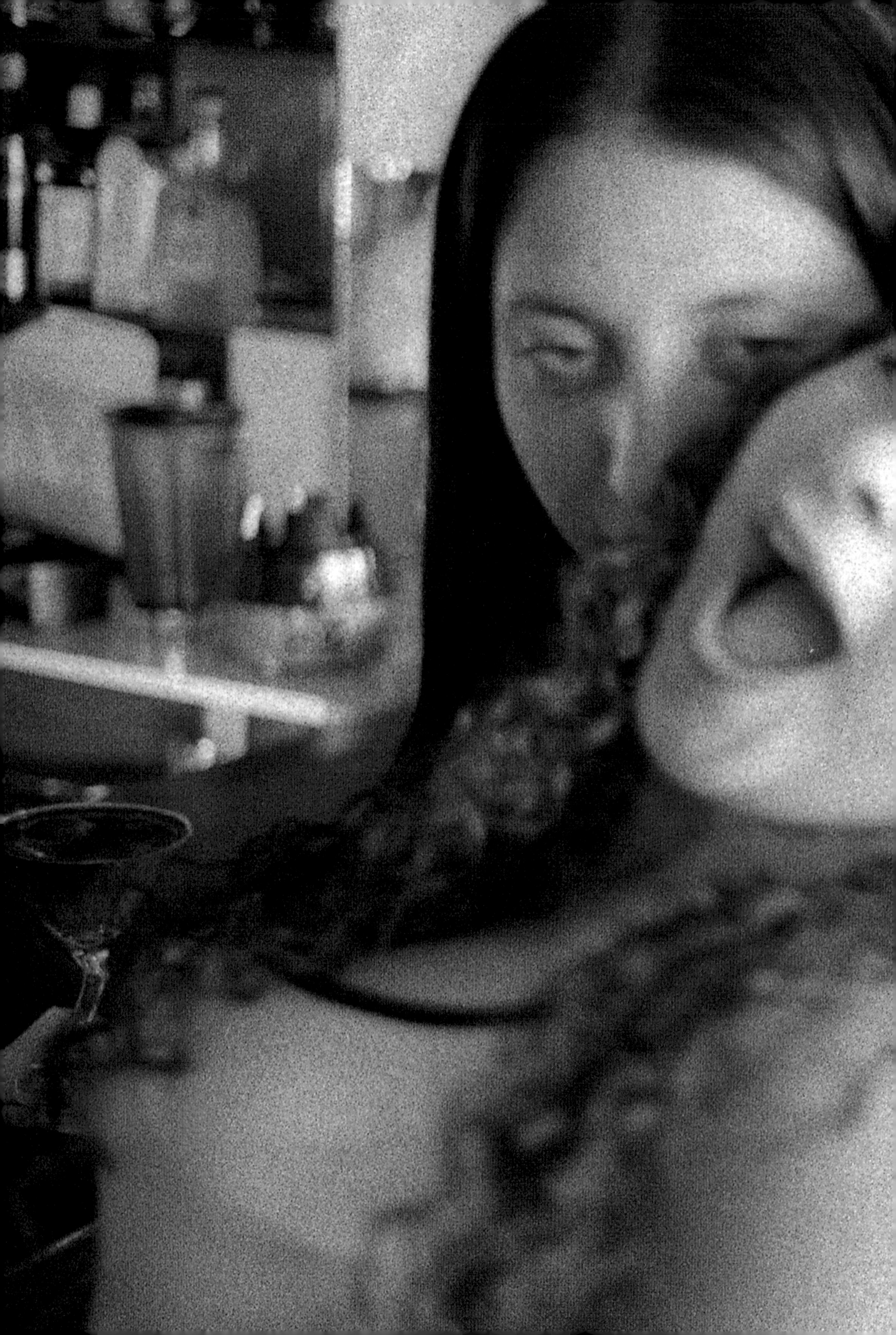

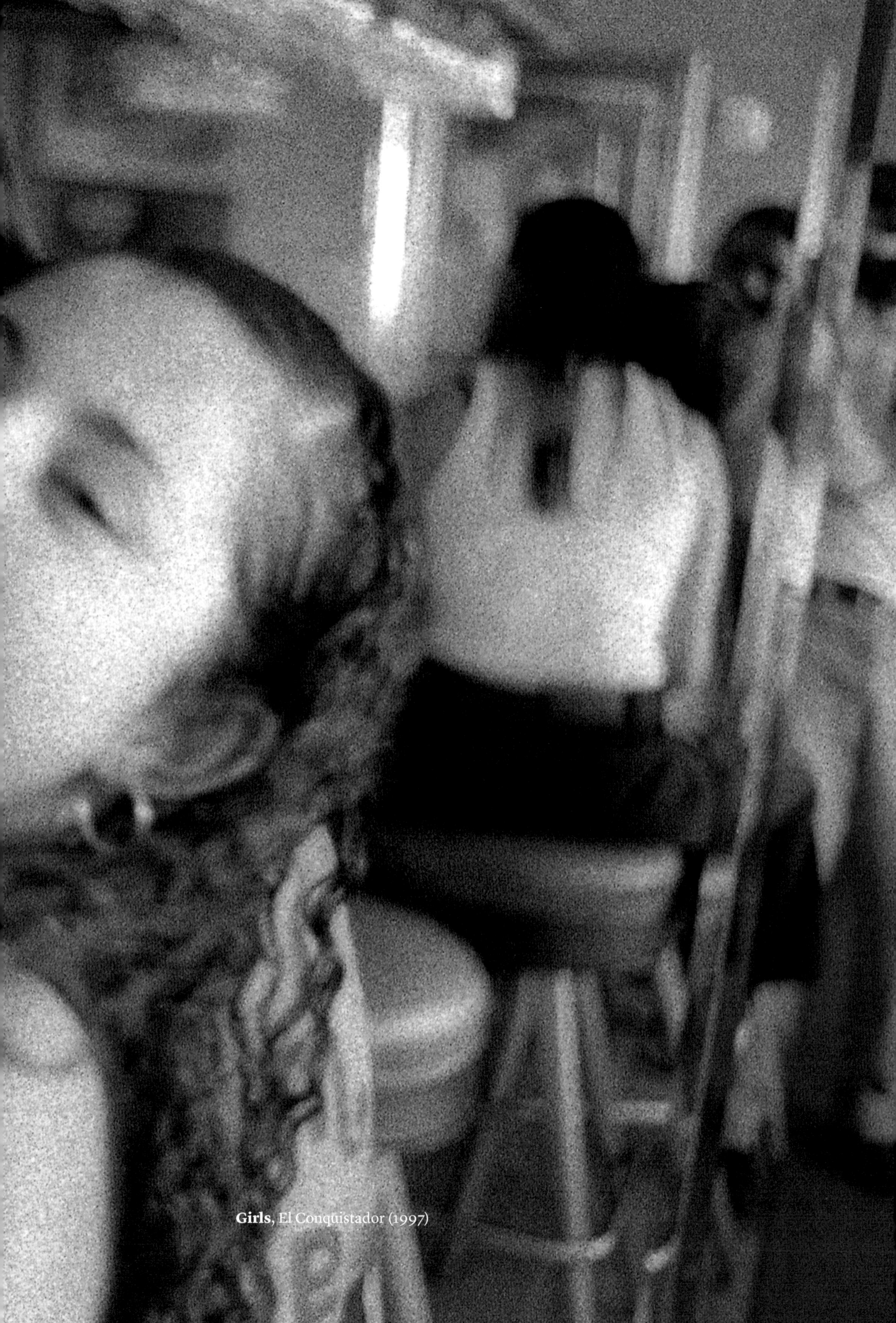

Girls, El Conquistador (1997)

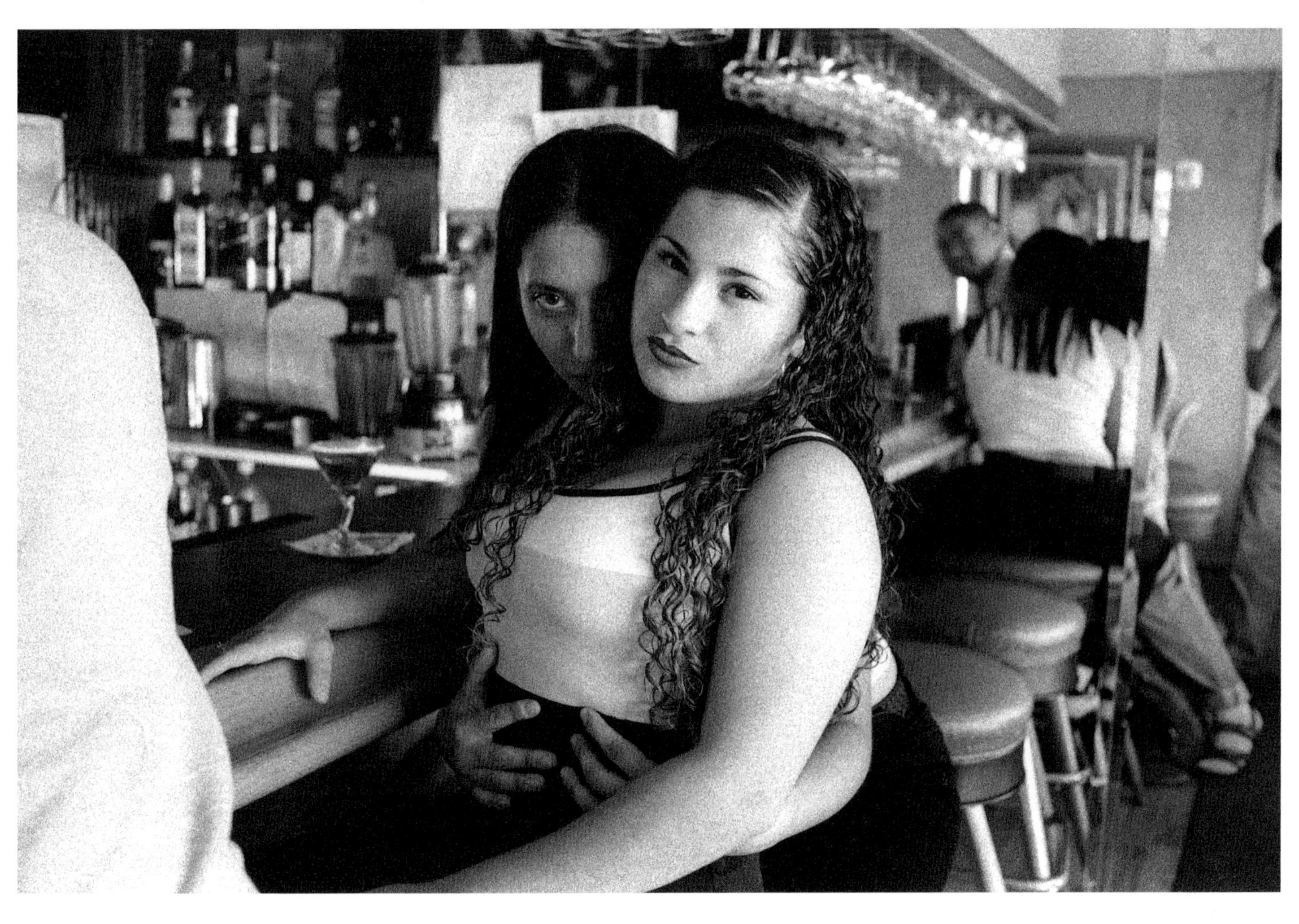

Girls, El Conquistador (1997)

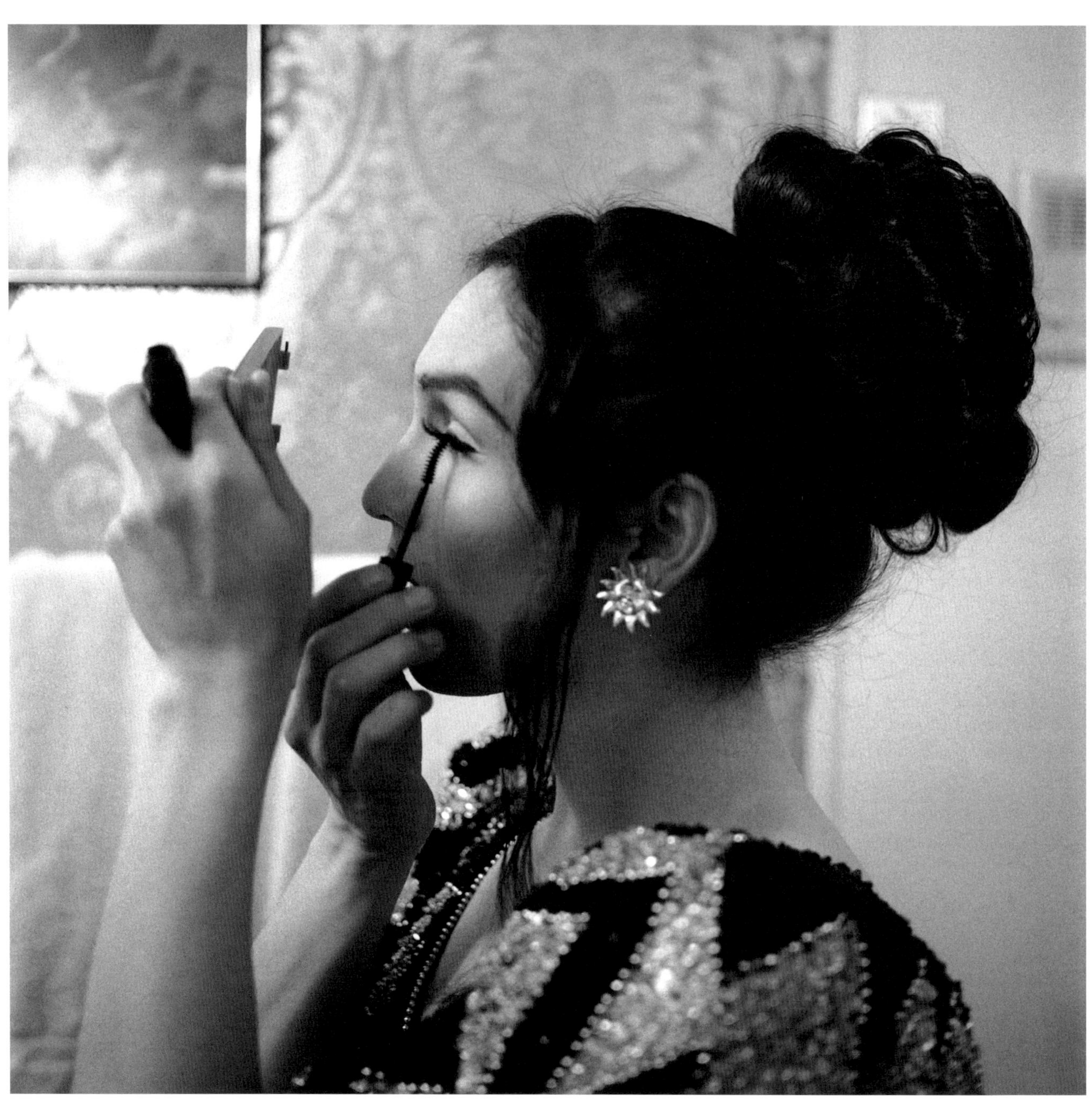

Stephanie, Echo Park (1994)

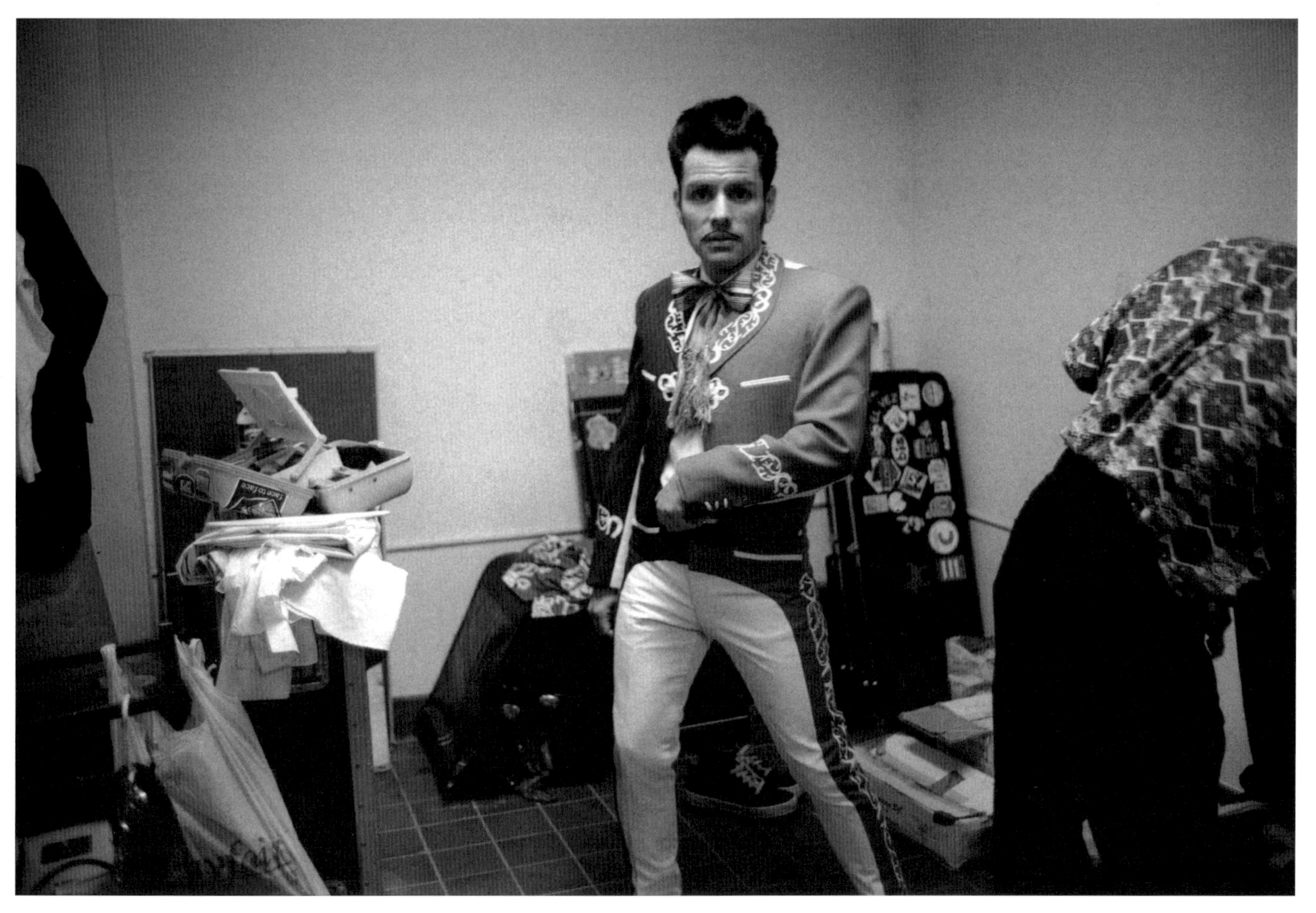

El Vez, Hollywood (1996)

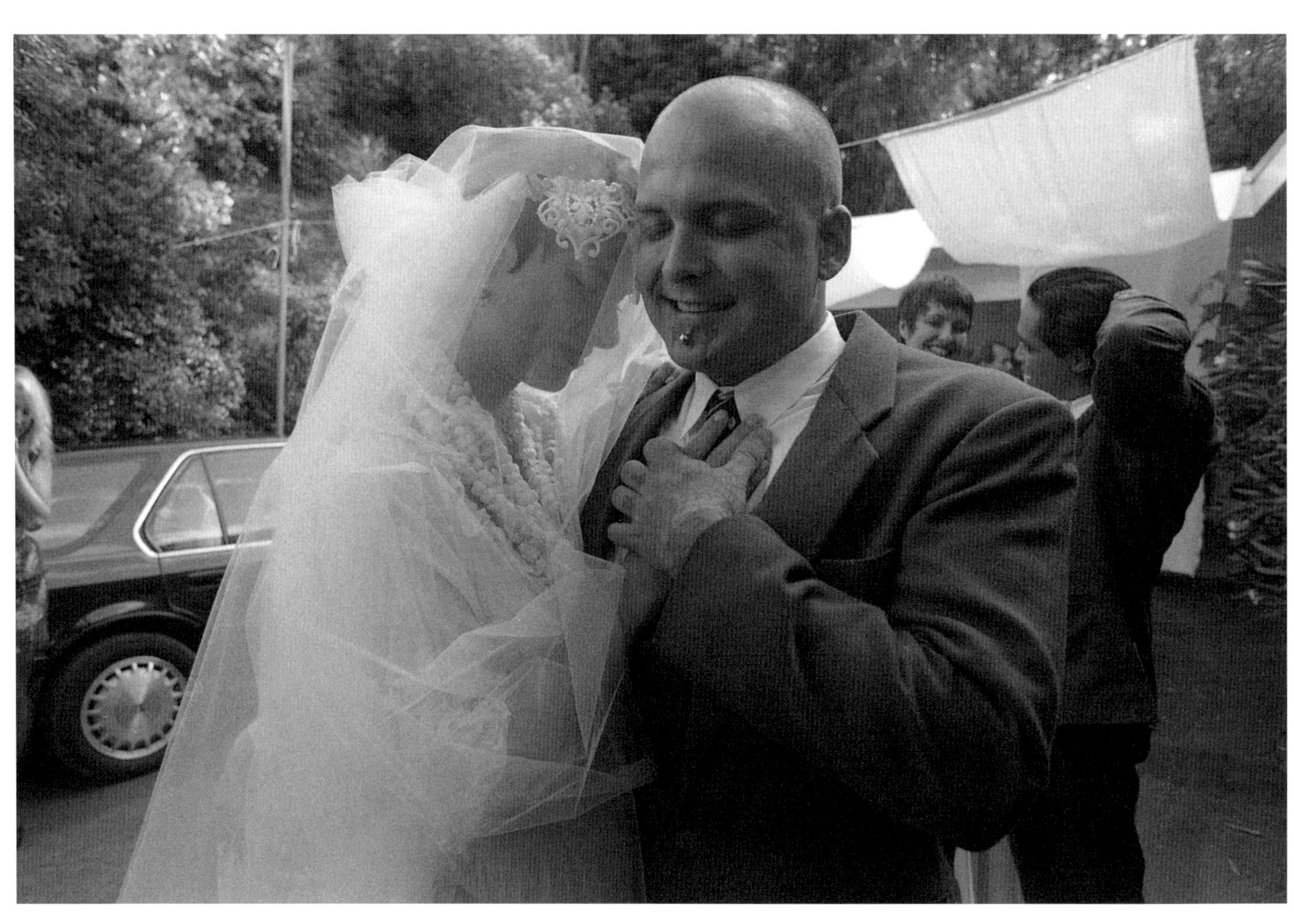

Ron Athey and Elyse Regehr, Hollywood Hills (1990)

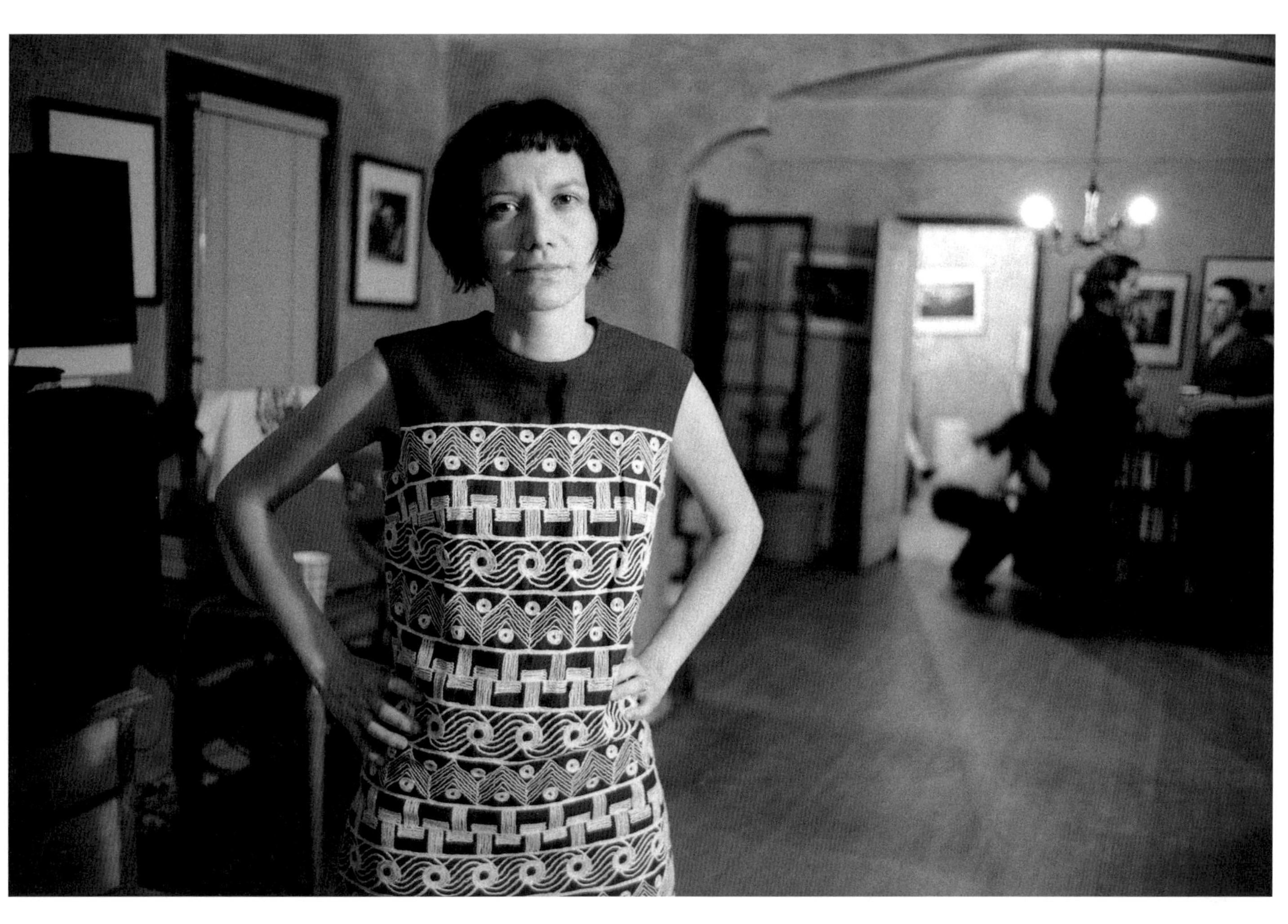

Rita Gonzales, Echo Park (1995)

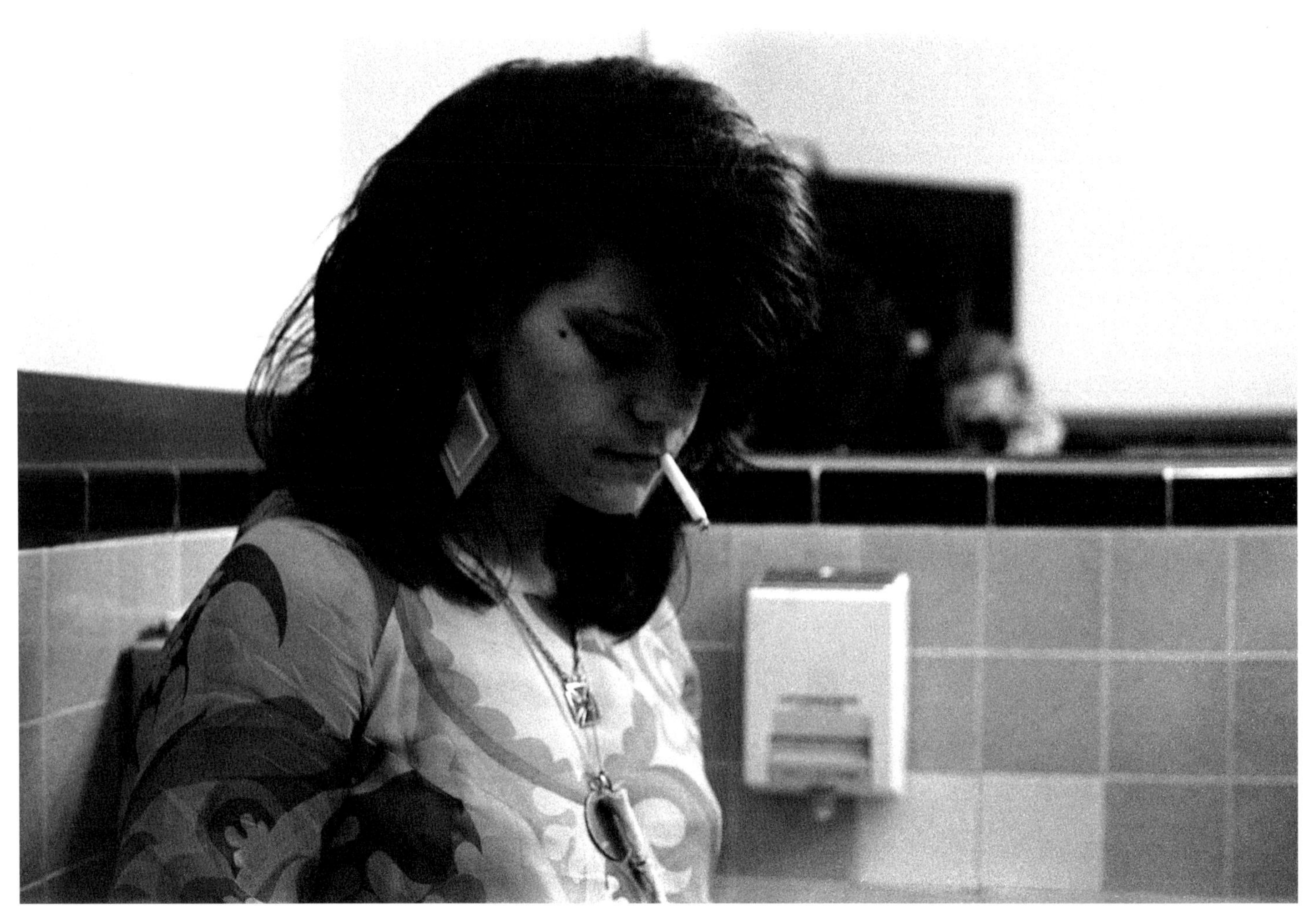

Julie, Hollywood (1985)

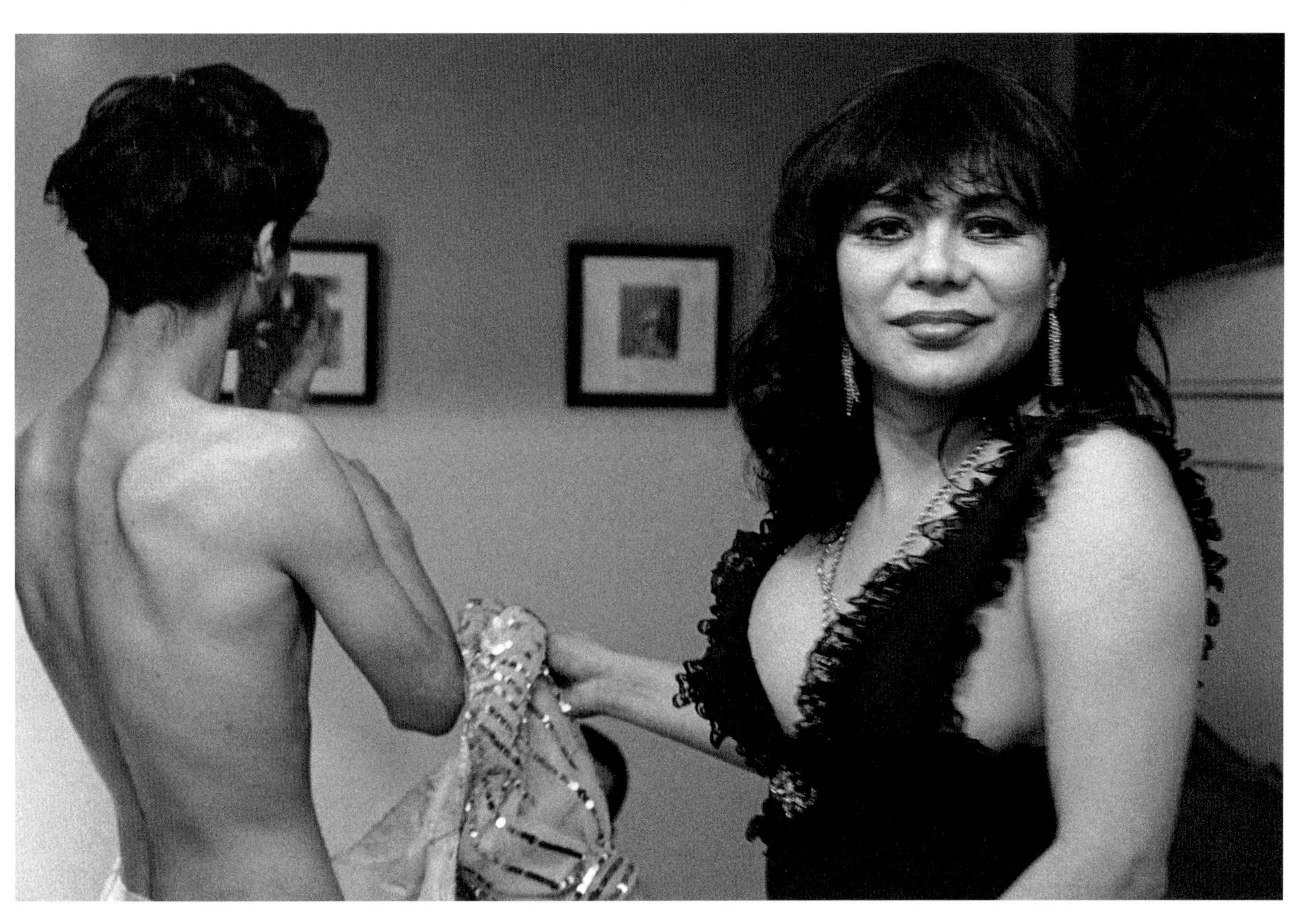

Miss Alex, Echo Park (1992)

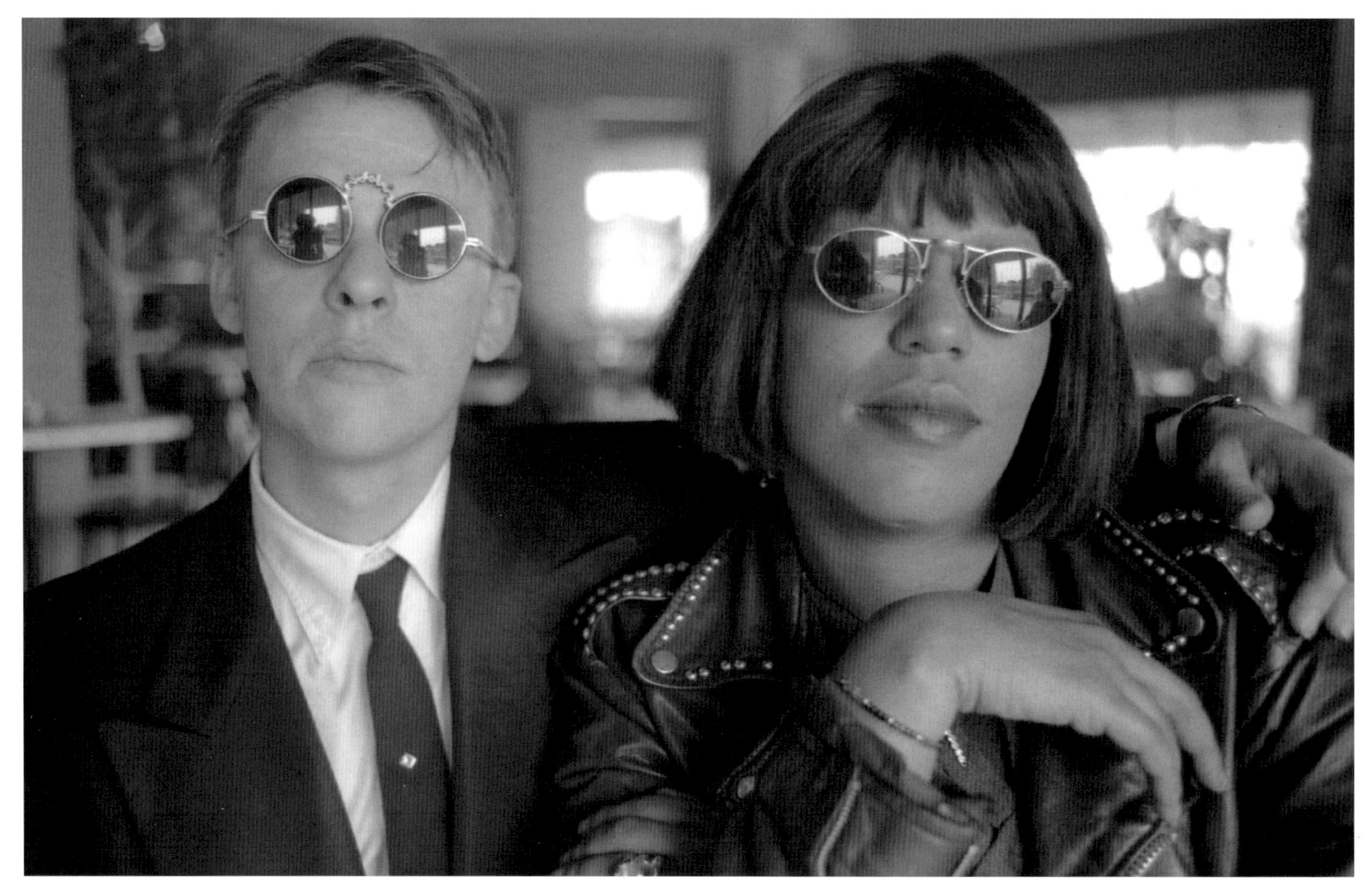

Paul Christian Kuhni and Taquila Mockingbird,
Atlas Bar and Grill (1992)

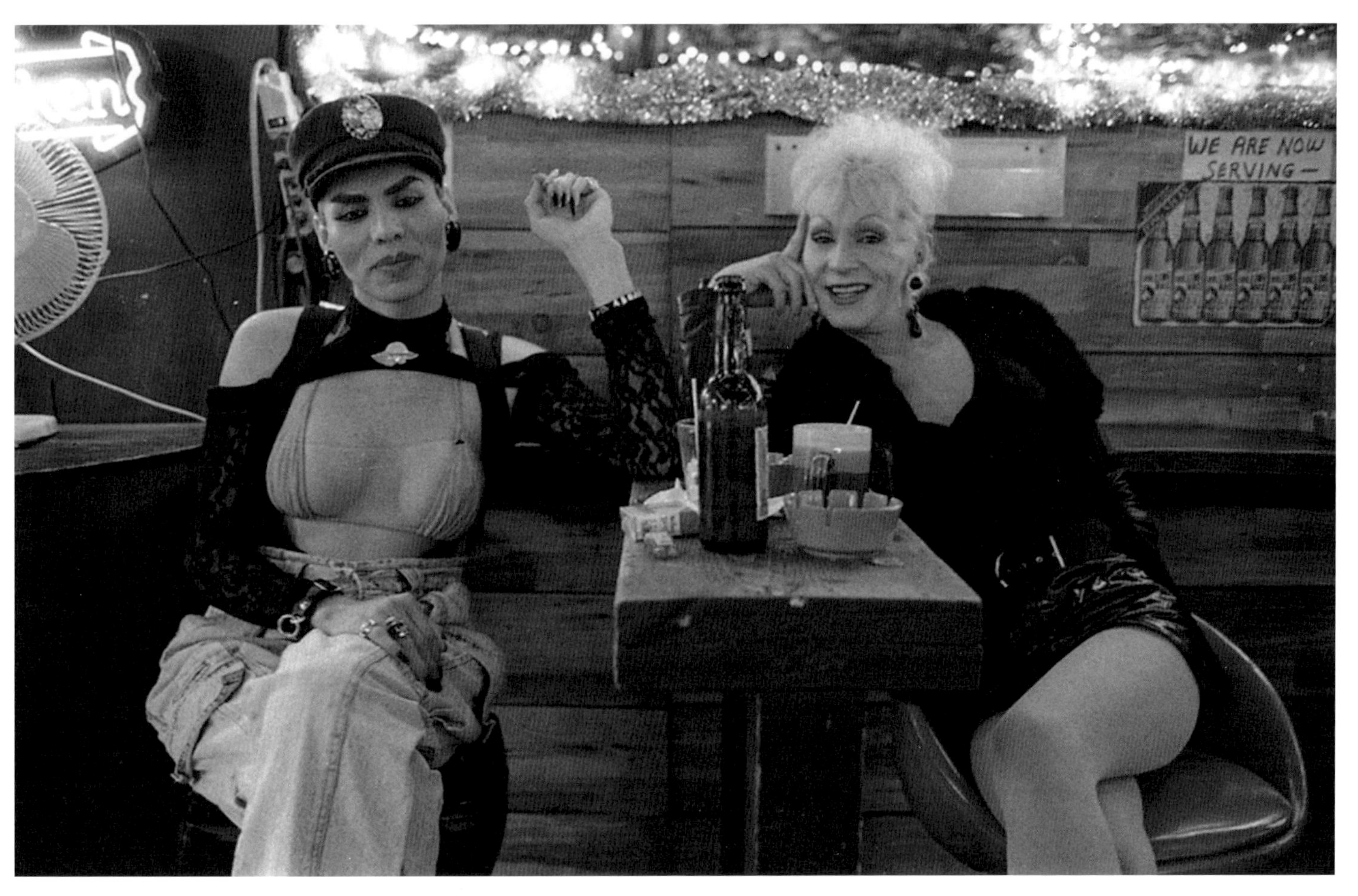

Untitled, Downtown (1993)

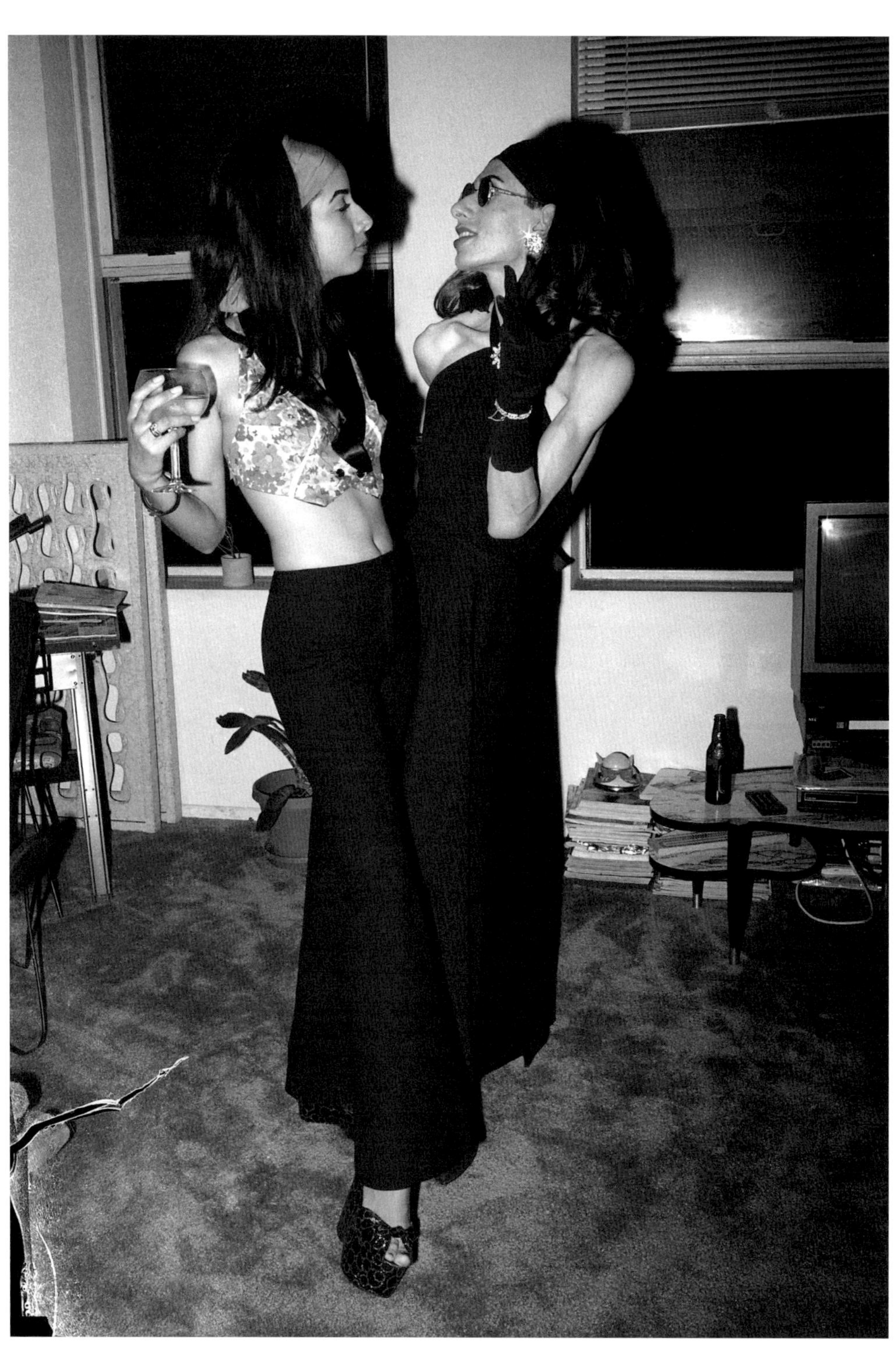

Cynthia and Juan, Downtown (1989)

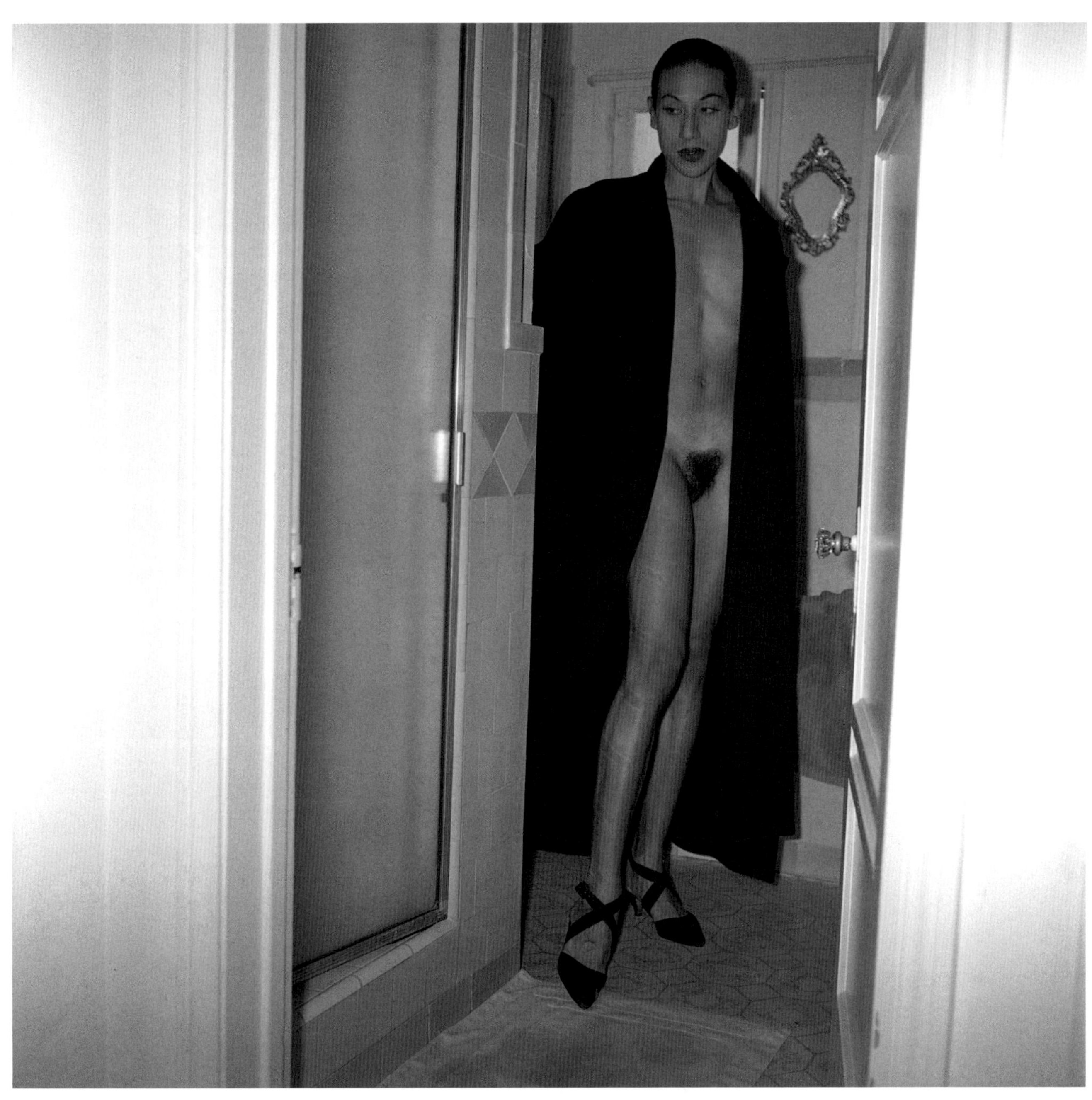

Javier, Miracle Mile (1993)

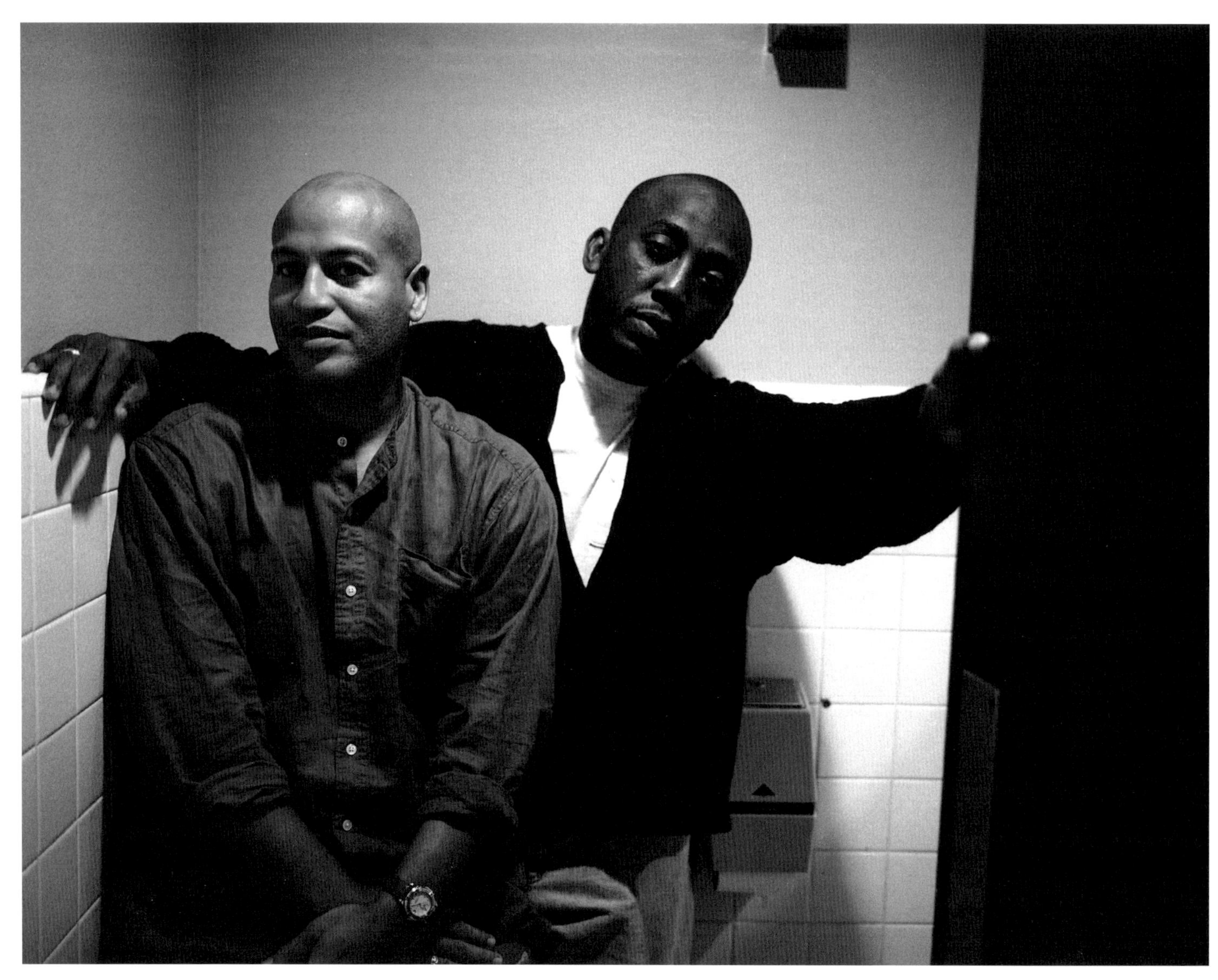

The Study, Hollywood (1996)

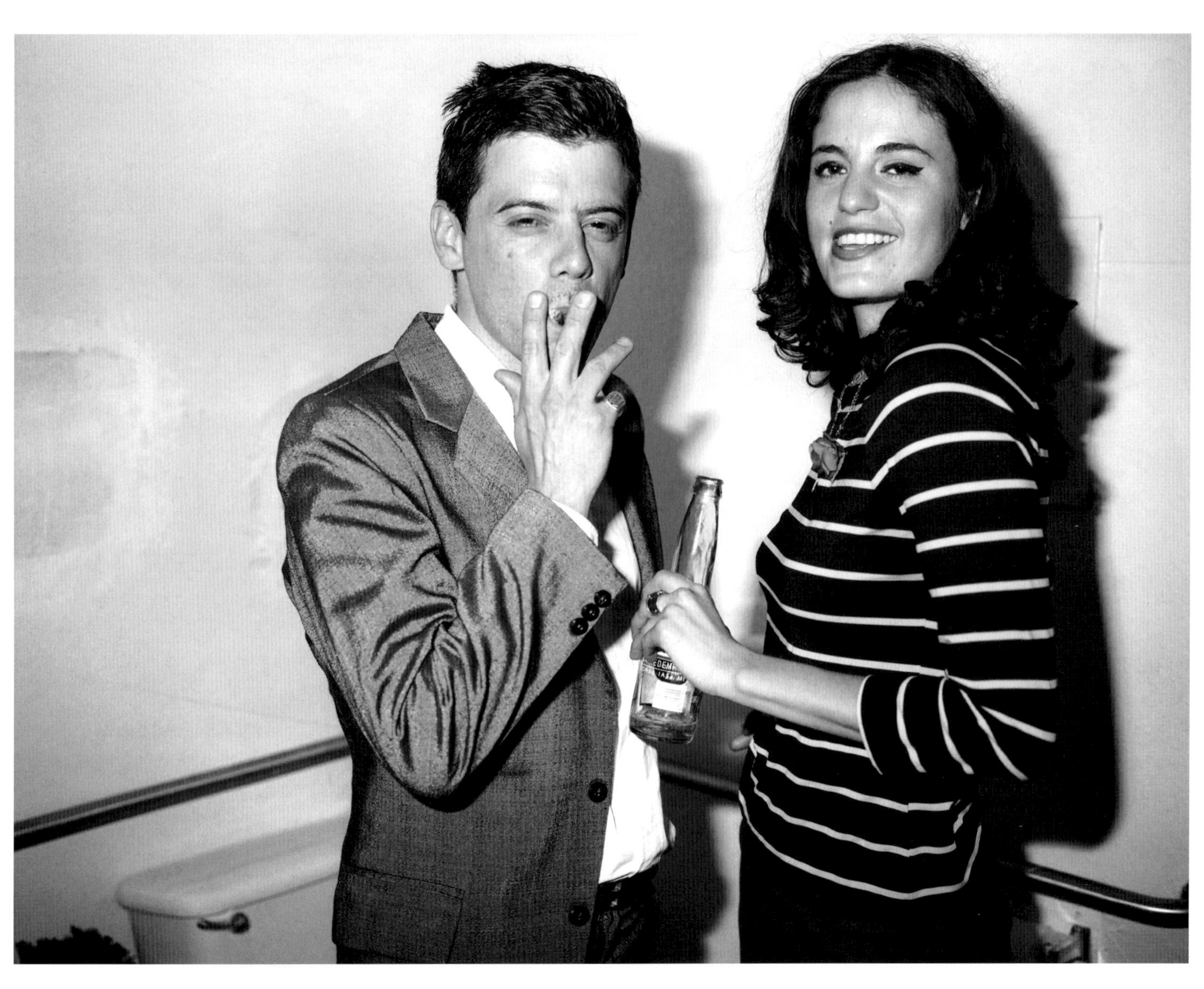

Martiniano and Milena, Los Super Elegantes,
Silverlake Lounge (1996)

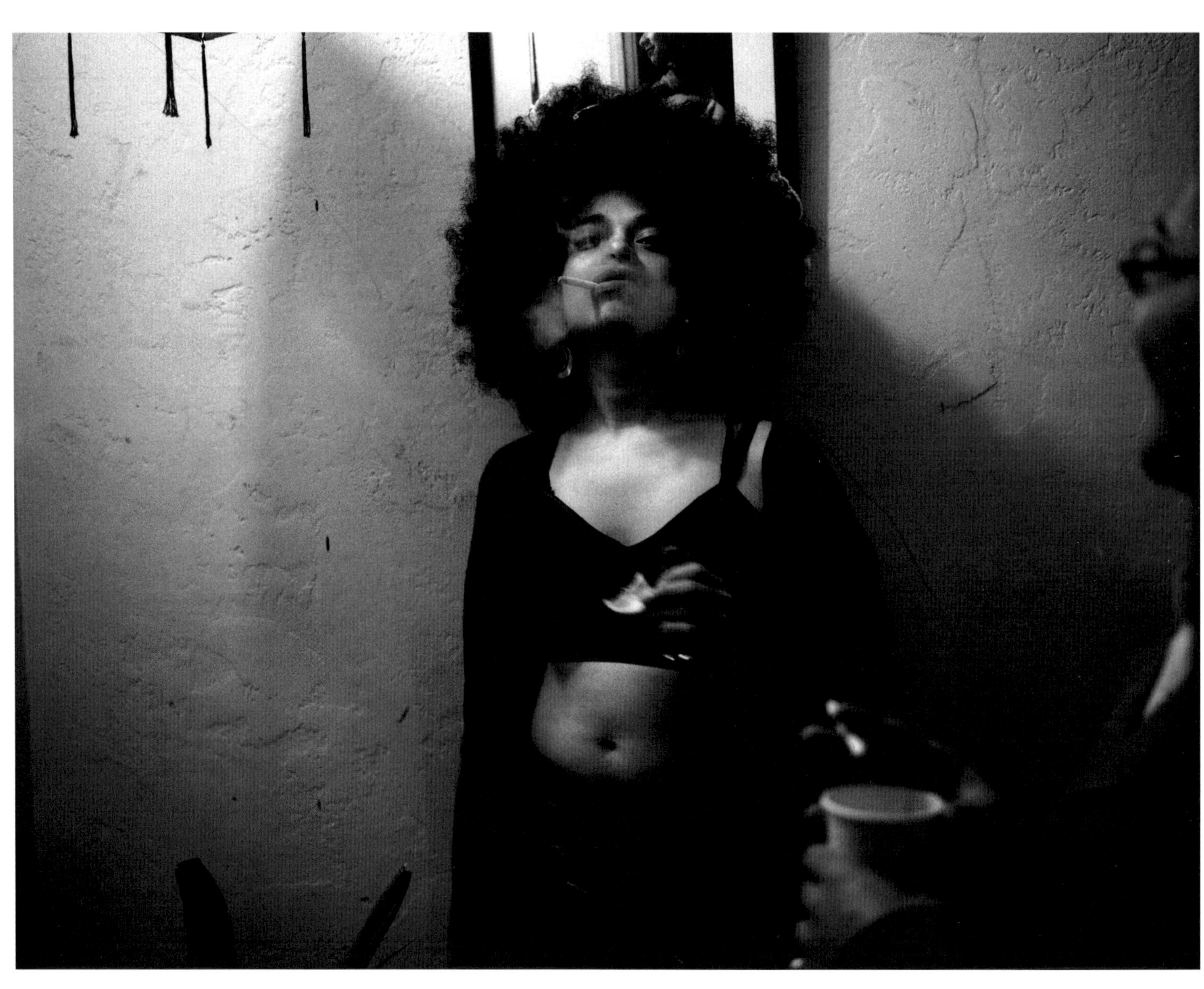

Ceri Zamora, Echo Park (1995)

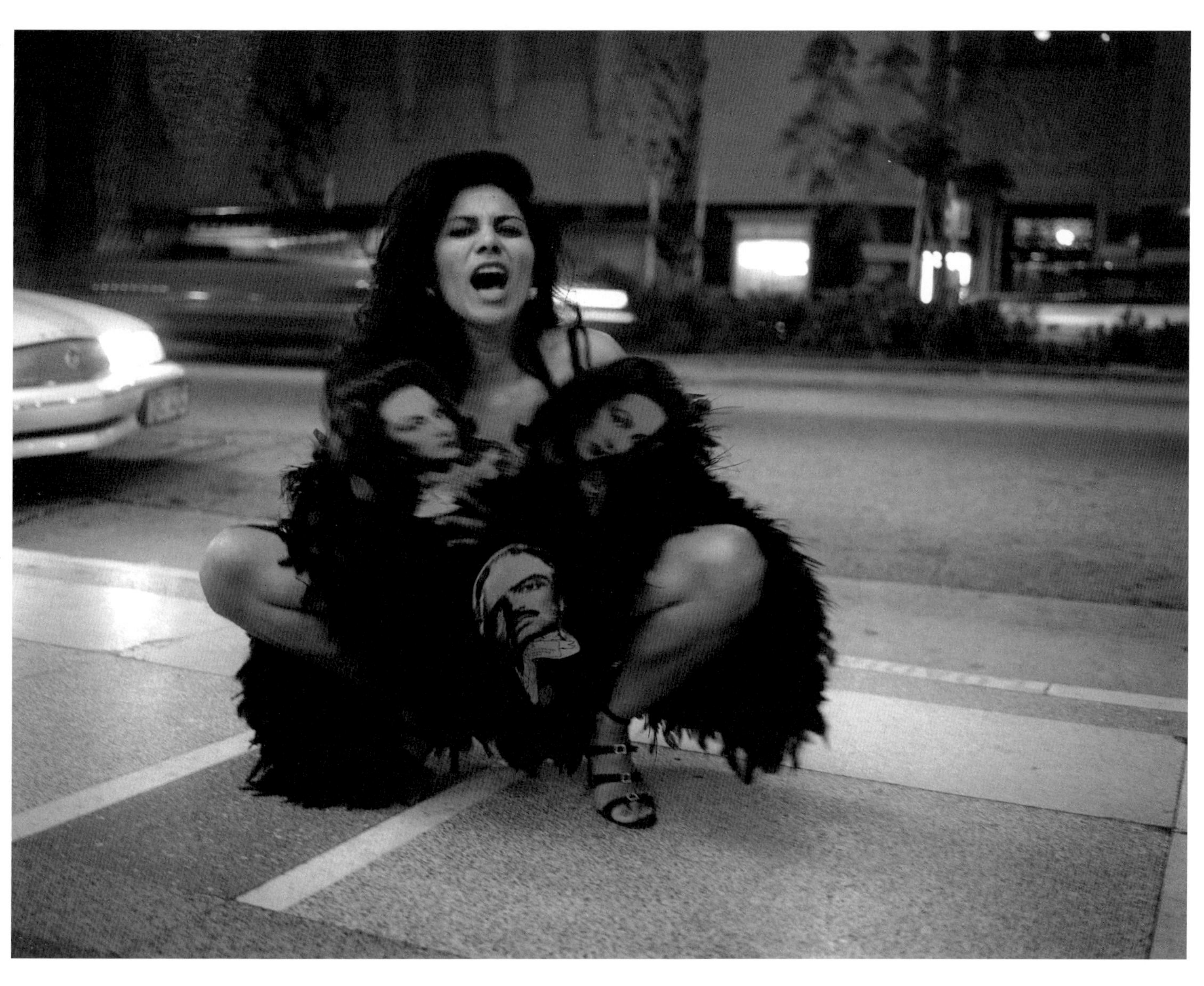

Xiomara, Korea Town (1993)

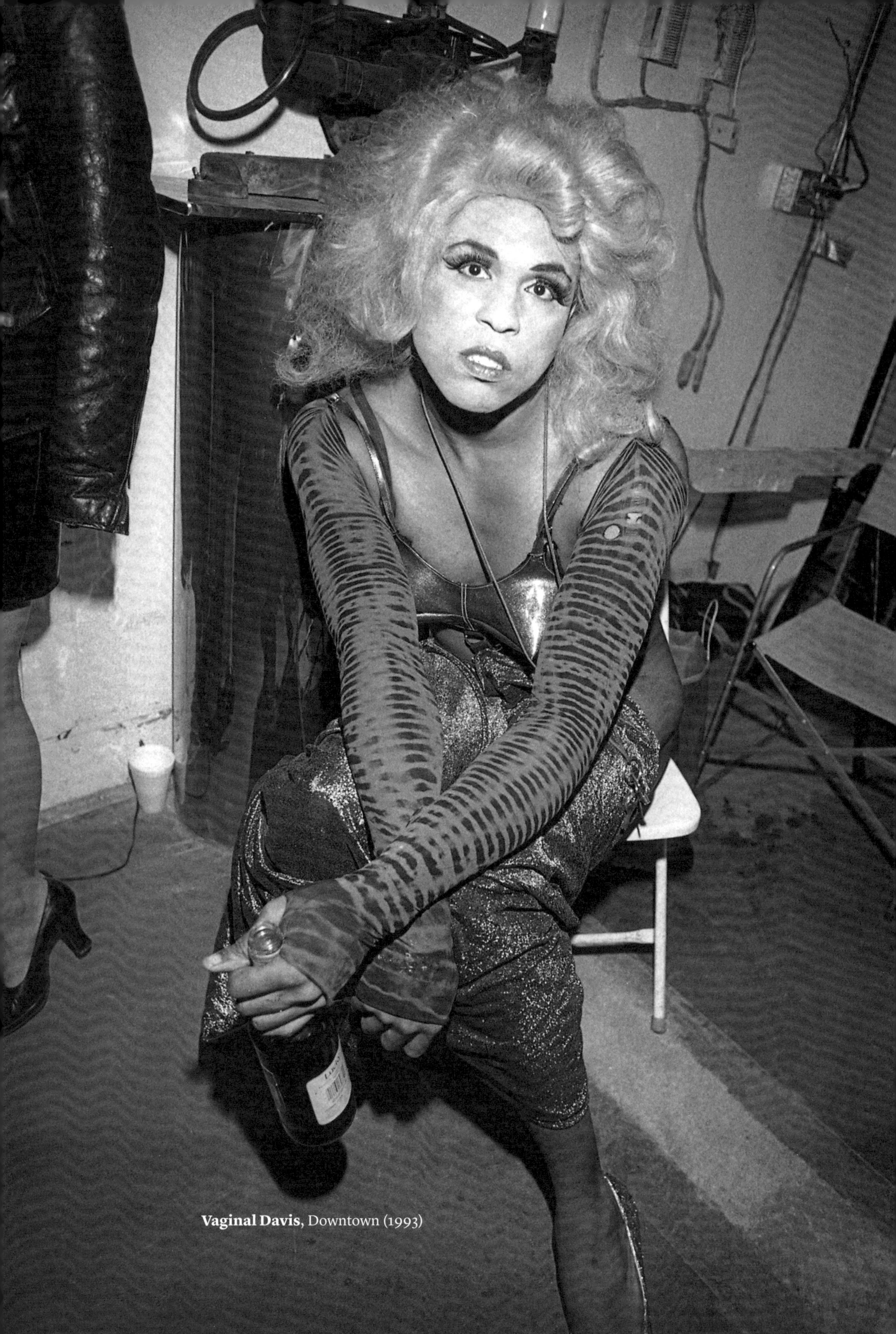

Vaginal Davis, Downtown (1993)

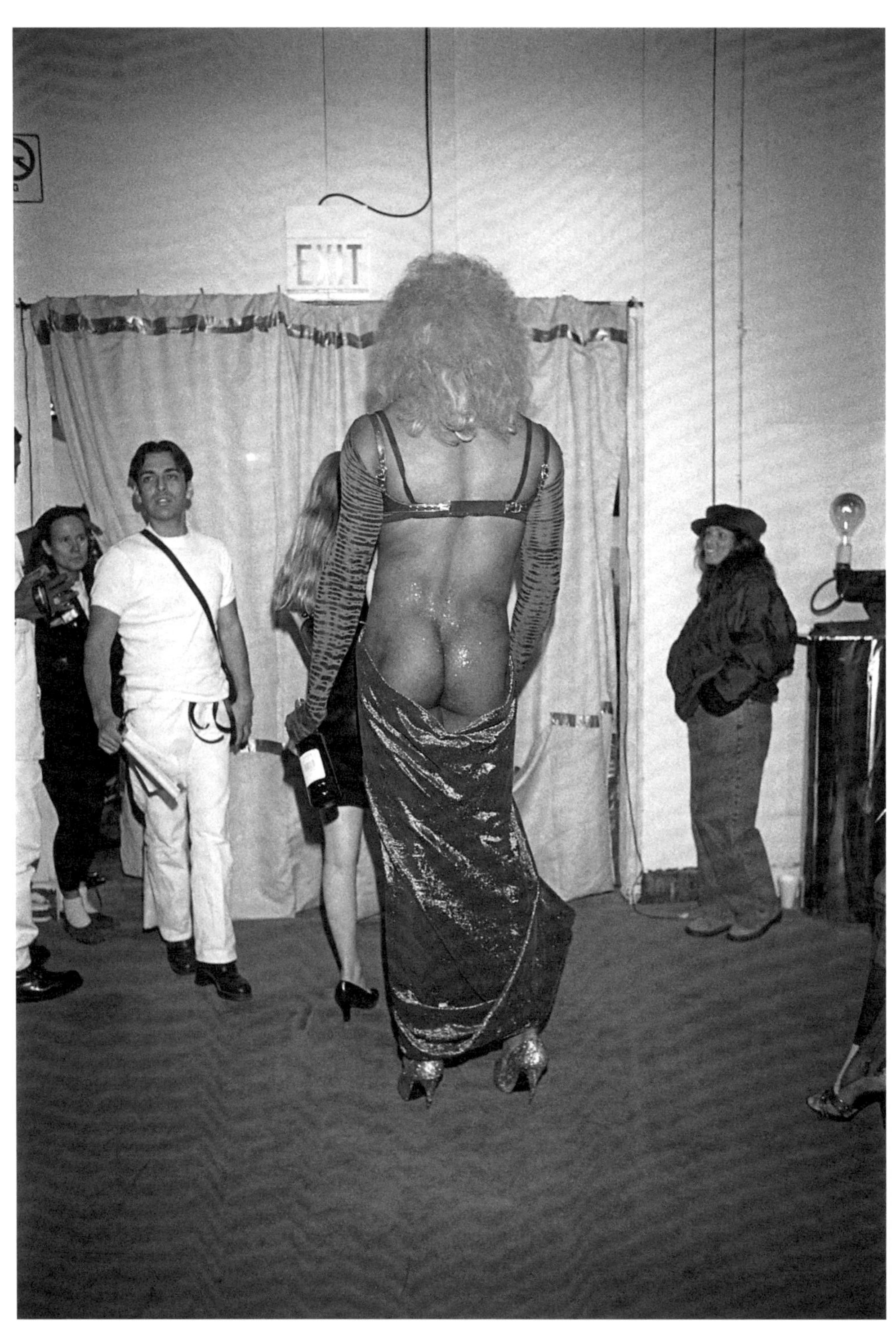

Vaginal Davis, Downtown (1993)

"Chicas de Hoy" A Conversation between Reynaldo Rivera & Vaginal Davis

From: Vaginal Davis
Date: November 7, 2018 at 10:46 PM,
To: Reynaldo Rivera
Subject: Re: Book project

Hey Darling,
 I got both of your emails, they came through to me.
I am teaching in Geneva where my phone doesn't work unless
I am connected to wifi. Switzerland isn't part of the EU.
 Let's chat via email. It can be like a volleyball game.
You can start stream of consciousness style and I can respond.
Or vice-versa. Does that sound good to you?
Hope all is well in your cosmos?
Love&kissyz
Duchess de Alba

From: Reynaldo Rivera
Date: November 8, 2018 at 1:51 PM,
To: Vaginal Davis
Subject: Re: Book project

I was thinking of writing my piece about how, growing up,
I thought about art as something white people do—and how
this perspective influenced my view of myself and what I
was doing. As far back as I've been able to trace my family
we've always lived in certain neighborhoods that seem to be
pathways of migration, kind of like the Wildebeest or other
migratory animals. Now these paths are no longer available
due to the cost and the difficulty of crossing this illegal border.
I was walking around Echo Park lake in front of the apartment
my moms lived in during the '60s, and I realized I could no
longer live in this neighborhood. I couldn't come back.
It was a strange feeling—I just don't make enough to be able to
live there. I'm actually gonna have someone write it for me
cuz I really do suck at putting ideas down on paper; I think
I just figured I have severe dyslexia. Have you seen the images
chosen for the book?

On November 8, 2018 at 1:37 PM
Reynaldo Rivera wrote:

Hello Frau Vaginal,
 I'm writing you from Lincoln Heights, I think it was
Alicia Armendariz's old neighborhood. I ran into her here
years ago. It's nice to hear her book and music are doing well.
I met her a year or two before meeting you. The first time we
actually spoke to each other was at an apt you had on Sunset
near Fairfax you had just moved into. I came over with Craig
Lee, he had been trying to introduce us. I will say—though at
the time I wouldn't have said it—that it was nice running into
other folk who weren't white. As with Alice—I loved running
into her at clubs, around 1985, '86, '87. I remember Cholita
performing in the kitchen of my house for my birthday, oh
the '80s!—but I guess that's another story.
 My idea about working with you was to just let you
write a story of this city that for better or worse fostered the
likes of us. Because it was a cheap place to live, and like Berlin
it allowed us to get by doing small jobs and still paying the
rent. I feel like, unlike New York or San Francisco, where you
become a New Yorker or San Franciscan, LA takes its shape
from its current inhabitants. Still, the city hasn't changed in
this magnitude at any time in my memory.
 This book is an attempt to leave a record that we were
here, since we tend to get erased and leave our neighborhoods
without any traces. Talking to a young Chicano in Pasadena
about growing up in Echo Park, this guy was surprised to
find out that it used to be a Latino neighborhood. We leave
very little written material behind. We're always found in the
footnotes of others'. Anyway mija, I am a terrible writer and
my spelling is even worse. I was just watching an interview you
gave in 2012. I liked the discussion about how you didn't fit in
with the mainstream gays, or the straights. And the thing about
your mama and the uncles? You know, in Mexico all the dyke
friends were our tias. In the US, I grew up around the lesbian
parties my mama would throw, and of course the lesbian fights
that always seemed to happen at the end, when they were
all drunk. All my cholo friends would just look at my mama's
friends dancing with each other. I think once somebody asked,
Why are they wearing three-piece suits? Meanwhile I went
from gangs to androgyny. I left the cholo thing behind around
1979 and started going to punk rock shows with my sister.
I, too, grew up around women: three sisters and two lesbian
parents.

On November 12, 2018 at 5:43 AM,
Vaginal Davis wrote:

Hey My Dearest Darling,
 I love what you wrote about your mamita and her
friends and their suits. Did they go to that lesbian bar The
Red Head on First Street? There was another lesbian bar in
Alhambra called the Plush Pony or the Pink Pony, not far from
Phil Spector's mansion. Isn't it crazy to build a mansion in
Alhambra, of all the suburbs in the world?
 It sounds like you grew up in a similar situation to my

lesbian mother Mary Magdalena DuPlantier. My mother was a barracuda femme top who ruled a bevy of proper butch women like a Creole Dona Herlinda. She was the ultimate femme. She always wore a dress or skirt suit with pearls and gloves, a matching hat and purse, orange red lipstick. She wore high heels to do housework! I never saw my mother use the toilet. She was born in April of 1919 in Shreveport Louisiana, a Black Creole on her father's side of the family. Her mother was a full-blooded Choctaw Indian who was born and raised on a reservation in Arkansas. My mother was older than my peers' mothers. She was about the same age as most of their grandmothers. Having an older mother was actually a blessing because it gave me knowledge of a different time (The Great Depression) and place outside my own reality. I was the baby, growing up in an all-female household with three older sisters and my lesbian uncles, who were part of my mother's lesbian witch-coven.

One of these uncles, Uncle Trash, owned a huge house on Bonnie Brae and 11th Street in the Pico Union district that was something of a lesbian commune in the late 1960s and '70s. The house was near the Bob Mizer Athletic Model Guild Compound that was notorious in the neighborhood. Uncle Trash was part of the group that opened the first Women's Building near MacArthur Park. Our apartment was a few miles west, around Pico Blvd and Western Avenue, but I spent a lot of time at Uncle Trash's huge old Queen Anne style house that was nicknamed the House of Seven Clark Gables. Uncle Trash was related to the Woolworth heiress Barbara Hutton, who at one time was married to Cary Grant. I never knew Uncle Trash's real name. But playing in this mansion as a child was always a lot of fun.

The women my mother ruled over were all stone cold butches who wore men's clothing in varying degrees. Uncle Trash came from a wealthy family, and always looked very dapper, smoking cigars and wearing expensively tailored suits and wingtip shoes. Uncle Trash nurtured my literary pretensions, taking me to fancy bookstores in downtown Los Angeles and giving me first editions of Louisa May Alcott, Frank L. Baum and Jane Austen. I was such a bookworm, and Uncle Trash encouraged this. Uncle Trash also spurred my artsy fartsy-ness.

A lot of the other lesbian uncles were from rough working class backgrounds. Uncle Spider chewed tobacco and dipped snuff and was always spitting, which I found a bit disgusting. My mother became radicalized in the late 1960s through her friendship with a Jesuit priest at St. Thomas Church who espoused liberation theology. As a Louisiana Creole, my mother was born Catholic but she experimented with a lot of different religions over the years. The one I enjoyed most was the Jehovah's Witness sect. I loved that Witnesses didn't celebrate holidays like Christmas or Easter, or even birthdays. Being that I was nosy, I loved proselytizing with them door-to-door, which in the religion was called Field Service. I also attended the Theocratic Ministry School, which I also loved since the Bible was taught as history and I love history. I always did well in school. I was the ultimate test taker. I was lucky to be placed in the Mentally Gifted Minors

program of the Los Angeles Unified School District. From elementary school to high school I was in classes with all these scholastically competitive Asian kids, which kept me on my toes.

Being a cute and precocious child I'd be invited inside during these Jehovah's Witness Field Service visits, and I loved seeing how other people lived. I don't remember anyone ever being rude to me. Instead they marveled that I was so sweet and well mannered. My mother wasn't very consistent in following the rules of any of the religions she took part in. We didn't celebrate Christmas, but my mother loved Christmas music, for some strange reason, and loved to play it during the holiday season. But we never had a tree or exchanged gifts, and I never went trick-or-treating for Halloween. Occasionally my mother would let me go to friends' birthday parties, but I never had one myself until my mid-thirties, when I'd host a party every year at a different dive bar with my "Club Sucker at the Garage" partner Frank Rodriguez. Frank and I would celebrate together, since our birthdays were on the same day: February 20th. Still, I never felt like I missed out on anything as a child. My Jehovah's Witness period was a great training ground for being outside of the mainstream: Eccentricity could be part of a resistance strategy.

I was back in Los Angeles in September because my nephew died suddenly. LA is so upscale now...all of these artisan coffee places and new restaurants with uncomfortable seating.

It's horrible. The only place that seemed the same was Café Tropical on Sunset Blvd in Silver Lake. I loved how the gorgeous young boy behind the counter was giving attitude to all the white people in the place. He wasn't necessarily being rude...he just wasn't featuring them. He served them with a blank and indifferent expression on his face. I was just gagging on the lovely extravaganza of it.

I was staying at my friend Hector Martinez's guest house in the Silver Lake Hills that he calls Plato del Lago, and made the mistake of walking from Café Tropical to the post office on Franklin and Vermont. By 9 a.m. it was so hot that I had to rest on a bus bench every couple of blocks. Walking from Silver Lake past the Junction into Los Feliz Village and East Hollywood, I didn't recognize the old neighborhood. The people I passed were either these well-off clueless young types or the very ragged and bedraggled, worn down by the harshness of what is life now in Los Angeles.

And then, the mini tent cities scattered about! With rents so high in what used to be one of the cheapest of the international cities, no wonder the homeless situation is out of control. My poor sister, who's ten years older than me, has lived in the same apartment in Hollywood at Santa Monica and Normandie since the late '70s, so she pays less than $600 a month for a one-bedroom dingbat flat. The new owners of the building want her out, because she pays way below market value. But if she gets kicked out, where can she go? She's way past retirement age, but she can't contemplate retiring from her government job at the Los Angeles County Housing Authority where she's worked for almost forty years. She'll have to keep working until she drops dead. And since she's handicapped, with many health issues, that will most likely be her fate—dropping dead on the job.

Her cute apartment building had one of those kidney-shaped mid century swimming pools but the new owners drained it and kicked out all of the hot muscular Latino boys, semi-hustlers who'd lived in the building and worked for the elderly gay white former owner. When he died and the building got sold, it lost its unique sexy flavor with the loss of the juicy Latino boys who made the place jump. The building was also lovely because of its intergenerational mix. People my sister's age and older got along well with the Latin queer boys who helped them be less lonely. So what if the boys didn't pay rent? They made up for it with the joy they lent to the atmosphere. The old gay owner got to chow down on the boy's huge pingas, and get an occasional mercy fuck. I never saw an elderly man look so happy and content. All the Latino boys loved my sister, who they called Teresita Maria—sister of the cholita diva.

When I lived in Los Angeles, my huge Koreatown homo-moderne apartment was owned by a woman who only rented to artists. She didn't care how long a flat stayed empty—she wanted the right person there, who had good energy. She never raised my rent and I probably would have stayed forever if her husband hadn't developed Alzheimer's, forcing her to sell the place to a horrible carpetbagger.

When you and I first met through Craig Lee in the '80s, he brought you to my tiny apartment at the La Villa Rosa on Sunset and Fairfax where I had my Hag Gallery: small, contemporary and haggard. My openings were always so much fun. I bought cheap jug wine from Smart & Final and those ultra cheap cans of beer. People would get so drunk, and met their significant other at my openings. Everyone accepted me, which was the main reason I turned my apartment into a gallery—I was hoping to find a boyfriend. Of course that plan backfired, and everyone got laid except me. But I did have some amazing exhibitions and film and video screenings that got a lot of great press. The first time I was written about in *Artforum* and *Art in America* was because of Hag Gallery. Before then, I'd never heard of those publications. I was so young and naïve in those days.

You are so right. I never thought of myself as an artist with a body of work. That was something I thought could only be done by white people. It's actually a miracle that I have an art career, coming from a poor background. These days you have to be rich or have a trust fund to have a career in art. It's not generally something poor people can take part in.

Do places like La Plaza on La Brea and Melrose still exist? That was always one of my favorite haunts. Do you know what happened to Olga? She choreographed the shows and was saving up money to move back to Mexico and open up her own hardware store. The first time a trendy white Hollywood crowd discovered La Plaza was through a Michèle Lamy fashion show where she used the girls as models. Did you document this?

On November 15, 2018 at 05:26 PST
Reynaldo Rivera wrote:

Oh lord Miss Vag, I just read what I wrote you and realized it's unreadable. Unfortunately I sent it without rereading. I got real stream-of-consciousness and it's all over the place so if I'm having a hard time it's going to be harder for you, plus I went into stuff that I maybe should have just kept it out. I'm going to pay more attention next time.
Sent from my iPhone

Subject: It's Brilliant!!! The Real Deal!
On November 16, 2018 at 6:15 AM,
Vaginal Davis wrote:

Darling Rey,
Please don't second-guess yourself. What you have written is visceral and immediate. Don't overthink it. It's delicious and raw. They can clean it up later. You just have to write straight from your soul. It's exciting to read and makes lots of sense. I have doctor appointments today but can't wait to formally respond tomorrow.
Keep it up and hard
Love&kissyz
Miss Vag
Sent from my iPhone

On November 17, 2018 at 7:05 AM,
Vaginal Davis wrote:

Oh my sweetness everything about your hot mama sounds divine! You are so lucky your mother is still alive. My mother Mary Magdalena died in June 2000. I was happy that she survived into the new century. Two of my sisters, Gloria Jean and Gracie Lee died in 2004 and 2009, followed by my oldest nephew, Mark Denning Taylor in 2010 and my youngest nephew, Brian Keith Taylor in September this year.

When my mother died I felt like an orphan, like I was alone in the world. Our lives were so intertwined. My mother was the real artist in the family. All I do is co-opt things she originally created. She was also an expert seamstress and used to make elaborate costumes for me to wear from primary school to high school. It's amazing what I got away with, but things were a bit looser in the 1960s and '70s.

I never really had a relationship with my Mexican-German-Jewish father Alberto Ruff, who died in the early 1990s in Argentina. My parents were never married. When they met, my father was 19 or 20 years old, and my mother was in her forties. She was working for my father's Jewish relatives at the Food Garden supermarket. Back then, our family lived in the famous Ramona Gardens Housing Projects in East Los Angeles. All my sisters attended Lincoln High School. When my mother first moved to Los Angeles during the great migration in 1945, she lived in Watts at the Jordan Downs Project House but they moved to Ramona Gardens in 1949. East Los Angeles was then the Jewish enclave of the city. Ramona Gardens was utopian housing for the poor, designed by Frank Lloyd Wright Jr., Rudolph Schindler and Richard Neutra. My mother was married to my sister's father, Sam Hall from 1937 to 1957. When they divorced he was still making

229

sexual demands on her, so she got preggers by my father and then her ex-husband left her alone.

My mother never wanted to be married or have children but back in those days it was just considered too weird not to conform. My father grew up in the Polanco district of Mexico City. His father was from Berlin but he hated his country of origin, leaving Germany in the early '30s before the Nazis fully assumed power. My grandfather would have hated that I live in Germany. He was the black sheep of his Prussian clan.

When I was growing up, my father would occasionally call the house. With his thick accent, he sounded like a cross between a vampire and Ricardo Montalbán. I remember him being tall with very pale, almost translucent skin, thin lips, slicked-back shiny black hair and a John Waters mustache. He smelled of vanilla wafers and cigarettes.

I've been dealing with a lot of questions in therapy concerning my father. My estrangement from my father is probably the main reason I've never had a boyfriend or relationship or fallen in love with anyone. I just have teenage girl crushes. I am permanently stilted, forever a teenager in perpetual longing. Ain't it sad?

When I hear of other people's romantic stories, dilemmas and love dramas I figure maybe I dodged a bullet. Coming of age during the AIDS crisis, maybe it was better that I never felt comfortable enough to engage in sex and relationships. Not that anyone ever really pursued me. I don't exactly exude sex appeal.

It's a bit embarrassing being almost 60 years old and still a virgin. But that's my reality. I never wanted to risk catching something that penicillin couldn't cure. Looking back over centuries of living. I think that never risking anything for love has left me a dried up fossil in amber. The only good thing I can say about my situation is that I have a sense of humor about it, and haven't turned completely bitter.

I like to focus on what I do have, which is a lot of wonderful friends scattered around the world, who are extremely loyal and protective of me. Over the years I've mentored a lot of younger artists and art students while teaching at colleges, art schools and universities. Since I will never have children of my own, the young people I mentor have become my progeny. I've turned into a big black mama with breasts that feed dying nations.

One thing I've always envied about Alice Bag and Ron Athey is that they let themselves go when it comes to love. Ron even married a young Italian/Argentine man and moved to London to be with him for six years. Alice's first marriage didn't go so well but then she met "Jailbait" Greg Velasquez and it's been the love of ages. I guess not everyone is meant to be partnered. If that were my destiny, it would have happened by now. I liked Craig Lee but I can certainly see that he had his dark side. Well there can't be light without dark. I never got too close to Craig even though he was very complimentary about my writing and performances. I've always been a little hesitant when it comes to dealing with people of the middle and upper classes. I guess I have a built-in disdain for the wealthy. My father's family was wealthy but they weren't really a part of my life.

In a way, Craig and Tomata du Plenty of the Screamers were mentors to me as well. My intuition at the time told me to keep a sense of mysterious distance with the Hollywood punk in-crowd. They were easily bored and could be quite dismissive of people.

Alice Bag was smart to leave the scene at the time when people were all strung out on heroin. Going to college and then Central America gave her a fantastic perspective on things. Alice possesses a fine sense of self-preservation, and she doesn't take excrement from anyone. When we did Cholita together she would call me out on my shit as well.

I am a natural freak. But a lot of people in the Hollywood crowd were poseurs with trust funds who came from good families. Actually coming from nothing is easier because there are no expectations placed upon you. I was the first person in my family to go to university. At university I met the children of movie stars, and they were all such big messes. I didn't need to take drugs or drink to be out there as a freakazoid. Even smoking mota, I had no interest in being a stoner chick, let alone all the other drugs. And drinking, well I enjoy a nice cocktail like an Old Fashioned, Vodka Gimlet or Whiskey Sour or a glass of white wine with dinner but luckily don't have an addictive personality. I am fortunate to always have been comfortable with my outsider status. I never fit in with the gays but I didn't fit in with the punks either.

Growing up in the city of cars and not knowing how to drive is something most people can't imagine. I knew at an early age I wasn't meant to be behind the wheel. I was content to ride my old 1940s vintage bicicleta and take public transport. I was so glad when they built the subway in LA, though at that time it didn't go very far. I didn't need to go to the tired San Fernando Valley for anything, or to the beaches, desert or mountains. I never learned how to swim, so you won't see me in anyone's pool. I do like ogling the hot surfer boys with their huge feet, broad shoulders and tiny waists. Even when I was young I never had a waist. Always a little bit of fat around the mid-section—the Mexican curse. And don't forget my childbearing hips. But I've always had a big booty, though no one has been interested in splitting it in two.

Yes, I remember Gil Cuadros. Wasn't he friends with that sexy artist Joey Terrill? I loved Joey's cartoon series *Chicos Modernos*. Gil was part of the same poetry reading series that Craig Lee and I performed in regularly at A Different Light Bookstore in Silver Lake. Those were some amazing events curated by the late James Carroll Pickett who also died of AIDS. James Carroll Picket wrote the play *Bathhouse Benediction*. I remember going to the famous bathhouse 8709 that was part of the Cedars-Sinai Hospital Complex with my friend Crystal Cross of the band the Speed Queens. Back then, Crystal was a butch lesbian; now he's a F2M going by the name Mr. Cross. We would sneak into the bathhouse to voyeur gay sex up close. We were so young. I was really titillated by how a big penis could disappear into a little tiny anus, and how the bottom could so easily take said member into his cavity.

We only got busted once, when one of the bathhouse em-ployees realized we weren't exactly men. He was cool with it though, and got a kick out of having us in that den of iniquity. Of course in that masculine space no one was interested in sex with me or Cross so we could just be little flies on the wall. I still remember the intoxicating smell of stale gym socks and poppers, and of course whenever someone had a mudslide that stench would raft through the place. The guy who worked there became our friend and co-conspirator. He was a sexy lean white trash kid originally from San Bernardino. He looked like Jan-Michael Vincent in the movie *Baby Blue Marine*. He had the flattest stomach I had ever seen in my life with what was a 16 pack, not just a six-pack of abs. His large bullet nipples were always inflamed and he wore a size 15 shoe. He was a true sex champion. After he got off duty he'd use the bathhouse himself and plow at least eight or nine guys, ejaculating into their bungholes. On several occasions he let Cross and I watch him in action. After he ejaculated, he'd still be rock hard. He wound up marrying a woman and moving to North Carolina.

On November 17, 2018 at 6:35 PM, Reynaldo Rivera wrote:

I used to record music off the radio and TV with a tape recorder I stole from a church parking lot in Pasadena. Eventually I traded it for half a Sherman, a cigarette dipped in PCP. Unfortunately, I didn't say no. Entre nous, I still haven't. I started very young, around 12. Btw I hope I didn't offend assuming you didn't have art training. I did know you went to university because I ran into you at UCLA in the early '90s. You were giving male-identified and wearing your trademark super-sized earrings. We chitchatted for a minute, god knows what about, and you went your way. I didn't know you had started before the '80s. I thought we were around same age. I lived through the '60s and '70s and I'd go out during the '70s, but I was a cholo so there wasn't much going on except house parties and occasionally picking my sister up at a disco. Later, she got me into punk rock. I was in Stockton working in the fields when she sent me the first B-52s album, and of course all the local stuff like 45 Grave, Christian Death, Dead Kennedys and the Germs.

Going to work up north helped me start the process of leaving gang life. I wonder if they'd go after me now? They didn't get to jump me out. Remember? Blood in, blood out. Believe it or not, I did the first part of the ritual—I got jumped, and blood was the requisite for the beating to stop and become part of this gang. Luckily by this point I'd befriended a veterano who was looking out for me, and he stopped the beating as soon as I bled. These guys were known to keep going until they were satisfied. His name was Gato. He was from the south side, super cool with his glass eye that he'd lost in a fight. I was living on the street around the time I got jumped and I remember him cooking for me. I was not used to anyone doing anything nice, especially someone like this dude. His death really affected me, and it was the real catalyst for leaving that life of violence behind. My sister and I had seen him that morning on Colorado and Fair Oaks getting a haircut. He'd gotten a job and seemed happy about it. He couldn't have been older than his early 20s, but that was the last time I would see him. He was murdered at a party that night. I went to his funeral, and that was the last time I associated with that scene.

On November 18, 2018 at 11:17 AM, Vaginal Davis wrote:

Hey Sweet Baby,

You could never offend me. You are so lovesexy!

You always reminded me of the handsome Mexican movie star Pedro Armendáriz in the María Félix film *Enamorada*. You're very suave and debonair like Gilbert Roland.

I am now writing on the iPhone.

Yes I am much older than you, probably by over a decade. On February 20th, I'll turn 58 so I will soon be 60. Forever Pisces. When you saw me on the UCLA campus in the early '90s it was because I had a day job working at the Placement & Career Planning Center. I worked there for over ten years, until 1994. It's hard to believe that someone as crazy as me could hold a normal job for that long. I used the Xerox machine at work to make my 'zine *Fertile La Toyah Jackson*. I was also freelancing for the *LA Weekly* and *LA Reader* and a British music mag called *ZigZag*. Since I could never get a boyfriend, I concentrated all of my energy on creative pursuits.

I guess nothing has changed much with respect to that. Working at UCLA wasn't a bad day job to have. I was a glorified secretary but only worked four days a week because I liked having Friday-Sunday off. I really got away with murder. At lunch we'd go to the men's swimming pool and ogle the water polo team as they were rehearsing in their Speedos. Yummy!!!!

You're right—I don't have any art training. I never went to art school. I'm still shocked to have commercial gallery representation on the West Coast, New York and London, and that my insane makeup paintings are in permanent collections of museums. If I hadn't left LA for Europe, I would have never been taken seriously as a visual artist. I'd be seen as just a kooky wing nut. To many, that's all I ever will be.

It's funny how I avoided gang violence. The gang-bangers were actually quite protective of me, The Clanton, Mara, Bloods, the AC/DCs—a queer street gang—the Crips and the girl gang the Criplettes. I was very friendly with everyone in the neighborhood. My older sister worked at juvie in East LA and everyone liked her, because she was very sweet to all the gang kids. I never had run-ins with the police because I never learned how to drive. If you don't drive, your chances of having an encounter with law enforcement are reduced. Both of my poor late nephews were arrested many times because they drove.

Will have to continue Monday when I can drag my laptop to the library.
Love&kissyz
Miss Gorda

Subject: Re: Fourth Round
On November 18, 2018 at 11:15 AM, Reynaldo Rivera wrote:

Mija, I'm 54, so we r just 4 yrs apart.
Sent from my iPhone

I want to say this before I forget: I always admired you and thought of your work as important, even back then before I knew what it was you were doing. And I still consider you a national treasure that had been overlooked for too long. It may not have been important to the art establishment at the time, but it was terribly important for ethnic queers like myself to see other ethnics being creative. It made me consider that maybe what I'm doing can and might be art. I think we created our own idea of what art was, and our own language, since we didn't get to go to art school and learn all the jargon. I didn't see what I was doing as "Art," but some other aesthetic thing. I did find beauty in it, but I just didn't think I could use the "Art" label since I didn't go to art school, or any school, for that matter. Art was something white people did. I learned aesthetics from watching silent movies and early talkies. That was my art education. I'd ditch school to watch a show called Hollywood Presents that was on at 12 in the afternoon. They showed movies with stars like Dietrich, Jean Harlow, ZaSu Pitts and Garbo. That was where it began for me. The silent movies were my teachers, and soon after this I bought my first camera from my dad. In the beginning, my mentors were movies, and later on I looked to music and singers like Toña la Negra, with songs like *Arráncame La Vida*, and *Mentira Salomé*. No I take it back, I think music came first, then cinema...it's almost 11 pm. Good night from Lincoln Heights.

Hey My Darling Rey,
     I was so moved by what you just sent I had to pick up my laptop and go to the public library where there is free wifi and respond immediately.
Love & kissy
Miss Vag

*

From the Cheese Endique Trifecta, the studio of Ms. Vaginal Davis in Berlina, Alamanya

     Oh my sexy gorgeous darling your lovely words are so meaningful to me. Reading about your struggles, trials and tribulations makes me just all out weep uncontrollably, something I have been doing a lot lately as my mortality looms large. Losing a relative who was younger than me—my nephew Brian Keith Taylor—who I took care of as a child makes me realize I don't have that much time on the clock either. Actually life on this planet is not guaranteed to anyone.
     I was the first one in my family to go to university, and I'd been taking courses through UCLA and USC since the early 1970s through a program called Upward Bound in conjunction with the MGM program within LAUSD. Ron Athey was also part of this program. I was very lucky that there was a social conscience for the underprivileged back in those days, because there were all these programs that you could take advantage of. There were wonderful librarians at the downtown main library who were mentors to me, and researched programs that were available. There was one program that sent students to Israel to live and work on a kibbutz for a school year. I loved hairy dark Jewish boys; I've always been a Hava Nagila queen. And there was another program where you could go to a fancy boarding school in Switzerland called Le Rosey, or attend Choate, a boarding school in Connecticut. I applied for everything because I had this hunger to see the world and I knew I'd have to find a grift of some kind to fulfill these outlandish dreams.
     I remember thinking my brother-in-law was a "nogoodnik" because he was a bookie and played the horses, never holding a regular job in his life. Now I see that things were stacked against him as a black man. Going against the system was the only thing available to him.
     My poor oldest sister Gracie Lee, the only one of my sisters to get married and have children, was always working three low-paying jobs. She was an LVN nurse at an olds folk's home, cleaning the patients and giving them sponge baths. She loved helping people, and she also worked as a waitress at the old J.J. Newberry's lunch counter at Pico and Rimpau. At night, she worked as a PBX operator for Rock Hudson, taking messages from his countless male lovers between the late 1960s and mid-'70s. Mr. Hudson was very generous to my sister, never forgetting her birthday or her children's birthdays, or her wedding anniversary. He also gave her a nice Christmas bonus and invited her to the Solstice Beauty Parties he gave at his mansion. My sister was one of few women who got to attend these famous soirees. The other women at the party were Mr. Hudson's black housekeeper, his black cook (he loved soul food), the actress/comedienne Nancy Walker who co-starred with him in the TV series *McMillan & Wife*, Doris Day and Elizabeth Taylor. The rest of the guests were the youngest and handsomest Hollywood studs, and as the witching hour approached, the parties would turn into huge orgies. My sister was a big fag hag and she loved watching gay men do each other.
     But getting back to what you were saying about forging an education by watching old films: that kind of self-educating is valid. Seeing old movies from the Golden Age of Hollywood was a great way to learn about classical cinema when we were young, even though the films were edited down for commercials. I loved watching Channel 52, which showed all the old Warner Bros. films, and Movie Greats on KTTV Channel 11, which showed a lot of MGM musicals. I used my little cheap tape recorder to tape the songs straight off my old black & white Emerson TV set, and this gave me knowledge of the Tin Pan Alley American Songbook of standards. My first loves were Hollywood musicals, show tunes and opera. Punk rock, pop and soul music came later.
     As a student in the MGM program I got to see opera for free at the Shrine Auditorium. I also got to see Josephine Baker perform at the old Hollywood Palace, Marlene Dietrich's last performance at the Music Center's Dorothy Chandler Pavilion, *Zoot Suit* at the Aquarius Theater, and Miss Eartha Kitt in *Timbuktu!* at the Pantages Theater on Hollywood Blvd.
     I didn't realize how fortunate I was that I didn't have to witness my mother being beat up by my sister's father. All

this happened before I was born. My mother also tried to kill her husband by lacing his food with rat poisons, but he had a cast iron stomach and he didn't even get sick. The few times she fought him back physically she wound up in jail. The police are more sympathetic with men in domestic abuse cases. Of course the abuse you suffered was on a much higher plane than anything that I had to deal with. You are such a survivor.

By the time I came on the scene my mother had nothing to do with men. I lived in a very tranquil, all female environment. There was very little so called "lesbian drama" with the group of lesbian women my mother ruled over.

Do you remember this butch Latina lesbian named Maria Dumbdumb who circulated in and around the punk scene? I always wondered what happened to her. She was a handsome dyke with a great sense of style. She never aged and always had rich girlfriends or rich faggots to support her. She never worked, as far as I could tell. I always admired her grift game of making sure she was taken care of financially and sexually. At one point I think she was going out with Chase Holiday, the lesbian club promoter Caroline Clone, and Joanne Smith who owned the only punk rock store in Beverly Hills. I have to admit I've been lucky in so many ways, since Miss LA can be a hard knock town. On the surface she seems lovely because of the sunshine and nice weather, but peel things back a bit and the evility emerges. If you don't have good intuition you can be hanging out with a crowd without even realizing that deep down, they can't stand you.

One thing I like about Germans is they can't pretend to like you if they don't. They're brutally upfront and honest, even to their own detriment. Sometimes you wish they wouldn't offer their opinions when they're not asked for. tIn Miss LA, it's all about keeping up the façade of niceness.

Did I mention that I was homeless for a bit in the early '80s? Once again I was lucky, as I figured out a way to stay in the hospital rooms they kept empty for doctors on night call at Cedars-Sinai. I hid my backpack in a utility box behind a design store on Robertson and Beverly. In the evening, I'd hang out at Studio One or The Odyssey until late, and then sleep at Cedars-Sinai. Their security was so lax, I could have easily stolen plenty of drugs if I'd wanted to. Sometimes my friend Tom Gallo let me sleep at his guest house in Beverly Hills. His father, Lew Gallo was a famous TV producer of successful crime shows.

**On November 18, 2018 at 8:50 AM,
Reynaldo Rivera wrote:**

How fortunate to have heard and seen La Baker and La Dietrich...how cool is that? I can't imagine what you went through kissing your mother goodbye. Someone told me your mother is what anchors you to this earth. Having so many friends die in the last few years has got me thinking about my own departure, plus being a very well lived 54. I'm surprised to still be here.

Did you know I lived in Berlin between the late '80s and '90s? I was there when the wall came down. I just couldn't hang with the winters, but back then Berlin was kinda like LA—a cheap city to live in. I was dating a woman who lived there so I moved between both places. I loved going to the flea markets all over the city. You'd think after all those years I'd be fluent. I did learn: *Eine tüte bitte tschüs...*

The year after the wall came down, the alte fraus were falling out of the skies like flies. I guess they panicked, thinking that no one was gonna take care of them and they started jumping out windows. One day I was waiting for my girlfriend to finish some work in Friedrichshafen in the formerly East Berlin, listening to Lucha Reyes on my headphones and something dropped. I thought maybe some punks had thrown a mannequin off the roof until I got closer and saw it was an elderly woman, still twitching, with a little stream of blood coming out of her mouth. I just panicked, started knocking on doors but I didn't know one word of German. I found the one and only business that was open there, a hairdresser, you can always count on us to bring life to a dead area—Anyway, a blonde queen came out. He had no clue what I was saying but he followed me, and took care of the poor old oma. I immediately called my psychic and asked her: Why did this happen to me? She told me that basically, this poor woman had died in front of me so I could have the extra years she would have had on this earth. I used to call her Hilda, and invoke her every time before getting on a plane, or when something crazy would happen. At the end of the day I am still Mexican. Goodnight mija once again from Lincoln Heights. Mija, are you really a Virginia? I would never have guessed—not that I thought you a slut, you just seemed like such a sexual or sensual being. All the strong, amazing and independent women seem to be single. I would think a man would want a strong, financially independent woman by their side, but maybe not. You know, there's a saying in Mexico, *Mejor sola que mal acompañada*, better alone than in bad company.

I wish I'd taken that to heart. Or the one my dad used to tell me: *hay gente que cruza el pantano y no se ensucia*, there are people who cross the swamp without getting dirty. I loved the Rock Hudson story. Actually I've loved all of your stories. I'm assuming you've published your memoirs? Memoirs of a Swan? Goodnight again. This feels kind of like group therapy, thank god for the editor.
Sent from my iPhone

**On November 19, 2018 at 1:00 AM,
Vaginal Davis wrote:**

More when I can get my lazy ass to the Bibliotech maybe Wednesday as I have therapy and a doctor's appointment tomorrow.
Love&kissyz
Graciela

**On November 19, 2018 at 3:15 AM,
Vaginal Davis wrote:**

Hey Darling,
It's so cold here in Berlin I don't feel like leaving the flat so I am writing to you on my phone.

Wasn't aware you had lived in Berlin. My first time here was in the early '80s, performing on a bill with Wieland Speck, who ran a section of the Berlin Film Festival for many years. I was also in Berlin before and just after the wall came down. I had a lot of weird successful performances in Germany, like at the Six Sex Weeks festival in Hamburg in 1996. And then I had a six-month residency here in 2001 that inadvertently led to my relocation in 2005. My art group, the CHEAP Kollektiv, was also created in 2001.

It's funny, the only one to clock me on my virginity is Ron Athey. He said it's only natural that someone who talks so much about sex hasn't experienced it. That's me in a nutshell. I feel there is a reason for everything, and I guess I never wanted to be a fool for love like my older sister was. I do resent that everything in the world is geared for couples and families.

Priscilla B still lives in Berlin. Remember her and Mary Mullen of the avant-punk group The Hesitations? And Lucas Reiner, the younger brother of movie director Rob Reiner, lives here. Lucas is an artist. He was part of the LA punk scene, and was very close with Tommy Gear of the Screamers. He also went to Beverly Hills High with Pleasant Gehman. I hear from Pleasant every once in a while via email.

Pleasant and I go all the way back to Judy's at the Century City Mall, the Biba makeup counter and Judy's Gear For Guys. Judy's also had a makeup line called Paint that had the most phenomenal colors. Yes I write and talk vividly about sex, but it's all from imagination, not praxis. I'm also a good listener and ask a lot of probing questions. I am so damn nosy, my mother used to call me her little attorney, since I always demanded more details after already intense questioning.

I'm not writing a memoir, but a novel that incorporates a lot of true stories. After Grace Dunham, Lena Dunham's sibling, did this New Yorker profile on me I was approached by a big literary agent and blah blah blah, so a lot has come pouring out of me...

Now you are the ultimate love god. Everything pouring out of you is sexy, sexy, and more sexy. I remember first meeting you and being mesmerized. With your style and dapper way of dressing you exuded big dick arrogance, which is always thrilling in a man. Warren Beatty has that, and Bill Clinton. I remember shaking the president's hand. He heard my name as "Reginald Davis" not Vaginal, and I didn't correct him—not with those big hands. He looks deep into your eyes. I'd probably let him spunk on my dress too.

Subject: 6th Round
On November 21, 2018 at 6:39 AM,
Vaginal Davis wrote:

From Freezing Cold Berlina

My Darling Beauty,

I remember the days when downtown LA was pretty much emptied in the evening except for artists. My friend Doug Gordon who now lives in Thailand but who used to be the art director of Tokyo Journal had a loft on Spring Street near Banco Popular you could ride your bicicleta in, and their rooftop garden was just major Miss Gorgeous. The rent for my first flat in Hollywood, The Karnak Apartments on La Mirada with the Egyptian pylon façade, was just $70 a month. It was a very large single or bedsit apartment with relief sculptures in the hallway and a snake motif banister in the stairwell. One of my neighbors was this sweet old man who used to work at the old Fox Studios on Sunset and Western that became Zody's Department Store. He'd retired from 20th Century Fox when it had that giant back lot in Century City. He told wonderful stories about old Hollywood that had me riveted. I lived on the second floor and he lived on the third, next to my Afro Sister "Pop That Cherry" Jefferson, aka Priscilla Hazelwood. She worked at the *LA Weekly* in the Art Department. Yes, I remember Jay Levin, the publisher of *LA Weekly*, giving drugs to the staff. When you worked at the *Weekly* at night, they provided dinner. I loved the offices on Hyperion, not far from the Frog Pond. That actor Barry Brown from the Peter Bogdanovich film *Daisy Miller* was the boyfriend of the owner, and he hung himself there. That was a tragedy. Remember the co-sexual bathhouse Healthworks on Hyperion? I always wanted to go there and see if a hot bisexual man would go for me.

My Afro Sister Pop That Cherry and I would go to Dreams (that later became Spaceland) for their happy hour with all you can eat tacos. Dreams, and that part of Silver Lake near the reservoir, used to be very white trash not at all upscale like it is now.

I also remember Gloria Ohland. She never liked me. I don't remember why, but it could be that I got Michael Lassell, one of the features editors, in trouble over an article I wrote. For a while I was persona non grata at the *Weekly* so I just wrote for the *LA Reader* under a different name. I had so many different personas! I wrote for the *Weekly* as Kayle Hilliard. Jay Levin didn't know that "Kayle" was actually Vaginal Davis. I wrote one of the Best of LA's for the late Jonathan Gold. He had me write about Funkytown...The Afro Sisters Take You Through Funkytown on the RTD Bus. Beulah Love took the photos in the bus yard. It was the first time the *Weekly* recognized South Central LA.

Gloria Ohland was good friends with Shelly da Cunha, who was married to the British punk musician Keith Levine. Donita Sparks, who was in the band the Shrews and later L7, and Kim Jones also worked at the *Weekly*. They were so cute and stylish. They always came to my Afro Sister shows. Kim married that hot punk boy dream Monty Messex who used to work at Flip of Hollywood. I had such a crush on Monty going back to when he was with Valerie, who worked with Ron Athey at Poseur on Melrose. Monty and Valerie were a very stylish young punk couple. The late artist Tim Smith was wildly in love with Monty.

For years, I never paid more than $200 in rent in LA. I always lucked out, finding very cheap flats that had interesting histories. The Karnak used to be owned by Paramount Pictures to house its junior stars. There were a series of Egyptian-themed apartments close to the Karnak and Paramount. A lot of rock bands like The Fiends, the Shadow Minstrels, The Nymphs and The Lazy Cowgirls lived at the Karnak. The

Happy Malaga Castle, that used to be owned by Greta Garbo, was not far away and hosted so many rock 'n roll parties. An Armenian family with two gorgeous and hunky sons lived in a house next door to the Karnak. I swooned over them—me and my schoolgirl-style crushes.

I also loved going with Cherry to the Armenian deli on Wilton Place to buy their cured meats and breads. Further down Wilton was the famous house where well hung Perry Farrell lived with the young hot boys he started the band Jane's Addiction with. Talk about a sex guru. He had all those boys dickmatized by his giant pecker. The Afro Sisters and Jane's Addiction used to perform together all the time at Theoretical Parties and at that big space under The Detour bar at the Junction. I was friends with Perry Farrell's young Orange County girlfriend Xiola Blue who od'd on heroin. She was such a beautiful, smart girl. She traveled with her best friends Mischa and Ix. Ix is still around—he goes by his real name, Stephan, now. He was in Berlin a few years ago and we reconnected. He'd lived with Buck in Hawaii for many years. Do you remember Buck? He was the sexy telephone repair guy in the punk scene with long blond hair and a muscular tight body. He was good friends with another boy, Pony who also had long hair but dark. Pony was very sweet and pretty and he hung out with Elliot of Industrial Revolution and Regina, a sexy punk "It" girl who sported a bald headed look.

I adored Tomato du Plenty. He was never two-faced like a lot of those people. He always called me doll face. I had some art objects and makeup paintings in a group show he curated at Cheap Racist Gallery. Do you remember that space? It was near the river.

I remember the Rosslyn, The Cecil and Alexandria Hotels—they were all SRO (Single Room Occupancy) flophouses where you could rent a room cheaply. Those days are over. When I got my first big apartment in Koreatown the rent was $500 and I thought that was a fortune!!!! I'd never paid that much before in my life. To think, having a three-bedroom/two bath split-level apartment with a garage and a terrace where on a clear day you could see all the way to Catalina Island! I also had a balcony with precious view of the Hollywood Sign. I didn't have a car but I used the garage to store costumes and sets from performance pieces. I always lived alone, except for a brief time in the early '80s when I shared a WeHo flat with my Afro Sister Uretha Franklin, aka Helen Bed O'Neill. She owned the store Retail Slut on Melrose. I only lived with her for three months because she was too scared to live alone. That apartment was great; it was around the former from the Bodhi Tree on Melrose, near San Vicente Blvd., down from the Pacific Design Center.

Our neighbor was an older black lady who still works at dry cleaners close to Hugo's on Santa Monica near La Cienega. She was amazing, in her mid-40s at that time. She had a young white hustler boyfriend who couldn't have been older than 20. He never wore a shirt even when it was cold and he had the most incredible tight sexy body. He wore Daisy Duke cut-off shorts with his giant white penis hanging out and for shoes, only flip flops or Vans tennis shoes with giant holes where his big toes stuck out. He had really sexy and thick, manly long

Fred Flintstone feet. He had an amazing sense of style with a buzz cut, broad shoulders, one long drop earring and turquoise jewelry on his chest and wrists.

Those were the days of odd interesting couples. In Edendale, there were always older white guys with younger Latino men. The boy would start out as the old white guy's lover in his teens, but the sex part of the relationship would end in his mid-20s. Often, he'd wind up marrying a woman and then his entire extended family would live with him and his white male ex-lover. That used to be a norm in Silver Lake, Echo Park, Edendale neighborhoods in the '70s, '80s and '90s!

Just before I moved to Berlin I rented a $160-per month office space at Wilshire and Alvarado in a medical building with an abortion clinic on the ground floor. The Semiotext(e) offices are in this building, or they used to be. I lived illegally in my office/studio and used the showers at the gym in the Biltmore Hotel. After I got gentrified out of my giant Koreatown place I had to use my ingenuity to find affordable housing. LA's rents had really started to get out of control. But when one door closed, another one opened and led me to Berlin, a place where I never expected to live.

You are certainly right. There were very few people of color in the underground scene. There was Robert Lopez aka El Vez, Trudy Aguellos, Alice Bag, and my lesbiana cousin Karla Duplantier, who was the drummer for The Controllers and in England for many years, where she modeled for Vivienne Westwood. Before moving back to LA, she was in a band called Jimmy the Hoover. Poor thing, she has multiple sclerosis now. There was crazy Taquila Mockingbird. I loved her—she was a magnificent grifter. And Marsha Hunt of Marsha and the Vendettas who had a kid with Mick Jagger; Tito Larriva; Gronk; the late Wagner Vieira who was the Brazilian David Wojnarowicz and used to design sets for Afro Sisters performances like *We're Taking Over*, *Interracial Dating Game* and *Salome's Last Dance*. There was Teresa Covarrubias of The Brat; the guys in Los Lobos; Angela of Odd Squad; Sean Carrillo; Art of Arts Building Jr.; The Tired Danielle aka Danielle of the Epiphany aka Baby Tenderlove of the Cosmetics; Michael Angelo of Gino's II and The Cosmetics; Michael Glass of Amok Books who used to run the bookstore at LACE when it was downtown; the guys in Fishbone; The Busboys and Roach from Roach and the Whiteboys...and that sexy black photographer, I can't remember his name, who got killed one night after picking up a trick at the One Way on Hoover. He got jumped while they were having sex at that park up the street. There was that cute black boy with the green eyes who was part of the Better Youth Organization of Youth Brigade and Godzilla's, what was his name? He went to UCLA at the same time I went there and we had some of the same friends, but we didn't know each other. He was in that punk rock documentary Another State of Mind along with Mike Ness of Social Distortion, who I had a huge crush on. I was distressed to see Mike Ness fucking Sean DeLear on the dance floor one year at that 666 New Year's Eve punk party at Vermont and Wilshire. Everyone was fucking at that party except me! Angelo of Fishbone was boning my Afro Sister Cherry, Stella of Straypop was with DJane, and I was so jealous that Sean D. lured Mike Ness into her sex web. She was wearing her fall, and those fake eyelashes and silver spray-painted stilettos. I loved her minimal makeup look. Well, she did have a big dick on that skinny body of hers, and she always had drugs, which was a big enticement for those messy white boys she favored. She was the ultimate snow queen.

I miss Sean D. who used to go by the name of Tony Cosmos. She always showed up wherever there was a scene. Her recent passing was definitely the end of an era. She'd moved to Vienna and was part of the Austrian artist collective Geliten. She died in Vienna. She's a face from the past I'll certainly miss. She sang backup on my PME EP from 1991. She wasn't asked—somehow she showed up with my drummer Big Dick Sneaky Pete Tomlinson and wound up on the record. That was her genius: always being in the right place at the right time.

**On November 21 2018 at 5:56 AM,
Reynaldo Rivera wrote:**

The '80s began with a bang fueled by PCP, crystal and coke. I was Mexican, so the late '70s were all about PCP angel dust—did I mention I said yes? By 1979 the angel dust craze was over, but I discovered speed up in Stockton through a guy I worked with at the cannery. I liked it because it allowed me to work all those hours, seven days a week—and the weight started coming off. At a certain point I thought I was glamorous like Jean Harlow. But I'd stop when I went back to LA.

I started hanging out with my cousin Tricia who was beautiful, glamorous and a massive drug addict. Money was no problem, she was supported by a sugar daddy, so eventually I stopped going to Stockton and started a serious speed/crystal run that lasted two years. I will say they were fun and tragic. So much happened in those years—days, weeks and months were packed with nonstop heavy living. That's when I met Craig at the *LA Weekly*. He hooked me like a carp with crystal. He'd come over to my house with speed till finally I gave in, and the rest is history. I got fired from the *Weekly* because I missed a week of work. I didn't go to work because Tricia's boyfriend made me go on a hideout from the FBI. I don't think that crazy honky had slept in a month. He saw FBI everywhere. I was young and I admired him, and he was the only photography person I knew. Still, I knew he was wacky. I may have been young, but by that point I'd been around the block a few thousand times. And I've gotta say, getting fired from the *Weekly* was quite a feat at that time. The paper would come out on Thursday, and we'd take alcohol breaks to go down the street to Casita del Campo or the Frog Pond. No one asked for ID and drunk driving was the norm until those mothers against drunk driving ruined it for all of us.

**On November 21, 2018 at 1:36 PM,
Vaginal Davis wrote:**

Dearest Mr. Juicy,
It is so damn cold in Berlina. It's usually never this cold till January or February. Earlier I wrote to you from the public library. I wish I hadn't ventured from my warm flat. I have doctor appointments tomorrow and Friday so I will have to go back outside and am dreading it. That's the thing with global warming—it's sometimes ultra warm and ultra cold. I never experienced such a hot summer this year in Germany so I bet we will have an extra harsh winter.

I remember when Robert Lopez ran La Luz de Jesus above Wacko on Melrose. Gorilla Rose worked at Wacko and so did Warhol Superstar Holly Woodlawn when she first moved from NY to LA. We did the first Cholita show at La Luz for Paul "Whitey" Glenn, the owner of Cowboys & Poodles, when he was living in Guatemala and making very interesting folk art. Slaight was his lover during that period, and when he got sick Whitey sent him back to LA. Slaight was so sexy, tall and beautiful. I was so crushed out on Slaight.

At a party at the Happy Malaga Castle I told Slaight how much I'd admired him for so long and how sexy he looked in the sailor outfit he wore in a performance with The New Marines and Christian Farrow at the LA Press Club on Vermont. I had just been featured in *Interview* magazine in a photo taken by Albert Sanchez, and Slaight said that he wished he could do what I did: all he'd ever done was be someone's boyfriend or trick.

I wanted so much back then to feel desired sexually.

Slaight was the ultimate boy beauty of the era. I didn't get until years later that what he was trying to say to me was that he felt like a passed around Patty...from one rich guy to the next, then discarded for a younger and prettier boy with a bigger dick.

When he got sick with AIDS the end of his reign as a sought-after Hollywood stud was brutal and abrupt. I remember visiting him at a rundown flophouse in Long Beach, and even with the Kaposi sarcoma lesions all over his face and body he looked so serene.
Love&kissyz
Graciela Grejalva

**On November 21, 2018 at 11:25 PM,
Reynaldo Rivera wrote:**

Mija are you planning on living the rest of your life in Berlina? Just wondering...

I did a job with Jonathan Gold back in 87 when he interviewed KRS-One. I took photos of him on Hollywood Blvd. Reading about LA in the '80s, you'd wonder how we survived all the violence. It was apparently one of the most violent cities in the US, with Rampart being the worst. I lived in the Rampart/MacArthur Park area in the later '80s...very convenient for gals on substances.

You can't talk about LA in the '80s without factoring in the violence and drugs. There was so much of both. We got the volk who'd been thrown out of prison by Castro—do you remember the Marielitos? And then, all the mentally ill people Ronald Reagan put out of hospitals while he was governor, and the Central Americans escaping genocide...Even the cholos thought twice about fucking with them. I felt the violence around me, but I'd lived with violence all my life. It does create a certain psychosis that you don't see until leaving. Arriving in Berlin, it felt strange to be walking at all hours of the night without the constant anxiety you feel in the US. My girlfriend say Rey, you're not in LA, stop being so paranoid. I hadn't realized it was so obvious…but this decade of the battering ram that the police used to crash into people's houses whenever they thought there might be drugs. The chief of police commented that all casual drug users should be shot.

I still think fondly of the '80s. I'd never really felt welcomed in the Latino or gay communities, not that I didn't want to. Having grown up a pariah, knowing everyone in my Mexican village would hate or even kill me if they found out what I was, I always wanted to belong. Being homo was the one thing everyone hated in that town—whenever one was found out, they'd get run out of town. Once, I was dragged by my feet through the town because they thought I was gay. I was in a small park with a kid I'd just met, the son of the Telegraph Director. This kid sat on my lap in a sexual manner. A group of men saw this and attacked me, and left the other kid to run home. I had no one to protect me. And I just realized, it was this kid's father who molested me when I was 7 or 8. I don't mean to get all Debbie Downer, it's all in the past. I remember a pair of maroon Levi's my aunt brought back from the US. Oh I loved them—they were a bit short and tight, so my aunt took them back after seeing me prance around with my tight red pants and my shirt tied around my waist. I was so bummed out. It's the story of my life, always loving the wrong thing. Every time I've allowed myself to love a human being totally, it has always been the wrong thing. But not with my dogs. I'd never had any pets until I got my three dogs and I'm thankful I'm finally able to just live without fear of it being used against me. Yes, love will tear us apart. How did I get from violent Los Angeles to love will tear us apart?

Who knows. I'm probably still waiting to be rescued by love.

Hmmmmm.

Subject: Round Seven
On November 21, 2018 at 11:35 PM,
Vaginal Davis wrote:

Such a good question as to whether I will always live in Miss Berlina Brunhilde. I know I could never live anywhere in the USA again especially missy El Lay. Probably I will want to live somewhere in Mexico like Guadalajara or Vera Cruz.

My poor late nephew—his second wife was a white girl from Washington State whose parents disowned her when she married my nephew. She left him several times running off with some wannabe rappers she met online. My nephew would always take her back after the rapper would dump her. He'd say, "but I LOVE her." I'd tell him, "Love isn't enough sweetie."

Jon Bok was the name of Paul Glynn and Robert Lopez's ex lover. He is a folk artist who puts bottle caps on old furniture. He did the old House of Blues and I think his husband is Mario Prietto's gay older brother—if they are still together. I think Paul Glynn and his Cowpoo partner Phil Heath have that store called Re-Mix on Beverly Blvd, if it's

still there. I never liked Phil but Whitey Paul could make a dog laugh. He's from Detroit, and has that Detroit thing that I like.

Yes the crack epidemic hit LA hard, things were so dangerous then. Surprised I was never mugged, especially shopping at those MacArthur Park outlets back then—people were so desperate. Berlin is pretty safe at night for a big city but I am still on alert from living in LA. You won't see me using my smartphone, zoning out in public. One must stay alert in the street.

Horrible Ronald Reagan. My mother use to say white people would joyfully eat the excrement directly out of his ass. And he used to be a Democrat.

Gotta prepare for taking my series of tests at the stomach doctor.

Love&kissyz

Anselma

On November 21, 2018, at 11:46 PM,
Vaginal Davis wrote:

Oh my Baron,

Preparing took less time than I expected. Didn't realize it was going to be so easy to knock out a stool sample for my doctor. Here in Germany doctors are so feces oriented in diagnosing what ails you.

You brought up a very important subject, in terms of gay, or so-called gay community. I'm always a little distrustful of "professional gays," now these homo-normative gays have started co-opting queerness, which I hate!

Gomorrah Wednesday aka Keith Holland who owned the indie label Amoeba Records and Filmworks lived next door to the late, great Harry Hay on Melrose Hill who started the Radical Fairies—now they were about community though they were a little too hippy-dippy for me.

Remember when gay bars in WeHo would ask for three pieces of ID to keep out women, femmes, blacks, Latinos and Asians? So much for being open. That's why I deal with people individually. I like to keep a critical eye on any group or movement, even the queercore scene that I'm the godmother of! When the scene started getting attention in the early '90s, so many people who had literary aspirations latched on. One guy I met around then who'd moved to LA from the Midwest accused me of keeping fun things away from him, like I was some divine arbiter of queer taste. As if I was purposely not letting him know about the most fun parties and clubs and preventing him from meeting sexy queer boys he could have sex with.

Like I have that much power.

Insane.

I actually liked this particular guy; he was cute and interesting but he got on my last raw nerve with his accusations.

Love&kissyz

Fetcha

Sent from my iPhone

Here at doctor's office waiting in between round of tests…
I knew I was going to be here for a while. I also have to come
tomorrow.

Oh the issue of drugs…I'm beginning to understand
more about why people want to be out of it. This life is so
difficult. I understand the need to check out, especially if you
are poor. Every few years mother would go on a bender. I'd
come home from school and hear jazz music playing loud
and see empty bottles of Michelob beer. The stress and strain
would get to her. Usually she never drank, never kept alcohol
in the home. My oldest sister Gracie Lee was a Champale
alcoholic. That's all she drank, but she did drink every day.
My other sister Gloria Jean became a Margarita mix alcoholic
later in life, but that wasn't till she discovered she had breast
cancer. When my mother got wasted she was a happy drunk,
but then, because alcohol is a depressive, she'd get sad and the
truth about her life would surface. My mother was filled with
so many Black Creole secrets I almost wish she'd gotten drunk
more often.

I was a little jealous of the punk rock junkies. I have
always been curious about heroin but I have an aversion to
needles. I never did acid, mushrooms, ecstasy, crystal, or
speed. I did try quaaludes and cocaine and loved both.

I'm sure if I ever did Ecstasy it would have the opposite
effect on me—I'd hate everyone. I never even did poppers.
I'm too much of a control queen for drugs. I have to be on
top of everything at all times—forever the over-achiever,
never allowing myself to be messy. Even drinking, I'm such
a lightweight: Very little gets me drunk and then I get sleepy.
A few times I've vomited from drinking and on those rare
occasions I don't touch alcohol for over a year. Mota I hate.
I don't like smoking anything and I've only been high once
from weed that I ate in cookies. Was high for what felt like a
week. Awful feeling that was. But I understand people's need
for the escape with drugs better.

Drugs should be legalized to get rid of the stigma
attached to criminalization. That tired prison industrial
complex that makes money off of black and brown bodies.
Makes me want to take my earrings off and throw down on
these Republicans and their three strikes and crime control
when crime has been down for over 20 years. Remember
when people would break in and steal a TV? That doesn't
happen anymore.

I never have fit in anywhere, so years ago I stopped.
I just create my own cosmos with the people who orbit it. Plus,
I can entertain myself and don't mind being alone. Some gays
can't even go to the toilet alone.
Smoochies
Fetchacita

On November 23, 2018 at 12:55 AM,
Reynaldo Rivera wrote:

Mija, you can't tease and not name names, who was this
Midwest queen that thought you were keeping him from being
entertained!? Do you remember the Flaming Colossus?
I think it was on 9th near Alvarado. I remember when the Frog
Pond closed because the owner hung himself after finding
out he had AIDS, like Jim Van Tyne from The Anti Club and
The Theoreticals. He got a room at that hotel on the corner of
Western and Hollywood Blvd. It's no longer there; it's been
replaced by a Thai mini-mall. Jim was a friend of Craig's.
I always wondered what happened to Tim Smith. I remember
the portrait he painted of Craig. You mentioned knowing
him…I wasn't a friend, I'm just being nosy. Do you miss LA?
How will you describe Los Angeles in your memoir?

On November 24, 2018 at 6:55 AM,
Vaginal Davis wrote:

Oh, the Midwesterner was this guy named Bill Bonifay. He did
a 'zine in Wisconsin that was quite interesting and then later,
he did a 'zine called *Evil Taco*, which was an unauthorized
biography of me, and it was hilarious. When I did that piece for
Pacific Standard Time in 2012 at the old Bullocks on Wilshire
produced by West of Rome, that's what I called the limited
edition artist book. Bill eventually created his own suburban
scene in LA with all these cute young Chicanos and black kids.
I spent a lot of time at Flaming Colossus with Michèle Lamy,
and the two French bros who owned the place, who I had a
mega-crush on. Those were fun times.

Jim Van Tyne attempted suicide at that motel but
the pills didn't kill him so Waylon & Randy finished the job.
The wages of sin are death, and they both died shortly after.
I miss Jim Van Tyne. He was definitely a mentor, and so
talented, with great taste in music. His legendary pancake
breakfasts—and those feasts he would create when Brad
Lapin was in town! Every freeloader in Hollywood came to
those spectacles. I stayed at Brad's and his lover's sumptuous
palazzo in Rome right near the Coliseum in 1999. The building
is from the 15th century. Brad was shocked when he read the
rave review I got in *la Repubblica*, the Italian national
newspaper. I think the only reason those Italian journalists
came was because it got leaked Marina Spadafora was going to
be there, and her family is royalty in Milan.

I miss my friends who still live in LA, although there
are not many left, because most got priced out. I miss good
Mexican and El Salvadoran food. I crave pupusas!!!!

Bruce Judy La Bruce is getting gay divorced from his
Afro Cuban husband. I remember when they met in a gay
bathhouse, the Cuban plowed Judy good with his 14 thick
inches of dinosaur dick. Judy was immediately dickmatized.
Cubans are so good at working it. I admire genius grift and this
Cubano played Judy like a violin. After they married, he fed
Judy rich foods until he got tubby and lost his sleek modern
dancer physique, and then the Cubano stopped fucking
him. So Judy took himself off the market because he was
embarrassed by his weight. He emailed me once from Brazil
bemoaning how sexy the boys were, and I said go to one of
those hustler bathhouses and lease yourself an Afro Brazilian

stud. I told him they don't care about your weight, just your billfold. So he did—he spent three days getting split in half, reopening his sex chakras with a different sex champion.

Frank Rodriguez had a very good-looking friend who was the most charming male courtesan to wealthy older men. This guy looked right at you when you talked, asking pertinent questions, gaining your trust. It didn't matter if he was genuinely interested; he just had mad communication skills. I loved that he was attractive with a nice build but wasn't overly muscled. He had a nice bulge in his pants but he was very presentable to parents, co-workers or board members. During the Club Sucker days he was about 30. If I had money, I would have given him my last dime. Yahoo. On bus headed to get a massage after being so long at doctor's office
Love&kissyz
Fetcha

**On November 24, 2018 at 4:11 PM,
Reynaldo Rivera wrote:**

I think my alienation from my Raza was my sexuality, and from gays...hmm, it was their exclusivity. When I first discovered West Hollywood I was giving androgyny and noticed I was invisible. A friend of Gloria's took me cuz she thought I would be a hit and she was surprised by the outcome. I was surprised too; I did want to have gay friends. At one time, I thought our gayness made us one. I also felt that gayness allowed me to wear a dress or not; paint my nails, wear a wig—it was all good because we were already gay and there was nothing worse! I couldn't possibly sink any lower. I didn't have many gay friends and the ones I did were like me—a bit artsy and just doing our own thing without the tight jeans and t-shirts so popular at the time. We were going to see the Plasmatics or Siouxsie, The Stranglers etc., but I found out I could sink lower, and within the so-called gay community, i.e., the white community: Being perceived as effeminate was even worse than being gay. I disagreed. At first I went out of my way to be the opposite and that caused a lot of trouble—people throwing shit at me from their cars or screaming insults. That's when wearing two earrings was crazy, or dying your hair or having long hair...that's why I fucking hate seeing heteros with earrings or anything else that would have meant a fight back then.

But I will say, my first boyfriend was one of those tight-clothes queens who listened to Altered Images. He was super good-looking, which ended up being the reason I ran the other way. There wasn't a mirror he didn't stare at and I was the opposite. The only time I did stare into the mirror was during my speed craze when I thought I was Dietrich, but otherwise I didn't like being reminded how ugly I was. I really had an issue with that but I hid it well, just as I hid love. I was afraid of letting anyone close. I wonder if I dated all those super good-looking men to remind me of my ugliness, so they would know the experience of being loved by a frog?

I tell you I love like a dog, there's no half way for me—it's all or nothing. I've only truly loved three men and dated five. People always assumed I was a whore but nothing was

farther from the truth. I was so afraid of catching cooties.

Maybe this book is more about leaving a body of beauty out of such an ugly life. I was determined to find beauty in places deemed ugly, or maybe I was just documenting the way that beauty can live side by side with violence and the ugliness of life, society and this country, a country that let millions of us die in the most inhumane way. We were rewriting the script we were given at birth. So many of us died without a trace, due to AIDS and other acts of violence. I've chosen to leave a trace. Recording their images as they re-imagined themselves and their stories in the '80s and '90s in Los Angeles, the city of dreams. Mrs Alex, Olga, Yoshi and all the rest of us were here, and we mattered. We made this city our city, if only for a brief time. And then we disappeared as quickly as we appeared. Still, our stories are woven into the story of this city—every alley and shitty bar, every empty lot where a rent-controlled building once stood.

**On November 24, 2018 at 04:35 PM,
Reynaldo Rivera wrote:**

I am always willing to lend a hand to my old queer brothers and sisters.
Sent from my iPhone

**November 24, 2018 at 8:58 PM,
Reynaldo Rivera wrote:**

I saw Les Rita Mitsouko at the Flaming Colossus. I think it was the only place they performed in LA. The singer Miss Ringer was the bomb. I was a huge fan.
Sent from my iPhone

**On November 25, 2018 at 3:16 AM,
Vaginal Davis wrote:**

My Darling Baron,
As Quentin Crisp would say, getting older is not for sissies. As a person of color, I feel like we go through several stages. The first is being ashamed and just wanting to become white and fit into the dominant culture, thinking that would solve all our woes. After we grow out of that stage, around our tweens, we go through the militant stage where we want to kill all white people and anything and everything associated with whiteness. I went through this stage in elementary school during the time that the Black Panthers came into our school and took over. This was the time I discovered Ms. Angela Davis, who was plastered all over the post office as the most wanted woman in America. By your mid-teens you go through a centrist period, which is also very confusing. You have a lot of righteous anger and nowhere to channel it. That's where being a bookworm came in handy for me. I lost myself in literature and escaped into my own inner world of fantasy.

Now as an old lady, I'm just one big giant bitcheta who vacillates between being very solitary, spending a lot of time alone in my own world, and then deciding I need to be more social, making an effort to be around people. Basically I am a mess. But at least I'm aware of my messiness and I am not deluded. Or not completely deluded. I do have my moments. I try to put things in perspective. Would my childhood self have ever imagined living the life I live now? It would have seemed like an impossibility. So I have to count my blessings, try not to become jaded and appreciate every moment. There are no guarantees in this life.

Working with, and mentoring young people by teaching my woolly brand of performance art keeps me in touch with a younger generation of artists. It's a lot of work and leaves me exhausted, but it's so worthwhile...exposing the children to my off-kilter worldview. They get really excited. Sometimes I wonder what things would have been like had I been a normal who had serial relationships...or if I'd married someone and had children. I find the thought of that really disgusting and limiting. Although I wouldn't mind having some big hunky man with a dinosaur penis stopping by once a week or so to devastate me in the bedroom. But maybe that fantasy would turn sour if it became a real, and I'm better off being alone.
love and kisses
Fetch

**On Nov 26, 2018, at 3:43 AM
Vaginal Davis wrote:**

My Dearest Darling Baron,
We are opposite on so many fronts. You have always had a partner and I have always been alone.

I loved the free lunch program in the LA Unified School District. I was always hungry growing up so getting that free lunch was very important to me. Back then, the cafeteria had workers who actually cooked fresh food everyday and it was quite good. Especially the hot cinnamon rolls for recess. In junior high and high school I worked in the cafeteria and had access to all the best food. All the cafeteria ladies loved me.

What you had to deal with on every level was much more serious. You are such a survivor, tackling adversity with grace and moxie. I really had nothing to complain about. Yes we were poor, on food stamps and Aid to Families with Dependent Children, but I was warm, with clothing and shelter and three simple meals a day. I had lots of supervision since for the most part, my mother didn't work and was at home after school every day. And I had my older sisters and lesbian uncles who all fussed over me and gave me lots of attention.

I wasn't a brat but I was given special attention because I did so well in school. I was the ultimate test taker and always scored high, so the teachers and administrators loved me using me to score points with politicians. I did get it from one sixth grade teacher, Mrs. Gichtin. I came to the defense of Linda Eng, a student who said in class that the principal deserved to get beaten up by a group of parents. Mrs. Gichtin attacked the girl verbally, and I said very quietly that she had a right to her opinion. This was when Mayor Bradley had been elected as the first black mayor of a major American city, and Mrs. Gichtin said she didn't like how the media made you feel that you were racist if you didn't vote for Mayor Bradley. The other candidate

was the very racist longtime mayor Sam Yorty, and I said in a mild and low voice that perhaps those who didn't vote for Mayor Bradley weren't fully aware of how racist they were. That didn't go over well with Mrs. Gichtin.

By the time I was at Berendo Jr. High, I had some major detractors. Some teachers thought I was stuck up, though one teacher defended me saying that I was tall and so carried myself in a way that made me appear stuck up, because I had such good posture and bearing. Your experience with teachers is typical for most black and brown kids. Teachers don't expect much, and consider them problems immediately, treating them as such. One black boy, Ray Brown, who I knew from elementary to high school got that kind of treatment. No matter what he did, he was frowned upon so after a while he just stopped trying. He was so sweet and confided many times that he felt dumb. I told him he was no dummy but he was never given a chance to shine.

I was an overachiever and I could code switch more easily and go into white voice, speaking very properly, which a lot of the other kids weren't able to do. If you can't code switch, you make white people uncomfortable and immediately get branded a problem. I got away with murder because I could code switch effortlessly. I used my voice to show displeasure with the inequities of the system in a way that was firm and authoritative. This was also a bit disturbing to white people, that at such a young age I gave off a confident air of authority. I just copied my mother's soft scholarly voice. My favorite phrase was This is not acceptable, spoken while giving them a horrified look, which basically said I thought they were racist, without actually saying the words out loud. This worked their white liberal guilt, and it was a powerful statement coming from a child. My mother used to always say she'd rather suck the dick of the Imperial Grand Wizard of the Ku Klux Klan than deal with any so-called well-meaning white liberals.

Even in my 20s, photographer Beulah Love always said that I got away with murder. I could say harsh, critical things without coming across as harsh. Whereas when he said similar things people immediately took violent offense. But once, I got clocked by Michèle Lamy. It was downtown at her studio on Traction Avenue near Al's Bar where Michèle had her knitwear line in the '80s. She was dying clothes, as she did whenever there was a problem and she needed to process. She'd just opened her store in the Beverly Center. I told her soon she'd have a store in every mall in America and she looked at me and said, "Get Out!"

**Subject: Round 11
On November 26, 2018 at 3:37 PM,
Vaginal Davis wrote:**

My Darling,
It's after midnight here in Berlin but I had to jump out of bed to ask you before I forget: did you ever take pictures of this amazingly incredible sexy go-go boy named Obregon who danced regularly at Chico's in Montebello, Arena and Circus?

I think his first name was Rich. He had a big tattoo

of his name in script. I was so crushed out on him. He was the
most beautiful boy with great lips and a bottom to build
a dream on and his muscles were beyond perfect. He was an
Adonis, and very sweet. The owner of Chico's sent him and
another exotic dancer to my fundraiser, Spicy Beef Curtains,
at my request. We were raising money to bring more artists
to LA for the Platinum Oasis that Ron and I curated for
the Outfest Film Festival. It was held at the fist fuck motel the
Coral Sands on Western and Hollywood Blvd back in 2002.

Whatever happened to Obregon? Did you take pics of
the go-go boys at Las Estrellas on Hollywood Blvd at Bronson?
I loved that lil dive bar. And Le Barcito on Glendale Blvd in
Edendale?
Ok I am going back to bed. Goodnight
Love&kissyz
Fetcha
Sent from my iPhone

**Date: 27 Nov 2018 at 1:40 PM,
Reynaldo Rivera wrote:**

My darling Vag,

I used to surprise white folk with my reading habits.
At the time, I thought it a compliment when they said how
interesting it was that I was reading de Sade...or that I read at
all! They were just surprised to see a Mexican reading.
I guess they didn't know there were bookstores on every
corner in the smallest Mexican town. If there's one thing
Mexican folk like, it's reading, from *¡Alarma!* to Foucault.
You know, I used to wonder, for a paper that spent most of its
time writing about minorities, mostly Latinos or black folk,
and being so politically correct—why didn't they have any
minority writers at the *LA Weekly* til they got Rubén Martinez?
Remember how popular the *Weekly* was? Everybody had the
Weekly at their house, at one point. That paper went down
the toilet when Jill Stewart took over.

What is your view of this city? What do you think of
the current changes, compared to the '80s and '90s? It's
amazing the extent of change happening here, and I imagine
for someone living abroad, it must be disconcerting. What
makes LA cool for me is also what makes it fucked up: the way
beautiful buildings are dumped for parking lots or those awful
apartment buildings that have sprung up all over downtown,
like the Orsini. Still,it allows for interesting possibilities.
I'm just waiting for them to happen. I do have faith that we'll
possibly build a better city this time. We've passed progressive
measures that wouldn't have passed a decade ago. At least
there are progressives in this new wave of young people
moving in, even though they might seem a bit suburban in
their quest for safety. Freedom is dangerous. The '80s were
violent but we had freedoms that seem impossible now.
I didn't even know I had to register my car; I drove it for years
with the same tags, like in New York when New York was a real
city. It was exciting and dangerous, and now it's just safe, like
Disneyworld is clean and safe, and full of young suburbanites,
like in LA. I just wonder if I like this new safety.
Sent from my iPhone

**On Nov 30, 2018 at 2:33 AM,
Vaginal Davis wrote:**

My sweetness and light,

The best time in LA for me was the late-'70s until the
mid-'80s after the Olympics. Everyone was expecting disaster
when LA won the bid for the Olympics but it turned out
magical. All the offices let their employees do half time and
there was absolutely no traffic—it was just gorgeous and the
weather was warm but not hellish. I've never cared for sports,
but I was able to score some free tickets to swimming events
and that was dreamy. Those broad shouldered swimmers with
their V-shape, tiny waists and huge feet with long finger-like
toes. Delicious.

And in the late '70s people used to run around almost
naked. Streets like Hollywood Blvd, Sunset, Santa Monica Blvd
and Wilshire had tons of pedestrians at all hours, especially
the Miracle Mile district. These hunky mimes used to perform
outside of LACMA on Sundays around the main pavilion or
near the tar pits. I hate mimes, but these dudes were built like
brick shithouses, wearing tight pants, suspenders and white
clown face. It was great.

And Westwood Village was even fun then. I spent a
lot of time in the Village because of the Upward Bound
program where I was taking classes at UCLA before I was
officially enrolled. I even had a playwriting class, and hunky
Tim Robbins was in class with me. This was before he started
The Actors' Gang. The teacher was Oscar Saul, who'd written
the screenplay for *A Streetcar Named Desire* in 1951, starring
Brando. Oscar Saul really complimented this little short one-
act I wrote about two Creole women based the interactions
between my mother and Mrs. Alain, our landlady.

My teachers at UCLA included Dorothy Arzner, an
openly lesbian film director, and one of only two women in the
Directors Guild during the Hollywood Golden era, the other
being Ida Lupino. Shirley Clarke also taught at UCLA, and
Haskell Wexler. I went with Tim Robbins to see a production
of an Arthur Schnitzler play at some Equity Waiver theater
in Hollywood on El Centro Street. The play was based on the
same novella that Stanley Kubrick later adapted into *Eyes
Wide Shut*. I remember seeing a WWI play at this same theater
in the '80s, starring Andrew Stevens and hunky Maxwell
Caulfield, who married Juliet Mills, who played Nanny in the
TV series *Nanny and the Professor*. And I saw the play *Vanities*
at the Music Center and a production of Wendy Wasserstein's
Uncommon Women and Others.

LA was so flirty in those days. I used to spend lots of
time at the California Record Store on Harvard and Pico,
which had a great selection of soundtracks. One time I was
looking through the racks and this middle-aged white man
came up next to me and whispered in my ear that I had a tight
little narrow ass that needed to get busted. I was probably 14 at
the time, and was frightened but also titillated that a dirty
old man had approached me in a lascivious manner.

I was taking ballet at the Stanley Holden Dance Studio
in West LA. I was so deluded, thinking I had a chance to
become a ballerina. Our teacher, Miss Denise had worked with

Gene Kelly. There were pictures of them together at MGM Studios from the '50s. I also took jazz and modern dance at the Marilyn Mask Dance Studios on Pico and Rimpau. Also on Pico was that old Sears Building, the police station and the swimming pool, where blonde surfer porn star Tim Kramer was a lifeguard. I remember seeing Tim Kramer at Studio One—he was so shy and sweet, not arrogant in the least. He had a sugar daddy who bought him a vitamin store in the shopping complex on Santa Monica Blvd near La Cienega where EZTV was housed.

One of the black gay dance instructors at Marilyn Mask also worked part-time at Disneyland, dancing in their stupid shows. He had a really muscular body and a huge dick bouncing around in his tights. Marilyn Mask was a Jehovah's Witness. In her younger years, she'd worked with Ben Vereen on his TV specials and in Las Vegas. The instructor with the huge cock once told me in class that I was way too tight and needed to get looser to do the dances properly...and he rolled this out in a very lewd manner. I guess it was very obvious I was a virgin. A few years later, the dancer/actor Gene Anthony Ray of the movie *Fame* took classes there. He was as sexy there as he was in the movie. I'd also see him with his dancer friends at Rage on Monday nights. Dancers have such amazing bodies but they have such horrible fashion sense.

Did you ever go to those upscale hustler bars—Numbers on Sunset Blvd, next to the Jewish deli Greenblatts; or The Carriage Trade on Beverly, that later became the restaurant Indochine? I loved both those places. I would go with my friend Doug Gordon who later moved to Japan and became art director for *Tokyo Journal*. Doug graduated from Chouinard Art Institute at MacArthur Park in 1970, before it became part of CalArts. Doug was a virgin like me, around 30 years old, and still an innocent. He loved being around a place that had a sexual milieu. We also went to the low-rent hustler bar Hunters & Collectors on Santa Monica and Gardner. At Numbers, you'd enter from the parking lot in back and walk down a mirrored staircase. Everyone sitting in the mirrored booths could see each new person arriving, and size him up from every possible angle. It was a trip. There were all these midwestern boys there—farm fresh and free-range looking, and the old men would pounce on them, especially if they were preppy, in a sweater. I remember seeing Robert Reed at Numbers. I couldn't believe Mr. Brady of *The Brady Bunch* was a big gay letch. I loved him on that TV show. He was so sexy, the ultimate hot dad. At Numbers he was a bitter old queen. Seeing him pounce on the boys was a revelation. I also saw Allan Carr, who produced the movies *Grease* and *Blue Lagoon*, at these bars. He always wore caftans from By George, the Hollywood Blvd haberdashery. Do you remember that store? I took Divine there and she loved it. She also loved Frederick's of Hollywood Bra Museum and the bargain basement of Playmates of Hollywood where everything was under $1.00. I also took Divine to Roscoe's Chicken & Waffles and for drinks at The Spotlight on Cahuenga and Selma. And The Firefly on Vine, where they lit the bar up on fire every hour and these other cute dive bars like My Place, the Lemon Drop Lounge and The Frolic Room, next to the Pantages Theatre. I think we also went to that black gay bar The Study on

Western, across from the Coral Sands fist fuck motel. I can't remember who was driving us around...maybe Rick Owens or Ricky Castro. I have a picture of Leigh Bowery and Michael Clark taken around this time when they were in LA for one of Michael's dance pieces. It's one of the few photos where the legendary Leigh Bowery is dressed casually and without makeup. He almost always wore outlandish outfits with matching hair and makeup. I took Leigh around to the Hollywood dive bars and Frederick's of Hollywood, too. You could get these 1940s reproduction pumps for only $10.00.

You are so right about all these new fugly apartment buildings popping up all over downtown LA and Hollywood. These flats are obviously cheaply made but sold as "luxury apartments." Everything in those places is just glued on. There's mold everywhere and they fall apart after a year. Berlin started building these too, but they overestimated the demand. Now the developers are losing money because anyone with any sense knows that it's a crock. I love it when developers lose money. They are such shysters, the ultimate crooks.

The building where I live in Berlin was built in 1880, with very high ceilings and sculptures in the foyer—just lovely. All these new buildings are just plain tacky. I would never want to live anywhere built after 1965. That is my cut-off date.

**Date: 8 Dec 2018 at 7:45 PM ,
Reynaldo Rivera wrote:**

I've been sick for days—will respond when I don't feel like hell.
Sent from my iPhone

**On December 9, 2018 at 2:51 AM,
Vaginal Davis wrote:**

Take your time sweetie. I am off to Geneva to teach and won't be back till Dec 16th.
Love&kissyz
Fetchacita
Sent from my iPhone

**Date: 13 Dec 2018 at 4:53 PM,
Reynaldo Rivera wrote:**

Hello Vag,
Do you think your kind of performance art could have flourished anywhere other than Los Angeles? Was it a product/side effect of your environment...of butch femmes dipped in urban violence with a side of ethnic plurality? Do you think your influences could have been rancheras as much as Darby Crash? I grew up hearing all the LA diss from people who assumed the whole city was made up of what we old school Angelinos call, "the west side." To most of the world, Los Angeles was a cultural wasteland. I think I trashed LA for a hot second, but quickly realized that somehow minorities were completely ignored in that dismissal, as if we didn't exist contributed or were a part of LA.

I think it was the anti-LA snobbishness, the narrative

of cultural superiority that got me hating on NY and SF. San Fran got super old, super fast. When I thought of SF I thought of poppers and fisting, so I guess I can forgive SF trespass. I wonder if the pre-AIDS queens hated Los Angeles as much as the ones that came after? In the late '80s and '90s one would hear about New York how culturally diverse it was. We heard about London and its musical importance, but for some reason Los Angeles was never measured by the same stick. Sorry bitches we gave you Brenton Wood, low-riders, Huggy boys, Raymond Chandler, gangster rap etc etc, and I'm not including the rest of the contributions from other cultures—the Armenians, Japanese, Chinese, etc. For our contributions one has to look at the footnotes. We never seem to be the main story.

The dominant culture has done a great job of erasing us culturally. We seem to have no recorded continuity in any neighborhood, and that's why we always feel as if we just arrived. There wasn't that much published by us (Latinos). And I don't mean publications like the *LA Weekly* that are just interested in the ghetto romantic notion of our story. Once again, we're being uprooted from areas like Echo Park, Boyle Heights and Highland Park. Young Latinos I've talked to are surprised to hear that Echo Park was once a Latino neighborhood, and that it was once very multicultural! Remember the San Francisco Mission district? Thank you!

I was thinking yesterday about how we're constantly being discovered by those at the top of the food chain...as if Mexican cinema began with Amorres Perros in the '90s. They put us back in the drawer until another decade goes by and then boom, they rediscover us.

I remember being at parties in the Mission during the '70s. I was treated like royalty then because I was a cholo from LA where low riders and Whittier Boulevard happened... I've had many influences, but I think my relationship with this city is the most important. LA was more multicultural than most of the cities in the '80s and '90s. We had Thai food on Friday, Ethiopian on Saturday, Cuban on Sunday and Italian, Filipino, Armenian, shall I go on? We took it for granted until we went to some of these international cities and had to put up with their terrible food and equally bad music. At least their food has gotten better since then. Thank you immigrants! And then there are the darling "Americans" who go to whatever third world country to learn to cook from some poor peasant in Oaxaca or Calcutta and return to the US to open a restaurant. Hey, I'm not dissing...I love that shit, guilt and all.

So tell me, how do you think this megalopolis influenced your style or art?

I'm curious about your non-white following, from early on. Did you have a black audience? I know you were quite popular with us Latinos, at least the people I knew. For those who seem to forget, we were there. We weren't just cleaning the clubs, or in my case cleaning the newspaper offices,we were also participants. Can you talk more about this?

From: Reynaldo Rivera
Date: 13 Dec 2018 at 8:49 PM,
To: Vaginal Davis

I just started feeling better but still feel unwell. Did you get last email? I sent it from a friend's computer. Hope you are well.
Sent from my iPhone

Subject: Re: Get well Darling
On December 13, 2018 at 12:48 PM,
Vaginal Davis wrote:

Hey Sweets,
Yes I received your last volley, I am teaching in Geneva—this gig keeps me exhausted. Will read and reply when I return to Berlin.
Glad you're feeling better
Love&kissyz
fetchacita
Sent from my iPhone

Subject: Winter Round—Late December
On December 20, 2018 at 4:41 AM,
Vaginal Davis wrote:

You hit it right square between the four eyes my lovely. I don't think I could exist without having been born and raised in Los Angeles. There is something in those Santa Ana winds. And I am certainly a product of rancheras as much as Miss Darby Crash and "es un punketa." Sheena es un punque rocker ahora!

I try not to diss Los Angeles though I have a love/hate relationship with the city because I'm too close to it. I was born here; I didn't come here trying to become a star in the commercial industrial entertainment industries. Those of us born here see through the facade. We know the limitations, because we were born into them.

I couldn't have been me without having grown up in LA. The same goes for Ron Athey, Beck, Alice Bag or Kembra Pfahler of the Voluptuous Horror of Karen Black, who grew up having surfer parents. We are all products of Southern California.

Ron Athey likes to refer to Santa Monica as "Aunt Monica." The tired Westside. When I was younger I never could figure out what it was about the Westside that irked me. Especially Santa Monica and Venice. Even when Venice was still rough. Maybe it's because I don't know how to swim. I was never a big fan of the beach, being terrified of large bodies of water. And the thought of laying out in the sun is a horror. Growing up with no car, the beach isn't easy to get to. It might as well be in Sacramento.

The first time I saw the ocean was on a second grade field trip to Cabrillo Beach. They used to have these bathhouses where people could shower and change, with a locker room set up. It was the first time I saw a grown man's penis. It was this blond hairy surfer dude. I was so entranced I ran up to him and grabbed his pinga. He picked me up and playfully tussled with me. I was in heaven. An adult male had never paid me so much attention. This surfer was very hairy with dark blonde thick hair all over his body and he had a thick bush of pubic hair and a chorizo that seemed gigantic to me with these hangy down Birkin Bag balls and a large mushroom headed circumcised cock. I was also fascinated by his chest hair, armpits and his large feet with long, finger-like toes that also had hair on them. He had an alpine/vanilla smell until his longish hair got wet and then he smelled like a wet dog. This must have been around 1968. I had been to Santa Monica's POP (Pacific Ocean Park) but that was at night. My brother-in-law took us to the midway, because he was the only one who had a car. At night I didn't notice the beach. Technically, Cabrillo Beach was my second time at the beach, but it was the first time I actually walked on the sand and stared at the water.

You are right—minorities are completely ignored in any discussion of culture in Los Angeles among New York intellectuals. It's so funny, all those kinds of critics of Los Angeles now live in LA. New York isn't the centre of the universe it used to be. It's still important but it's lost its zest.

Oh and San Francisco. It's easy to be a big fish in a small pond, as they say. It's pretty in San Francisco but I could never live in the Bay Area, and now it's impossible. I had never had much of an institutional presence in the Bay Area until I moved to Berlin. Then, I was invited to be in an exhibition at the Yerba Buena Museum. When I was based in LA, the institutions up north ignored me. Which was just as well.

When I was doing the Afro Sisters, the only other artist working in a similar vein at the time was Michael Franti. I believe the name of his San Francisco-based group was the Beatnigs. He went on to become better known with the hip hop band Disposable Heroes of Hiphoprisy.

One time the Afro Sisters performed at this space on Robertson Blvd that was used for Narcotics Anonymous and AA meetings. We had a very large black urban audience at this gig. and they loved us and converged on us after the show and bought every copy of *Fertile LaToyah Jackson* magazine. It was not our usual audience of art and music people. This black audience was made up of people of a lot of different ages, from elderly to tweens. One of the people in attendance was that guy who formed the Hittite Empire. Later, he became part of the Highways performance art scene in Santa Monica. Do you remember graffiti that was everywhere in the early '90s that said Tim Miller=Death? Whatever happened to him? Is he still around? He was billed as the boy-next-door of performance art.

I never performed much at Highways but I did shows at Beyond Baroque and it was one of the few places on the west side that I liked. Also, Angel's Gate in San Pedro. I performed a lot there when I was on the poetry circuit.

LA used to have so many little weird performance art and poetry circuits that criss-crossed each other. Like the Photography Centre in MacArthur Park and all these wonderful little spaces that attracted a lovely crowd of diverse people. Even Be Bop in the Valley was like that, and there were a few places in Pasadena. There's such a big difference between black people who grew up in South Central LA and those who grew up in Pasadena. Like night and day. And no one ever mentions the black population of the San Fernando Valley, and the other valleys beyond, like Simi Valley, which I think produced Sean DeLear. There was also a group of black punk kids who were part of the Better Youth Organization of the hardcore punk band Youth Brigade. Two of them were in the documentary *Another State of Mind*. Then there was that club in the valley called Godzilla's. I am really stretching my memory banks.

It was always nice to see that there were other black freaks out there, even though sometimes you thought you were the only one. People fail to mention the eccentricity of the black freak as a form of resistance. There is a history. Someone like George Clinton—who produced a record with the Red Hot Chili Peppers—and Super Freak Rick James, Sun Ra and Afrofuturism. No one mentions the queerness of Sun Ra, or the forgotten black new wavers like Gary Allen who was the boyfriend of Flea of the Red Hot Chili Peppers. He used to be a hustler when he and Anthony were at Fairy Fax High School. They didn't call that school Fairy Fax for nothing. And the connections between punks and the hustling scene on Santa Monica Blvd and Selma Avenue, and on Polk Street in San Francisco and 53rd and Third in New York City. All of this is very important.

In LA a lot of early punk shows were at halls in South Central and industrial spaces in Funkytown on Jefferson Blvd, Adams Blvd, Exposition and Pico. These shows mixed punk white artists, who were urban pioneers living in dirt cheap storefronts in South Central with the S & M scene and its dungeons and sex clubs like the LA Water Polo Team. It was almost like the buffet flats of Harlem and Central Avenue in the 1920s. Someone needs to write about the Dunbar Hotel and the Club Alabam. My mother use to go there in the 1940s with her pachuca and Filipino girlfriends. She used to talk about how mixed it was on Central Avenue with Latinos, blacks, Asians, and whites at the Dunbar and Club Alabam seeing Lester Young perform.

I could go on and on but I have to go and see my German tax lady, as I haven't done 2017 taxes.
love and kisses
"Fetcha"

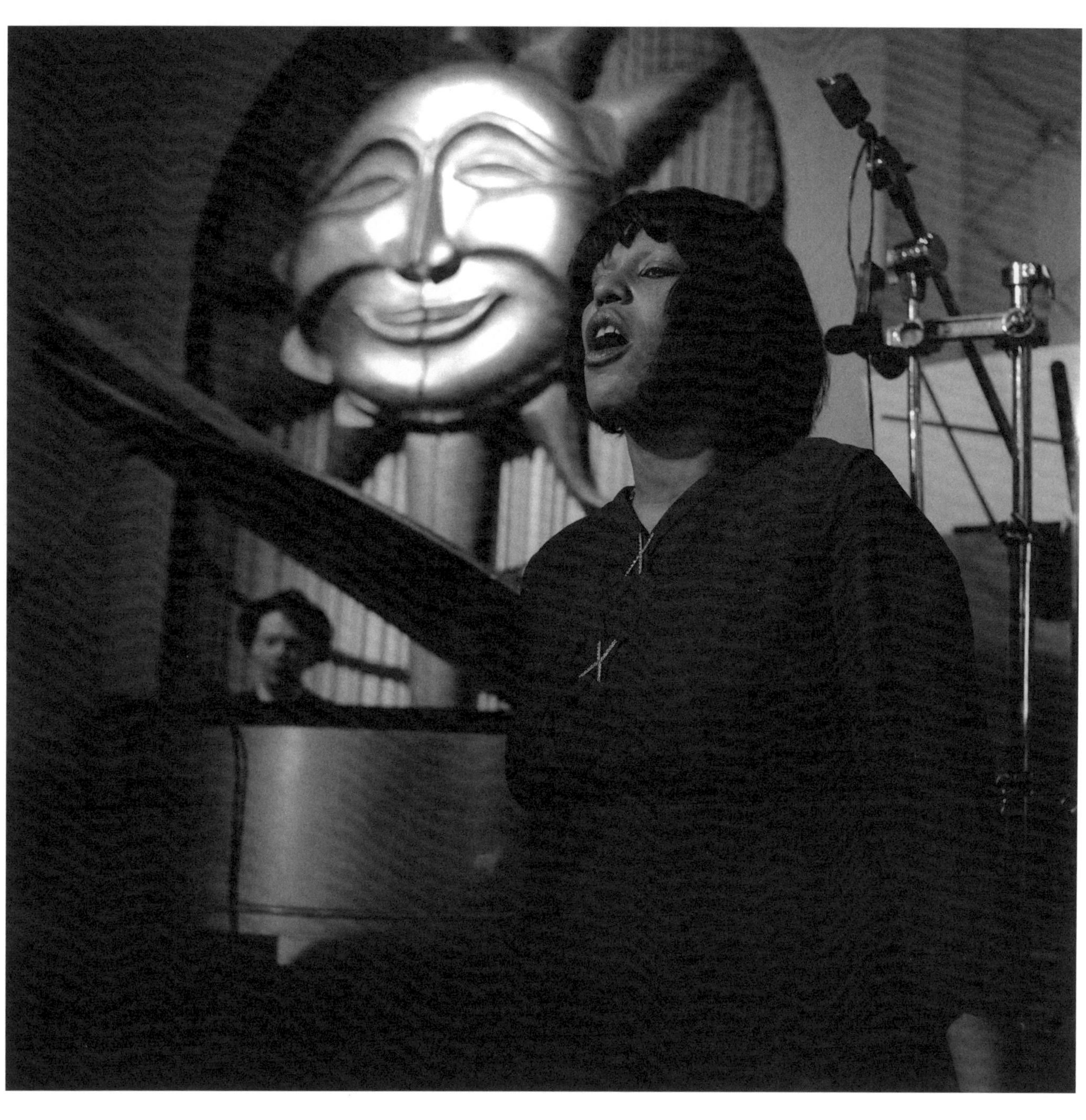

Paul Christian Kuhni and Taquila Mockingbird,
Atlas Bar and Grill (1992)

245

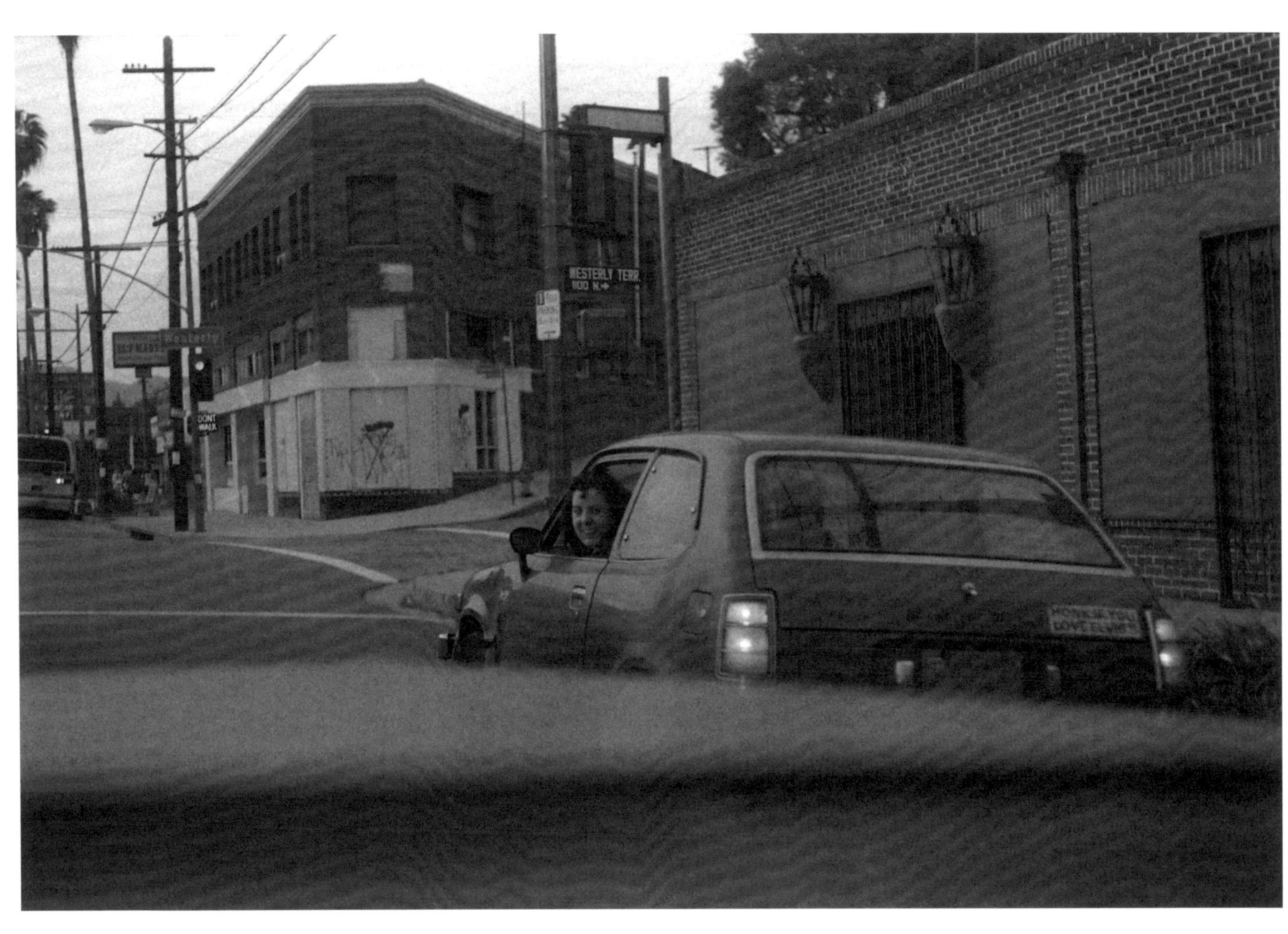

Echo Park (1989)

Acknowledgments

I dedicate this book to, I would say the *girls*, from La Plaza
but it's probably incorrect so I'll say to the *performers* from La
Plaza. Miss Alex, Gaby, Olga, Melissa del Llano, Angela, and
Paloma. To the girls from Mugy's, Tina and Yoshi, and from
the Silverlake Lounge, Vanessa, Olga, La Montenegro, and all
the others whose names I've forgotten.

Special thanks to Chris Kraus and Hedi El Kholti
for believing in this project and all the work they've done way
beyond the call of duty. And for being super cool. To Miss
Lauren Mackler for her patience and dedication.

To my bff, Joseph Stewart, for all the digital help and
for pushing me in the beginning when I wanted to quit. And to
la Gracie for making sense of my terrible writing.

To my daughters, Ceri Zamora and Annette Weber,
my sisters, herminia Connie and Kathy Rivera. To my amazing
mother, Catalina Martin and Marisol Aynat. And to my
husband Christopher Arellano.

Published by Semiotext(e)
PO BOX 629. South Pasadena, CA 91031
www.semiotexte.com

Designed by Lauren Mackler
Editorial assistance by Sarah Yanni

Chris Kraus would like to thank the Kone Foundation
for a residency and support at the Saari Residence in western
Finland.

Special thanks to Juliana Halpert and Gracie Hadland.

ISBN: 978-1-63590-112-2

Distributed by The MIT Press, Cambridge, Mass.
and London, England

Printed in Belgium

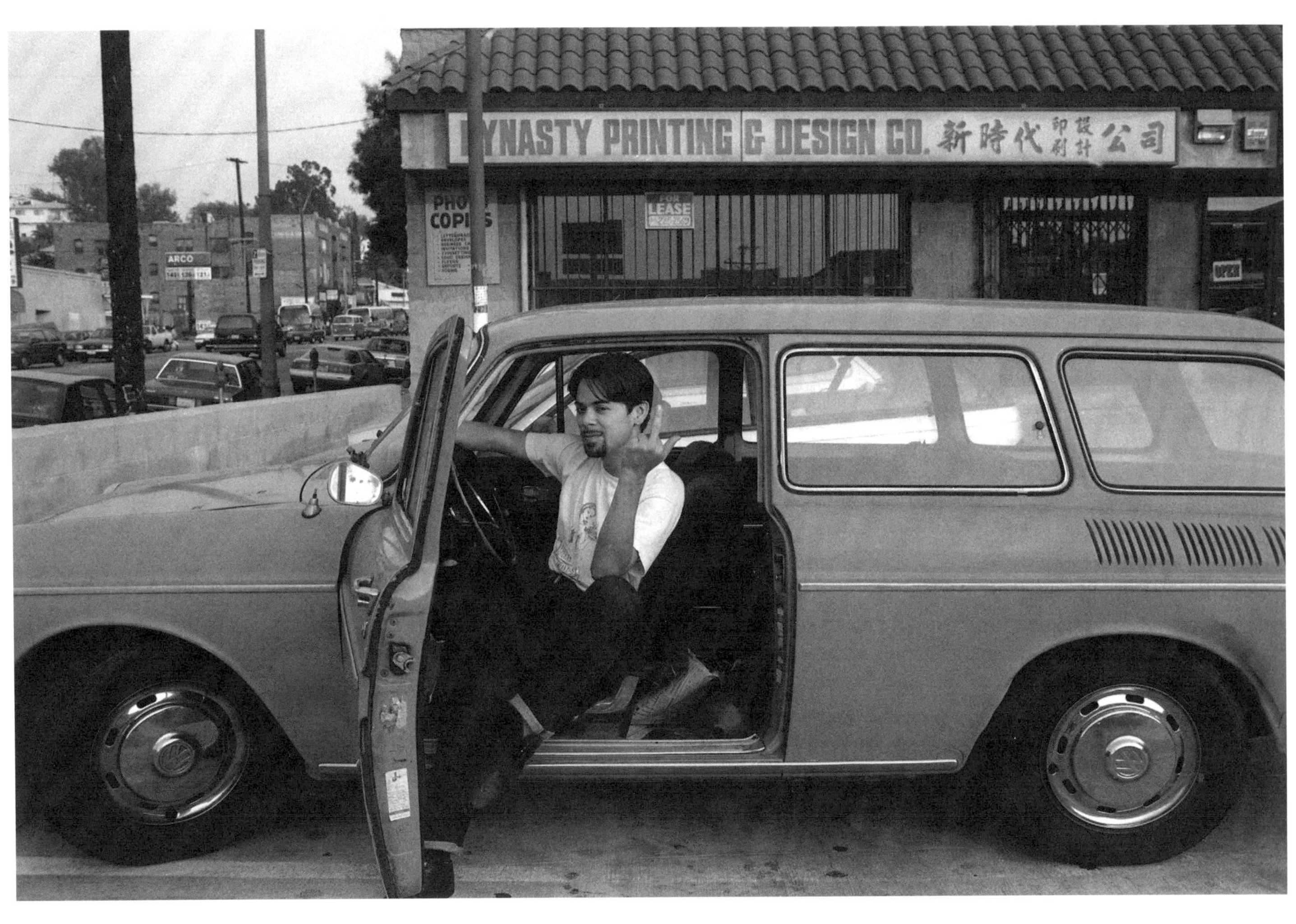

Reynaldo Rivera, Echo Park (1989)

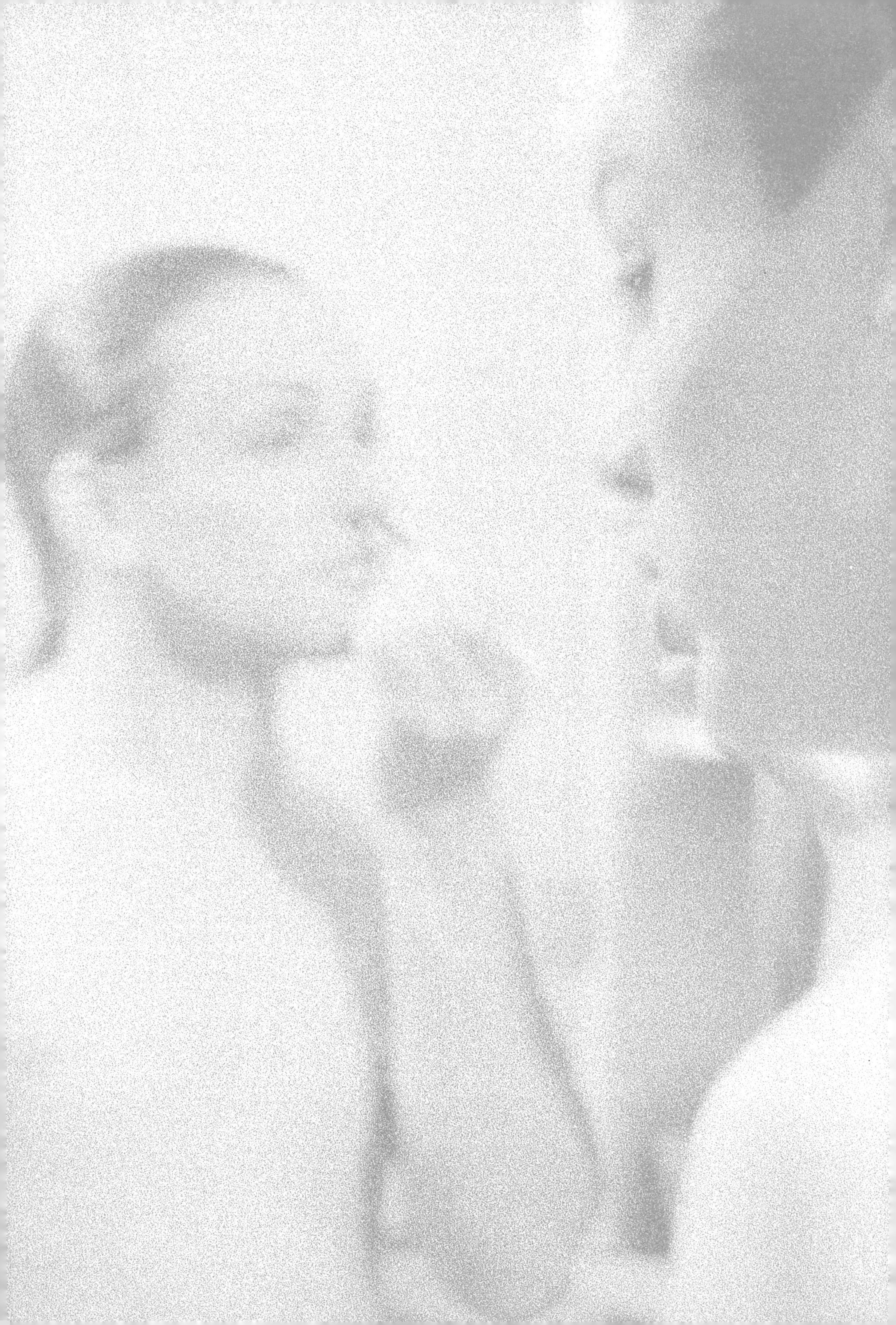